John Clark Marshman

The History of India, from the Earliest Period to the Close of Lord Dalhousie's Administration,

Vol. II

John Clark Marshman

The History of India, from the Earliest Period to the Close of Lord Dalhousie's Administration,
Vol. II

ISBN/EAN: 9783348014229

Printed in Europe, USA, Canada, Australia, Japan

Cover: Foto ©ninafisch / pixelio.de

More available books at **www.hansebooks.com**

THE

HISTORY OF INDIA,

FROM

THE EARLIEST PERIOD TO THE CLOSE OF

LORD DALHOUSIE'S ADMINISTRATION.

BY

JOHN CLARK MARSHMAN.

VOL. II.

LONDON:

LONGMANS, GREEN, READER & DYER.

1867.

[The right of Translation is reserved.]

CONTENTS

OF

THE SECOND VOLUME.

CHAPTER XVI.

LORD CORNWALLIS'S ADMINISTRATION.—THE THIRD MYSORE WAR.
1786—1793.

Date

...puts out... Sindia...

1785—1792 Sindia...

1790 H... 42

1792...

1786 En... of Sindia...

1788...

1796 N...

The M...

...99 Gre...

...69 R...

CHAPTER XIX.

LORD WELLESLEY'S ADMINISTRATION.—FOURTH AND LAST MYSORE WAR, 1798—1799.

CHAPTER XX.

LORD WELLESLEY'S ADMINISTRATION (continued), 1799—1802.

II. B

CHAPTER XXI.

LORD WELLESLEY'S ADMINISTRATION.—MAHRATTA AFFAIRS, 1800 - 1803.

CHAPTER XXII.

LORD WELLESLEY'S ADMINISTRATION (continued), 1804–5.

B 2

CHAPTER XXIV.

LORD MINTO'S ADMINISTRATION.

CHAPTER XXV.

Administration of Lord Minto (continued), 1809-13.

CHAPTER XXVI.

CHARTER OF 1813.—LORD HASTINGS'S ADMINISTRATION.—NEPAL WAR. 1814—1816.

CHAPTER XXVII.

TRANSACTIONS WITH NATIVE PRINCES, 1814—17.—PINDAREE AND MAHRATTA WAR, 1817.

CHAPTER XXVIII.

THE PINDAREE AND MAHRATTA WAR—MISCELLANEOUS NOTICES, 1817—
1822.

CHAPTER XXIX.

ADMINISTRATION OF MR. ADAM AND LORD AMHERST.

THE HISTORY OF INDIA.

CHAPTER XVI.

LORD CORNWALLIS'S ADMINISTRATION—THE THIRD MYSORE
WAR—1786—1793.

Sir John
Macpherson's
administration,
1785.

HASTINGS left the government in the hands of Mr.,
afterwards Sir John, Macpherson, who presided
over it for twenty months. He came out to
Madras at the age of twenty-two, as purser in one of the
Company's ships, but soon after his arrival quitted the sea
for more lucrative employment at the court of the Nabob of
the Carnatic, where he obtained great consideration. Under
his influence the Nabob was induced to make a direct appeal
to the Minister in England, as the most effectual means of
regaining his political independence, and throwing off the
restraints of the Madras government. Mr. Macpherson
was charged with this mission, and accredited by a letter
to the Duke of Grafton, which gained little for his patron,
but a Madras writership for his young agent. Soon after his
arrival at the Presidency he obtained one of the most
lucrative appointments in the service, that of military paymaster, but was expelled from it by Lord Pigot, in 1776, on
the ground that he was still a partizan of the Nabob. With
his usual sagacity, he persuaded the Nabob to make his will,
and appoint the king of England his executor and the

guardian of his children—an office which was most injudiciously accepted. Mr. Macpherson, who returned to
England as the representative of the Nabob, with a full
purse, was not long in obtaining a seat in Parliament, and
made himself so useful to the Minister by his eloquent pen
and his servile vote, as to obtain the appointment of second
member of Council at Calcutta. The war with the Mahrattas
and Hyder had produced the same effect on the finances of
India as the war which England had been waging with the
North American colonies produced on her finances. Troops
to the number of 70,000 had been maintained for several
years in provinces the most remote from each other, and a
debt had been accumulated to the extent of six crores of
rupees. The army and civil establishments were fifty lacs of
rupees in arrears, and the whole machinery of government
was in a state of disorder. Mr. Macpherson applied himself
with great energy to financial reform, and effected reductions
exceeding a crore of rupees. He received thanks from the
Court of Directors, and a baronetcy from the Crown; but it
is not to be concealed that his two successors, Lord Cornwallis
and Sir John Shore, considered his pretensions to economy,
except with regard to the reduction of salaries, a mere
delusion, and his whole administration a failure.

Wars between
Tippoo, the
Mahrattas, and
the Nizam,
1786.

The treaty of Mangalore left Tippoo with
unimpaired resources, and augmented his arrogance. The ink was scarcely dry, when he
wrote to his French allies at Pondicherry that
he was only waiting for an opportunity of crushing the
Nizam and the Mahrattas, and exterminating the English.
His first act after the pacification was to seize 30,000 native
Christians on the Malabar coast, and cause them to be circumcised. The Hindoos south of the Kistna were treated with
the same violence, and 2,000 brahmins destroyed themselves
to avoid the indignity. Of the population of Coorg, 70,000
of all ages and both sexes were ruthlessly driven off to
Seringapatam. Tippoo then proceeded to demand the cession

of Beejapore from the Nizam, on some frivolous pretext, and •
attacked the Mahratta garrison of Nurgoond, of which he
obtained possession by an act of perfidy. Nana Furnuvese,
finding Tippoo a more dangerous neighbour than his father
had been, proceeded to form an alliance with the Nizam early
in 1786, for the conquest and partition of his whole territory.
The allied army opened the campaign on the 1st of May, by
the siege of Badamee, which surrendered before the end of
the month. After various assaults and repulses, which
generally terminated to the advantage of Tippoo, he brought
this campaign of nine months to an unexpected termination
by a voluntary offer of peace. A treaty was accordingly concluded between the belligerents in April, 1787, by which
Tippoo engaged to pay forty-five lacs of rupees of tribute,
and to surrender many of the places he had captured. This
sudden change of policy was subsequently explained by the
great efficiency given to the military establishments of the
Company by the new Governor-General, Lord Cornwallis, and
which led Tippoo to suppose that the English were about to
take part in the war against him.

Lord Macartney   Lord Macartney, who had taken Calcutta on
offered the   his way to England, was detained there by severe
Governor-
Generalship,   illness, and was agreeably surprised on his re-
1786.   covery to ·receive the unsolicited offer of the
Governor-Generalship, as a token of the estimation in which
his services were held by Mr. Pitt and Mr. Dundas. Instead,
·however, of accepting the appointment, and taking the oaths
and his seat in Council, he postponed the acceptance of it
till he had an opportunity of conferring with the Ministry on
the additional powers which he deemed necessary to impart
dignity and efficiency to the office. He embarked therefore
for England, and on his arrival submitted his views, which
were in every respect judicious, to the Court of Directors
and to the Prime Minister, by whom they were entertained
with great complacency. But all his prospects were at once
blighted when he proceeded farther to solicit such token of

the royal favour as should demonstrate that he entered upon this responsible office with the entire confidence of the Ministers of the Crown, as well as of the Court of Directors. The request was not only in itself reasonable, but essential to the efficiency and vigour of the government. It was the absence of this support which had subjected the administration of Hastings to the greatest embarrassment. But Mr. Dundas, who had sustained the nomination of Lord Macarteny against a violent opposition in the Cabinet, took umbrage that "he did not rather repose his future fortunes in our ·hands than make it the subject of a *sine qua non* preliminary." Within three days of the receipt of this request, Lord Cornwallis was gazetted Governor-General of India.

Change in the system of government. The government of the Company's affairs in India had hitherto been entrusted to one of their own servants, on the ground that local experience was the most important qualification for the office. But this principle of selection, though well suited to the requirements of a factory, was ill adapted to the government of an empire. The advantage arising from this knowledge of the country and the people, however great, was found to be over-balanced by the ·trammels of local associations, and the difficulty of exercising due control over those who had previously been in the position of equals. The transcendant ability of Hastings himself had been too often neutralized by these connections, and he had been obliged to meet the cabals and intrigues which beset him in the Council chamber by compromises, which weakened the authority of government, and strengthened abuses. These considerations induced the Ministry to place the government in the hands of ·a nobleman of elevated rank and high character, and unfettered by any local ties. The choice fell on Lord Cornwallis, who had. filled several posts of importance, both military and diplomatic, and who stood so high in the estimation of the country that even the surrender of a British army to Washington at Yorktown, which decided the question of American independence,

had not shaken his credit. It was within eight months of
that disaster, that his name was mentioned by Mr. Dundas,
in reference to the future government of India, and was
received with great satisfaction by both parties in the House
of Commons, who united in paying homage to his talents.
He was appointed Governor-General in February, 1786, and
reached Calcutta in the month of September. Thus, by the
singular caprice of circumstances, the man who had lost
America was sent out to govern India, and the man who had
saved India was subjected to a prosecution for high crimes
and misdemeanours. Lord Cornwallis's government commenced under the happiest auspices. He enjoyed the entire
confidence of Mr. Pitt, and, more especially, of Mr. Dundas,
the Indian Minister, who remarked in one of his letters, that
they "never before had a government in India and in
England acting in perfect harmony, on principles of perfect
purity and independence." The spirit of insubordination and
faction which had deranged Hastings's administration was
at once subdued by the dignity and firmness of Lord Cornwallis's character, and the current of public business began
to run smoothly, as soon as he assumed the charge of it.

Correction of
abuses,
1786-88.
The first three years of his administration were
devoted to the correction of abuses, to which it is
necessary to advert more particularly, to indicate
the progress of integrity in the public service. The Court of
of Directors still continued to act on the old and vicious principle of "small salaries and large perquisites." The salaries
came from their own treasury, which they guarded with the
parsimony of a miser, the perquisites came from the people,
and excited little observation, though they served to vitiate
the whole system of government. Every man who returned
to England rich was considered a rogue, and every man who
came home poor was set down as a fool. Hastings made
some effort to correct these abuses, but he had not sufficient
official strength to stem the tide, and he was often obliged to
allay opposition by the bribe of places and emoluments. The

Court of Directors nominated their friends and relatives to the most lucrative appointments in India, and the connection thus established between the patrons in Leadenhall-street, and the nominees in India, was too often fatal to the authority of the Governor-General. Lord Cornwallis was determined to put an end to this practice, but his efforts were not successful until he threatened, if it was persisted in, to resign the government, "that he might preserve his own character, and avoid witnessing the ruin of the national interests."

Instances of abuse, 1786. Lord Cornwallis found the system of official depredation in full bloom. The sub-treasurer was, as he remarked, playing with the deposits; that is, lending out lacs upon lacs of the public money, at twelve per cent. interest. The Commander-in-Chief had given two of his favourites the profitable privilege of raising two regiments, which Lord Cornwallis ordered to be disbanded soon after his arrival. The two commandants immediately demanded compensation, but after the most diligent inquiry, it could not be discovered that either of the regiments had ever existed, except on the paymaster's books. The collectors of the revenue were still engaged in trade, in the name of some friend or relative, and as they were also judges and magistrates, and possessed of irresistible influence in their districts, they were enabled to amass enormous fortunes; and one of them did not hesitate to admit, that his emoluments exceeded his salary more than twenty fold. The raja of Benares is described by Lord Cornwallis as a fool, and his servants as knaves, and the Resident, supreme in power, monopolized the commerce of the province, and realized four lacs a year, though his regular allowance did not exceed 1,000 rupees a month. It was the old process, so well understood in the east, of turning power into money, which now gave fortunes to a new race of conquerors, as it had enriched the Afghan, the Tartar, the Mogul, and the Abysinian conquerors, who preceded them. There was, however, this material difference in the two cases; the Asiatic invader settled in the country, and his acquisitions were expended in it, while the European transported his gains to his own country, and was seen no more. The fortunes thus imported into England will not, it is true, bear any comparison with those which have been subsequently realized in manufactures and railroads. With one exception, there were not a dozen of the Company's servants, from first to last, who took home so large a sum as forty lacs of rupees, but, for the time, their wealth was considered prodigious; and serious apprehensions were entertained by many in England, that eastern gold would undermine its constitution. But it is the peculiar merit of the British administration in India, that it has succeeded in surmounting these abuses, under which previous dynasties had perished, and that, instead of becoming more corrupt with the progress of time, it has worked itself pure, and now presents a model of official integrity, which has, perhaps, no parallel in the world.

The salaries of the public servants augmented, 1788.
To the task of reform Lord Cornwallis applied himself with the greatest assiduity. He hunted out frauds in every department, and abolished jobbing agencies, and contracts and sinecures. His greatest difficulty arose from the importunity of men of power and influence in England who had been in the habit of quartering their friends and kindred, and even their victims at the gambling-table, on the revenues of India. But the Governor-General was inexorable, and he had the courage to decline the recommendations of the Prince of Wales himself, afterwards George the Fourth, who, as he remarked, " was always pressing some infamous and unjustifiable job on him." These reforms, however, were not consummated till he had convinced the Court of Directors of the truth, which Clive and Hastings had in vain pressed on them, that " it was not good economy to put men into places of the greatest confidence, where they have it in their power to make their fortunes in a few months, without giving them

adequate salaries." The Court parted with the traditionary policy of two centuries with great reluctance; but Lord Cornwallis at length succeeded in "annexing liberal salaries to these offices, and in giving gentlemen a prospect of acquiring, by economy, a moderate fortune from the savings of their allowances."

Arrangement with Oude. 1786.

" On the arrival of Lord Cornwallis, the Vizier hastened to send his minister to Calcutta, to renew the request to be relieved from the expense of the British troops stationed in his dominions. But the rapid encroachments of Sindia in Hindostan, and the growing power of the Sikhs, convinced the Governor-General that the brigade could not be withdrawn from Futtygur without great risk. He consented, however, to reduce the demand on the treasury of Lucknow for their support, from seventy-four to fifty lacs of rupees a year, provided it was paid with punctuality. The higher sum had never been realised, and the Company lost nothing by the arrangement, while the defence of Oude from foreign invasion, was provided for at a charge of less than a fourth of its entire revenue. The Vizier was, at the same time, relieved from the pressure of the European harpies who had long been preying on him, and of the monopolies they had inflicted on his country, under the influence of British supremacy. He was likewise exonerated from the payment of ten lacs of rupees a year, which had been allotted by Hastings for the office of the private agent of the Governor-General at the durbar, Major Palmer, of which his own share amounted to two lacs. Lord Cornwallis also conferred an inestimable boon on Oude by peremptorily refusing to recognize the claims of any of the private creditors of the Vizier, and thus rescued that kingdom from the fate of the Carnatic. But he could not fail to perceive the glaring abuses of the government, in which the Vizier took no further interest than to give the sanction of his authority to the acts of his servants, when they could prevail on him—which was rarely the case—to look into the affairs of the kingdom.

The Vizier'sonly care was to obtain money for boundless dissi-
pation; and so the zemindars were allowed to squeeze the
ryots, the ministers squeezed the zemindars, and the Vizier
extorted every rupee he could obtain from his ministers, and
squandered it in cock-fighting and debaucheries, in maintaining a thousand horses in his private stables, which he never
used, and a whole brigade of elephants. —

Demand of the Lord Cornwallis, on leaving England, was espe-
Guntoor Sirkar, cially enjoined to amalgamate the King's and the
1788 Company's troops, and to secure the possession of
the Guntoor Sirkar. The project of amalgamation was warmly
espoused by the king and supported by his Ministers; no
efforts, however, were made during the administration of Lord
Cornwallis to carry it into effect, but on his return to England,
after seven years of experience, he earnestly recommended
the adoption of it to Mr. Dundas and the Court of Directors.
The reversion of the Guntoor Sirkar, it will be remembered,
was assigned by the Nizam to the Company by the treaty of
1768, after the death of his brother, Basalut Jung. He died
in 1782, but the Nizam constantly evaded the surrender.
Lord Cornwallis found him in 1786 involved in a war with
Tippoo, and considered it inopportune to press the cession at
the time. But in 1788, the prospect of continued peace with
France, which removed all fear of European interference, and
the aspect of politics in the Deccan, seemed to present a
suitable occasion for making the demand. To obviate every
difficulty, troops were drawn to the frontier, and Captain
Kennaway, the Governor-General's aide-de-camp, was despatched to Hyderabad., "to demand the full execution of the
treaty of 1768," with the intimation, that a British force was
prepared to enter Guntoor in a fortnight. To the surprise of
Lord Cornwallis, the Nizam ordered the immediate surrender
of the district without any hesitation, as well as the adjustment of all accounts; but at the same time he expressed his
confidence that the Company's government would be prepared,
with equal alacrity, to fulfil the obligations to which they

were bound by it; namely, to send two battalions of sepoys
and six pieces of artillery, manned by Europeans, whenever
the Nizam should require them, and to reduce and transfer to
him the province of the Carnatic Balaghaut, "then usurped
by Hyder Naik." With his usual duplicity, the Nizam sent
an envoy at the same time to Tippoo, to propose an alliance
for the extirpation of the English. Tippoo readily assented
to the proposal, on condition of receiving a daughter of
the Nizam in marriage; but the Tartar blood of the son of
Chin Kilich Khan boiled at the idea of a matrimonial alliance
with the son of a naik, or head constable, and the negotiation
fell to the ground.

Perplexity of   Lord Cornwallis was not a little perplexed by
Lord Cornwallis, this manœuvre on the part of the Nizam. Since
1789.   the treaty of 1768, the British Government had
in two successive treaties acknowledged Hyder and Tippoo
as the lawful sovereigns of the Carnatic Balaghaut. The
Act of 1784 had, moreover, strictly prohibited the formation
of alliances with native princes without sanction from home.
But Lord Cornwallis deemed it important to British interests
to secure the co-operation both of the Nizam and the Peshwa
against the hostile designs of Tippoo, which were daily becoming more palpable. To meet the difficulties of the case, he
addressed a letter to the Nizám, which was avowed to have
the full force of a treaty, though it professed to be simply a
clearer definition of the old compact. In this letter he stated
that if the province in question should at any time come into
the possession of the Company, with the assistance of his
Highness, the stipulation of the treaty would be faithfully
observed. The brigade of British troops, he said, should be
furnished whenever the Nizam applied for its services, but
with the understanding that it was not to be employed
against any power in alliance with the English. A list of
these powers was added to the document, but the name of
Tippoo was omitted. This memorable letter, dated the 7th
of July, 1789, has been considered by some writers of con-

siderable note, as the cause of the war which broke out with Tippoo six months after. That an engagement which contemplated the partition of his dominions, and placed an English force at the disposal of the Nizam, with liberty to employ it against him, while he himself was excluded from the register of British allies, must have given him great annoyance, will not be denied. But, before the treaty of Mangalore was a day old, he had assured the French governor of Pondicherry that he would renew the war with the English on the first occasion. He had fitted out an expedition to attack the king of Travancore, an ally of the English, long before he heard of the letter. It was certain that whenever he was ready for the struggle, he would neither want a pretext, nor wait for one. As to the Act of Parliament intended to isolate us from all the other powers of India, even the author of it, Mr. Dundas, had begun to consider it a mistake, and had recently written to Lord Cornwallis that "an alliance with the Mahrattas of the closest kind was all that was requisite to keep the whole world in awe respecting India.".

Proceedings of the Madras government, 1789. The little principality of Travancore, at the southern extremity of the Malabar coast, had been placed under British protection by the treaty of Mangalore. Tippoo, who had long coveted the possession of it, had been for some time assembling a large force in the vicinity, and the raja, anxious to strengthen the defences of his kingdom, had recently purchased the towns of Cranganore and Ayacottah of the Dutch. Tippoo immediately demanded the surrender of them on the plea that that they belonged to his vassal, the chief of Cochin. The raja refused to resign them, and applied to the British authorities for support. Lord Cornwallis directed the President at Madras to inform both Tippoo and the raja that if the Dutch had held independent and unreserved possession of them, he was instructed to assist the raja in maintaining and defending them. Unfortunate as Madras had been in its Presidents for a long series of years, Mr. Holland, who now occupied the chair, appears to have been the very worst of the lot. He not only withheld this communication from Tippoo, but sent a disheartening letter to the raja, and, at the same time, demanded a lac of pagodas for himself, as the condition of aiding him with a British detachment. To promote this profligate negotiation, he kept the army in such a state of inefficiency as to encourage Tippoo's aggression. Holland was deeply implicated in all the criminality of the Nabob's loans, and, although he had been ordered to suspend all payments to the creditors as soon as there was any probability of a war with Tippoo, he chose to continue these disbursements, allowed the pay of the troops to fall into arrears, and neglected to make any preparation for the impending war. ·

Tippoo attacks Travancore, 28th December, 1789.
Emboldened by this negligence, Tippoo suddenly attacked the "lines of Travancore," consisting of the defensive wall which the raja had erected; but after a severe action was repulsed with disgrace, and with the loss of 2,000 men. He immediately ordered down a battering train from Seringapatam, and reinforcements from every quarter. Even the detachments employed in dragooning "the infidels of Malabar," who refused circumcision, were recalled from their mission, and the next three months and a half were wasted in preparation for the attack of this miserable wall. Holland, after he had received information of this attack, which was equivalent to a declaration of war, actually proposed to appoint commissioners for the pacific adjustment of all differences with Tippoo, and persisted in declining to provide cattle for the army which was to take field. Soon after, he fled from his post and embarked for England.

Treaties formed by Lord Cornwallis, 1790.
During the three years of Lord Cornwallis's administration he had been eminently successful in his financial reforms. The income of Bengal now exceeded its expenditure by two crores of rupees, and he was enabled not only to supply the wants of the other Presi-

dencies, but to send home an investment from territorial revenue, of a crore and thirty lacs, which was calculated to realise two crores in the London market. But however much he regretted that the fruit of three years of economy should be swept away at a stroke, he determined to lose no time in bringing all the resources of the country to the prosecution of the war which Tippoo had wantonly provoked. It was not a time for pottering over Acts of Parliament, and he proceeded at once to form alliances, offensive and defensive, with the two other powers of the Deccan. Although Nana Furnuvese had hitherto treated the friendly advances of Lord Cornwallis with coldness, so great was the animosity of the Mahrattas against Tippoo, that they now agreed to co-operate heartily with the British Government in reducing his power. The hatred and dread of Tippoo also quickened the zeal of the Nizam, and a tripartite treaty was concluded between the parties, which provided that the Nizam and the Mahrattas should attack Tippoo's dominions both during and after the rains, and prosecute the war with all vigour; that they should join the British army if required, with 10,000 horse, for which they were to be fully reimbursed; that a British contingent should accompany their troops, and that the territories and forts conquered by their united arms should be equally divided among them. Of the three powers in the Deccan, the Nizam was the most feeble, and he knew but too well that as soon as the strength of Tippoo was broken, and the balance of power destroyed, he would be exposed to the encroachments of the Mahrattas, who kept open a long account against him of arrears due for *chout* and tribute. He, therefore, delayed the ratification of the treaty while he endeavoured to obtain from Lord Cornwallis, not only the guarantee of his own dominions during the war, but the promise of full protection from the claims of the Poona durbar after its termination. Lord Cornwallis could not, however, consent to this proposal without giving umbrage to his Mahratta allies, and the Nizam was obliged to rest satisfied with the general assurance of friendly support, as far as might be compatible with the engagements of the Company.

Campaign of 1790.   Lord Cornwallis was desirous of taking the field in person, but, finding that General Medows, an officer of acknowledged ability, in whom he placed great confidence, had been appointed Governor and General-in-Chief at Madras, he determined to leave the campaign to his management. The General reached Madras late in February, and prepared to commence operations with a body of 15,000 troops, " the finest and best English army," in the opinion of Lord Cornwallis, " which had ever been assembled in India." The plan of the campaign was similar to that framed by Colonel Fullarton, in 1783, of proceeding southward to Coimbatore, and after reducing the forts and occupying that rich district, of ascending the ghauts to Seringapatam. Another division, when reinforced from Bengal, was to march on the capital through the Baramahal. So great, however, was the deficiency of supplies, owing to the criminal neglect of Holland, that General Medows was unable to move from Trichinopoly before the 26th of May, and was nearly three weeks in reaching Caroor, the frontier station, only fifty miles distant. The army arrived at Coimbetore on the 23rd of July; Dindigul was captured on the 21st of August, and Palghaut, deemed by the natives impregnable, surrendered on the 21st of September, with sixty guns of various calibre. But here the success of the campaign terminated. General Medows injudiciously separated his force into three divisions, and placed them at too great a distance from each other for mutual support. Tippoo took advantage of this error, and, by a masterly movement, descended the Gujelhutty pass, attacked the foremost division under Colonel Floyd, and obliged him to fall back with the loss of some of his guns. " We lost time," said Lord Cornwallis, " in 1790, and Tippoo gained reputation." Several forts stored with provisions likewise fell into his hands; but the subsequent junction of the three divisions baffled his plans, and he moved northward to oppose the army advancing from Bengal.

The Bengal division— Hartley's exploit, 1790.

On the breaking out of the war, Lord Cornwallis adopted the bold plan of Hastings, and despatched a large expedition from the Bengal Presidency along the coast down to Madras. It reached Conjeveram on the 1st of August without accident, under the command of Colonel Maxwell, and there it was reinforced by several regiments from Madras, which raised its strength to 9,500 men. The object of General Medows was to form a junction with this force, and that of Tippoo was to prevent it. But, notwithstanding the rapid march and able dispositions of the Mysore army, a union was effected of the two bodies of English troops on the 17th of November. Tippoo then marched south to attack Trichinopoly, and the chain of English posts and depôts in that quarter, and General Medows closely followed his track. In these desultory movements the troops were subjected to unprofitable fatigue, and began to lose confidence in their commander, who was evidently unequal to the direction of operations on a large scale. The character of the campaign was, however, redeemed by the brilliant exploit of Colonel Hartley, who will be remembered as having earned the highest distinction twelve years before, in the war with the Mahrattas. In the present year, he was stationed on the Malabar coast, with a body of 1,500 men and a few guns, to watch the movements of Hussein Ali, the Mysore general, who guarded the province with a force of 7,000 or 8,000 men, and a large body of fanatic Moplas. On the 8th of December he ventured to attack Colonel Hartley's little band under the walls of Calicut, but was signally defeated, with the loss of more than 1,000 men, and obliged soon after to surrender, together with 2,500 of his force. The loss, on the side of the English, did not exceed fifty-two. General Medows, who was totally devoid of any feeling of professional jealousy, in announcing this success to Lord Cornwallis, exclaimed, "Oh, to eclipse the brilliant action of Colonel Hartley."

Lord Cornwallis takes the field in person, 1791. Lord Cornwallis, mortified by the futility of the campaign, resolved to resume his original design of taking the command of the war in person, and arrived at Madras on the 12th of December, 1790. General Medows returned to the Presidency with his army, without expressing a murmur on the trying occasion of being superseded in the command. Tippoo quitted the neighbourhood of Trichinopoly, and proceeded northward into the heart of the Carnatic, marking his progress by the desolation of the province. He then advanced to Pondicherry, where he wasted several weeks in negotiations with the French governor, through whom he sent a mission to Louis the Sixteenth, then in the vortex of the French revolution. Though the French and English were at the time at peace, he requested that a body of 6,000 troops should be sent to his assistance, for whose conveyance and support he offered to make suitable provision, and with whose aid he engaged to capture the English settlements and transfer them to the French. The unhappy king revolted from the proposal, and remarked: "This resembles the affair of America, of which I never think without regret, my youth was taken advantage of at that time, and we suffer for it now; the lesson is too severe to be forgotten." Meanwhile, Lord Cornwallis was making the greatest efforts to resume operations in the field. It was the first time the British armies in India had been led by a Governor-General in person, who enjoyed the undivided exercise of all the civil and military powers of the state, and commanded the resources of all the Presidencies. His presence was considered by the allies the strongest pledge of sincerity, and gave them every confidence of success.

Capture of Bangalore, 21st March,1791. The British army was concentrated at Vellore on the 11th of February, and Lord Cornwallis made a demonstration of advancing to Seringapatam through the Amboor pass, while his force, with its convoys, passed undiscovered and unopposed through the more easy pass of Mooglee, and on the 17th of February, stood on the table land of Mysore, only ninety miles from Bangalore, without having fired a shot. Tippoo, who had manifested unaccountable indecision while Lord Cornwallis was organizing his plans, hastened, by forced marches to rescue his seraglio and treasures which had been deposited in that fortress, and was only just in time to save them from capture. Bangalore capitulated on the 21st of March, but the pleasure of success was damped by the loss, during the siege, of Colonel Moorhouse, who, though he had risen from the ranks, exhibited all the characteristics of a gallant and most accomplished soldier.

Arrival of the Nizam's contingent, 1791. The Nizam's contingent of 10,000 horse assembled in the neighbourhood of Hyderabad, in May, 1790, in accordance with the conditions of the treaty of alliance; but they never moved beyond their own frontier, till they heard, in September, that Tippoo had gone southward to Coimbetore. When there was no longer any risk of encountering his army, the Nizam's troops entered the Mysore territory, spreading desolation and ruin in their course. But, instead of marching on to join the English army, they sat down before Copaul, a tremendous rock a few miles north of the Toombudra, and twenty miles west of the ancient ruins of Vijuynugur, which detained them nearly six months. As soon, however, as intelligence of the capture of Bangalore reached their camp, they hastened forward, and joined Lord Cornwallis's army on the 13th of April, 1791. They are described as mounted on horses in excellent condition, and clothed in armour of every conceivable variety, including the Parthian bow and arrow, the iron club of Scythia, sabres of every age and nation, lances of every length and description, and matchlocks of every form. But there was neither order, nor discipline, nor valour among them; and the gay cavaliers were so utterly unsuited for field work that they were unable to protect their own foragers, and soon ceased to move beyond the English pickets.

Lord Cornwallis was now in full march on the capital; and Tippoo, yielding to the representa- tions of his officers, and the remonstrances of his women, resolved not to allow it to be invested without a struggle. His father had always advised him to avoid a regular engagement with the English, but he determined on this occa- sion to disregard this salutary injunction. He drew up his whole army at a short distance from Seringapatam, with the Cavery on his right and a ridge of hills on his left; and there, on the 13th of May, was fought the battle of Arikera. Although Tippoo executed his movements with great promptitude and military judgment, he was entirely discomfited. On the sum- mit of the hill, where the last shot was fired, the island of Seringapatam and the eastern face of the fortress became visible to the victors; but here terminated the triumph of the campaign. For many weeks the British army had been suffer- ing the extremity of want. The scanty stores which accom- panied it had been exhausted, and Tippoo's light horse cut off all supplies of provision or forage, and created a desert around it. After the engagement of the 13th, Lord Cornwallis felt, as Sir Eyre Coote had felt ten years before, that he would gladly exchange the trophies of victory for a few days' rice. The Nizam's horse, which was unable to make any effort for its own subsistence, increased the calamity by consuming forage and grain. General Abercromby, with the Bombay army sent to co-operate with Lord Cornwallis, had proceeded down the Malabar coast, and, passing through the friendly country of Coorg, had arrived at Periapatam, forty miles distant from Seringapatam; and Lord Cornwallis, after the engagement, advanced to Caniambady, with the view of forming a junction with him. But, on the 20th of May, his commissariat officers reported that it was utterly impossible to move his heavy guns a step farther with bullocks reduced to the condition of skeletons. The whole camp was falling a prey to want and disease; and Lord Cornwallis was constrained to accept the conclusion that the object of the campaign was no longer practicable, and that the salvation of the army depended on an immediate retreat. On the 21st of May instructions were sent to General Abercromby to retrace his steps to the coast, which he reached in safety, after having destroyed a portion of his siege guns, and buried the remainder at the head of the pass. The next day Lord Cornwallis issued a general order, explaining to the soldiers, European and native, the true motives of this measure, in order to avoid misapprehensions, and then destroyed his own battering train and heavy equipments. On the 26th the army began its melancholy march back to Madras.

Progress of the Mahratta contingent, 1790. The dispirited force had scarcely accomplished half a short march, when a body of about 2,000 horse made its appearance on the left flank. It was supposed at first to be a portion of the enemy's troops advancing to make an attempt on the stores and baggage on the line of retreat, and prompt dispositions were made to frustrate it, but a single horseman soon after galloped up and announced that it was the advanced guard of their Mahratta allies. By the coalition treaty the Mahratta cabinet had engaged to furnish a body 10,000 horse for the prosecution of the war with Tippoo, and the Governor-General had engaged to strengthen their main army with a British detachment. Captain Little accordingly embarked at Bombay, with two battalions of sepoys and one company of European and two of native artillery, with which he reached the rendezvous at Coompta on the 18th of June, but found that not more than 2,000 Mahratta horse had been assembled. This was explained by the fact that, although the treaty, offensive and defensive, had been actually signed by Nana Furnuvese on the 1st of June, the envoys of Tippoo were still entertained at Poona, in the hope, which the ministers did not attempt to conceal, that he might be induced even at the eleventh hour to purchase their neutrality by a concession of territory. This hope was at length dispelled; the vakeels were dismissed on the 5th of August, and Pureshram Bhao, the Mahratta commandant, crossed the Kistna six days after and joined the army. But it soon became evident that his intention was not so much to promote the general object of the confederacy in the humiliation of Tippoo, as to take advantage of the co-operation of the British artillery to recover the fortresses and territories which Tippoo had wrested from the Mahrattas. On the 18th of September, he sat down before Dharwar, a mud fort, but well fortified, and garrisoned by 10,000 Mysore troops, under the command of one of Tippoo's ablest generals. The fort held out till the 30th of March, when the garrison capitulated, on hearing of the fall of Bangalore. On the 1st of January, 1791, a second Mahratta army, consisting of 25,000 horse and 5,000 foot, marched from Poona, under Hurry Punt, the commander-in-chief of the armies of the state, and advanced into Mysore by a more easterly route, capturing a number of forts in its progress.

Junction of the Mahratta and English armies, 1791.   These two bodies were united on the 24th of May, 1791, and marched towards Milgota, where two days later they came up with the English army on the first day of its retreat. Great was the astonishment of Lord Cornwallis to find the Mahratta forces, which he supposed to be a hundred and fifty miles distant, in his immediate vicinity. But, his intelligence department, to which only 2,000 rupees a month had been allotted, was wretched beyond example, while the admirable organization of Tippoo's troop of spies intercepted all communication, and kept the allies mutually ignorant of each others movements. Had the approach of the Mahratta armies been announced a week earlier, the campaign would have presented a very different prospect. The provisions which they brought with them, though sold at an exorbitant rate, proved a seasonable relief to Lord Cornwallis's famished soldiers. The bazaar of the Mahratta camp presented the greatest variety of articles; English broadcloths and Birmingham penknives, the richest Cashmere shawls, and the most rare and costly jewellery, together with oxen, and sheep, and poultry, and all that the best

bazaars of the most flourishing towns could furnish, the result
of long and unscrupulous plunder; while the carpets of the
money-changers in the public street of the encampment,
spread with the coins of every kingdom and province in the
east, indicated the systematic rapine of these incomparable
freebooters. But, though the Mahratta sirdars had been enrich-
ing themselves with plunder from the day on which they took
the field, they set up a plea of poverty, and demanded a loan
of fourteen lacs of rupees. Lord Cornwallis had no time to
examine the morality of this request; he had only to consider the consequence of refusing it—the transfer of their
alliance to Tippoo, who was ready to purchase it at any price.
He, therefore, sent an express to Madras, and took out of the
hold of the ships then about to sail for China, the specie
intended for the annual investment.

Operations of
the Mahratta,
the Nizam's and
the English
forces, 1791.

Hurry Punt, the Mahratta general-in-chief,
accompanied the English army on its retirement,
but lost no opportunity of indulging in plunder.
The main body of the Mahratta army, under
Pureshram Bhao, moved to the north west, subjecting the
Mysore districts to indiscriminate spoliation. The siege of
Simoga, in which he engaged, was rendered memorable by
the skill and heroism of Capt. Little's detachment which accompanied his force, who, after thirty-six hours of hard fighting, without food or rest, placed the fortress in his hands. The
Bhao had left Lord Cornwallis in July, under a solemn promise to return to the army whenever required; but nothing
was farther from his intentions; his object was to avail himself of the aid of the English force to recover the territory
which the Mahrattas had lost; and he was importuning
Captain Little to attack Bednore, when another and more
peremptory requisition obliged him to return to the south;
but he did not join the English camp till a fortnight after the
termination of the war. The army of the Nizam, on the
retreat of Lord Cornwallis, proceeded to the north-east, and
laid siege to Goorumconda, where it was detained many

months. The fort was at length captured by the English auxiliary force, and Hafiz-jee, who had been the bearer of Tippoo's offer of an alliance with the Nizam's family four years before, which was rejected with indignation, was made prisoner and cut to pieces by the Nizam's commander, to revenge that deep felt indignity. Soon after, the Hyderabad army was summoned to join Lord Cornwallis, then advancing a second time against Seringapatam. After his retirement from the capital in May, 1791, he employed the remainder of the year in the conquest of the Baramahal, and the reduction of the fortresses with which the country was studded, and the fortifications of which had been improved by Tippoo with so much skill and assiduity as to excite Lord Cornwallis's warm admiration. Nothing, indeed, filled the princes of the country with such awe of the British power as the ease and rapidity with which fortresses, absolutely impregnable to the assaults of any native force, were mastered, and which they attributed to the power of magic. While the Mahrattas had been six months and a half besieging Dharwar, and the Nizam's army had been detained five months before Copaul, such fortresses as Kistnagherry, Nundidroog, Severndroog, and others, which seemed to defy all human approach on their inaccessible peaks, were captured in a few days.

The grand con-voy, January, 1792.   The arrangements of Lord Cornwallis for the campaign of 1792 were completed early in January, and he took the field with a convoy which surpassed in magnitude anything which had ever accompanied a British force in India, and struck the Deccan with amazement. First and foremost, marched a hundred elephants laden with treasure, followed by a hundred carts supplied with liquor, and 60,000 bullocks laden with provisions belonging to the *brinjarees*, the professional and hereditary carriers of India, more than one-fourth of which number had been serving in Tippoo's army the preceding year. Then in three parallel columns came the battering train and heavy carriages, the infantry and the field-pieces, the baggage and the camp followers. The appearance of these vast supplies, partly received from England, and partly drawn from the other Presidencies, within six months after Lord Cornwallis had been obliged to retreat for want of provisions, might well justify the exclamation of Tippoo, "It is not what I see of the resources of the English that I dread, but what I do not see."

Siege of Serin-gapatam, 6th February, 1792. On the 25th of January, the Nizam's army, consisting of about 8,000 men, under the command of his son, but more gaudy than serviceable, together with a small body of Hurry Punt's Mahrattas, joined the camp of Lord Cornwallis, when he moved forward with a force, consisting exclusive of allies, of 22,000 men, 44 field-pieces, and 42 siege guns. On the 5th of February the whole force reached an elevated ground which commanded a view of Seringapatam, standing on an island formed by two branches of the Cavery. The defences, which had been greatly improved by Tippoo, consisted of three lines protected by 300 pieces of cannon, the earthwork being covered by a bound hedge of thorny plants, absolutely impenetrable to man or beast. Tippoo's force was encamped on the northern face of the stream, and his position was so admirably fortified that it appeared an act of rashness to attack it. Lord Cornwallis reconnoitred the works on the 6th, and determined to storm them that same night. The generals of the allies were astounded when they heard that the English commander had gone out in person, like an ordinary captain, in a dark night, without guns, to assail these formidable lines. But the attack was planned with the greatest skill, and rewarded with complete success. The contest raged throughout the night, and by the morning Lord Cornwallis had obtained possession of the whole of the enemy's redoubts, and established himself in the island, with the loss of 530 killed and wounded, of whom 36 were officers. The casualties in Tippoo's army were estimated at 4,000, but as the conscripts whom he had pressed into his service took advantage of

II.   D this reverse to desert it, his total loss did not fall short of 20,000.

Treaty of peace, 1792. Tippoo now began to tremble for his capital and his kingdom, and hastened to release Lt. Chambers, whom he had detained, contrary to the capitulation of Coimbetore,—which that officer had defended to the last extremity,—and sent him with overtures to Lord Cornwallis. On the 16th of February, General Abercromby joined the camp with a reinforcement of 6,000 men from the Malabar coast. The operations of the siege were prosecuted with unabated vigour during the negotiations, and on the 23rd the works were so far completed that fifty pieces of cannon were brought to bear on the fortifications. Tippoo assembled his principal officers, and adjured them on the Koran to advise him in all sincerity and good faith, and to inform him whether, in their opinion, he ought to accede to the demands of the confederates. They replied that no reliance could any longer be placed on his soldiers, and that submission was inevitable. Tippoo felt that he had to choose between the loss of his throne, and submission to the severe terms dictated by Lord Cornwallis; which were, that he should cede half his territories, pay three crores of rupees towards the expenses of the war, and give up two of his sons as hostages. The confederates left Sir John Kennaway, the British plenipotentiary, to settle the conditions of the treaty, but when it was completed, Hurry Punt, the Mahratta general-in-chief added a supplemental demand of sixty lacs of rupees for himself and the Nizam's general, as a reasonable fee for their labours in the negotiation. This sum was subsequently reduced to one-half that amount. From documents found on the capture of Seringapatam, in 1799, it was discovered that both the Mahrattas and the Nizam were all this time engaged in a clandestine correspondence with Tippoo, the object of which was unconsciously but effectually defeated by the signature of the preliminaries by Lord Cornwallis on the 23rd, and the arrival of the hostages on the 25th of

February.   The youths were conveyed with much ceremony
to the Governor-General's tent, and received with distinguished
courtesy.   A crore of rupees had also been sent in, when
Tippoo, finding that the little principality of Coorg which he
had destined to destruction for the assistance afforded to the
English was to be included in the territory he was required
to cede, not only remonstrated against the demand of what
he termed one of the gates of Seringapatam, but manifested
a disposition to renew hostilities.   Lord Cornwallis, however,
made preparations for pressing the siege with such promptitude, that Tippoo was speedily brought to reason.   The
tripartite treaty had provided that the territories conquered by
the joint exertions of the allies should be equally divided among
them.   The Mahrattas, as the preceding narrative will show,
had given no assistance in the war, and the Nizam's force
had done nothing but consume provisions and forage, but
Lord Cornwallis was determined to adhere to the original
compact with the most scrupulous fidelity, and made over a
third of the indemnity, as well as of the territory, to each of
the confederates, annexing another third, of the value of forty
lacs of rupees a year, to the dominions of the Company.   It
comprised the district of Dindigul in the south, and of the
Baramahal in the east, including several important passes
into Mysore, and a large strip of fertile territory with great
commercial resources on the western coast, which was
annexed to Bombay, and formed the first real domain of
that Presidency.   *Dindigul, Baramahal & Wainad.*

Proposals to   This was the first acquisition of territory since
relinquish terri-   it had been resolved to control the growth of the
tory,
1780-1793.   British empire in India by Acts of Parliament.
Mr. Pitt, on the introduction of his India Bill, in 1784, stated that
his first and principal object would be to prevent the Governor
of Bengal from being ambitious, and bent on conquest; and
his chief objection to Hastings was, that he had endeavoured
to extend the British dominions in India.   The dread of territorial expansion was, in fact, the prevailing bugbear of the

day. But neither Hastings, nor any other statesman in England or in India, had ever entertained any such design. On the contrary, Hastings was at one time prepared to relinquish all the Northern Sircars. Clive had given back the entire kingdom of Oude, when it had been forfeited by the result of the war which the Nabob vizier had wantonly waged against the . Company, and he denounced any attempt to extend the British territories beyond the Curumnussa. Lord Cornwallis, soon after he assumed office, expressed his wish to withdraw from the Malabar coast, and to reduce Bombay to a mere factory, subordinate to Calcutta or Madras; and Lord Shelburne, when Prime Minister of England in 1782, proposed to give up everything except Bombay and Bengal; and, had Lord Cornwallis accepted the office of Governor-General when it was first proposed to him, he would probably have taken out orders to abandon the Madras Presidency. If the extent of the British dominions in India had depended, therefore, on the wishes, or the policy of its rulers, so far from being ambitiously expanded, it would apparently have been reduced within very narrow limits.

Encroachments of native princes, 1793.
Those who took the lead in the government of India at this period, had evidently but a partial knowledge of its early history and polity, of the character of its princes, or of the position in which England was placed. From time immemorial, aggression had been the life-blood of all Indian monarchies. Twenty-five centuries before Mr. Pitt's time, the father of Hindoo legislation had placed conquest among the foremost of regal virtues. "What the king," says Munoo, "has not gained, let him strive to gain by military strength;" and this is, perhaps, the only injunction of the Hindoo shastras, which Hindoo princes have never forgotten. The same aggressive principle was adopted by the Mahomedan conquerors, not only in reference to infidel princes, but to those of the "true faith." Every new dynasty, as it arose with the elastic vigour of youth, continued to attack and appropriate the territories of its neighbours, till

it became itself effete, and was in its turn absorbed by new adventurers. For more than ten centuries there had been no settled kingdom, guarded by a respect for prescriptive rights, anxious to maintain peace with its neighbours, and content with its ancient boundaries. In every direction, the continent had presented an unbroken series of intrigue, violence and aggression.

The position of the English, 1756—1793.   At the period which this narrative has reached, the political cauldron in India was seething with more than ordinary violence. The four chief powers, the Peshwa, the Nizam, Tippoo, and Sindia, had been established within the brief period of sixty years by usurpation, and were kept alive by the impulse of aggression. Every year had witnessed some invasion of the right of some prince in Hindostan or the Deccan. It was at this juncture that the English appeared on the scene, and took up arms to defend their factories. By the superiority of their valour and discipline, they became a first-rate military power, and, consequently, an object of jealousy to all the belligerent princes of India. It was the restlessness and encroachment of those princes, and not the ambition of English governors which gave rise to nearly all the wars in which they were engaged. Admitting that they had any right to be in India at all, the increase of their power and possessions was the inevitable effect of that law of progression to which all new dynasties were subject. From the very first they were placed in a state of antagonism to all those who dreaded their power, and coveted their possessions. The slightest appearance of weakness, and, too often, even the exhibition of moderation—a virtue unknown in India—became the signal of aggressive assaults. When the aggressor was conquered, it appeared to be the dictate of prudence to prevent the renewal of hostilities by reducing his resources, and appropriating a part of his territories. And thus was the British empire in India gradually extended by a mysterious but inexorable necessity, which overpowered, not only the reluctance of English governors, and the denunciations of patriots, but even the omnipotence of Parliament.

Censure of Lord Cornwallis in the House, 1793.   The conduct of Lord Cornwallis was not allowed to pass without censure in the House of Commons, more especially from Mr. Francis, who had been the instrument of annexing the province of Benares to the Company's territories.   The war which Lord Cornwallis 'considered "an absolute and cruel necessity," forced on him by the ungovernable ambition and violence of Tippoo, was stigmatised as unjust and ambitious, and the treaties of alliance he had formed with the Nizam and the Poona durbar were affirmed to be infamous.   Lord Porchester went so far as to assert that the war was founded on avarice, but the charge was triumphantly refuted by the fact that Lord Cornwallis had not only been subject to a loss of nearly three lacs of rupees by it, but had relinquished his share of the prize-money, which came to four lacs and a half more—a generous act which was nobly emulated by General Medows. The House ratified all the measures of the Governor-General, including the large acquisition of territory which he had made, and the king conferred on him the dignity of Marquis. The precedent has been scrupulously maintained since that time, and every Governor-General who has enlarged the British empire in India, has received the thanks of Parliament, and has been decorated with honours by the Crown.

Reduction of Tippoo's power, 1793.   The progress of the war demonstrated beyond question, that of the three native powers in the Deccan, Tippoo was by far the strongest.   Both the Nizam and the Mahrattas were found to entertain the most lively dread of his power and his ambition, and, they were brought to feel that they could not have defended themselves effectually from his encroachments, without the aid of an English army.   The power of Tippoo was effectually reduced by the alienation of one-half his territorial resources, which, before the peace, were reckoned at about two crores and a half of rupees. The Nizam and the Poona durbar had exhibited such inefficiency during the campaigns, as to reduce themselves to a very subordinate political position, and the prestige of British power had been in a corresponding degree augmented. The deference paid to the Governor-General both by friends and enemies placed the British name and consequence in a light never known before in India. After this period, for half a century, there were no more treaties of Mangalore, or conventions of Wurgaum, but the British authorities dictated their own terms in every negotiation.

CHAPTER XVII.

LORD CORNWALLIS'S ADMINISTRATION—REVENUE AND JUDICIAL REFORMS—POWER OF SINDIA.

Lord Cornwallis's revenue reforms, 1793.   THE brilliant success of the Mysore war reflected the highest credit on Lord Cornwallis, but the permanent renown of his administration rests upon his revenue and judicial institutions, which form one of the most important epochs in the history of British India.

Rise of the zemindars.   The resources of government in India had been derived from time immemorial, almost exclusively from the land, a certain proportion of the produce of which was considered the inalienable right of the sovereign. The settlement of the land revenue was, therefore, a question of the greatest magnitude, and embraced, not only the financial strength of the state, but the prosperity of its subjects. Two centuries before the period of which we treat, Toder Mull, the great financier of Akbar, had made a settlement of the lower provinces, directly with the cultivators, after an accurate survey and valuation of the lands. To collect the rents from the ryots, and transmit them of the treasury, agents were placed in various revenue circles, and remunerated for their labour by a per centage on the collections. The office of collector speedily became hereditary, from the constant tendency of every office in India to become so, and, also from the obvious convenience of continuing the agency in the family which was in possession of the local records, and acquainted with the position of the ryots, and the nature of the lands. The collector thus became responsible for the government rent, and was entrusted with all the powers necessary for realising it. He was permitted to entertain a military force, which it was his constant aim to augment, to increase his own consequence. His functions were gradually enlarged, and came eventually to embrace the control of the police and the adjudication of rights. The collector was thus transformed into a zemindar, and assumed the title and dignity of · raja, and became, in effect, the master of the district.

Evils of the revenue system, 1772—1790. The English government had from the first treated the zemindars as simple collectors, and ousted them without hesitation when others offered more for the lands than they were prepared to pay. But this uncertainty of tenure, and this repeated change of agency was found to be equally detrimental to the improvement of the lands, the welfare of the ryots, and the interests of the state. Under such a system there could be no application of capital to the operations of agriculture; the estates became deteriorated, while the remissions which Government was obliged to make from time to time, overbalanced any profits arising from competition. The Court of Directors complained that the revenue was steadily diminishing, and that the country itself was becoming impoverished and exhausted. Lord Cornwallis, soon after his arrival, declared that agriculture and internal commerce were in a state of rapid decay, that no class of society appeared to be flourishing, except the money-lenders, and that both cultivators and landlords were sinking into poverty and wretchedness. The evils under which the people groaned, he affirmed to be enormous. ✗

Remedy proposed by the Court of Directors, 1786.

The Court of Directors felt the necessity of adopting some bold and decisive measure to arrest the progress of ruin, and, under this impression, framed their memorable letter of the 12th of April, 1786, which became the basis of the important revenue settlement, begun and completed by Lord Cornwallis. They condemned the employment of farmers of the revenue and temporary renters, who had no interest in the land, and defrauded the state, while they oppressed the ryots. They directed that the engagements should be made with the old zemindars, not, however, as a matter of right, but of fiscal policy. On the presumption, moreover, that sufficient information must have been acquired regarding the estates, they desired that the settlement should be made for a period of ten years, and eventually declared permanent, if it appeared to be satisfactory. But Lord Cornwallis found that the Court had been essentially mistaken in this conclusion. Twenty years had been employed in efforts to procure information regarding the land, and five schemes had been devised for the purpose, but the Government was still as ignorant as ever on the subject. The Collectors had no knowledge of the value of the lands, of the nature of tenures, or of the rights of landlord and tenant. They had no intercourse with the people, and were ignorant of their language. They saw only through the eyes of their *omlas*, or native officers, whose sole object was to mystify them, in order the more effectually to plunder the country. Lord Cornwallis, therefore, suspended the execution of the orders of the Court, and circulated interrogatories with the view of obtaining the necessary information, and, in the mean time, made the settlements annual.

Proprietary right in the lands, 1793.

The proprietary right in the land had been considered, from time immemorial, to be vested in the sovereign; and although Mr. Francis and some others had thought fit to adopt a different opinion, the great

majority of the public servants adhered to the ancient
doctrine. But, after the investigations were completed, the
Governmemt, acting upon a generous and enlightened policy,
determined to confer on the zemindars the unexpected boon of
a permanent interest in the soil. Before this concession, the zemindars, from the highest to the lowest, had been mere tenants
at will, liable at any time to be deprived by the state landlord
of the estates they occupied. But the regulations of 1793,
in which the new fiscal policy was embodied, converted the
soil into a property, and bestowed it upon them. A large
and opulent class of landholders was thus created, in the
hope that they would seek the welfare of the ryot, stimu-
late cultivation, and augment the general wealth of the
country. It was found, however, to be much more easy to
determine the relation between the government and the landlord, than between the landlord and his tenant. The rights
of the cultivators were more ancient and absolute than those
of the zemindar; but the zemindar had always practised
every species of oppression on them, extorting every cowrie
which could be squeezed from them by violence, and leaving
them little beyond a rag and a hovel. Mr. Shore, who super-
intended the settlement, maintained that some interference
on the part of government was indispensably necessary to
effect an adjustment of the demands of the zemindar on the
ryot. Lord Cornwallis affirmed that whoever cultivated the
land, the zemindar *could* receive no more than the established
rate, which in most cases was equal to what the cultivator
could pay. The difficulty was compromised rather than
adjusted by declaring that the zemindar should not be at
liberty to enhance the rents of the "independent
talookdars" and two other classes of renters who
paid the fixed sums due to the state through him,
simply for the convenience of government. The zemindar
was also restricted from enhancing the rent of the class of
tenants called *khoodkast*, who cultivated the lands of the
village in which they resided, except when their rents were

below the current rates, or when their tenures had been improperly obtained. The remaining lands of the estate he was at liberty to let in any manner and at any rate he pleased. For the protection of the resident cultivators it was enacted that the zemindar should keep a register of their tenures, and grant them pottahs, or leases, specifying the rent they were to pay, and that for any infringment of these rules the ryot was to seek a remedy in an action against him in the civil courts. But the registers were not kept, and pottahs were rarely given; and, as to the remedy, a poor man has little chance against his wealthy oppressor in courts where the native officers are universally venal, and their influence is paramount. By the unremitted contrivances of the zemindar, and changes of residence on the part of the ryot,—which extinguished all his rights,—the class of resident cultivators has been gradually diminished; and the ryots have been placed at the mercy of the zemindar. The absence of any clear and defined rules for the protection of the cultivator in his ancient right not to pay more than a limited and moderate rent, and to be kept in possession of his fields as long as he did so, is an unquestionable blot on a system which in other respects was highly beneficial.

Settlement
made perma-
nent, 1793.

After the settlement had been completed, the great and all important question came on whether it should be decennial or permanent. Mr. Shore, the highest authority in all revenue questions in India at the time, strenuously opposed every proposal to make it irrevocable. He argued that government did not yet possess sufficient knowledge of the capabilities of the land, and of the collections, to make an equitable distribution of the assessment. But Lord Cornwallis replied, with great force, that if we had not acquired this knowledge after twenty years of research, and after the collectors had been employed especially for three years in seeking for it, we could never expect to obtain it, and the settlement must be indefinitely postponed. He considered that the boon which it was proposed to confer

on the zemindars would give them an irresistible inducement
to promote cultivation, and to render their ryots comfortable.
Mr. Shore, with a more correct appreciation of the character
of the zemindars, affirmed that they had never been alive to
their true interests; that they were utterly ignorant of the
rudiments of agricultural science; that the whole zemindary
system was a mere conflict of extortion on their part and
resistance on the part of the ryot, the zemindar exacting
whatever he had any chance of wringing from him, and the
ryot refusing every cowrie he could withhold; and he argued
that the zemindar would not assume new principles of action
because his tenure was made permanent. But Lord Cornwallis was resolute in his opinion that a fixed and unalterable
assessment was the only panacea for the evils which afflicted
the country, and he strongly urged it upon Mr. Dundas.
Some of the leading members of the Court of Directors,
partly influenced by the weighty opinion of Mr. Shore, and
partly by their own convictions, adopted a contrary opinion;
but, as a body, they could not be persuaded to give their attention to the measure. Mr. Dundas resolved, therefore, that
it should originate with the Board of Control. Mr. Pitt,
who had for many years studied every Indian question with
great assiduity, shut himself up with Mr. Dundas at his
country seat at Wimbledon, determined to master the subject
in all its bearings and results. Mr. Charles Grant, who had
passed many years of his life in India, and combined the
largest experience with the most enlightened views,—though
he had not been considered worthy a place among the Directors,—was invited to assist Mr. Pitt and Mr. Dundas in these
deliberations, and he gave his suffrage for the perpetuity of
the settlement. Mr. Pitt at length declared his conviction
of the wisdom of this measure, and a despatch was accordingly drawn up by Mr. Dundas and sent to the Court of
Directors. The subject was too large for their consideration
in general, and the few who understood it, finding that the
Ministers of the Crown had made up their minds on the point,

thought it best to acquiesce, and the dispatch was sent out to India.

Result of the settlement. The permanent settlement of Bengal and Behar was promulgated in Calcutta on the 22nd of March, 1793. It was the broadest and most important administrative act which the British government had adopted since its establishment in India. At a period when the revenue derived from the land formed the bone and muscle of the public resources, and while one-third of the country was a jungle, the assessment was fixed for ever. No margin was allowed for the inevitable increase of expenditure in the defence of the country, and in the development of civilised institutions; and there was moreover the unquestionable conviction that where the rent happened to be excessive, it must be reduced; where it was inadequate, it could not be increased. With the experience of seventy years before us, we are enabled to discover many defects and inequalities in the settlement, and it would be a miracle if this were not the case; but we must not forget the impending ruin of the country which it was intended to avert. It was a bold, brave, and wise measure. Under the genial influence of this territorial charter, which for the first time created indefeasable rights and interests in the soil, population has increased, cultivation has been extended, and a gradual improvement has become visible in the habits and comfort of the people; and the revenues of the provinces of Bengal and Behar have increased to fourteen crores of rupees a-year, of which only four crores are derived from the lands. Before dismissing the subject it may be worthy of remark, that with all his benevolent and generous sympathies for the natives, Lord Cornwallis was not able to advance beyond the traditional creed of England, that all her colonial and foreign possessions were to be administered primarily and emphatically for her benefit. No effort was to be spared to secure the protection, the improvement, and the happiness of the people; but it was with an eye exclusively to the credit and the interests of the governing power. He closes his great minute

on the permanent settlement with this characteristic remark:
" The real value of Bengal and Behar to Britain depends on
the continuance of its ability to furnish a large annual investment to Europe, to assist in providing an investment for
China, and to supply the pressing wants of the other presidencies."

Reform of the civil courts, 1793. The administration of Lord Cornwallis was also
rendered memorable by the great changes intro-
duced into the judicial institutions of the Presidency. The collector of the revenue had hitherto acted also
as judge and magistrate. Lord Cornwallis separated the
financial from the judicial functions, and confined the collector
to his fiscal duties, placing him under a Board of Revenue at
the Presidency. A civil court was established in each district
and in the principal cities, with a judge, a register to determine cases of inferior value, and one or more covenanted assistants. Every person in the country was placed under the
jurisdiction of these courts, with the exception of British
subjects, who were, by Act of Parliament, amenable to the
Supreme Court. To receive appeals from the zillah and city
courts, four Courts of Appeal were constituted at Calcutta,
Dacca, Moorshedabad, and Patna, and from their decisions
an appeal lay to the Sudder Court at the Presidency, nominally
composed of the Governor-General and the members of
Council. All fees of every description were abolished, and
the expenses of a suit restricted to the remuneration of
pleaders and the expense of witnesses.

Criminal courts, 1793. For the administration of criminal law, it was
ordained that the judges of the four Courts of
Appeal should proceed on circuit, from zillah to zillah, within
their respective circles, and hold jail deliveries twice in the
year. The Mahomedan law, divested of some of its most
revolting precepts, was the criminal code of the courts, and
the Mahomedan law officer, on the completion of the trial at
which he had been present, was required to declare the sentence prescribed by that code, which was carried into execu-

tion if the judge concurred in it, and if he did not, it was referred to the Sudder Court, which was also constituted a Court of Appeal in criminal cases. The zillah judges were likewise invested with the powers of a magistrate, and authorized to pass and execute sentences in trivial offences, and, in other cases, to apprehend the delinquent and commit him for trial before the judges of circuit. Each zillah was divided into districts of about twenty miles square, to each of which an officer called a _daroga_ was appointed, with authority to arrest offenders on a written charge, and when the offence was bailable, to take security for appearance before the magistrate. Of all the provisions of the new system this proved to be the most baneful. The daroga, who was often fifty miles from the seat of control, enjoyed almost unlimited power of extortion, and became the scourge of the country.

The code of 1793.

For more than ten years, the clear and simple rules for the administration of justice, drawn up by Sir Elijah Impey, in 1781, had been the guide of the Courts. Lord Cornwallis considered it important that his new institutions should have all the certainty of fixed rules. " It was essential," he said, " to the future prosperity of the British in Bengal that all regulations affecting the rights, persons, and property of their subjects, should be formed into a code, and printed, with translations, in the country languages." Mr. George Barlow, a civil servant of mark at the time, and subsequently Governor-General, _ad interim_, and Governor of Madras, had the chief hand in manipulating the code of 1793, more especially in the police and judicial departments. He was ignorant of the principles or practice of law, except as he might have picked up some notion of them in the country courts. He expanded the ordinances of Sir Elijah into an elaborate volume of regulations, altering the original rules, without improving them. This code, however valuable as a monument of British benevolence, was altogether unsuited to a people who had been accustomed to have justice distributed by simple and rational enquiry. The course of procedure was loaded with formalities, and the multiplication of puzzling and pedantic rules only served to bewilder the mind, and to defeat the object in view. There was, in fact, too much law for there to be much justice. Every suit became a game of chess, and afforded the amplest scope for oriental ingenuity and chicanery. "Justice was thus made sour" by delay, and equity was smothered by legal processes. To add to the impediments thrown in the course of justice, it was administered in a language equally foreign to the judge and the suitors.

Exclusion of natives from power, 1793.

Notwithstanding the wisdom exhibited in Lord Cornwallis's institutions, they were deformed by one great and radical error. He considered it necessary that the whole administration of the country should be placed exclusively in the hands of covenanted servants of the Company, to the entire exclusion of all native agency. In the criminal department, the only native officer entrusted with any power was the Daroga, upon an allowance of twenty-five rupees a month. In the administration of civil justice, cases of only the most trivial amount were made over to a native judge, under the title of Moonsiff; but while the salary of the European judge was raised to 2,500 rupees a month, the Moonsiff was deprived of all pay, and left to find a subsistence by a small commission on the value of suits; in other words, by the encouragement of litigation. Under all former conquerors, civil and military offices, with few exceptions, were open to the natives of the country, who might aspire, with confidence, to the post of minister, and to the command of armies. But under the impolitic system established in 1793, the prospects of legitimate and honourable ambition were altogether closed against the natives of the country. If the peculiar nature of British rule rendered it necessary to retain all political and military power in the hands of Europeans, this was no reason for denying the natives every opportunity of rising to distinction in the judicial departments, for which they were eminently qualified by their industrious habits, and their natural sagacity, not less than by the knowledge they possessed of the language and character of their fellow-countrymen. The fatal effects of this exclusion were speedily visible in the disrepute and in-efficiency of the whole administration. With only three or four European functionaries in a district, which often contained a million of inhabitants, the machine of government must have stood still without the services of natives. But this power and influence from which it was impossible to exclude them, being exercised without responsibility, was used for the purposes of oppression, and the courts of every description became the hot-bed of corruption and venality.

Capture of
Pondicherry,
1793

The remaining events of 1793 are few and un-important. Information having been received that France had declared war against England, Lord Cornwallis issued orders for the assemblage of a large force at Madras, intending to take the command of it in person, and march against Pondicherry. He embarked at Calcutta on the 25th of August, but was twenty-five days in reaching Madras. On his arrival there, he found that Colonel Brathwaite had proceeded to invest Pondicherry, and that, in consequence of the insubordination of the French troops, the governor had been obliged to capitulate a few days before. Lord Cornwallis embarked for England in October, after a memorable reign of seven years, during which period he had given strength and stability to the power established by the daring of Clive, and consolidated by the genius of Hastings. The dignity and firmness which he exhibited in his intercourse with the princes of India conciliated and overawed them, while the supreme authority which he exercised over all the Presidencies, convinced them that a new element of vigour had been introduced into the British government in India, which rendered it more formidable than ever.

Progress of
Sindia's en-
croachments,
1784.

The treaty of Salbye, which Sindia had con-cluded with Hastings, on the part of the Mah-ratta powers in 1782, raised him to a commanding

position in the politics of India. He was no longer a mere
feudatory of the Peshwa, but an independent chief, the ally
of the British Government, who had honoured his capital with
the presence of their representative. He determined to lose
no time in improving these advantages, and of pushing his
schemes of ambition in Hindostan. The state of affairs at
Delhi was eminently favourable to these views. The imbecile
emperor was a puppet in the hands of Afrasiab Khan, who
invoked the aid of Sindia, in his master's name, to demolish
the power of his rival, Mahomed Beg. Sindia accepted the invitation with alacrity, and advanced with a large force to Agra,
where he had a meeting with the emperor in October, 1784.
Afrasiab was soon after assassinated, and the authority of
the imperial court, and the influence connected with it, were at
once transferred to Sindia. He refused the title of Ameer-ool-
omrah, but accepted that of Vakeel-ool-mutluk, or Regent of
the empire, for the Peshwa, and the post of deputy for himself,
and was thus nominally invested with the executive authority
of the Mogul throne. The emperor likewise conferred on him
the command of the imperial forces, and assigned to him the
provinces of Agra and Delhi, out of which he agreed to pay
65,000 rupees monthly, for the expenditure of the emperor's
household. His ambitious views were thus gratified sooner
than he had expected, and in the elation of success, and
encouraged likewise by the departure of Hastings, he demanded the arrears of *chout* for Bengal and Behar, but
Mr. Macpherson not only rejected the claim with indignation,
but constrained him to offer a humble apology for having
made it.

Sindia attacks
the Rajpoots,
and is defeated,
1787

The resources of the provinces of Agra and Delhi,
which had been exhausted by constant hostilities,
were found inadequate to the maintenance of the
large force which Sindia entertained, and he sequestered the
jaygeers of the Mahomedan nobles of the court. A powerful
party was thus raised against him, which received secret
encouragement from the emperor himself. Sindia then pro-

ceded to despoil the Rajpoots, and at the gates of Jeypore made a demand of sixty lacs of rupees, as tribute due to the imperial treasury. The greater portion of this sum was paid, but when his general appeared to claim the remainder, the Rajpoot tribes made common cause, and attacked and routed him. Sindia advanced with all his troops to encounter them, but Mahomed Beg, who joined his standard after the murder of Afrasiab, fearing that the confiscation of his estates would not be long delayed, if Sindia were victorious, chose the eve of the battle for going over to the Rajpoots. He was killed in the engagement which followed, but his gallant nephew, Ismael Beg, one of the best native soldiers of the age, rallied the troops, and Sindia was obliged to retire. He was preparing to renew the conflict, on the third day, when the whole of the emperor's troops went over in a body to Ismael Beg, with eighty pieces of cannon. Sindia had not been reduced to such straits since he fled from the field of Paniput, but in no emergency did he evince greater fortitude and conduct. Fortunately for him, the Rajpoots, satisfied with their success, retired to their respective homes, instead of following up the victory. They left Ismael Beg to conduct the war alone, and he laid siege to Agra, the fortifications of which had been greatly strengthened by Sindia. In this extremity, he addressed Nana Furnuvese, and importuned him to aid him in maintaining the Mahratta ascendancy in Hindostan. But Nana was jealous of the growing power of Sindia, who he knew was aiming at the supreme control of the Mahratta commonwealth, and although he did not fail to send forward troops under Holkar and Ali Bahadoor, they were intended rather to watch and check his movements than to assist them.

Gholam Kadir, 1788.   In this position of affairs, the infamous Gholam Kadir, a turbulent soldier of fortune, the son of the Rohilla chief, Zabita Khan, who had died in June, 1785, appeared on the scene. Ismael Beg was still engaged in the siege of Agra. Gholam Kadir, with his body of free

E 2

lances joined him there, and Sindia advanced to attack them
both. On the 24th of April, they raised the siege and advanced sixteen miles to meet him; Sindia was completely
overpowered, and obliged to retreat to Bhurtpore, the capital
of the friendly Jauts. Gholam Kadir was soon after called
off to defend his own jaygeer from the encroachments of the
Sikhs, by whom it was invaded at the instigation of Sindia,
who took advantage of the circumstance to attack Ismael
Beg, under the walls of Agra. The battle was fought on the
18th day of June, 1788, and terminated in the complete dis·
persion of Ismael's troops. He immediately joined the camp
of Gholam Kadir, and they advanced together towards Delhi,
but the emperor refused to admit either of them into it.
Gholam Kadir, however, succeeded in corrupting one of the
emperor's confidential officers, seized the gates of the city,
and occupied the palace and the citadel. He then let loose
his licentious soldiers on the city, which was for two months
subjected to a degree of violence, rapine and barbarity, unexampled even in the gloomy annals of that imperial metropolis, which had been so repeatedly devoted to spoliation.
The wives and daughters, and female relatives of the emperor
were exposed and dishonoured, while some were, more mer-
cifully, put to death. To crown his infamy, the
ruffian put out the eyes of the wretched monarch
in their sockets with his dagger. Ismael Beg
turned with horror from the sight of these atrocities, and on
receiving the promise of a jaygeer, entered the service of
Sindia, who advanced to Delhi, reseated the emperor on the
throne, and did everything that humanity could suggest, to
alleviate the sorrows of the old man, then in his sixty-fifth
year. A force was sent after Gholam Kadir who took shelter
in Meerut, where he defended himself with vigour, but seeing
his case desperate, mounted a swift horse and fled across the
country, but was captured and brought into the presence of
Sindia, who subjected him to the most barbarous mutilations,
under which he expired.

Gholam Kadir blinds the emperor, 1788.

Sindia's European force, 1785—1791. The success which had attended the exertions of Sindia was owing, in a great measure, to the force which he had organised under European officers. He could not fail to perceive that the native Mahratta soldier, though admirably adapted for marauding expeditions, was ill suited for regular warfare, or for the maintenance of such a power as he was endeavouring to establish; and he resolved to create a Sepoy army on the model of the English battalions. The Count de Boigne, a native of Savoy, had come to India in quest of service, and circumstances brought him to the camp of Sindia, by whom he was immediately entertained. He was an officer of distinguished talents and great military experience, having served both in Europe and in India, and a large force was gradually formed under his direction, consisting chiefly of Rajpoots and Mahomedans, commanded and disciplined by European officers, many of whom were English adventurers. The force was eventually raised to 18,000 regular infantry, 6,000 irregular and 2,000 regular cavalry, and 600 Persian horse. With the aid of these regiments Sindia was enabled to fight pitched battles, and to capture towns and forts, as no Mahratta chief had ever done before. A foundry was likewise established, and 200 cannon cast. The equipment of this formidable force completely established Sindia's authority in Hindostan, and made him the most powerful member of the Mahratta confederation.

Battle of Patun, June 17, 1790. The turbulent Ismael Beg did not long remain faithful to Sindia, and he was joined by the Rajpoot rajas of Jeypore and Joudhpore. Sindia attacked the allies at Patun, on the 20th of June, 1790. Ismael fought with his usual bravery, and thrice charged through Sindia's regular infantry, cutting down the artillerymen at their guns. Holkar's force stood aloof during the engagement, and the issue of the battle was for a time doubtful, but the personal gallantry of De Boigne and his European officers, and the firmness of his disciplined troops, secured the day to his

master, though not, as it was affirmed, without the loss of
11,000 men. Ismael Beg fled with a small retinue to Jeypore, all his guns were captured, and ten of his battalions
grounded their arms and surrendered. The Rajpoots, how-
Battle of Mairta, ever, still continued to maintain the war, and in
12th Sept., 1791. the succeeding year a second battle was fought,
at Mairta, in which De Boigne achieved another victory. The
Rajpoot tribes were now apparently at Sindia's mercy, but
the equivocal conduct of Holkar induced him to grant them
peace on the payment of a moderate tribute. The raja of
Joudhpore, however, who had assassinated Sindia's brother,
Jayapa, thirty-two years before, was now required to surrender Ajmere to atone for the deed.

Sindia marches   Sindia had offered to join the alliance against
to Poona, 1792. Tippoo, in 1790, on the condition that two battalions of English troops should accompany him to Poona,
that his own conquests in Hindostan should be guaranteed,
and that he should be assisted to effect the complete subjugation of the Rajpoot states. Lord Cornwallis necessarily
rejected these terms, upon which he entered into correspondence with Tippoo—all the while, however, professsing the
warmest attachment for the Company—and assumed a
threatening attitude towards the Peshwa; and, if the arms
of the allies had met with any serious reverse in the war with
Tippoo, would doubtless have made common cause with that
prince against them. That he might be in a position to take
advantage of circumstances, and establish his authority at the
Mahratta capital, he resolved to proceed thither, much against
the wishes of Nana Furnuvese, who was justly apprehensive
of his designs. After the battle of Patun, he had obtained
from the emperor, for the third time, patents constituting the
Peshwa Vakeel-ool-mootluk, or regent of the empire, and
Sindia and his descendants, hereditary deputies. It may
serve to give some idea of the prestige which still lingered
about the Mogul throne, that, at a time when the emperor
was dependant on Sindia for the daily expenses of his house-

hold, such a sunnud as this was considered an important acquisition in the Deccan. As a pretext for appearing at . Poona, he gave out that he was proceeding to invest the Peshwa with the robes of his new office. He arrived at the capital on the 11th of June, 1792, and in order to exhibit his influence over the imperial house, as well as to gratify the feelings of the Hindoos, he published an edict he had extorted from the emperor, forbidding the slaughter of bullocks and cows throughout the Mogul dominions. Nana Furnuvese used every effort to prevent the Peshwa's accepting the title conferred on him, but Sindia had brought a large variety of rarities with him from Hindostan which delighted the fancy of the young prince, and, by making constant arrangements for his amusement, obtained a complete ascendancy over him. A day was accordingly fixed for the investiture.

The grand investiture, July, 1792.
Sindia spared no pains to render the ceremony imposing. A grand suite of tents was pitched in the vicinity of the town, and the Peshwa proceeded to them with the greatest pomp. At the farthest end of the great tent of state a throne was erected to represent that of the Great Mogul, on which the imperial sunnud and the insignia were placed. The Peshwa approached it and placed on it the usual offering of a hundred and one gold mohurs, and took his seat on the right, when Sindia's secretary read out the patent, as well as the edict abolishing the slaughter of kine. The Peshwa was then invested with the gorgeous robes and splendid jewels of the office, and returned to Poona amidst the acclamations of thousands, and salvos of artillery. The grandeur of the scene exceeded everything which had ever been seen in the Mahratta capital before. It was on this occasion that Sindia exhibited one of the most extraordinary specimens of mock humility recorded in Indian history. It must be borne in mind that three months before this time, Tippoo had been stripped of half his dominions, and that Sindia was now the most powerful native prince in India, and master of an army composed of sixteen battalions

of regular infantry, five hundred pieces of cannon, and a
.hundred thousand horse. But he dismounted from his elephant
at the gates of Poona, and in the great hall of audience
placed himself below all the. hereditary nobles of the state.
The Peshwa entered the room, and desired him to take his seat
among the highest dignitaries, when he replied that he was
unworthy of that honour, and untying a bundle which he
carried under his arm, produced a pair of slippers, which he
put before the Peshwa, saying, "This is my occupation; it
was that of my father," and it was with great apparent reluctance that he allowed himself to be conducted to the
honourable seat prepared for him.

Battle with   Sindia and Nana Furnuvese, after this trans-
Holkar, 1792.   action, maintained an outward appearance of
respect and civility, though plotting each other's destruction;
but their respective forces in Hindostan could not be restrained
from open hostility. They had been engaged together in
levying tribute from the Rajpoots, and had captured two forts,
but quarrelled about the division of the spoil. De Boigne,
with.20,000 horse and 9,000 regular infantry, fell on Holkar's
army of 30,000 horse, and four battalions disciplined by Europeans. The conflict was desperate, and the four battalions
were completely annihilated, only one European officer escaping the carnage. Holkar retreated with the wreck of his
army, and on his route sacked and burnt Sindia's capital,
Oojein. This battle rendered Sindia absolute in Hindostan,
and served to aggravate the intrigues at Poona, and to deepen
the alarm of Nana Furnuvese. But he was unexpectedly re-
Death of   lieved from all-anxiety by the death of Sindia, on
Sindia, 12th   the 12th of February, 1794. Had he lived a few
Feb., 1794.   months longer, a contest for the office of chief
minister of the Peshwa, and the supreme command of the
Mahratta power would have been inevitable. For thirty-
five years he may be said to have passed his life in the camp,
devoting himself to the improvement of his army, and the
increase of his resources. His character has been aptly.

summed up in a few words, by the great historian of the Mahrattas, "he was a man of great political sagacity, and considerable genius, of deep artifice, restless ambition and implacable revenge." He received from his father a small
principality; he bequeathed to his successor, a lad of thirteen,
a kingdom comprising all the territory from the Sutlege to
Allahabad, two-thirds of Malwa, and the fairest provinces in
the Deccan, as well as the finest native army in India.

Enlargement
of the powers
of the Gover-
nor-General,
1786.

The proceedings in England in connection with
the government of India, subsequent to Mr. Pitt's
Bill in 1784, will now claim attention.   The
Regulating Act of 1773, which created the office
of Governor-General, made him responsible for the safety of
India, but gave him only a single vote in Council, and rendered him liable, on every occasion, to be overruled by his
colleagues.   The distractions of Hastings's administration
are to be attributed, in a great measure, to this anomalous
clause, which frequently brought the Government to a dead
lock.   Lord Cornwallis therefore refused to accept the office,
subject to this encumbrance, and a Bill was introduced and
passed in 1786 to enable the Governor-General and the Governors of the minor Presidencies to act in opposition to the
opinion of the Council, when they deemed it necessary for
the welfare of the country, the counsellors being at liberty
to record the reasons of their dissent.   Of the wisdom of
this measure no better proof can be offered than the fact
that it has worked beneficially for nearly eighty years.

The Declara-
tory Act, 1788.

The gravest movement of this period, however,
was the consummation of Mr. Pitt's plan of trans-
ferring the powers of government from the Company to the
Crown.   In the year 1787, a conflict of parties arose in the
republic of Holland; the French and the English Governments
espoused opposite sides, and there was every prospect of a
rupture between them.   The interference of France in the
politics of India, had been for half a century the great object
of dread to the Court of Directors, and under the apprehen-

sion that they might have again to encounter it, they now solicited the Ministry to augment the European force in India, and four regiments were immediately raised for their service. Happily, the peace with France was not interrupted, but, as soon as the storm had blown over, the Court of Directors, anxious to save the cost of the regiments, declared that they were no longer necessary. Lord Cornwallis had earnestly recommended the augmentation of the European force in India, to give greater security to our position, and the Board of Control therefore determined that the regiments should be sent out. The Court of Directors, however, refused to allow them to embark in their ships, and as the contest, which thus arose between the India House and the Ministry, involved the great question of the substantial powers of government, Mr. Pitt referred the question to the decision of Parliament.

Discussions in Parliament, 1788.

On the 25th of February, 1788, Mr. Pitt introduced a Bill to declare the meaning of the Act of 1784, and affirmed that "there was no step which could have been taken by the Court of Directors before the passing of that Bill, touching the military and political concerns of India, and the collection, management, and application of the revenues, which the Board of Control had not a right to take by the provisions of that Bill." He stated, moreover, that in proposing his Bill of 1784 it was his intention thus to transfer the whole powers of government to the Crown. The organs of the Court of Directors in the House stated that they never would have supported that measure, if they had supposed such to have been its intent; and they discovered, when too late, that in voting for Mr. Pitt's Bill they had committed an act of suicide. An objection was raised to the despatch of the regiments on the constitutional doctrine that no troops could belong to the King for which Parliament had not voted the money. Mr. Pitt thereupon stated his conviction that the army in India ought to be on one establishment, and to belong to the King, and that it was not without an eye to such an arrangement that he had brought forward the present motion. But, notwithstanding the boundless influence which he enjoyed in the House, the members were alarmed at the immense power which he attempted to grasp. Many of his stanch supporters deserted him, and the Opposition were very sanguine in their hopes of being able to overthrow the Ministry on this occasion. There were four tempestuous debates on the question, one of which was prolonged to eight o'clock in the morning. Mr. Pitt had encountered no such opposition in the present Parliament, and to prevent being beaten in the successive stages of the Bill, was under the necessity of making great concessions, and adding several conciliatory clauses to it. The Declaratory Act of 1788 rivetted on the East India Company the fetters which had been forged by the Act of 1784.

The Charter of 1793. The period for which the exclusive privileges had been granted to the East India Company expired in 1793, and on the 23rd of April, the Court of Directors presented a petition to Parliament for the renewal of them. But new commercial and manufacturing interests had been springing up in England with great vigour since the last concession, and petitions poured into the House from Liverpool, Glasgow, Manchester, Bristol, and other seats of industry and enterprize, protesting against the continuance of a monopoly in so large a trade, and the exclusion of the country in general from any share in it. The Court of Directors appointed a Committee to draw up a reply to the petitioners, and to demonstrate that it was essential to the national interests that the East India Company should continue to be the sole agent for managing the commerce and government of India. The Ministry found the existing state of things, more especially since the Declaratory Act, exceedingly convenient to themselves, and resolved to oppose all innovation. Fortunately for the Company, Lord Cornwallis, notwithstanding the Mysore war, had placed the finances of India in a more flourishing condition than they had ever been in before;

and, it may be said, than they have ever been in since.
Mr. Dundas was thus enabled to ask the House, with an air
of triumph, whether they were prepared to stop the tide of
this prosperity, for a mere theory.

Arguments for
renewing the
Charter, 1793.

The arguments which he adduced for continuing the power and privileges of the East
India Company were, that to throw the trade
open to all England would retard the payment of the Company's debts; that it would check the growing commerce of
India, and that it would inevitably lead to colonization and
ensure the loss of the country to England. He objected to
the dissolution of the Company, because the patronage of
India, added to the other sources of influence in the Crown,
would destroy the balance of the Constitution. These arguments, solemnly propounded by the Ministers, at a period
when free trade was considered the direct road to ruin, were
received with blind confidence by the House, and the privileges
of the Company were renewed, with little modification, for a
period of twenty years. To meet the clamours of the merchants and manufacturers of England, the Company was
directed to allot 3,000 tons a year for private trade, but as the
privilege was hampered with the heavy charges and delays
of their commercial system, it was little prized, and seldom
used. An effort was made by Mr. Wilberforce, one of the
ablest and most enlightened members of the House, to obtain
permission for missionaries and schoolmasters to proceed to
India, and give voluntary instruction to the people, but he
was vehemently opposed by the old Indians in the Court of
Directors, who had imbibed the fantastic notion that the
diffusion of knowledge would be fatal to British rule in India,
and that the presence of missionaries would be followed by
rebellion; and the House was persuaded by Mr. Dundas to
reject the proposal.

Remarks on the
Charter, 1793.

The Charter, as it is called, of 1793, may be
regarded as a faithful reflection of the narrow
views of the age, which, considered that the introduction of

free trade and Europeans, of missionaries and schoolmasters,
into India, would sap the foundation of British authority.
The experience of nearly three-quarters of a century has
dispelled this hallucination. Since the extinction of the
Company's monopoly, the trade, instead of being diminished,
has increased twenty fold. The free admission of Europeans
into India has not endangered the dominion of England; on
the contrary, during the great mutiny of 1857, India was
nearly lost for want of Europeans. The patronage of India
has been trebled in value, and the Company has been
abolished, yet, owing to the happy discovery of the principle
of competitive appointments, the power of the Crown has not
been increased, and the independence of Parliament has not
diminished. Christian missionaries have been admitted into
India and placed on the same footing as the Hindoo priest
and the Mahomedan mollah, and allowed to offer instruction to
the natives; and, the education of the people is now considered
as much a duty of the state as the maintenance of the police;
—yet the feeling of allegiance to the Crown of England has
not been impaired.

CHAPTER XVIII.

ADMINISTRATION OF SIR JOHN SHORE, 1793—1798.

Sir John Shore
Governor-Gene-
ral, 1793.

Sir John Shore, a distinguished member of the
Company's civil service, and the author of the
revenue settlement of 1793, succeeded to the government, on the departure of Lord Cornwallis, who, in a
letter to Mr. Dundas on the choice of his successor, had given
it as his opinion, that "nobody but a person who had never
been in the service, and who was essentially unconnected
with its members, who was of a rank far surpassing his asso-
ciates in the government, and who had the full support of
the Ministry at home, was competent for the office of Gover-

nor-General." Subsequently to the date of this letter, Sir
John, then Mr. Shore, had visited England, and on his return,
Lord Cornwallis wrote again to Mr. Dundas, that "seeing
how greatly Mr. Shore's mind had been enlarged and improved
by the visit, he desired to make an exception in his favour."
Mr. Pitt, who had taken great interest in the question of the
revenue settlement, had been much struck with the industry,
candour and talent exhibited by Sir John Shore, and, believing him to be well suited to carry out the views of Lord
Cornwallis, mentioned his name to the King as his successor.
The King replied, that "No one could have been so properly
thought of as Mr. Shore, unless a very proper man of distinction could be found to be Governor General at Bengal."
Sir John Shore, therefore, received the appointment, and entered on the duties of his office on the 28th of October, 1793.

Guarantee treaty accepted by the Nizam, 1792–93.
The first question of importance which came up
to test his powers, was connected with the politics
of the Deccan. The treaty of alliance concluded
with the Nizam and the Mahrattas by Lord Corn-
wallis in 1790, stipulated, that "if after the conclusion of the
peace with Tippoo, he should attack or molest either of the
contracting parties, the others shall join to punish him, the
mode or conditions of effecting which shall be hereafter settled
by the contracting parties." To avoid future complications,
Lord Cornwallis was anxious, after the termination of the
war, that the grounds on which the allied powers could demand
mutual support, should be distinctly defined. He accordingly
sent the draft of a "treaty of guarantee," to Poona and
Hyderabad, in which he proposed that if any difference should
arise between any of the confederates and Tippoo, the nature
and circumstances should be communicated to the others,
and that they should not be bound to take up arms till they
were convinced that he had justice on his side, and that every
effort for conciliation had been exhausted. The proposal was
highly acceptable to the Nizam. The Mahrattas had a long
account against him, and their envoys were pressing the

settlement of it at Hyderabad, at the time when his army was employed conjointly with theirs against Tippoo. The Nizam brought forward a counter-claim of larger amount, under thirty-four heads, for contributions unjustly exacted, and revenue unjustly withheld. But he proposed to postpone the adjustment of these accounts till the war had terminated, hoping thereby to obtain the friendly interposition of the English government. He therefore welcomed the treaty of guarantee with much avidity, under the impression that it would serve to strengthen his influence with Lord Cornwallis, and counteract the hostility of the Poona durbar, who were already preparing to invade his territories.

Rejected by the Mahrattas, 1793.   The Mahrattas, on the other hand, declined any engagements which might in any measure interfere with their designs on the Nizam. Mahdajee Sindia was then at Poona, exercising a powerful influence in the councils of the state, and he did not conceal his opinion that the Company had become too powerful, and that Tippoo ought to be supported as a counterpoise to them. He denounced the proposed treaty as an arrogant assumption of authority. Nana Furnuvese, however, was anxious to cultivate a good understanding with the English government, as a check on the ambitious projects of Sindia, and prolonged the negotiations for several months. He then drew up the outline of another treaty, including in it the demand of arrears of *chout* from Tippoo, which he was well aware Lord Cornwallis would never sanction. After a twelvemonth vainly spent in these wearisome discussions, the Governor-General was obliged to abandon all hope of obtaining the concurrence of the Mahrattas in any arrangement, and to remain content with a vague and verbal assurance, that they would abide by their engagements.

Sir John Shore's neutrality, 1794-95.   At the beginning of 1794, the death of Mahdajee Sindia, the chief opponent of the Guarantee treaty, and the succession of his grand-nephew Dowlut Rao, a youth of thirteen, to his power and resources, appeared to present a favourable opportunity for the energetic interposition of British influence to preserve the peace of India. But Sir John Shore determined to remain quiescent. The Mahrattas, who expected some decisive movement on this occasion, were not slow to perceive that the sceptre of the British power had fallen into feeble hands; and as soon as they discovered that Lord Cornwallis's successor was resolved to limit his interference to "good offices," they hastened their preparations for war with the Nizam. Tippoo likewise announced his intention of joining them to crush the Nizam, who immediately claimed from the Government of Calcutta the fulfilment of the 10th article of the treaty of 1790, which bound the contracting parties to unite in repelling his aggressions. There can be little doubt that if Lord Cornwallis had been in India at this time, his manly representations, backed by the assembly of an army on the frontier, would have been sufficient to maintain peace between the parties. But Sir John Shore lacked his spirit and resolution; he had a morbid dread of giving offence to the Mahrattas, which might end in a war, and drain the treasury, then full to the brim; and he was above all anxious to exhibit a most exemplary obedience to the Act of Parliament which discountenanced native alliances. The question which he put to himself was "whether we were bound by treaty to defend the Nizam, if Tippoo should attack him while engaged in hostilities with the Mahrattas, either as their ally or independently of them." Strange to say, his opinion was in the negative. The Nizam pleaded that in becoming a party to the treaty of 1790, he had trusted to the good faith of the English Government, not to the treachery of the Mahrattas. But Sir John Shore persuaded himself that the defection of one of the parties from a tripartite alliance, offensive and defensive, and his union with the power against whom the treaty was made, cancelled the obligation of the remaining party. It is, however due to his memory to state that his judgment was evidently influenced, to a considerable extent, by the incompetence of his Commander-in-chief to take charge of a war with Tippoo and the Mahrattas. He resolved,

therefore, to remain neuter, and leave the Nizam to his fate.
And thus the high reputation which the British Government
had acquired throughout India by the prompt succour of the
raja of Travancore when attacked by the armies of Tippoo,
was sacrificed by his successor, from motives of expedience
and economy, and too obsequious a submission to an Act of
Parliament through which Lord Cornwallis had boldly driven
his coach, and had, nevertheless, received the thanks of both
Houses.

Expedition against the Nizam, 1795.   To assemble a Mahratta army when there was
a prospect of plunder had never presented any
difficulty. On the present occasion the young
Peshwa resolved to accompany the expedition, and summoned
all the feudatories into the field; and it proved to be the last
time they were mustered under the national standard. Dowlut
Rao Sindia brought up a force of 25,000, of whom 10,000 consisted of De Boigne's regular infantry. The Raja of Berar
contributed 15,000 horse and foot. Holkar's contingent was
only 10,000, but of these 2,000 were disciplined by European
officers; and he had, moreover, a following of 10,000 Pindarrees.
Govind Rao Guickwar likewise sent a detachment of troops,
and all the southern Jaygeerdars furnished their quota. The
whole army mustered 130,000 horse and foot, and 150 pieces
of cannon. The Nizam, abandoned by his English allies,
threw himself into the hands of their European rivals, with
whom they were then at war. A French officer of the name
of Raymond, who had come out to India with Lally, twenty-
five years before, and fully shared his animosity towards the
English, had entered the service of the Nizam; and organised
two battalions, which did good service in the Mysore war.
When the struggle with the Mahrattas appeared inevitable,
he was directed to increase his force to the fullest possible
extent. The procrastination of the Mahrattas, arising from
the dissensions created by the death of Mahdajee Sindia,
enabled Raymond to raise this body of troops to 18,000, all
of whom were trained and commanded by European officers.

II.   F

The war with the Mahrattas, while at a distance, was popular with the Hyderabad army. The disorderly soldiers indulged in the wildest gasconade, threatening to plunder and burn Poona; the dancing girls moved through the camp chaunting the triumphs the army was about to achieve, and even the chief minister, forgetting his own dignity, boasted that the Peshwa should be banished to Benares, with a cloth about his loins and a water-pot in his hand, to mutter incantations on the banks of the sacred stream.

Defeat of the Nizam at Kurdla, 11th March, 1795. The Nizam was the first in the field, and advanced from Beder, where he had established his camp, towards the Mahratta frontier. The Peshwa quitted Poona in January, and the two armies approached each other on the 10th of March. On that evening the Nizam sat in durbar, and received congratulations for the victory of the morrow. The forces joined issue on the 11th, a little in advance of the village of Kurdla, which has given its name to the battle. The Nizam's Patan cavalry drove the centre division of the Mahratta army, commanded by Pureshram Bhao, from the field, and a large portion of his army was seized with a panic and fled. By this time the regular battalions on both sides approached within musket shot of each other, and the Nizam's cavalry were advancing steadily to the support of their infantry, when Rughoojee Bhonslay assailed them with a shower of rockets, and Perron, who commanded Sindia's disciplined troops, poured in a destructive fire from thirty-five pieces of cannon he had judiciously planted on an eminence. The cavalry was put to the route, but Raymond's infantry stood their ground, and had even obtained some advantage over Perron's battalions, when he was obliged, in consequence of repeated and pressing orders, to follow the Nizam, who had retraced his steps, to Kurdla. The Nizam was accompanied on this expedition by his zenana, and the favourite Sultana, terrified by the roar of the artillery, insisted on his retiring beyond the reach of it, and threatened, if he refused, to disgrace him by exposing herself to public gaze. The dotard

yielded to her importunities, and the whole army retreated in
wild confusion. The greater portion of the troops fled from
the field, after having plundered the baggage of their own
army, but the Pindarrees pursued them, and stripped them of
everything they possessed. The next morning the Mahrattas
advanced over the field, and found it strewed with guns,
stores, baggage, and all the equipments of the army. Only a
tenth of the Nizam's force remained about Kurdla, in which he
had taken refuge, and where, after sustaining the cannonade
of the Mahrattas for two days, he solicited a cessation of
arms. The Mahrattas demanded territorial cessions of the
value of thirty-five lacs of rupees a-year, together with an
indemnity of three crores of rupees, one-third to be paid down
immediately, as well as the surrender of Musheer-ool-moolk,
his chief minister, and the ablest man at his court, on the
pretext that amends must be made for some insulting language
he was reported to have used in reference to Nana Furnuvese.
With these hard conditions the Nizam was constrained to
comply, and he affixed his signature to the humiliating treaty
on the 13th of March, 1795.

The Nizam in-
creases his
French force,
1795.

During these transactions the British ministers
at the court of the Nizam and the Peshwa removed from their camps, and remained in the
neighbourhood, mere spectators of the event. Neither were
the two English battalions in the pay of the Nizam allowed
to take any part in the war, notwithstanding his earnest
entreaty. He returned to his capital highly incensed at this
neutrality, and immediately dismissed the battalions, while
Raymond was directed to increase his force with all diligence.
He and his officers lost no opportunity of manifesting their
hatred of the English; they carried the colours of the French
republic, then at war with England, and wore the cap of
liberty on their buttons. Raymond made the greatest and
most successful exertions to improve the discipline and efficiency of his corps, and the power and resources of the
Hyderabad state, which Lord Cornwallis had endeavoured to

F 2

secure for the interests of the British nation, were thus transferred to its enemies. The Nizam, following the example of Sindia, determined to assign districts for the support of this foreign force, and Raymond made his selection of Kurpa, because it lay on the confines of the Company's territories, and was comparatively adjacent to the coast, from which he would be enabled to receive recruits, and possibly co-operate with a regiment then expected from France. But even the pacific Shore could not brook the presumption of the Nizam in planting a hostile force in the immediate neighbourhood of the British territories. He peremptorily insisted on their removal, and threatened to enforce the demand by a military demonstration. Just at this juncture an unexpected event—the rebellion of the Nizam's son, Ali Jah—served in some measure to restore a good understanding between him and the government of Calcutta. On the night of the 28th of June that prince abruptly quitted Hyderabad, and proceeded to Beder, where he raised the standard of revolt. The Nizam was thrown into a fever of alarm, and recalled the English battalions in all haste, and offered immediately to remove the French force from the frontier. The battalions were directed to march against the prince with the utmost expedition; but before they could reach Beder, Raymond's corps had extinguished the revolt.

Death of the Peshwa relieves the Nizam, 1795.   The battle of Kurdla completely prostrated the Nizam, and left him at the mercy of the Mahrattas, who would doubtless have returned to complete his humiliation after the division of the spoil, had not the sudden death of the Peshwa given a new direction to the current of events, and restored to him much of his previous consequence. By the success of the recent campaign Nana Furnuvese had gained the summit of his wishes. He had restored the Mahratta supremacy in the Deccan, and gratified the Mahratta chiefs with plunder. Dowlut Rao Sindia manifested the greatest deference to him; the raja of Berar and the great brahmin feudatories were entirely subservient to him. He was without a rival in the Mahratta commonwealth; but his love of power, and his anxiety to monopolise it, produced an event which brought him to the grave in misery and disgrace. During the minority of the Peshwa, Madhoo Rao, the second, Nana had for twenty years enjoyed, with occasional interruptions, the chief control of Mahratta affairs at the capital. But though the Peshwa was now of age he was still kept by the minister in a state of the most stringent and galling tutelage, and in a fit of impatience threw himself from a terrace of the palace on the 22nd of October, 1795. He died two days after, bequeathing his throne to his cousin Bajee Rao, the son of the luckless Raghoba, and the last of the Peshwas. Bajee Rao was a prince of many accomplishments, mental and bodily, graceful in person, mild in his demeanour, and of the most insinuating address, but distinguished above every prince of the age by his profound dissimulation, and his utter unscrupulousness. As he grew up Nana Furnuvese had watched his movements with great jealousy, and had for some time detained him a close prisoner. The unexpected death of the Peshwa confounded all the plans of Nana, and gave rise to a series of complications unmatched even in Mahratta history, of which, however, we can find room for only a brief outline.

Chimnajee,   Immediately after the catastrophe Nana as-
Peshwa, 1796.   sembled the Mahratta chiefs, carefully suppressed
the dying bequest of the late Peshwa in favour of Bajee Rao, and proposed that his widow should be required to adopt Chimnajee, the younger brother of Bajee Rao, in whose name he himself intended to continue to administer the government. Bajee Rao, on receiving intimation of this plot, which, if successful, would have deprived him of all his rights, opened a secret correspondence with young Sindia and his minister, Balloba Tantia, and offered them jaygeers of the value of four lacs of rupees a year if they would support his claim to the succession. Nana Furnuvese discovered this negotiation, and resolved to circumvent Sindia by releasing Bajee Rao of

his own accord, and placing him on the vacant throne. That prince was accordingly conducted to Poona, and reconciled to Nana, whom he engaged to maintain as his minister. Meanwhile Balloba, Sindia's chief adviser, who resented this proceeding, resolved to counteract the designs of Nana, and directed the army, then encamped on the banks of the Godavery, to march up to Poona. Nana, who was as remarkable for political talent as for personal cowardice, immediately fled to Poorunder. Balloba, now master of the situation, proposed to Pureshram Bhao, the commander-in-chief, that Bajee Rao should be set aside, and placed in confinement, that the widow of the late Peshwa should adopt Chimnajee, and that Pureshram himself should be the chief minister. He sought advice of Nana in his retreat, and that wily statesman not only gave his approval of the adoption, but proceeded in person to Satara to procure the investiture from the descendant of Sevajee. Bajee Rao, ignorant of these machinations, repaired to Sindia's camp, where he was detained as a prisoner, while Chimnajee, greatly against his own will, was installed as Peshwa on the 26th of May, 1796.

Pureshram Bhao, now at the head of the government, immediately released the minister of the Nizam, who had been held as a hostage for fourteen months since the battle of Kurdla.

Bajee Rao raised to the throne, 4th December, 1796.

The great object of all the parties in power at Poona at this time was to obtain possession of the person of Nana, who was obliged to fly for security to the fortress of Mhar. His fortunes now seemed to be at the lowest ebb, but they were restored by his extraordinary tact. "The vigour of his judgment," as the historian of the Mahrattas observes, "the fertility of his resources, the extent of his influence, and the combination of instruments he called into action, surprised all India." He renewed his communications with Bajee Rao. He entered into an engagement with the Nizam, which is generally known as the treaty of Mhar, and was dated the 8th of October, 1796, in which it was provided that a body of 15,000 Hyderabad troops and a train of artillery should be sent to assist in establishing Bajee Rao as Peshwa, and Nana as minister, and that, in return for this assistance, the territory the Nizam had been constrained to cede to the Mahrattas should be restored, and the balance of the indemnity remitted. Balloba, the inveterate foe of Nana, having received some intimation of these schemes, determined to frustrate them by sending Bajee Rao as a prisoner into Hindostan. He was sent under the charge of Sirjee Rao Ghatkay, and on the route succeeded in corrupting him, by promising his master, Sindia, a donative of two crores if he obtained his liberty and his crown; he was liberated accordingly. The schemes of Nana were now matured. He had secured the co-operation of Roghoojee Bhonslay, and Holkar. He had gained over Sindia by the promise of Pureshram's jaygeers, worth ten lacs of rupees a year, and on the 27th of October, 1796, that chief commenced the revolution by seizing his own minister Balloba. Pureshram took to flight; Nana marched in triumph to Poona, and on the 4th of December placed Bajee Rao on the throne of his ancestors, and canoelled the adoption of Chimnajee.

Nana seized and confined, December, 1797.   Bajee Rao, whose nature was to trust no one and to deceive all, was no sooner in possession of power than he began to plot the destruction of the two men who had been the chief instruments of his elevation. The agency of Sindia was employed against Nana, who was induced by the representations of the infamous Sirjee Rao to pay his master a visit of ceremony, when he was seized and confined in the fort of Ahmednugur. His escort, consisting of a thousand persons, was stripped, maimed, killed, or dispersed. Troops were sent to pillage his adherents, and the capital presented a scene of confusion and bloodshed. Having thus disposed, as he thought, of Nana, Bajee Rao began to devise means of ridding himself of Sindia, who had recently espoused the beautiful daughter of Sirjee Rao Ghatkay. The wedding was celebrated with extra-

ordinary display and expense. The monthly cost of his army
at Poona, moreover, did not fall short of twenty lacs of
rupees. He began to be straitened for money, and was constrained to press Bajee Rao for the two crores which had been
agreed on as the price of his release and elevation. Bajee
Rao pleaded the emptiness of his treasury, but advised him
to constitute Ghatkay his chief minister, and instruct him to
levy this sum from the wealthy inhabitants of Poona. The
advice was taken; the ruffian was let loose on the capital,
and, as long as it exists, his name will be remembered with
horror and execration. He proceeded in the first instance to
the Peshwa's palace, where he seized the ex-ministers of the
party of Nana, and scourged them until they gave up their
property. The rich bankers and merchants, and all who
were suspected of the possession of wealth, were tortured till
it was surrendered. For many days the city of Poona was
given up to plunder and violence. Amrit Rao, the illegitimate
son of Raghoba, who had been placed in the office of minister
on the imprisonment of Nana, not knowing that the infamous
Ghatkay had been set on these atrocious proceedings by the
advice of his own brother, Bajee Rao, attributed them to the
malevolence of Sindia, and proposed to assassinate him.
Bajee Rao readily entered into a project so entirely in accordance with his own wishes, and one Abba Kally was
selected to despatch him, at a public interview, in the
Peshwa's palace. Sindia was summoned to the audience
chamber, and Bajee Rao upbraided him with the arrogance and
cruelty which he and his servants exhibited, and declared that
he would no longer endure the contempt shown to his authority,
ordering him at the same time peremptorily to depart from the
capital. Sindia replied, with the greatest modesty, that he
was anxious to obey, but could not remove his camp for want
of funds, and solicited payment of the large sum which had
been expended in seating Bajee Rao on the throne. At this
moment Amrit Rao inquired whether he should give the signal
to the executioner, but Bajee Rao's courage failed him, and

Sindia was allowed to depart in peace. This was the first occasion on which the Peshwa manifested that irresolution of purpose which marked his character through life, and rendered him an object of general contempt. It was in the midst of this scene of intrigue and confusion that Lord Wellesley assumed the office of Governor - General, and speedily convinced the native princes of India that the energy of Hastings and Cornwallis was restored to the British Government.

Amalgamation of the army, 1794. One of the two points on which Lord Cornwallis had received specific instructions before he embarked for India, had reference to the amalgamation of the King's and the Company's army. Mr. Dundas considered that India could be retained only by a large European force; and as the number of European soldiers in India, in 1788, was only 12,000, to about 58,000 native sepoys, he deemed it necessary, in order to create a feeling of perfect security, to augment it to about 17,000, so as to establish the proportion of one to three. He considered it important that the whole of this force should be under the Crown, and " act in concert with the general strength of the empire." Lord Cornwallis, during his residence in India, collected a mass of information on the subject, which he embodied in an elaborate minute on his return to England. He proposed that the whole army, European and native, should be transferred to the Crown; but he considered it indispensable that the European officers of the native army should remain an essentially distinct body; that they should go out to India early in life, and devote themselves entirely to the Indian service, in which a perfect knowledge of the language, and attention to the customs and religious prejudices of the sepoys, was absolutely necessary. This plan of amalgamation, which appears to have been drawn up in November, 1794, was rejected by the Court of Directors, who were not disposed to transfer their entire military establishment to the Crown; and it did not receive the full concurrence of the Board of Control.

Mutiny of the Bengal officers, 1795-96.

Before this plan was ready for consideration, the officers of the Bengal army were in a state of open mutiny. Lord Cornwallis had been employed during his administration in abolishing sinecure offices, and lessening the sources of illegitimate gain, both in the civil and military branches of the service. The civilians had been compensated for these reductions by increased salaries, but it was impossible to adopt the same rule with regard to a body of officers counted by thousands. The command of a regiment was still worth 80,000 rupees a year, but the general disproportion in the remuneration of the two services, was a source of constant envy and discontent to the military branch. This feeling was inflamed by the superior advantages of rank enjoyed by the King's officers. Sir John Shore, on assuming the government, found that he had to deal, not with the discontent, but with the actual insubordination of the Bengal army, and, in a country in which he felt that "the civil authority was at the mercy of the military." This spirit of mutiny continued to increase throughout the year 1794; but the officers refrained from any overt act of rebellion, while they waited to ascertain how far the new regulations which Mr. Dundas was drawing up in lieu of Lord Cornwallis's amalgamation scheme, proved agreeable to their wishes. The regulations, however, were delayed so long, that the patience of the officers was exhausted, and on Christmas-day, 1795, Sir John Shore convened the Council, and laid before them the alarming intelligence he had just received. Delegates had been elected from each regiment to form an executive board, and the whole army was bound by the most solemn obligations to protect their persons, and make good their losses by a general subscription. This board was authorized to treat with government on these terms:—that the Company's regiments should not be reduced; that the King's troops should be limited by law to a small number; that promotion should invariably go by seniority; and that all allowances which had at any time been granted to the army, including double batta, should be restored. If these conditions were not accepted, they were prepared to seize the Governor-General and the Commander-in-chief, and take possession of the government.

Conciliatory measures of Government, 1795.   The Council was thunderstruck at this state of affairs. It was a crisis of the same magnitude as that which Clive had quelled thirty years before by his undaunted bearing; but there was no Clive at Calcutta. The Governor-General instantly dispatched orders for troops to the Cape and Madras, and directed the Admiral to bring up his whole squadron to Calcutta without delay; he likewise accepted an offer from De Boigne, of the services of a corps of Sindia's cavalry, commanded by European officers. The Commander-in-chief, Sir Robert Abercromby, proceeded to Cawnpore. Though he was not the man for the emergency, his official character and his courteous manner effected some good; but it was the firmness of the artillery in Calcutta, and the manly resistance of several officers at Cawnpore, that stemmed the tide of mutiny for the time. The long-expected regulations arrived at length, in May, 1796, and disgusted all parties. Sir John Shore described them as a mass of confusion, calculated neither to gratify the officers, nor to improve the discipline of the army. The spirit of revolt blazed forth afresh. Remonstrances poured in upon the bewildered government from every quarter, and on the 30th of June, Sir John Shore wrote to his superiors at home stating, that the pressure on him had been so great, as to oblige him to give way, partly, and to modify the regulations. In a minute which he promulgated in India, he expressed a hope that the general code which he had drawn up would be acceptable to the officers. The regulations were so modified, that there was little of them left. The concessions went even beyond the expectations of the army. Arrears of batta to the extent of seven lacs of rupees, were granted unasked; the arrears of brevet rank were gratuitously bestowed, and such an addition made to the allowances of the officers of all grades, as to entail a permanent addition of seven lacs of annual expenditure. The weakness of government had, in fact, surrendered everything up to a factious army. In a letter to Lord Cornwallis, immediately after this transaction, Sir John Shore admitted that he was little qualified by habit or experience, to contend with a discontented army, and the responsibility of these wretched measures, must, therefore, rest chiefly with the Commander-in-chief.

Alarm of the Ministry in England, 1796.   The intelligence of these concessions, which reached England in December, 1796, filled the Ministry with alarm, and they determined immediately to supersede Sir John Shore. Lord Cornwallis was importuned to proceed forthwith to India, and he was assured by Mr. Dundas, that if he could bring himself to forego his comforts at home for only a twelvemonth, and spend three months at Calcutta, and three months at Madras, he would do the greatest service to his country that ever any man had it in his power to do. So urgent did the necessity of the case appear, that Mr. Dundas offered his own services, in case of Lord Cornwallis's refusal, and stated his readiness to go out to Bengal as Governor-General; but Mr. Pitt refused to part with his colleague, and Lord Cornwallis determined "to sacrifice all personal consideration of comfort and happiness, to the service of the public." He was sworn in as Governor-General on the 1st of February, 1797, and the appointment was immediately announced to all the Presidencies in India. On the first intelligence of this spirit of insubordination, Mr. Dundas declared himself averse to all concessions, and resolved to put it down with a high hand. But he met with serious obstructions in various quarters, and was obliged, at length, to succumb to circumstances. There was a regularly organised committee of Bengal officers then sitting in London, as the representatives of the mutineers in India, and the Court of Directors and Mr. Dundas, strange to say, entered into negotiations with them, and passed, what Lord Cornwallis designated, a "milk-and-water order," with which they desired him to embark for India and assume the government, which he refused to do. They proceeded further to make concession after concession to the London committee, and even promoted one of the ringleaders to a confidential post at the India House. Lord Cornwallis therefore resigned the office of Governor-General in disgust, on the 2nd of August.

Affairs of Oude; death of the Vizier, 1797. The most memorable event of Sir John Shore's administration was the change which he made in the Oude succession. Hyder Beg Khan, the chief minister, was a native statesman of vast energy and singular ability, and sustained the sinking fortunes of the state with great vigour. His death in 1795, and the appointment of a successor totally devoid of principle, put an end to all hope of reform in the government. By nature, the Vizier was a man of good disposition, but spoiled by the enjoyment of absolute power, and by the fools, knaves, and sycophants, who composed his court. During the seventeen years of his reign he had lived only for one object—the gratification of his personal appetites. Some English adventurer who visited his court introduced to his notice the diversion of a race by old women in sacks. The Vizier was enchanted with this new pleasure, and exclaimed, that though he had expended a crore of rupees in procuring amusement, he had never found anything so much to his taste. The government was completely effete, and, but for the protection of the English battalions, the country would long since have been absorbed by Sindia. Sir John Shore, before he resigned the government, paid a visit to the Nabob at Lucknow, and prevailed on him to appoint Tufuzzil Hussein, his minister. He had been his master's representative in Calcutta, and had obtained the entire confidence of Sir John Shore by the simplicity of his character, his unblemished integrity, and his great abilities. In his various interviews with the Vizier, Sir John endeavoured to inculcate on him the necessity of endeavouring to promote the prosperity of the country and the happiness of his people; but he found that such questions had never come within the

scope of his imagination. Whatever favourable impression
the Governor-General might produce in the morning, was
completely effaced in the evening, when the Vizier was again
closeted with his buffoons and parasites, or stupified with opium.
After a residence of six weeks at Lucknow, Sir John returned
to Calcutta, and the Nabob, worn out with excesses, died in
the course of the year.

Vizier Ali,   The succession of his reputed son, Vizier Ali,
Nabob, 1797.   was ratified by Sir John Shore on the ground that
the old Nabob had acknowledged his title, that the Nabob's
mother had given it her sanction, and that it was generally ac-
quiesced in by the people.   But he subsequently received
information of his spurious birth and violent character, and,
from that feeling of conscientiousness which had always guided
his conduct, proceeded to Lucknow to investigate the case.
Before he reached it, he was met by the minister, Tufuzzil
Hussein, who assured him that Vizier Ali was not even the illegitimate son of the late Vizier, but the offspring of a man of
the lowest caste; that his elevation had created astonishment
and disgust, and that the succession belonged of right to
Sadut Ali, the brother of the late prince.   The province of
Oude was considered by the people of Hindostan to stand in
a position altogether different from that of any other principality in India.   In 1764 it had been conquered by the
British arms, and forfeited by the laws of eastern warfare.
It was afterwards voluntarily restored to the family of the
Vizier by Lord Clive, and was ever after considered a dependency of the British Government, and the appointment of
its Nabobs was held to rest on the will of the Governor-
General.   Sir John felt the full responsibility of his situation,
and was most anxious to do justice.   He consulted all those
who were likely to give impartial testimony, and he found
the statement of the minister regarding the ignoble birth of
Vizier Ali fully confirmed.   He learned, likewise, that since
his elevation he had exhibited great violence and unsteadiness
of character, and the most hostile designs towards the English

Government. Sir John, therefore, came to the conclusion that it would be injurious to the country, and disgraceful to the British name to support him, and that, as all the children of the late Nabob were illegitimate, the throne ought to descend to his brother.

Arrangement with Saadut Ali, 1798. That prince was at the time residing at Benares, and Sir John Shore deputed Mr. Cherry, the Resident, to announce the intentions of the British Government to him. He was likewise presented with the draft of a treaty, which, with some subsequent modifications, embraced the following provisions: that the defence of the Oude dominions should remain exclusively with the British Government; that the number of British troops stationed in Oude should consist of 10,000; and that the annual payment for them should be seventy-six lacs of rupees, which was to vary according to the increase or diminution of the force; that the fortress of Allahabad, the key of the province which the English were to defend, should be made over to them, that the Nabob should not maintain more than 35,000 troops, and should enter into no negotiation with any foreign power, without the consent of the British Government. The treaty made such arrangements as a superior would dictate to a subordinate, and fully bore out the impression that Oude was subject to the Company. During this negotiation, Sir John was encamped in the immediate neighbourhood of Lucknow, and exposed to no little peril from Vizier Ali, who was surrounded by bands of desperate men, who openly talked of his assassination. The city was then supposed to contain 800,000 inhabitants; the streets were narrow lanes and intricate passages, capable of being strongly defended, and every house was filled with armed men. Ibrahim Beg, a bold and reckless adventurer, commanded the troops of Vizier Ali, and had 300 pieces of ordnance, of which 30 were so posted that they could not be seized without great danger. Sir John Shore was strongly advised by the minister and the nobles to anticipate the designs of Vizier Ali, and seize him in the city, but he felt that the firing of a single shot might lead to the massacre of thousands. In the midst of these dangers, his escape from which was pronounced by his successor in the government to be miraculous, he maintained the utmost calmness and composure, and his conduct throughout this transaction exhibited a pattern of courage and resolution.

Sadut Ali at length reached Cawnpore, and was escorted from thence to Lucknow, a distance of 50 miles, by a large British force, and all the embarrassments of Sir John Shore at once terminated. Vizier Ali was deserted by his servants and followers as Sadut Ali approached the city, in which he was proclaimed Nabob Vizier on the 21st of January, 1798. Vizier Ali was removed to Benares, where he resided some time on his pension of a lac and a half of rupees a year, cherishing the most inveterate feelings towards the English Government. The revolution was hailed by Europeans and natives as an act of justice, and the general feeling in Oude was that "the right had come to the rightful." The Court of Directors recorded that "in circumstances of great delicacy and embarrassment, Sir John Shore had conducted himself with great temper, ability, and firmness." Dr. Lawrence, a friend of Mr. Burke's and one of the managers of the impeachment of Hastings, threatened Sir John with an indictment for his proceedings in Oude, but it was never carried into execution; and the impartial voice of posterity has paid homage to the honesty, the wisdom, and the vigour manifested by him on this occasion. Immediately after Saadut Ali had been placed on the throne, Sir John Shore, who had been created Lord Teignmouth, returned to Calcutta, and embarked for England on the 25th of March, 1798.

CHAPTER XIX.

LORD WELLESLEY'S ADMINISTRATION—FOURTH AND LAST
MYSORE WAR, 1798, 1799.

Lord Wellesley, SIR JOHN SHORE was succeeded in the govern-
Governor-
General, 1798, ment of India by Lord Mornington, subsequently
1799. created Marquess of Wellesley, then in his thirty-
eighth year. He was born in Ireland in 1760, and placed at an
early age at Eton, where he became one of its most distinguished scholars. On coming of age he took his seat in the Irish
House of Peers, and engaged in the most important debates
of the time. Soon after, he was elected a member of the British
House of Commons, and was brought into communion with the
great men of genius who then adorned the senate, and who
have shed an imperishable lustre on that period of English
history. At the age of twenty-six he was nominated one of
the Lords of the Treasury. In January, 1794, he delivered a
brilliant speech against French jacobinism, which stamped him
as one of the rising men of the day, and was supposed to have
mainly conduced to his Indian appointment. He had likewise
enjoyed the advantage of a seat at the Board of Control for
four years, which gave him a comprehensive knowledge of the
politics of India. He was, moreover, the intimate friend of
Mr. Pitt, the prime minister, and possessed the confidence of
Mr. Dundas, the President of the Board of Control, an association of inestimable value to a Governor-General. He embarked for India in November, 1797, and landed at the Cape
in February 1798, where he found Lord Macartney, who had
been Governor of Madras during the second Mysore War, as
well as Lord Hobart, who had recently been recalled from that
post, and was thus put in possession of their views regarding
British interests in the Deccan. At the Cape he also met with
Major Kirkpatrick, formerly minister at Sindia's court, and
latterly the Resident at Hyderabad, and obtained from him the

II.   G most important information respecting the strength of the various native powers, and the objects of their policy. While Lord Wellesley—we anticipate his superior title—was detained at the Cape, a vessel from Calcutta touched there, with the despatches of the Government to the Court of Directors, which he did not hesitate to open, that he might obtain the latest intelligence of the actual position of affairs in the empire he was going out to govern. With the information derived from these various sources, he composed his first despatch to Mr. Dundas, embodying his own views of the course of policy which it was advisable to pursue. This letter afforded the clearest evidence of his extraordinary genius for government.

After the humiliation of Tippoo, in 1792, the *Extinction of the balance of power, 1798.* Indian authorities in London had been encouraged by Lord Cornwallis to believe that the security of the Company's interests depended on that balance of power which he had established among the princes of the Deccan, and which he considered both stable and permanent. But the first survey which Lord Wellesley was enabled to take of the country powers convinced him that a greater fallacy had never been harboured in Leadenhall-street. There never had, in fact, been, and, considering the policy of the native courts, there never could be, anything like a real balance of power in India. With the princes of India, rapine and conquest had been from time immemorial the only avowed principle of action. War was considered the chief source of glory; it was sanctioned by the ordinances of religion, both Hindoo and Mahomedan; it was prosecuted without any pretext or semblance of justice, and restrained only by the power of resistance. The Court of Directors, trusting to this imaginary safeguard, had prohibited all alliances with the native princes, and all interference in their affairs. Sir John Shore was determined to carry out their system with conscientious fidelity; but, before he had been eighteen months in office, he saw the whole fabric of the balance of power crumble to pieces before his eyes. At the battle of Kurdla, the Peshwa and the other Mahratta princes completely demolished the power of the Nizam, while Sir John Shore looked on, and refused him the aid even of the British battalion which was in his pay. Soon after, the Peshwa was, in his turn, reduced to extremity by the encroachments of Sindia, and implored the protection of the Governor-General. It was refused from a servile deference to the orders of the Court of Directors, and the power of the Peshwa was reduced to the same state of prostration as that of the Nizam. The balance of power in the Deccan was thus irretrievably desstroyed. The British Government became the object of derision to the princes of India, who were fain to conclude that it contained the same elements of decay as all Asiatic sovereigntics, and that the energy which had raised it to the summit of power was now exhausted. "Its moon," they said, "was already in the wane;" and a brief prolongation of Sir John Shore's feeble administration would have brought the British empire in India to the brink of destruction.

State of India, 1798. To estimate the difficulties of Lord Wellesley's position on assuming the government, it is only necessary to glance at the state of the chief native powers. In the south, Tippoo was brooding over his misfortunes and thirsting for an opportunity of gratifying his hostility to the English,—the ruling passion of his life. The five years of peace he had enjoyed were assiduously devoted to the improvement of his resources. Though deprived by Lord Cornwallis of half his dominions, he was still able to maintain a formidable army in a state of the highest efficiency. He had entertained a body of French officers, and, as the anxiety of France to regain her former power in India had revived with the ambition of the Revolution, he expected material assistance from a French alliance, The Nizam, finding the assistance of the British regiment he subsidised denied him by Sir John Shore in the hour of his utmost need, had increased the strength of his French battalions, under Raymond, to 14,000 men and 36 field pieces, and assigned districts yielding eighteen lacs of rupees for their support. They constituted the only military force of any importance in his dominions, and were gradually assuming the authority and tone natural to such a position. They carried the colours of the French republic, then at war with England, and wore the cap of liberty on their buttons. Sindia, who was supreme at Poona, had likewise obtained possession of the person of the emperor at Delhi, and was strengthened by all the influence still connected with the Mogul throne. His territory in the Deccan extended to the banks of the Toombudra, and skirted the frontiers of the Nizam and the Peshwa, while in the north his possessions abutted on those of the Company and the Nabob of Oude: The French battalions raised by De Boigne, he had augmented to 40,000 men, with 464 guns, and assigned an entire province for their maintenance. The organization of this force included all the requirements of war, fortresses, arsenals, founderies, and depôts, and it was in no respects inferior to the British army in Hindostan. To add to Lord Wellesley's embarrassments, the European officers of the Company were in a state of complete insubordination, the spirit of the community was depressed by the visible weakness of the Government, and public credit was at so low an ebb that it was not possible to obtain money under twelve per cent. Lord Cornwallis had bequeathed a surplus revenue of a hundred and eighty-five lacs of rupees a-year to his successor, but under Sir John Shore's administration it had dwindled down, year after year, without any war expenditure, and for the first time in the history of British India peace had created a deficit.

The Mauritius proclamation, 1798.   Lord Wellesley landed in Calcutta on the 17th May, and within three weeks was startled by the appearance in one of the Calcutta journals of a proclamation issued by General Malartic, the Governor of the Mauritius. It stated that two envoys had arrived in the island from Tippoo Sultan with despatches for the Government in Paris, proposing an alliance offensive and defensive, and requesting a body of troops without delay to assist him in ex-

pelling the English from India, and it invited volunteers to
enrol themselves under the Sultan's colours. The document
was at first deemed spurious, as it was difficult to suppose
that Tippoo would thus publicly proclaim his hostile intentions, and prepare the British Government to defeat them;
but the receipt of a second copy of it from the Cape dispelled
every doubt. Soon after, it was announced that a French
frigate at the Mauritius had taken on board about a hundred
men, including civil and military officers, and landed them at
Mangalore, on the Malabar coast, after capturing two East-
Indiamen on the route. On reaching the capital, the French
officers organised a Jacobin club under the auspices of the
Sultan, whom they dignified with the title of Citizen Tippoo.
The tree of liberty was planted with due ceremonials, and
surmounted with the cap of equality; the emblems of royalty
were burned, and the French republic, one and indivisible, was
consecrated on the public parade.

The Coast army   Lord Wellesley determined to anticipate the
ordered to   designs of Tippoo, and directed General Harris,
assemble, 1798.   the officiating Governor of Madras, to assemble
the Coast army to march directly on Seringapatam. At the
same time, he called on the Nizam and the Peshwa, the
signataries of the treaty of Seringapatam, to furnish their
quota of troops in accordance with the 12th article. The
Presidency of Madras was thunderstruck at this daring project. General Harris trembled to commit the Government in
so hazardous a conflict, and cautioned the Governor-General
against the error of putting any trust in these dilatory and
timid native allies, the only advantage of enlisting whose
services was to prevent their being transferred to the enemy.
Even the governing spirit of Madras, Mr. Webbe, a young
civilian of thirty-one, of whom the Duke of Wellington, then
General Wellesley, affirmed that he was one of the ablest men
he ever knew, and, withal, the most honest, was appalled at
such an enterprize. He had a lively dread of the Mysore
power, which had, within memory, annihilated Baillie's detach-

ment, devastated the Carnatic, and burned the suburbs of
Madras. In a very elaborate state paper, he enumerated all
the dangers and disasters which had attended our former wars
with Hyder and Tippoo. In 1791, Lord Cornwallis, he said,
took the field with an army completely equipped, but had failed
to reach Seringapatam. At present, the entire disposable
force of the Presidency did not exceed 8,000 men, and they
were without draft cattle, supplies, or commissariat. This
army, far from being in a condition to march upon the enemy's
capital, was unequal even to the defence of the Company's
territories, if Tippoo should think fit to invade them, which he
would not fail to do when he heard of our preparations. The
treasury, moreover, was bankrupt; the public debt had increased in eight years from seventeen to fifty lacs of pagodas,
and the twelve per cent. paper was at a discount of five per
cent. On the other hand, Tippoo numbered 60,000 troops, a
large portion of whom consisted of the celebrated Mysore
horse. His infantry was, in part, disciplined by French
officers. He possessed 144 field-pieces, a rocket brigade, a
long train of elephants, and a superb muster of carriage and
draft cattle. Any movement of troops which might give umbrage to Tippoo could only end in fearful disasters, and in
the impeachment of Lord Wellesley. These representations,
however, instead of deterring him from his purpose, only
served to demonstrate more clearly the imperative necessity
of extricating the affairs of the Company from this perilous
position. If, he argued, we were not strong enough to repel
the assaults of Tippoo, he was virtually master of the Deccan,
and there could be no real security as long as it depended
simply on the moderation of an inveterate foe. Though constrained, therefore, from the weakness of the Madras Presidency, to fold up the idea of striking an immediate blow at
Tippoo's power, he issued peremptory orders for the equipment
of the army, and threatened with his severest displeasure, and
in his most imperious style, those who "presumed to thwart
him, and arrogated to themselves the power of governing the

empire committed to his charge." Meanwhile, he called on Tippoo to disavow his embassy to the Mauritius. ·

Lord Wellesley's vigorous policy, 1798. — The state of affairs at Hyderabad demanded the immediate attention of the Governor-General. Raymond, who organized the French force of the Nizam, had died in the spring of the year. His successor, Piron, who was considered an abler soldier, was animated by a stronger feeling of jacobinical hatred to England. Lord Wellesley felt that in the approaching conflict with Tippoo, he could not take this body of troops into the field as a part of the Nizam's contingent, without the hazard of their joining the Sultan, with whose French officers they were in constant communication. To leave them behind without a large force to watch their movements, appeared equally dangerous. The French force at Hyderabad was, moreover, the nucleus of the power which France was endeavouring to establish in the Deccan. The junction of this body with the French troops in Mysore, and those in the service of Sindia, might at any time extinguish the power of the Nizam and the Peshwa, and enable the French to bring the resources of the Deccan and of Hindostan to bear on the dominions of the Company. The extinction of the French army at Hyderabad was, therefore, an object of the first importance. At this critical juncture, Lord Wellesley received a letter from Zemaun Shah, announcing his intention to cross the Indus and invade Hindostan, and demanding the assistance of the English Government to drive the Mahrattas back into the Deccan. Zemaun Shah was the grandson of the renowned Ahmed Shah Abdalee, whose victory at Paniput, forty years before, was still remembered with a feeling of terror throughout India. The intrinsic weakness of his power had not then been discovered, and another Abdalee invasion could not be contemplated without alarm. Lord Wellesley was thus menaced with dangers in every direction, but he never feared the bugbear of responsibility, and he determined to carry out the plans he had formed for the protection of the empire, without waiting

for the sanction of the Court of Directors or the Board of
Control. He found that the Company had not augmented their
security, by curtailing their influence, but had drifted into a
position where it was less perilous to advance than to stand
still or to recede. He resolved at once to terminate that policy
of isolation which had been erroneously considered the safeguard of British power, and to abandon the system of non-
interference which was held sacred in Leadenhall-street.
Within three months after he had taken his seat at the
Council board, active negotiations were commenced through
the country; every durbar from Cape Comorin to the banks
of the Jumna was electrified by the revival of that energy
which was supposed to be extinct, and the princes of India
soon felt that the spirit of Clive and of Hastings again
animated the Government of Calcutta.

Proposed alli-
ance with the
Nizam, 1798.
      Lord Wellesley's first negotiation was with the
court of Hyderabad. The minister, Musheer-ool-
moolk, more commonly designated Meer Allum,
fell into the hands of the Mahrattas at the battle of Kurdla,
and was kept in confinement, in order to deprive his master of
the benefit of his great abilities. He had recently obtained his
liberty, and resumed the management of the Nizam's affairs.
Alarmed at the ascendency which the French officers had
acquired during his captivity, and disgusted at their arrogance,
he had resumed the lands allotted for their maintenance, and
had repeatedly proposed to the Company's Resident that an
English subsidiary force should be substituted for the French
battalions. The proposal was refused by Sir John Shore, but
Lord Wellesley now eagerly embraced it, and offered to
augment the corps of British troops in the Nizam's pay to
6,000, with a proper complement of artillery, on condition that
a provision of twenty-four lacs of rupees a-year should be
made for their support, and that the French force should be
promptly disbanded. He likewise offered his mediation on all
matters in dispute with the Peshwa, and engaged to protect
the state from his unjust claims. The Nizam, then in his

sixty-fifth year, more feeble in body and in mind than his
illustrious father at the age of a hundred, manifested considerable repugnance to so close an alliance with a power which,
since he ascended the throne, had risen to be the most formidable in India. The minister himself was not insensible of the
danger which might be incurred by this connection ; but he
argued that the Hyderabad state was utterly defenceless, and
that it was more advisable to be dependent on a power distinguished by good faith than to remain exposed to the
ambitious views of Tippoo on the one hand, and the insatiable
rapacity of the Mahrattas on the other. The influence of the
minister was paramount, and the reluctant consent of the
Nizam was at length obtained to the treaty.

Proposal to the   The proposal of a similar alliance was likewise
Peshwa, 1798.   made to the Peshwa, Bajee Rao. In the preceding year, he had solicited the aid of a British force to protect
him from the designs of Sindia, who had fixed his head-
quarters near Poona, but Sir John Shore, in deference to the
policy then in the ascendant at the India House, had refused
to comply with his wishes, and the opportunity of establishing
an influence at the Mahratta court was lost. Bajee Rao
then entered into negotiations with the Nizam, and concluded an alliance with him, ceding territory valued at
eight lacs of rupees a-year, as the price of his assistance
against Sindia. Sindia avenged himself by despatching
envoys to Tippoo, to invite him to attack the Nizam, and
by releasing the great minister, Nana Furnuvese, whom the
Peshwa feared as much as he detested. On the Nana's
arrival at Poona, a strong feeling of mistrust of the Peshwa
led him to decline all connection with public affairs. The
Peshwa, therefore, repaired to his residence in the dead of
night, with only a single domestic, and employed all those
insinuating arts of which he was so perfect a master, laid his
head at the feet of the Nana, swore to consider him in future
as his father and his counsellor, and, in a flood of tears, conjured him not to abandon the brahmin sovereignty, but to

assume the office of minister. The appeal was successful;
but the Nana had no sooner entered on his duties, than the
Peshwa began to plot his destruction, and urged Sindia to
place him again in confinement. The minister discovered the
intrigue, and repairing to the palace, upbraided Bajee Rao
with his unparalleled treachery, and begged him to cease
plotting against the liberty and life of an old man, but to
allow him to retire into obscurity. The Peshwa protested his
innocence, threw the blame on his officers, and persuaded the
Nana to resume his post. It was at this period that the
Resident brought forward the proposition which he was
instructed by Lord Wellesley to make, of a subsidiary alliance
to liberate the Peshwa from the thraldom of Sindia. It provided that a large British force should be received into the
service of the Peshwa, and due arrangements made for their
support; that the French should be for ever excluded from
his dominions; and that all differences with the Nizam and
Sindia should be submitted to the arbitration of the British
Government. It has been supposed that the eagerness manifested on this occasion by the Governor-General tended to
defeat his object. But Bajee Rao had no desire for the final
settlement of such claims, which had been the source of
Mahratta greatness, and which it was the national policy
never to close. The alliance proposed by Lord Wellesley was
designated by him a restoration of the Peshwa to his due
authority and power, but he and the other princes to whom
the offer was made were too astute not to perceive that it
involved the complete extinction of their political independence
and of their military power. The Peshwa would, it is true, have
been relieved from the domination of Sindia, but it would only
have been a change of collars, the substitution of one which
he could never shake off, for another which, however galling,
might yet be temporary. It is not surprising that princes
with whom independence had a charm, the value of which was
often enhanced by its risks, should have been loth to part
with it. The Peshwa, therefore, acting upon the advice of

Nana Furnuvese, evaded the proposal of an alliance, but assured the Resident that he would faithfully observe the engagements of the triple alliance. A large Mahratta force was ostensibly ordered to assemble and join the expedition which the Governor-General was fitting out against Tippoo, but it was never intended to act, and the Mahrattas took no part in the campaign.

_{Negotiations with Sindia and Poona, Nagpore, 1798.} While these negotiations were in progress at Poona, Colonel Collins, the Resident at the court of Sindia, was instructed to lay before him the letter of Zemaun Shah, requesting the co-operation of the British Government in driving the Mahrattas from Hindostan, liberating the emperor from bondage, and restoring him to the throne. The Resident was instructed to assure Sindia that the Governor-General was determined to resist this attempt to disturb the established states of India in their actual possessions, and to invite him to unite in a defensive league against the Abdalee. Sindia was also urged to quit Poona and return to Hindostan, where he would find an English army ready to join him. He declined the alliance, but promised to proceed to his own provinces in the north, a promise he did not intend to fulfil. The raja of Nagpore had maintained a friendly disposition towards the Company, and Mr. Colebrooke, the most eminent Oriental scholar of the day, was sent to his court to improve it, but the raja refused to entangle himself with an alliance.

_{Extinction of the French force at Hyderabad, 1798.} To give effect to the subsidiary treaty with the Nizam, four Madras regiments, with proportionate artillery, were ordered to march to Hyderabad, but the Madras treasury was so empty, that the Governor was obliged to raise funds for their equipment on his own personal responsibility. They reached Hyderabad on the 10th October, but the difficulties of the transaction were not past. Every artifice and intrigue was employed for nine days to evade the performance of the treaty and the dismissal of the French corps. The vacillation of the Nizam and his minister arose,

not only from the dread of a collision between the two forces, English and French, but also from a feeling of reluctance at the last moment to descend to a state of helpless and irretrievable dependence on a superior power. The Nizam, under the influence of personal terror, took refuge in the neighbouring fortress of Golconda. The British Resident, Captain Kirkpatrick, was obliged to assume a high tone, and to assure the minister that it was now too late to recede, and that the Nizam would be held responsible for the consequences of this breach of faith. Colonel Roberts, who commanded the British force, was anxious to bring the question to an issue before the arrival of the Nizam's household cavalry, who were known to be friendly to the French interests, and had been ordered up from the country. The minister was at length convinced that there was more danger in evading than in performing the engagement his master had entered into, and a proclamation was issued dismissing the French officers from the service, and releasing the sepoys from the obligation of obedience to them. Both officers and men were thrown into a state of confusion and dismay by this unexpected announcement. The British force was moved into a position which completely commanded the French encampment, and from which, if necessary, the French storehouses and magazines could be set on fire by red hot shot. The French commandant, Mons. Piron, on receiving his dismissal from the Nizam, sent a messenger to inform Captain Kirkpatrick that he and his officers were ready to place themselves under British protection, and expected to be treated according to the usages of civilised nations. But the men, to whom considerable arrears were due, rose in a body on their officers and placed them in confinement, and it was not without great difficulty they succeeded in escaping during the night to the English camp. Captain Malcolm, a young officer of great spirit and ambition, then rising to notice, was sent to quell the excitement of the native troops, and to offer them the payment of their arrears. By his great tact in the management of natives, he prevailed on them to accept these terms, and before the evening this large body of 14,000 disciplined troops, possessed of a powerful train of artillery and well-stored arsenals, was disarmed without the loss of a single life. This great achievement, the foremost of the new administration, filled the native princes, who were calculating on the downfall of the Company's power, with amazement, while it gave fresh confidence to their native subjects. The ability with which it was planned, and the promptitude with which it was executed, removed all cause of anxiety from the minds of the European functionaries of government at all the Presidencies, and created a spirit of confidence and devotion, which contributed essentially to the success of the Governor-General's plans.

While Lord Wellesley was engaged in pre-*Mysore War sanctioned in England, 1798.* parations for war, he was so happy as to receive a despatch from the Court of Directors, written on the receipt of the Mauritius proclamation. The dread of the Mysore power, which they had thrice encountered in thirty years, still haunted their imaginations, and they began to tremble anew for the security of their possessions in the Deccan. They stated that if Tippoo had actually entered into a league with France, it would be neither politic nor prudent to wait till he commenced hostilities, but they also enjoined the utmost discretion in resorting to arms. Mr. Dundas considered that this breach of faith fully warranted a · declaration of war, and Lord Wellesley was thus enabled to commence the campaign with the full concurrence of the authorities in England. On the 18th October he received intelligence that Bonaparte had landed in Egypt with the object of establishing a French empire in the East, and two days after issued orders to Madras to press forward the organisation of the army in every department, and to send the battering train and heavy stores to the frontier without delay. He likewise announced his intention to strengthen the Coast army with 3,000 volunteer sepoys, and, above all, with His Majesty's 33rd Regiment, commanded by Colonel Wellesley, afterwards the Duke of Wellington, in himself a

First letter to Tippoo, November 8, 1798. host. On the 8th of November, intelligence of the complete success of the movement for the suppression of the French force at Hyderabad, reached Calcutta, and Lord Wellesley despatched his first communication to Tippoo Sultan. The British Government, he said, could not be ignorant of the intercourse he had formed with the French, the inveterate enemies of the Company, and then actually at war with England; and he was cautioned against a connection which "must subvert the foundations of friendship between him and the Company, and introduce into the heart of his kingdom the principles of anarchy and confusion." The Governor-General had, consequently, been obliged to adopt measures of precaution and defence, though he was anxious to live in peace and amity with all his neighbours. He was, however, desirous of propounding a plan which would remove all distrust and suspicion, and establish a good understanding between the Company and the Sultan, on the most stable foundations; and he proposed to depute Major Doveton for this purpose to his durbar. Lord Wellesley likewise resolved to proceed to Madras in person to obviate the delay inseparable from a distant correspondence, and to bring the authority of the Supreme Government to bear upon the military preparations. Sir Alured Clarke, the Commander-in-chief, was to be left in Bengal to watch the movements of Zemaun Shah, who had already crossed the Indus and reached Lahore. The Calcutta militia, an old institution which had fallen into disuse, was embodied to the number of 1,500. Lord Wellesley then embarked for Madras, which he reached on the last day of the year, and assumed the control of all the political and military arrangements, leaving the local administration undisturbed in the hands of the Governor.

Correspondence of Lord Wellesley and Tippoo, 1799. Lord Wellesley found Tippoo's reply to his letter at Madras. With regard to the embassy, the Sultan observed that the agents of a mercantile tribe, who had purchased a two-masted vessel, happened to go with a cargo to the Mauritius, and forty persons, French, and of a dark colour, ten or twelve of whom were artificers and the rest servants, had embarked in her for Mysore in search of employment. Some of these had entered his service, and the others had left the country. The French, "who were full of vice and deceit, had perhaps taken advantage of the departure of the ship to put about reports, with the view to ruffle the minds of both Sircars." The proposed conference with Major Doveton he evaded, under the pretence that "the treaties and engagements entered into among the four Sircars"—the English, the Nizam, the Peshwa, and himself—"were so firmly established and confirmed, as ever to remain fixed and durable, and be an example to the rulers of the age. No means more effectual than these could be adopted to give stability to the foundations of friendship and harmony." To this letter Lord Wellesley replied on the 9th of January, giving a full detail of all the transactions by which Tippoo had violated the treaties subsisting between him and the Company, and manifested the hostility of his designs. He stated that the new engagements which the Sultan had entered into with the common enemy, necessarily demanded new arrangements on the part of the allies. He solemnly admonished him to assent to the conciliatory mission of Major Doveton, and warned him of the dangerous consequences of delay in arduous affairs, entreating him not to postpone his reply for more than one day after the letter should reach his presence. Before the arrival of this communication, Tippoo had again written to the Governor-General to lull him into security, assuring him that "the sincerity of his friendship and regard, together with proofs of his solicitude for tranquillity and peace (his friendly heart being bent on their increase) had been made apparent." At the time when this letter was written, he was despatching Dubuc, one of his French officers, through the Danish settlement of Tranquebar, to the Executive Directory at Paris, to solicit the aid of 10,000 or 15,000 troops, who were to be maintained at his expense, and employed in expelling the English from India. He was likewise inviting Zemaun Shah to cross the Indus, and join him in prosecuting "a holy war against the infidels, polytheists, and heretics." "Please God," he said, "the English shall become food for the unrelenting sword of the pious warriors." Lord Wellesley's letter of the 9th January appears to have given him the first clear monition of the danger which he had incurred by his negotiations with the French, and his first impulse was to receive the mission of Major Doveton, and throw himself on the consideration of the Governor-General. The letter addressed to him by Bonaparte, from Egypt, stating "that he had arrived on the borders of the Red Sea, with an innumerable and invincible army, full of the desire of delivering him from the iron yoke of England," had not as yet reached him; but his French officers assured him that the army of Bonaparte must already have embarked for India, and might be daily expected. After many days of alternate hope and fear, he forwarded his reply with this significant expression : " Being frequently disposed to make excursions and hunt, I am, accordingly, proceeding on a hunting excursion. You will be pleased to despatch Major Doveton, slightly attended (or unattended)."

Strength and progress of the British Army, 1799.   But Tippoo had miscalculated the character of the man he had now to deal with, and the length to which he might venture to procrastinate. Lord Wellesley had determined to bring the war to a close in a single campaign, by one vigorous and decisive blow at the capital. Seringapatam was the great object of Tippoo's pride, the centre of his power, his principal granary, and his only arsenal, on the preservation of which he considered the fate of his kingdom to depend. Unlike any other fort in India, it was impregnable from June to November, owing to the rise of the Cavery around the island on which it was erected. Unless, therefore, it could be reduced before the rains set in, the campaign must prove abortive, and the intolerable expense of a second season of military operations must be incurred. As the year advanced, every moment became increasingly important, and Lord Wellesley, after waiting in vain for the early reply he had solicited from Tippoo, on the 3rd February ordered the army to break ground. In reply to the cold and ungracious letter of the Sultan, when it arrived, he expressed regret that his earnest representations of the dangers of delay had not been heeded. The mission of Major Doveton, he said, was no longer expedient; but General Harris, who was advancing at the head of an army into Mysore, would be prepared to receive any embassy Tippoo might think fit to send. The army which was now about to take the field was considered the best appointed, and the most perfect in point of equipment and discipline which had ever been collected in India under the British standard. Only six months before, the Madras functionaries had declared that it would be impossible to assemble a force of more than 8,000 men, which would be scarcely equal to the defence of the Carnatic, if it were invaded by the Sultan. But the commanding energy of Lord Wellesley, seconded by the indefatigable exertions of his brother, Colonel Wellesley, and of the son of the great Clive, now Governor of Madras, had called into existence an army of 20,802 men, of whom 6,000 were Europeans, with a battering train of 40 guns and 64 field-pieces and howitzers. To this number was added 10,000 of the Nizam's cavalry and the Hyderabad subsidiary force, which included 3,600 of Raymond's disciplined sepoys, and made up another body of 10,000 foot, under the direction of European officers, and commanded by Colonel Wellesley and Captain Malcolm. It thus became an efficient auxiliary, instead of the dead weight it had proved during the campaign of Lord Cornwallis. The army was fortunate in its superior officers, all of whom, with one exception, enjoyed the advantage of the experience acquired in the previous Mysore war; while General Harris, the General-in-chief, was personally acquainted with all the localities on the route. Lord Wellesley possessed in an eminent degree two of the greatest qualifications for command, great discernment in the

selection of his instruments, and the wisdom of reposing unreserved confidence in them; and never were these talents
more distinctly exhibited than on the present occasion, by
the accordance of unfettered authority to General Harris, and
the able officers associated with him. The Bombay division of
6,420 troops was assembled under General Stuart at Canna-
nore, on the Malabar coast, to advance simultaneously on the
capital.

Tippoo marches
to the western
coast, 1799.
Tippoo, who had made several marches to the
eastward to meet Major Doveton, at length assembled his chief officers, and expressed his vexation
that while the English were closing on him from the east and
the west he was losing invaluable time, and pointed out the
necessity of "marching, and striking some decisive blow."
He determined, therefore, to leave Poornea and Syud Sahib
with a sufficient force to watch the movements of General
Harris, and to march in person with the flower of his army
across the peninsula and engage the army of General Stuart,
whose advanced post was then at Seedasere. It was diligently
propagated throughout the country that Tippoo was proceeding against General Harris, and nothing was so little expected
by the Bombay army as his appearance in its neighbourhood.
On the morning of the 5th March, however, the raja of
Coorg, a gallant prince, the grateful ally of the Company, and
the mortal enemy of the family of Hyder, who had always
oppressed him, ascended the hill of Seedasere, and to his
amazement beheld the plain below covered with Tippoo's encampment. Preparations were immediately made to meet
the attack of the enemy by General Hartley, the second in
command, a name of ancient and high renown on that coast.
On the morning of the 6th the advanced brigade was vigorously assailed by the Sultan's entire force, and three battalions
under the gallant Colonel Montresor sustained the assault for
six hours with such cool and determined bravery, that the
utmost efforts of Tippoo's best officers and troops could make
no impression on their ranks. General Stuart, who was ten

miles in the rear, hastened to their assistance, and found them
exhausted with fatigue and reduced to their last cartridge.
His timely arrival decided the fortune of the day. Within
half an hour Tippoo's army retreated through the wood with
the loss of 2,000 men. He continued for six days to linger in
the vicinity in a state of great perplexity, and on the 11th
March turned his back on the Bombay force, and marched to
oppose the advance of General Harris.

Progress of   General Harris reached Bangalore on the 15th
General Harris, March, with the heavy charge of conveying the
1799.   vast and cumbrous equipage for the siege in
safety to its destination. Of the three routes which led
from Bangalore to Seringapatam he had chosen the most
southern. It presented many points where a bold and
skilful enemy might have seriously obstructed his progress,
more especially on the banks of the Madoor, which
afforded an excellent position for opposing the passage of an
army. But, throughout the campaign, the Sultan appeared to
be bewildered, if not infatuated; and, in direct opposition to
the advice of his own most experienced officers, and of his
French commandant, he fixed upon Malavelly as the field for
encountering the English force. The battle, in which Colonel
Wellesley particularly distinguished himself, terminated in
the complete discomfiture of Tippoo, with the loss of 1,000
men. After the defeat he moved his encampment in a northern direction, not doubting that General Harris would adopt
the route to Seringapatam which had been taken in the previous war by Lord Cornwallis. It had therefore been laid
waste under his own inspection, and not a particle of dry
forage or a pile of grass was left unconsumed. But the
chief of the guide corps, Major Allen, whose exertions contributed pre-eminently to the success of the campaign, and
Captain Macaulay, were sent southward to examine the road
which led to the Cavery, twelve miles distant; and they
returned at midnight with the report that it presented a fine
and open tract of country, and that the ford at Sosilla afforded

every facility for the passage of an army. The next morning
the whole force marched down with all promptitude, and before
nightfall one wing was across the river, while Tippoo was
twenty miles distant, in an opposite direction, waiting to
oppose General Harris's progress towards the capital. The
happy choice of this route gave the famished cattle an abundance of rich pasturage; it facilitated the junction of the Bombay army, and it rendered abortive the dispositions which
Tippoo had made for defending the northern face of Seringapatam. Nothing could exceed his dismay and rage when
he found all his plans frustrated by this admirable strategy.
He summoned his principal officers, and said, " We have now
arrived at our last stage ; what is your determination?"
·" To die with you," was their unanimous reply. Every one
present was deeply affected at the distress of his sovereign,
who was bathed in tears, and the meeting broke up with the
firm resolution to make one last and desperate effort for the
defence of the capital and the kingdom, with no alternative
but victory or death.

The Army before
Seringapatam,
April 6th, 1799.
No farther opposition was made to the progress
of the British army, the advanced post of which
was established within 1,600 yards of the fort on
the 6th April. This direct march on the capital with a heavy
siege train, through a hundred and fifty miles of the enemy's
territory, without establishing a single intermediate post, was
in accordance with that daring spirit which had won our
dominion in India, and which, when conducted by such men as
Harris, and Baird, and Wellesley, and Malcolm, could scarcely
be considered rash ; but it was not effected without the greatest
· risks. If Tippoo's resources had been directed with any
degree of ability, this attempt to reach the capital, with an
unwieldy convoy, might have ended in disaster. Though
extraordinary efforts had been made to perfect the equipment
of the force, and the number of cattle provided for its use
exceeded 60,000, not including a countless multitude of
brinjarees and provision dealers, the army had no sooner begun

to move than it experienced the same kind of embarrassments which had defeated Lord Cornwallis's first expedition in 1791. On the third day of the march, every store which could possibly be dispensed with was destroyed to increase the available carriage. As the army advanced, the loss of powder and shot and other military stores, from the failure of the cattle, created, very serious alarm. This was attributed to the climate and water of Mysore, which were said to be unfavourable to the cattle of the Carnatic. It was owing to these impediments that the army was only able to advance at the rate of five miles a-day, when every hour was of increasing importance. Two days after the Bombay division had effected a junction with General Harris, it was found, on weighing the rice bags, that the stock was mysteriously diminished—such mysteries are by no means uncommon in the commissariat department— and there remained only eighteen days' consumption, even for the combatants. It was evident that unless the supplies which Colonel Read was then employed in collecting in the southern districts could reach the camp before the 6th of May, it would be reduced to a state of starvation. General Floyd was therefore despatched with a large force to convoy them.

Progress of the siege, 17th April to 4th May, 1799. For any details of the siege, which may be considered as having commenced on the 17th of April, we cannot find room. It was pushed on with such vigour that the Sultan was induced, within three days, to make proposals for a conference. General Harris, in his reply, dwelt on the repeated efforts made by Lord Wellesley to avert the war by negotiations, and informed him that the only conditions on which he was now authorised to treat, were, the cession of half his dominions, the payment of two crores of rupees in two instalments, and the delivery of four of his sons, and four of his chief officers, as hostages. The Sultan, who still appeared to have no just conception of his danger, raved at what he termed the arrogance and tyranny of the proposition, and did not deign to return any reply to it. "Better," he exclaimed, "to die like a soldier, than to

live a miserable dependant on the infidels, and to be placed
in the roll of their pensioned rajas and nabobs." Yet,
throughout the siege, he exhibited none of that mental or
physical energy which was to have been expected of him,
and, instead of making due preparations for the impending
assault, busied himself in consultation with his astrologers.
On the 3rd of May it was reported that there were provisions
only for two days left in the English camp: but it was likewise reported that the breach was practicable, and it was
determined at once to bring the contest to an issue. The
troops destined for the storm, 4,376 in number, took up their
appointed stations in the trenches the next morning. General
Baird, a gallant and distinguished officer, who had been for
four years confined in irons in a dungeon in Seringapatam, was
very appropriately selected to lead the assault. Tippoo, who
directed all the operations of the defence himself, had discarded
the advice of his most experienced officers, and surrounded
himself with boys and parasites, who flattered his vanity.
They assured him that the attack would not be made before the
evening, and he had just sat down to his mid-day meal, when
intelligence was brought him that it had already begun. After
a few moments of silent and awful expectation in the trenches,
General Baird ascended the parapet at one o'clock, and exhibited
his noble military figure to the view of both forces, and then,
drawing his sword, desired his men " to follow him, and show
themselves worthy of the name of British soldiers." A small
and resolute band of Tippoo's troops met the forlorn hope on the
slope of the breach, and the greater portion on either side fell
in the desperate struggle, but within seven minutes after the
soldiers emerged from the trenches, the British ensign was
floating over the breach. The works, however, were defended
with great valour, and the carnage was terrific at the rampart
where the Sultan had taken his station, and was animating
his troops. The two columns of assailants, which after
storming the breach, had wheeled to the right and left, were
gradually gaining ground; the Mysore sepoys borne down by

them, at length lost confidence, and every avenue was choked up with fugitives.

Death and in-terment of Tippoo, 4-5th May, 1798. The column commanded by General Baird at length made its way to the front of the palace, and Major Allen climbed over an unfinished wall with a flag of truce, and was conducted to an apartment where two of Tippoo's sons were surrounded by officers and attendants in a state of the deepest consternation. The Major gave them and their adherents the assurance of complete safety, and endeavoured to convince them that the only chance of saving the life of their father was his immediate surrender; but they declared most solemnly that he was not in the palace. He then requested that the outer gate should be opened to prevent its being forced by the victorious soldiers, to which they at length consented, but not without great hesitation. In front of it Major Allen found General Baird with a large body of European troops, who had just learned that on the preceding night Tippoo caused twelve of their comrades who had fallen into his hands to be murdered in cold blood, and they were frantic to avenge them. The General, however, succeeded in preventing their entrance into the palace, where no life would have been sacred, and he requested that the young princes should be brought out to him. They were received with great humanity and kindness, and conveyed with suitable honours to the presence of the General-in-chief. General Baird now proceeded to search the palace for the Sultan, when the commandant offered to point out the place where he was said to be lying, though, as he had heard, only wounded. He accompanied the General to the gateway which had been the great scene of conflict and carnage, and which presented a ghastly spectacle. It was already night, and the bodies lay heaped in masses on each other; they were separately drawn out and examined by the light of torches. One man alone, the personal attendant of the Sultan, was found alive, and he pointed out the spot where the body of his master lay. It was immediately recog-

nised by the native commandant, and conveyed to the palace.
It appeared, on enquiry, that Tippoo had received three
wounds in succession, and was then placed by his faithful
attendants in his palankeen, but the spot soon became so
blocked up with dead and dying combatants that it was found
impossible to remove it. Tippoo then appears to have crept
out, when a European soldier, entering the gateway, endeavoured to snatch his brilliant sword-belt. Though fainting
from loss of blood, the Sultan grasped a sword which lay near
him, and aimed a blow at the soldier, who immediately lodged
a ball in his temples, and deprived him of life. His remains
were conveyed through the city, and the inhabitants crowded
the streets and prostrated themselves before the bier of their
late sovereign. He was interred in the superb mausoleum of
the family, by the side of his father, with all the imposing
rites of Mahomedan sepulture, and the honours of an European
military funeral.

Character of   Thus, in the space of a few hours, fell the
Tippoo, 1799.   capital of Mysore, though garrisoned by 20,000
troops, defended by 287 pieces of ordnance, and provided with
well-stored arsenals and every munition of war. It was the
opinion of Lord Wellesley and of the best military authorities
around him, that with a thousand French troops well commanded, Seringapatam, through the strength of its fortifications and the difficulties of approach, would have been impregnable. With the capital fell the dynasty of Hyder, after
a career of thirty-eight years. Tippoo, who was forty-six at
the time of his death, possessed none of his father's abilities,
either for war or for peace; he exhibited neither the same
moderation in prosperity, nor the same equanimity in adversity.
In the opinion of the Mysoreans, the one was born to create
an empire, and the other to lose it. Tippoo died bravely in
the defence of his throne, but it was the death of a soldier, not
of a general or a sovereign. He was distinguished by bigotry
and intolerance, and was the only Mahomedan sovereign since
Aurungzebe who determined to propagate his creed by perse-

cution. Both father and son exhibited for thirty years the same rancorous hatred of the English, and it was a dread of their projects throughout this period which mainly influenced the policy of the Company's Government. The animosity of Hyder was occasioned by the follies of the Madras council; that of Tippoo sprung from his natural malevolence. The expulsion of the English from India was the ruling passion of his life, and to accomplish this object he intrigued in every durbar in India, and sent his emissaries to Cabul and Paris.

Remarks on the transactions of 1799. For half a century the Deccan had been the source of constant anxiety to the Court of Directors, and the theatre of perpetual warfare. The safety of the British possessions had always been precarious, even in the intervals of peace. Lord Wellesley terminated this state of insecurity. Within a twelvemonth after landing in Calcutta he extinguished the French party and influence at Hyderabad, and made all the Nizam's resources subservient to British interests; he annihilated the kingdom of Mysore, and he established the Company's authority from Cape Comorin to the Kistna on so solid a basis that it has never since been interrupted. The capture of Seringapatam, an event second in importance only to the battle of Plassy, resounded through the whole continent, and the sudden and complete extinction of one of the substantive powers of India, struck terror into the hearts of its princes, and exalted the prestige of the British Government. But these advantages were not obtained with out the violation of those solemn injunctions which the wisdom or the fears of Parliament, the Ministry, and the East India Company, had issued to restrain the growth of the British empire in India. "I suppose," said Lord Wellesley, in writing to Mr. Pitt on the subject of these transactions, "You will either hang me or magnificently honour me for my deeds. In either case I shall be gratified; for an English gallows is better than an Indian throne." He was magnificently honoured, by the King with a step in the peerage, by the Parliament with its thanks.

Lord Wellesley entertained no views of territorial aggrandisement when he entered upon the war with Tippoo, but the issue of it had placed the whole of his dominions at the absolute disposal of the Company, and the right of conquest was exercised with great wisdom and moderation. Lord Wellesley, who acted in this matter exclusively on his own judgment, without consulting his ally the Nizam, felt that the appropriation of the whole territory to the Company would have raised a flame of discontent at Hyderabad and Poona, which it might have cost another war to quench. To have divided it equally between the Nizam and the Company would have inflamed the jealousy of the Mahrattas, and enlarged the territories of a prince who was incompetent for the management of those he already possessed. To have given the Peshwa a proportionate share of the conquered districts when he had not participated either in the expense or the risk of the war, would have been an act of inconsistency, and it would, moreover, have imprudently strengthened a power of very doubtful fidelity. Lord Wellesley, therefore, determined to make over a portion of the territory to the ancient dynasty of Mysore, whom Tippoo had reduced to a state of abject poverty and humiliation. The family had passed out of all recollection in the country, which rendered the act the more generous. A child of five years of age—the present rajah—was drawn from obscurity and placed upon the throne, to which districts yielding fourteen lacs of pagodas a-year were attached. It was intended that the new state should be essentially native in its character and administration, and the brahmin Poornea, who, although a Hindoo, had been for a quarter of a century the most efficient of the ministers of Hyder and Tippoo, and was the model of an Indian statesman, was appointed to the chief control of affairs, while Colonel Close acted as the representative of the British Government. The military force, for the maintenance of which the sum of seven lacs of pagodas were appropriated, was to be disciplined and commanded by British officers. The Company

was, moreover, at liberty to take over the entire management
of the state, or of any portion of it, if the mal-administration
of the raja should endanger the subsidy. Though Lord Wellesley deemed it expedient to associate the Nizam with the
Company in the preliminary convention for the disposal of the
conquered territory, the treaty with the Mysore raja was concluded in the name of the British Government alone, from
whom he received the kingdom as a free gift, bestowed on
him personally, without any mention of heirs. The whole
arrangement was merely a screen to cloak the appropriation
of the resources of the kingdom to the objects of the British
Government; and Lord Wellesley did not hesitate to affirm
that the territories thus placed under the nominal sovereignty
of the raja of Mysore constituted substantially an integral
portion of our own dominions. But he did not fail to do justice
to the interests of the country in the selection of the members
of the commission appointed to complete the organization and
settlement of it. It included Colonel Barry Close, the prince
of the Indian diplomatists of the time; Captain Malcolm, afterwards Governor of Bombay; Captain Munro, subsequently
Governor of Madras; Henry Wellesley, eventually Lord
Cowley, ambassador in Paris; and the Duke of Wellington;
—the largest number of men of genius ever assembled at the
same board in India, either before or since.

The remaining districts of Mysore were thus
Allotment of
the remaining partitioned. Territory of the annual value of
territory, 1799. 777,000 star-pagodas was allotted to the Company, but charged with the payment of 240,000 pagodas to
the families of Hyder and Tippoo, with the proviso that the
British Government should be at liberty to make such deduc-
tions from time to time from the sums allotted for their maintenance as might appear proper on the decease of any member
of the various branches of the family, and to limit, and if advisable, to suspend entirely the payment of the whole or any
part of the stipend, in the event of any hostile attempt on the
part of the family, or any member of it, against the peace of

the territories of the Company, or its allies. The provision thus made for the royal family of Mysore gave them a more liberal allowance than they had ever enjoyed before. Districts yielding 600,000 star-pagodas a-year were transferred to the Nizam, charged, however, with the payment of 70,000 pagodas annually to Kumur-ood-deen, one of the most eminent of Tippoo's generals, who had thrown himself unconditionally on the generosity of the British Government. A tract of country, yielding 263,000 star-pagodas a-year, was reserved for the acceptance of the Peshwa, on conditions which will be presently noticed. The additions thus made to the Company's dominions consisted of districts which gave them the absolute command of the Malabar coast, and the exclusive possession of the southern division of the Peninsula from coast to coast. It included also the capital, on which both Tippoo and Lord ·Wellesley set a high value, but which has been subsequently abandoned as a military station, from its unhealthiness. The population has dwindled down from 150,000, when it was the seat of Tippoo's government, to about 12,000.

Prize money, 1799.
The property captured at Seringapatam was at first estimated at ten crores of rupees. The assignment of so prodigious a sum as prize money could not have failed to demoralize the army, but it was fortunately found not to exceed a tenth of this amount. In 1758, when intelligence of the battle of Plassy reached England, the Crown made a grant to the Company of all booty captured by their own soldiers, with a reservation of the royal prerogative when the King's troops happened to be associated with them. Lord Wellesley, thinking the army might become impatient if the distribution of the Seringapatam prize money had to await the receipt of instructions from England, which in such cases are scandalously delayed, took upon himself the responsibility of "anticipating" the royal assent and the sanction of Leadenhall-street, and directed the immediate division of it. This procedure received the sanction both of the Crown and 'the Company. The Court of Directors, moreover, anxious to

manifest their sense of the merits of Lord Wellesley, offered him a donation of ten lacs of rupees from the proceeds of the captured grain, which appertained to the state, but his high sense of honour induced him to decline the gift, on which they settled an annuity of £5,000 a-year on him for twenty years. But the Commander-in-chief, General Harris, far from exhibiting the same magnanimity allotted to his own use double the usual share of his rank, or thirteen lacs of rupees. The general officers followed his example. The injustice of / depriving the rest of the army of their legitimate dues by (this unfair appropriation was so palpable, that the law officers of the Crown to whom the case was referred—the Attorney-General, subsequently Prime Minister of England, and the Solicitor-General, afterwards Speaker of the House of Commons—advised the parties to refund the excess, of their own accord, but they refused to relinquish a cowrie. A suit was therefore commenced against them in Chancery, which, however, was not successful; but the stigma of this rapacity tarnished the laurels of Seringapatam.

Peshwa refuses the offered territory, 1799. On the eve of the war with Tippoo, Lord Wellesley demanded of the Peshwa the aid of the contingent which he was bound by the treaty of 1792 to furnish, and he ostensibly ordered Pureshram Bhao, one of the great feudatory chiefs of the Mahratta empire, to join the British army with his force. At the same time, however, Bajee Rao, with his usual duplicity, received two vakeels at his court from Tippoo, and accepted a douceur of thirteen lacs of rupees, unknown to his minister, Nana Furnuvese. The Mahratta contingent consequently took no part in the campaign. On the contrary, the Peshwa and Sindia concerted a plan for attacking the dominions of the Nizam, while his army and that of his British ally were occupied with the siege of Seringapatam; and on the 26th April, 1799, Lord Wellesley, who was fully apprized of their machinations, considered a rupture with them imminent. But before their plans could be matured they were astounded by the intelligence that Tippoo was slain and his power extinguished. Bajee Rao affected great delight at this intelligence, and Sindia offered his congratulations to the Governor-General, but took care to dispatch his emissaries into Mysore to encourage the partizans of the late government to resist the British authorities. Notwithstanding the hypocrisy of Peshwa, however, Colonel Palmer, the Resident at his court, was instructed to inform him, that although he had forfeited all claim to a share of the conquered territory, the Governor-General was prepared to assign him districts valued at 263,000 pagodas a-year, on his consenting to admit the mediation of the British government on every question in dispute between him and the Nizam, and to exclude the French from his dominions. He replied, that he should be happy to accept the territory, as a commutation of the *chout*, to which the Mahrattas were entitled from the whole kingdom of Mysore,. but the two conditions he positively rejected. After a protracted discussion which led •to no result, the reserved territory was divided between the Company and the Nizam, and Lord Wellesley, disgusted with what he considered the "systematic jealousy, suspicion and insincerity" of the Peshwa, took leave of Mahratta politics, till a more favourable opportunity should turn up in the course of events for his intervention.

Dhoondia Waug, 1800. It only remains to be noticed that the settlement of Mysore was accomplished without any of those embarrassments which usually attend the introduction of a new government. The only opposition was offered by one Dhoondia Waug, who had been confined in irons in Seringapatam for various depredations in Mysore, and was inconsiderately released on the capture of the town. He was a daring adventurer, and having collected together some of Tippoo's disbanded cavalry, and a body of men of desperate fortunes, proceeded northward, plundering the towns and villages in his progress. Success brought crowds to his standard, and he was enabled to obtain possession of the

rich district of Bednore with its important fortresses., Two
British armies were sent against him, who succeeded in
recovering the district, and driving him to the frontier of the
Peshwa's dominions, where the pursuit necessarily ended.
The distractions which prevailed among the Mahratta chiefs
enabled him to collect another and a larger body, and the
revolt began to assume formidable dimensions. It was manifest that there could be no tranquillity in the Deccan while
this bold chieftain was roaming through it, at the head of an
increasing force of marauders. Colonel Wellesley was,
therefore, directed to take the field against him, and with his
usual energy and promptitude, pursued him without the relaxation of a day for four months, from district to district, and
at length brought him to bay on the 10th September, 1800.
With four regiments of cavalry, European and Native, he
completely defeated and dispersed 5,000 of Dhoondia's horse.
The freebooter fell in the action, and the insurrection, which,
without this vigorous effort, might have ended in the establishment of a hostile power, was completely suppressed.

Cession of Terri-
tory by the
Nizam. By the treaty concluded with the Nizam, on the
1st September, 1798, the new subsidiary force,
which took the place of the disbanded French
battalions, was placed on the same footing with the regiments
previously in his service, and restricted from acting against
the Mahrattas. The minister was no stranger to their insatiable rapacity, and the recent refusal of the Peshwa to
admit the arbitration of the British Government for the settlement of his demands on the Nizam, plainly indicated the
treatment which he had to expect from the Mahratta powers.
He therefore proposed to the Resident that the subsidiary
force should be augmented, more especially in the cavalry arm,
and that territory should be substituted for the subsidy in
money which was then paid for its maintenance. The proposal was most welcome to Lord Wellesley. He felt that the
cash payments might be precarious, and that the conveyance
of so large a sum month by month from the treasury to the

residency would be a source of constant irritation, which might ripen into political embarrassments. The negotiation occupied little time, and it was speedily arranged that in lieu of the payment of forty lacs of rupees a-year, districts yielding sixty-three lacs of annual revenue should be ceded in perpetual sovereignty to the Company, and that the remaining territories of the Nizam should be unreservedly guaranteed by the British Government against the encroachment of every enemy. The territory thus transferred by him consisted of the districts he had obtained from Mysore by his alliance with the British in the wars of 1792 and 1799. The exchange was beneficial to both parties. The dominions of the Company were extended on the north to the Toombudra and the Kistna, and being surrounded on three sides by the sea, included every harbour in the peninsula. The Nizam was relieved from all further anxiety regarding the interminable demands of the Mahrattas, without the alienation of any portion of his patrimonial possessions; and although, by relinquishing the military defence of his kingdom, and the right of foreign negotiations, he ceased to be one of the substantial powers of India, the transaction proved the salvation of his throne. Every other native power throughout the Deccan, from the Nerbudda to Cape Comorin, has been blotted out of existence, while the descendant of the Tartar Chin Kilich Khan still continues to occupy the musnud of Hyderabad, though with diminished splendour.

CHAPTER XX.

LORD WELLESLEY'S ADMINISTRATION CONTINUED, 1799—
1802.

Tanjore, 1800.   THE remaining transactions in the Deccan are few. Tuljajee, the raja of Tanjore, adopted Serfojee, and died in 1786; but the validity of the adoption was controverted, on the ground that the raja himself was in a state of mental incapacity at the time, that Serfojee was an only son, and that he was beyond the age of ten. Ameer Sing, the half-brother of the deceased prince, was accordingly placed on the throne, with the full concurrence of the Court of Directors. Serfojee, who had been educated by the missionary Swartz, and was a youth of many accomplishments, did not cease to press his claims on the British Government, and they were indirectly strengthened by the gross misconduct of Ameer Sing, who was a mere Asiatic voluptuary and tyrant. Sir John Shore was at length induced to submit the case anew to the most renowned pundits in Hindoostan, as well as in the Deccan, and they concurred in pronouncing the adoption of Serfojee unexceptional, according to the precepts of Hindoo law. The Court of Directors, persuaded that they had given their sanction to an act of injustice by his exclusion, instructed Lord Wellesley to place him on the throne, on condition that he should accept any arrangement the Government might think fit to dictate regarding the more punctual payment of the debts due to the Company, and the better management of the country. Commissioners were appointed to examine the condition and the resources of Tanjore, and on their report, Lord Wellesley assumed the entire administration of the country, and settled on the raja an annual allowance of one lac of pagodas, together with a fifth of its net revenue. Thus expired this little independent principality, a hundred and fifty years after it had been founded by Shahjee, the father of Sevajee.

The state of the Carnatic, 1799. In the treaty made by Lord Cornwallis, in 1792, with the Nabob of the Carnatic, it was provided that an annual subsidy should be paid for the support of the British troops to whom the defence of the country was committed, and that certain districts should be pledged to the Company, on which no assignments should be given. Mahomed Ali, the reigning prince, whom the Company had set up as "their own nabob of the Carnatic" in the days of Clive and

Coote, in opposition to the nominee of the French, occupied the throne for nearly half a century, and died in 1795. His son and successor, Omdut-ool-omrah, was surrounded, as his father had been, by a swarm of unscrupulous and rapacious Europeans, who fed his extravagance by loans at exorbitant interest, and received by way of security, assignments on the revenue of districts, which were rack-rented by their profligate agents. The Company's servants at the Madras Presidency were very inadequately paid, and the traffic in loans to the Nabob presented the shortest and surest road to fortune. The moral atmosphere of the Presidency had been polluted for forty years with the corruption of these nefarious transactions, and it was believed that some of the public servants still continued to participate in them. The European creditors of the Nabob had instilled into his mind the idea that a distinction both of interest and of powers existed between the Crown and the Company, and that the one might be advantageously played off against the other; the Company's Government was, therefore, treated by him with habitual contumely. Their representations were strengthened by the letters addressed to him, from time to time, as to an equal, by the King of England and, more particularly, by the Prince of Wales, which were treasured up in the palace as the most precious gems. This royal correspondence, which was not vouchsafed to any other native prince, tended to lower the character and weaken the authority of the local Government to such an extent that Lord Wellesley ventured to remonstrate with his royal highness on the injurious effect of his letters on the public interests. The advances with which the Nabob was liberally supplied by the European and native money-lenders who haunted his court, enabled him to pay the subsidy with punctuality. But this aid only served to postpone the crisis of his embarrassments, and was sure to aggravate it when it came. The wretched cultivators were ground down by the local agents of the creditors; the prosperity of the country was rapidly declining, and the resources of Government were threatened with extinction. In 1795, Lord Hobart, the Governor of Madras, endeavoured, at the particular request of the Court of Directors, to obtain a modification of the treaty of 1792, and proposed that the mortgaged districts, on which the Nabob continued to grant assignments contrary to his engagement, should be transferred to the Company in lieu of the subsidy. To secure the concurrence of the Nabob, he offered to relinquish debts due to the Company to the extent of a crore of rupees, but his creditors constrained him to reject the proposal, because, though highly "advantageous to his interests, it would have extinguished their own flagitious profits. Lord Hobart then proposed to resort to coercion, on the ground that the treaty of 1792 had been violated by the Nabob, and ceased to be binding on the Company, but Sir John Shore, peremptorily refused his concurrence; and the acrimonious correspondence which grew out of the proposition, induced the Court of Directors to recall Lord Hobart.

They had, however, set their heart on this measure, and they requested Lord Wellesley to call at Madras on his way to Calcutta, and make a second effort to procure the Nabob's consent to it. But under the interested counsel of the harpies around him, he not only spurned the proposals, but went so far as to raise the question whether the Company had any claim whatever upon the revenues of the Carnatic. The negotiation consequently fell to the ground; but the treaty of 1792, had, likewise, given the Governor-General authority, in the event of a war on the Coast, to assume the entire government and resources of the Carnatic, with the reservation of a fifth for the support of the Nabob's dignity. In the prospect of a war with Tippoo, the Court of Directors had, moreover, directed the Government of India to take possession of the Carnatic, and not·to relinquish it without special instructions from them. But Lord Wellesley was unwilling to adopt so extreme a measure, and made the milder request of a contribution of three lacs of pagodas for the use of the army then about to

Lord Wellesley's proposals to the Nabob, 1799.

I 2

take the field. The Nabob made a solemn promise to furnish this supply, but violated it "with every circumstance of infamy." In reliance on his pledge, the scanty funds in the Madras treasury had been fully appropriated to the equipment of the army, and his failure might have proved most disastrous to the military operations of the campaign, if a supply of treasure had not opportunely arrived from Bengal. Lord Wellesley next proposed to the Nabob to renounce for ever the right of the Company to assume the management of the Carnatic, on the occurrence of war, if he would consent to transfer in perpetuity territory yielding an annual revenue equal to the subsidy he was bound to contribute for the military defence of the country, he receiving the benefit of whatever additional rents the districts might yield under improved management. Lord Wellesley likewise offered a liberal and generous arrangement respecting the debts due by the Nabob to the Company, which fell little short of two crores of rupees. But this proposal was likewise rejected, and the Governor-General was rebuked for having ventured to make it, at a time when the instalments were punctually paid, although with money raised at usurious interest.

Discovery of the Nabob's intrigues, 1799.
By the treaty of 1792, the Nabob was bound "not to enter into any negotiation·or political correspondence with any European or native power, without the consent of the Company." But, on the fall of Seringapatam, papers were discovered which showed that both the late and the present Nabob had been engaged in a clandestine correspondence with Tippoo, by means of a cypher—which was found—and had conveyed secret intelligence, and friendly admonition, and important advice to him. The fact of this intrigue was established by the clearest oral and documentary evidence; nor will it appear incredible except to a European mind. Intrigue is the aliment of native courts, and there was not a native prince in India who would have considered such a plot dishonourable under any circumstances, or felt any regret except on its failure. On examining the

documents, Lord Wellesley came to the conclusion that the Nabobs, father and son, had not only violated the treaty by negotiating a separate connection with Tippoo, but had placed themselves in the position of enemies of the Company by endeavouring to establish a unity of interests with "their most implacable foe." The obligations of the treaty, he said, were thus extinguished, and the British Government was at liberty to exercise its rights in whatever manner might be most conducive to the general interests of the Company in the Carnatic. The "combination of fortunate circumstances" which had revealed the correspondence, removed every difficulty from his mind, and satisfied him of the justice and equity of depriving the Nabob of the civil and military government of the Carnatic, reserving a suitable proportion of its revenues for his support. But the negotiations then on foot with the court of Hyderabad, regarding the commutation of territory for the subsidy, were not, as yet, complete, and it appeared advisable to postpone the assumption of the Carnatic. This delay afforded time for receiving the direct sanction of the Court of Directors and of the Board of Control for this bold measure. But when the period for action arrived, the Nabob Omdut-ool-omrah was on his death-bed, and it was deemed indelicate to disturb his last moments with a painful discussion. On his death, the Governor of Madras communicated to his reputed son, whom he had nominated as his heir, the proofs of his father's and grandfather's infidelity, by which all claim to the consideration of the Company had been forfeited. He was informed that the succession to the musnud was now a question of favour and not of right, and that it could be conceded only on condition that the entire civil and military power of the state should be resigned to the British Government. Acting under the advice of the guardians whom his father had appointed, he refused to accept these conditions. They were then offered to Azim-ool-omrah, the son of the deceased Nabob's brother, who acceded to them without hesitation; and, in the pompous language of the proclamation, "this prince, the immediate great grandson of the Nabob Anwur-ood-deen khan, of blessed memory, had renewed the alliance between the Company and his illustrious ancestors, and established an adequate security for the British interests in the Carnatic; and the British The Carnatic Government had resolved to exercise its rights annexed, 1801. and its powers, under Providence, in supporting and establishing the hereditary pretensions of the prince in the Soobadaree of the territories of Arcot and the Carnatic Payenghaut." In plain English, the Nabob was mediatized, and the Carnatic became a British province. A fifth of its revenues was allotted for his support; but the arrangement was distinctly and intentionally limited to him and to his own family, instead of being extended, as in the case of former treaties, to his heirs and successors. The annexation of the Deccan to the dominions of the Company was thus consummated. Out of the territories acquired from Mysore, the Nizam, the Nabob of the Carnatic, and the rajah of Tanjore, Lord Wellesley created the Presidency of Madras. Of the population, which, according to a late census amounted to more than twenty-two millions, eighteen millions belong to Lord Wellesley's annexations, and though they were made in direct contravention of the resolutions of all the public authorities in England, they were honoured with their hearty concurrence.

Native embassy While Zemaun Shah was advancing towards to Persia, 1800. Delhi, Lord Wellesley despatched a native envoy, Mehndy Ali, to the court of Persia, to instigate the king to threaten his hereditary dominions in Central Asia, and induce him to recross the Indus for their defence. The unscrupulous vakeel, who considered lying the first qualification of an Oriental diplomatist, assured the king that the Governor-General was not in the smallest degree annoyed at the invasion of Zemaun Shah, but rather wished him to advance into the country, and thus afford an opportunity of showing how easily he could be expelled. But, he remarked, the Abdalee was a Soonee, and had grievously oppressed the Sheahs, the ruling sect in Persia, and constrained thousands of them to

take refuge in the Company's territories. To arrest the
progress of so heterodox a prince would be an acceptable service both to God and man. The pious monarch swallowed the
bait, and lost no time in giving encouragement to Mahomed
Shah to invade the dominions of his brother, Zemaun Shah,
who was thus obliged to retreat in haste across the Indus, in
the course of the year 1799.

Malcolm's em-   But Lord Wellesley considered it advisable to
bassy to Persia, send a more imposing embassy to Persia, with the
1800.   view of establishing a British influence in Central
Asia, and preventing the periodical alarm of an invasion by
Zemaun Shah, with his horde of Turks and Tartars, Oosbegs
and Ghiljies. The officer selected for this mission was
Captain Malcolm, then not more than thirty, who had
attracted the notice of Lord Wellesley by the talent he had
exhibited during the late critical transactions at Hyderabad,
and the ardour of his professional ambition. He was peculiarly adapted for a mission to a court like that of Persia,
by his thorough knowledge of the oriental languages,
character, and weaknesses, his admirable tact, and his invariable good humour. No accredited agent had visited that
court since the days of Queen Elizabeth, when the name of
England was utterly unknown in Asia, and Lord Wellesley
was anxious to impress the Persians with a due sense of the
power and wealth of the British empire in the east. The
envoy's suite comprised more than five hundred persons,
European and native. The embassy was equipped in the most
magnificent style, and supplied with watches glittering with
jewels, caskets of gold beautifully enamelled, lustres of
variegated glass, richly chased pistols, and massive mirrors
in gorgeous frames, which twelve hundred men were daily impressed to convey from the coast to the capital, and a hundred
and forty maunds of sugar and sugar-candy. Though impeded at every step by the frivolities of Persian etiquette,
Captain Malcolm was treated with distinguished honour during
his progress through the country. On his arrival at Teheran,

he was received in full durbar by the king, decked with the
jewels of which his ancestor, Nadir Shah, had plundered
Delhi in 1739, and arrayed in a robe studded with precious
stones, the value of which was computed at a crore of
rupees. The ulterior purpose of the mission was to establish
a predominant influence at the Persian court, and this could
be accomplished only by a lavish expenditure; the envoy,
therefore, "bribed like a king, and not a pedlar," upon a
scale which made the Court of Directors wince. But, when
he came to open his commission, he found that his immediate
object had been already accomplished, by the humble native
vakeel who preceded him, and who had been instrumental
in compelling Zemaun Shah to recross the Indus, by foment-
ing the rebellion of his brothers, and suggesting an attack
on Balkh. A political treaty was nevertheless made, which
provided that the king of Persia should labour to counteract
any future attempt to invade Hindostan; that if Zemaun
Shah invaded Persia, the Company should aid the king with
stores, and that neither the French, nor any power in alliance
with them, should be allowed to erect a fort in any part of
the Persian dominions. It stipulated, moreover, that if any
of the French nation should endeavour to establish themselves in the country, the king's officers should disgrace,
expel and exterminate them. To extenuate this truculent
order, Captain Malcolm explained that it was a mere eastern
hyperbole, and, in reality, meant nothing. He likewise concluded a commercial treaty, granting various privileges,
which were, however, of no value, as the trade of Persia,
in its most palmy days, had never been worth maintaining.
The result of the embassy fell miserably short of its cost.
Indeed, the political treaty, so far as it revealed our fears of
the invasion of India by a European power, through Persia,
may be considered positively mischievous. The Government
of India, however, experienced no further molestation from
Zemaun Shah, who perished in battle two years after.

Proposed expe-   On the fall of Seringapatam, Lord Wellesley

dition to the suggested to Mr. Dundas the propriety of sending
Mauritius, 1799. a force from India to co-operate in any attempt
which the Ministry might make to expel the French from
Egypt. But the communication between England and India,
was at that period so dilatory and precarious, that he was for
seven months without any authentic information from home.
He limited his exertions, therefore, to the assemblage of a
large body of European troops at Trincomalee, the noblest
harbour in Ceylon, to be ready to proceed in any direction
which Mr. Dundas might indicate. In the reply which he
subsequently received from Downing Street, no notice was
taken of the proposed expedition to Egypt, and Lord Wellesley resolved to employ the armament collected at Trincomalee in the capture of the Mauritius and Bourbon. The
possession of these islands, at an easy distance from the
continent of India, greatly facilitated the hostile projects of
the French, and exposed the political and commercial interests
of England in the east to no small risk. The privateers
fitted out in them preyed incessantly on British trade in
every part of the eastern seas. The losses sustained by the
merchants of Calcutta alone, since the beginning of the war,
were moderately estimated at two crores of rupees. The rate
of insurance had reached a point which almost suspended the
trade of the port. The Indian squadron, under Admiral
Rainier was unable to protect the Bay of Bengal, in which five
merchant vessels had recently been taken. On the 7th of
October, 1800, the Company's ship the "Kent," armed with
eighteen guns, was captured by a French vessel of war, at
the mouth of the Hooghly, after an action of an hour and
three-quarters, in which fifty-five of her crew were killed or
wounded. Lord Wellesley could not brook this insult at the
very threshold of his capital, and determined at once to send
the Trincomalee fleet and army to the islands, and extinguish
this nest of corsairs. But, the design was unfortunately
frustrated by Admiral Rainier. He thought fit to keep the
letter soliciting the co-operation of the fleet, for six weeks

without acknowledgment, though the lateness of the monsoon
required the utmost despatch, and at length positively refused
to take part in the expedition, without the express commands
of his Majesty, signified through the usual channel of the
Admiralty.   As the Ministry were not prepared to displace
him for this misconduct they gave him official credit for having
acted under a sense of public duty.   To every one besides
it was palpable, that he was actuated only by that feeling of
contemptible jealousy which had so often led the officers of
the royal navy to treat the instructions received from a
Governor of the Company with contempt.   The expedition
was necessarily abandoned when the aid of the navy was
denied.   The islands remained in possession of the French
for eight years longer, and the priggish conceit of the Admiral
entailed on the commerce of India an additional loss of two
crores of rupees.   The recurrence of such acts of folly was
subsequently prevented by an Act of Parliament which placed
the king's navy, equally with his army, at the disposal of his
representative in the east.

Expedition to
the Red Sea,
1800.
At length, Lord Wellesley received a despatch
from Downing-street, stating that Sir Ralph Abercromby had been despatched with a force of
15,000 men, to co-operate with the Turkish army in expelling
the French from Egypt, and that it was deemed advisable to
support his operations with an Indian force.   The armament
collected at Trincomalee was, therefore, ordered to the Red
Sea, together with a large addition of Bombay troops.   The
army, consisting altogether of 4,000 Europeans and 5,000
volunteer sepoys, was entrusted to General Baird, with the
animating remark of Lord Wellesley, that a "more worthy
sequel to the storm of Seringapatam could not be presented to
his genius and valour."   The expedition touched at Mocha,
and proceeded up the Red Sea to Cosseir, where the troops
performed one of the most extraordinary feats ever achieved
by an army, that of traversing a hundred and twenty miles of
the arid and pathless desert to Ghennah, on the Nile.   General

Baird reached Cairo on the 10th August, and on the 27th encamped on the shores of the Mediterranean. The history of British India teems with romance, but there is no incident more romantic than the appearance of sepoys from the banks of the Ganges, in the land of the Pharaohs, marching in the footsteps of Alexander and Cæsar, under an English commander, to encounter the veterans of the army of Italy. Before the Indian contingent, however, could be brought into action, the report of its approach, combined with the energy of Sir John Hutchinson, who had succeeded to the command on the death of Sir Ralph Abercromby, induced the French general to capitulate. But the power and the resources of the British empire were most conspicuously exhibited to the world by this concentration of troops from Europe and Asia on the banks of the Nile.

The Peace of Amiens, 1802.   Within a month of the surrender of the French army in Egypt, the preliminaries of peace between England and France were signed at Amiens. All the foreign settlements which had been captured in India, Ceylon excepted, were restored, as well as the Cape of Good Hope, then considered, and with reason, the maritime gate of India. The Court of Directors, under the influence of a short-sighted economy, immediately ordered their military establishments in India to be reduced, but Lord Wellesley, not considering the British dominions sufficiently secure to justify such a measure, hesitated to comply with their order, and the course of events fully vindicated his sagacity. The treaty of Amiens was no sooner ratified than Bonaparte despatched a large armament to Pondicherry, with the determination of re-establishing the power and influence of France in India. It consisted of two ships of the line, two frigates, and two corvettes, with a military staff of several general officers, and a due proportion of subordinate officers, with 1,400 European troops, and ten lacs of treasure, under the direction of Mons. Leger, who was designated Captain-General of the French establishments to the east of the Cape. It was to be followed by a second squadron of three ships of the line and two frigates. Lord Wellesley had brought with him to India the intense anti-gallican feeling of the day. It had been his constant aim for three years to exclude French influence from every native durbar. He had completely succeeded in closing the Deccan against it, and the feelings with which he now witnessed the arrival of a powerful French force on the Coromandel coast, directed by the supreme genius of Bonaparte, may be readily conceived. He felt that all our relations with the native princes would be at once deranged, and the seeds of another conflict for supremacy planted in the soil of India, ever fruitful in revolutions. There was already a formidable French force in Sindia's pay in Hindostan, equal in numbers and strength to the British army in that quarter, and he could not contemplate the co-operation of the two bodies in the north and south without a feeling of just alarm. He determined, therefore, by an act of unexampled audacity, to disregard the royal warrant, which preremptorily directed him to restore to the French Republic "all the countries, territories, and factories which had belonged to it in India." On the arrival of Admiral Linois with his squadron in the roadstead of Pondicherry, Lord Clive, the Governor of Madras, was directed to inform him that the Governor-General had resolved to postpone the restitution of the French settlements till he could communicate with the Ministry in England. The fleet returned to the Mauritius, and before a reply could be received to the reference, hostilities had recommenced in Europe, and the British interests in India were thus saved from the dangers they must have been exposed to if the continuance of peace had enabled Bonaparte to give full scope to his ambitious schemes.

Vizier Ali as- We turn now to the affairs of Oude. One of
sassinates Mr. the latest acts of Sir John Shore's administration
Cherry, 14th
January, 1799. was the elevation of Sadut Ali to the musnud, in the room of the profligate Vizier Ali, who was sent to Benares, with an annual pension of a lac and a half of rupees. The turbulence of his disposition, however, rendered it imprudent

to permit him to reside so near the frontier of Oude, and it was
resolved to remove him to Calcutta. He spared no effort to
procure a reversal of the order, but without success. A day
or two before the period fixed for his departure, he called on
Mr. Cherry, the British Resident, under whose superintendence
he had been placed, and complained in very intemperate language of the harshness of this procedure. Mr. Cherry endeavoured to calm his violence, and remarked that he was simply.
carrying out the orders of his superiors, for which he was not
himself responsible. The youth started up in a rage from his
seat, and struck Mr. Cherry with his sword. His attendants,
who were waiting for the signal, rushed in and butchered him,
as well as several other gentlemen residing in the house.
From thence they hurried to the houses of other Europeans,
several of whom fell victims to their fury ; but on the arrival
of a troop of horse, they took to flight, and eventually sought
refuge in the woody district of Bootwul. Vizier Ali was soon
after joined by several zemindars, and was enabled to take
possession of the eastern districts of Oude with a considerable
force. Sadut Ali had lost all popularity by his exactions, and
in the hour of need discovered that both his subjects and his
troops were disposed to desert him, and join the standard of
his rival. He was constrained, therefore, to apply for a
British detachment to protect his own person. Another detachment was sent against Vizier Ali; his followers rapidly
dispersed, and he fled for protection to the Rajpoot raja of
Jeypore, who delivered him up on the demand of Lord Wellesley. But even in that age of anarchy and treachery, the surrender of one to whom an asylum had once been granted, was
considered an act of unpardonable baseness, and the raja
became an object of contempt in every kingdom and province
of India.

Augmentation   On the approach of Zemaun Shah to the Indus,
of British   which has already been noticed, Lord Wellesley
troops in Oude,
1800.   requested Sir James Craig, the commandant in
Oude, to communicate his views on the defence of that king-

dom, which was certain to be the first object of spoliation, more especially as the discontented Rohillas in its northern districts would not fail to join their fellow-countrymen in the camp of the invader. Sir James replied that the rabble of troops maintained by the Vizier was not merely useless, but dangerous, and that if he were required to march against Zemaun Shah, he should be as unwilling to leave them behind, as to leave a fortress in the possession of an enemy. Sadut Ali was bound by the treaty which seated him on the throne to provide seventy-six lacs of rupees a-year for the subsistence of British troops, 13,000 in number, employed in the defence of his country. The home authorities had more than once informed the Governor-General that they considered this force too small for the protection of the kingdom, and that it could be rendered secure only by the substitution of a well organised force commanded by their own officers, for the disorderly regiments of the Vizier. Lord Wellesley, who fully concurred in these views, had frequently brought the subject before the Nabob. On his return to Calcutta, in November, 1799, he renewed his representations in greater detail. The British Government, he said, was bound to defend the Nabob Vizier's territories against all enemies; the present British force was insufficient for this purpose, and required a large augmentation. The treaty had provided for this contingency, out of the revenues of the country. The cost of additional troops would amount to fifty lacs of rupees a-year, and the proper course for the Nabob to adopt was to discharge his own disorderly troops, and thus effect a saving equivalent to the new demand.

The Nabob pro-
poses to abdi-
cate, 1800.

The proposed reform would have transferred the entire military power of Oude to the Company, which was precisely the object which Lord Wellesley had in his eye, but which the Nabob was most anxious to prevent. To evade the question, he proposed to retire from the Government. The refractory and perverse disposition of the people, he said, combined with the want of zeal and fidelity in his servants, had filled him with disgust. Neither was he pleased with his subjects, nor they with him. From the first he had been indisposed to the cares of government, and he was not reconciled to them by experience. He expected that one of his sons would be placed on the throne, as a matter of course, to perpetuate his name, and that suitable allowances would be granted to the other members of the family. As for himself, the treasure which he had accumulated—estimated at a crore of rupees—would procure him all the gratification he could desire in a private station. Lord Wellesley eagerly caught at the proposal of the Nabob Vizier, and hastened to inform the Court of Directors that he intended to turn it to account, and establish the Company's exclusive authority in Oude. He informed the Nabob that he was fully prepared to sanction the proposed abdication, provided he took up his residence in the British dominions, and vested the government of Oude absolutely and permanently in the Company, but he could not permit the public treasure, which belonged to the state and was liable for its obligations, to be removed.

He withdraws his abdication, 1800.

But the Nabob Vizier had never seriously contemplated the resignation of his kingdom to his son, and still less to the Company. His ruling passion was avarice, and nowhere could it be more amply gratified than on an Asiatic throne. On the receipt of Lord Wellesley's proposal, he assured the Resident that he would not bring on himself the odium and disgrace of having sold his country for money, and had therefore abandoned all thought of retirement. Lord Wellesley expressed great indignation at the insincerity and duplicity, as he termed it, of the Vizier, and charged him with having made a proposal which was from the first illusory, and designed only to defeat the reform of his military establishment by artificial delays. The Governor-General resolved to proceed at once to action. Several regiments were ordered to move to different stations in the Oude territories, and the Nabob was called on to make provision for their maintenance, according to the terms of the treaty. He immediately addressed a memorial to the Governor-General, acknowledging that he was the creature and dependent of the Company, but remonstrating against a measure to which he had never given his consent. The seventh article of the treaty, he said, provided that no augmentation of the British force should be made without necessity, yet a large increase was now needlessly forced upon him. By the seventeenth article he was to enjoy full authority over his household affairs, his subjects, and his troops; whereas he was now required to relinquish the control of the military force in his dominions, which would not fail to annihilate his authority, and expose him to the contempt of his people. This remonstrance excited the highest displeasure of Lord Wellesley, who ordered it to be returned to the Nabob, as being deficient in that respect which was due to the first British authority in India, and he was informed that "if he should think proper again to impeach the honour and justice of the British Government in such terms, the Governor-General would consider how such unfounded calumnies and gross misrepresentations, both of facts and arguments, ought to be noticed."

Submission of the Nabob— Second demand, 1800.

The Nabob Vizier yielded to necessity, and began to disband a part of his own troops, in order to obtain funds for the payment of the British regiments. But, in November, 1800, he was required to make provision for a second body of troops, "to complete the augmentation." He pleaded the extreme difficulty with which the collections were realized, and refused to become responsible for any further payments till he was assured that his resources were sufficient to meet them, lest he should be chargeable with a breach of faith. At the same time, he ordered a schedule of his revenues to be drawn up by his treasurer, and submitted through the Resident to Lord Wellesley, who, on receiving the statement, replied that "if the alarming crisis be now approaching in which his Excellency can no longer fulfil his public engagements to the Company . . . it became the duty of the British Government to interpose effectually for the protection

of his interests, as well as those of the Company, which were
menaced with common and speedy destruction by the rapid
decline of the general resources of his Excellency's dominions."
The Resident was then instructed to propose either that he
should resign the entire management of the civil and military
government to the Company, a suitable provision being made
for his own maintenance and that of his family, or that he
should cede to the Company in perpetual sovereignty a section
of his territories sufficient to cover the expense of the entire
British force. The Nabob manifested the strongest repugnance
to both proposals, and a tedious correspondence ensued, which
was marked, on the part of Lord Wellesley, by that imperious
tone which had characterized the transaction throughout. The
Nabob, unable to obtain any relaxation of the demand, entreated
Lord Wellesley to allow him to go on pilgrimage, the pretext
by which Hindoos and Mahomedans endeavour to escape from
an embarrassing position. The whole of his territories and
treasure, he said, was at the disposal of the Company, and he
had neither inclination nor strength to resist them, but he could
not yield his consent to a proposal so injurious to his royal
character. Lord Wellesley was desirous, if possible, to avoid
the appearance of a compulsory cession of territory, and despatched his brother and private secretary, Mr. Henry Wellesley, to Lucknow, in the hope that the presence of a member
of his own family would overcome the repugnance of the
Nabob. Every form of ingenuity was exhausted to obtain the
voluntary surrender of the districts, but the Nabob still persisted in asserting that it would inflict an indelible stain on his
reputation throughout India to deprive one of its royal houses of
such a dominion. The Resident at length brought the discussion
to an issue by ordering the intendants of the districts which had
been selected to hold themselves in readiness to transfer their
collections and their allegiance to the Company.

Annexation of the Oude terri-tories, 1801.   The Vizier deemed it vain any longer to contend
with negotiators who could bring such arguments
to bear on him, and on the 10th November, after

two years of weary discussion, simply, as he said, "to gratify the wishes of Lord Wellesley, and in submission to the earnest solicitations of his brother," signed the treaty which transferred to the Company for ever districts yielding a hundred and thirty-five.lacs of rupees a-year, leaving him a territory, guaranteed against all invaders, valued at a little over a crore of rupees.

Remarks on this transaction, 1801.
The security which this transfer of military power in Oude gave to the possessions both of the Nabob and the Company will admit of no question. A British force, fully adequate to the defence of the frontier was substituted for the miserable legions of the Nabob, always an object of more dread to their masters than to their enemies. An important addition was made to the resources of the Company, and a large population was rescued from the oppression of native officers, whose only remuneration consisted of the sums they could extort from the people. But of all the transactions of Lord Wellesley's administration, this acquisition of territory from the Nabob by the process of coercion has been considered most open to censure, as an arbitrary, if not unjust proceeding. For any justification of it we must look to the peculiar position of the country and the political obligations which it created. The throne of the Nabob was upheld only by British bayonets, and if at any period during the previous fifteen years they had been withdrawn, the dynasty of Oude would have ceased to exist. The safety of Oude was menaced not only by Zemaun Shah, and the hordes of Central Asia ready to follow his stirrup, but also by Sindia, who had planted a formidable force of 30 or, 40,000 disciplined troops, commanded by European officers on its frontier, and only waited for an opportunity to spring on its inviting districts. It was necessary, therefore, to maintain a powerful force, permanently, against the probabilities of a Mahratta invasion. For the Company to continue responsible for the defence of the whole kingdom of Oude, with only a third of its revenues, the realization of which was subject to all the corruption and abuses of the system of

misrule, dignified with the name of government at Lucknow, was not only unreasonable, but financially impracticable. The fidelity of the troops depended on punctual pay, and this punctuality required the solid basis of territorial revenues, honestly administered by British officers. This is the sinew of the argument by which this high-handed—or as the natives would call it, *zuburdust*—proceeding has been vindicated, and it will be readily conceded that it is by no means deficient in strength. Nor should it be forgotten that the kingdom of Oude fell to the Company by right of conquest in 1763, and was restored to the reigning family as a matter of grace; and that according to the prescriptive maxims of eastern policy, it was considered ever after subject to the control, if not even at the disposal, of the British Government, who had accordingly made and unmade Nabobs at its own pleasure. It was doubtless on this principle that Lord Wellesley told the Nabob on one occasion during these negotiations, that he had a right to take over, not a part only, but the whole of his country.

Appointment and dismissal of Mr. Henry Wellesley, 1801.   The settlement of the districts ceded by the Nabob Vizier was entrusted to a commission consisting of the Company's civil servants, of which Mr. Henry Wellesley, the brother of the Governor-General, who combined great administrative talent with much firmness and discretion, was made President. In announcing this arrangement to the Court of Directors, Lord Wellesley stated that the labours of the commission would probably be completed within a twelvemonth, perhaps in a shorter period, and that his brother would receive no allowance beyond the salary of his post as private secretary. The Directors expressed their cordial approbation of the terms of the treaty, which was calculated to promote their interests, and which created thirty new appointments for their civil service, but they denounced even the temporary appointment of Mr. Wellesley as "a virtual supersession of the just rights" of that favourite service, and they hastened to give vent to their jealous feeling in a despatch, which peremptorily ordered his dismissal. The

K 2

President of the Board of Control, Lord Wellesley's personal
friend, Lord Castlereagh, drew his pen across the despatch and
returned it to the India House, with the remark that the appointment was not in the fixed and ordinary line of the Company's service; that it was only decent to await an explanation
from the Governor-General, and that Mr. Wellesley would
probably have relinquished the office before the despatch could
reach India. The labours of the commission were in fact completed, and Mr. Wellesley had resigned the office, even before
the despatch was drafted.

The Sudder   On Lord Wellesley's return from the Coast, he
Court, 1800.   devoted his attention to various measures of internal administration with his accustomed ardour. Of these,
one of the most important was the reconstruction of the
Sudder Court at Calcutta. This was not only the highest local
court of appeal, but was charged with the duty of superin-
tending the administration of justice, and the operations of the
police throughout the whole of the Presidency. Under the
native governments, the prince had always united the legislative, executive, and judicial powers of the state in his own
person. The Company acted on the principle of introducing
as few changes as possible in the existing system of administration, and it was accordingly provided that the Governor-
General in Council should, in like manner, exercise the highest
judicial functions, in addition to those of the executive
government and of legislation. The Sudder Court was
accordingly held in the Council Chamber, with closed doors,
and without the presence either of the suitors or of their
pleaders. The proceedings of the lower courts were translated into English and read to the members of Council, and
the decisions they passed in each case, were recorded and promulgated by the register. To this system of procedure,
Lord Wellesley saw many grave objections: The translation
of the papers occasioned a vexatious delay, and the union of the
judicial and the legislative functions in the same body was
repugnant to sound principle; a conscientious discharge of

the duties of the Sudder Court would absorb all the time of
the Governor-General, while the administration of justice with
closed doors deprived it of one of its most important safe-
guards, and impaired the confidence of the country. On the
other hand, to throw open the Council Chamber while suits
were under examination, would not be without its disadvan-
tages. The presence of the Governor-General on the bench
would necessarily interfere with the freedom of advocacy ;
few native pleaders would be found to contest his opinions,
and his will, rather than the law, would too often be the rule
of decision. It was resolved, therefore, to divest the
Governor-General and Council of their judicial functions, and
to select the ablest judicial officers in the service to preside
in the Court. Lord Wellesley was anxious that the chief
judge should be invested with the same emblem of dignity
which the chief justice of the Crown Court enjoyed, but he
was unable to procure the distinction of knighthood for him.
The Sudder Court, however, was rendered illustrious by the
appointment of Mr. Henry Thomas Colebrooke, the most
profound Oriental scholar of the day, and one of the most
distinguished of the public servants, to preside over its proceedings.

The College of
Fort William,
1800.

It became evident, moreover, to Lord Wellesley's mind, that there could be no substantive
improvement in the administration of the country,
without providing a succession of men, sufficiently qualified
to conduct it. The civil service had produced not a few men of
first-rate ability, but it was in its origin only a mercantile
staff, and it had not been deemed necessary to accommo-
date the training of the civilians, as a body, to the more
important duties which now devolved upon them. India was
still considered rather in the light of a commercial factory,
than an imperial domain. For men who were to act as
magistrates, collectors, judges, political agents, and ambassadors, it was still deemed sufficient if they were well versed
in the mysteries of the counting-house, understood book-

keeping by double entry, and wrote a hand which the Directors could read. The system which Burke had reprobated fifteen years before was still unchanged, and lads of fifteen were sent out to the Indian service before their education was finished, with no opportunity or inducement after their arrival, to complete it. Of the languages of the people, whose affairs they were to administer, they were not required to know even the rudiments. To supply these palpable deficiencies in the system of government, Lord Wellesley was determined to found a College in Calcutta, and assemble in it the young writers, as the embryo civilians were designated, from the three Presidencies, and set them to continue and complete their European education, and to study the laws, literature, and languages of the people they were to govern. The institution was projected on that scale of magnificence which marked all Lord Wellesley's plans, and in the medal which was struck on the occasion, the date of its establishment was thrown back a twelvemonth, to associate it with the memorable event of the capture of Seringapatam. A provost and vice-provost were appointed, with salaries of Indian magnitude, and the sum of 5,000 rupees a-month was allotted for the public table of the collegians. Learned men were invited to join it from all parts of India, and in the minds of the natives the halcyon days of the great Mahomedan and Hindoo princes, who had sought to render their courts illustrious by the assemblage of the literati, appeared now to be revived in the metropolis of British India. Four disputations were to be held annually in the grand edifice which Lord Wellesley had erected, " in an august assembly," composed of the natives of rank and learning, pundits and moonshees, rajas and foreign ambassadors. Such an institution was at the time essentially necessary to give the stamp of efficiency to the institutions of the British Government; but it was very costly, and, it was erected without the sanction, or even the cognizance, of the Court of Directors. Accordingly, on the 29th January, 1802, they passed a

peremptory order for its immediate abolition. Lord Wellesley
was mortified to an extreme degree by this subversion of one
of his most cherished schemes, which exposed him to the
contempt of India, and he gave vent to his feelings in a
passionate appeal to his friends in the Ministry. He likewise
placed on the records of the Council an elaborate minute, in
which he combated the arguments of the India House, and
maintained the necessity of such an institution with irresistible
force. The objection which the Court of Directors had raised,
on the ground of expense, had been obviated, he said, by
the imposition of a new tax, which would produce a sum
equal to the charge of the College establishment. This was
no other than the renewal of the transit duty on the conveyance of produce from district to district, which Hindoo and
Mahomedan Governments had been in the habit of imposing.
At the present day it appears incredible, that one of the most
liberal and enlightened statesmen of that period, should have
taken credit to himself for the establishment of one of the
most barbarous and mischievous taxes ever devised, and
sought to make provision for his noble college by the interruption of inland commerce. He proceeded to pass an order
for the abolition of the College, " as an act of necessary submission to the controlling authority of the Court," but immediately after, issued a second order directing that the abolition
should be gradually effected, in the next eighteen months.
At the same time, he entreated Lord Castlereagh to use his
utmost endeavours to save from destruction the institution
which he regarded with feelings of greater exultation, than
even the kingdom he had built up in the Deccan, and to the
consolidation of which he vowed to devote his political life.
Under the pressure of the Board of Control, the Court of
Directors were induced to qualify their orders, and permit the
continuance of the College, but on a reduced scale, limiting its
agency to the students of the Bengal Presidency, and to the
cultivation of the native languages. To complete the
European education of the students, and impart to them the

rudiments of the eastern tongues, they set up an expensive College of their own at Haileybury.

Private Trade, 1793—1801. At the renewal of the charter in 1793, Parliament endeavoured to silence the clamours of the merchants and manufacturers of England for a participation in the Indian trade, by obliging the Court of Directors to allot them 3,000 tons of freight annually. Though this concession was saddled with extravagant charges and vexatious restrictions, the private trade soon increased, under its operation, to 5,000 tons a-year. The commerce of India was, in fact, bursting the bonds of the monopoly, which, however valuable during the period of its infancy, was totally unsuited to an age of development and maturity. The subject was forced on the attention of Lord Wellesley as soon as he landed in Calcutta, and on the 5th October, 1798, he issued his first notification for the encouragement of free trade between India and the port of London, to which, at that time, all imports were restricted. Ship-building had recently attained great perfection on the banks of the Hooghly, and a vessel of 1,400 tons, a vast size for a merchantman of that period, was then on the stocks. Lord Wellesley, on the part of Government, chartered a number of country-built vessels, and relet them to the private merchants, with liberty to make arrangements with the proprietors to suit their own convenience, and secure those advantages which could not be enjoyed in the privileged tonnage of the Company. This indulgence was discontinued in 1799, but it was found necessary to renew it in the succeeding year. The evils of the monopoly were daily becoming more palpable. The trade of Calcutta was increasing beyond all example, and forcing a passage in foreign vessels which were freighted by English capital, the funds of the merchants, and the savings of the services. In the previous year, the imports and exports of American, Portuguese, and Danish vessels had exceeded a crore and a half of rupees, and in September, 1800, there were 8,500 tons of shipping, under foreign colours, lying in the Hooghly. By these ships the produce of India was conveyed to Europe with great expedition and economy, and the East India Company was thus beaten out of the markets on the continent. Lord Wellesley considered it important to secure this valuable commerce to British interests. . There were 10,000 tons of India-built shipping then anchored in Calcutta, and he determined, as in 1798, to engage a large portion of this tonnage to convey the produce of the country, belonging to private merchants, to the port of London.

In his despatch to the Court of Directors on the subject, he stated that "it would be equally unjust and impolitic to extend any facility to the trade of the British merchants in India by sacrificing or hazarding the Company's rights or privileges, by injuring its commercial interests, or by departing from any of the fundamental principles of policy which now govern the British establishments in India; but the increasing commercial resources of Great Britain claimed for her subjects the largest attainable share of the valuable and extensive commerce of such articles of Indian produce and manufacture as were necessarily excluded from the Company's investments." He recorded his decided opinion that a well-organised system of intercourse between the ports of India and London was indispensable to the interests both of the Company and of the nation. These liberal views met with the entire concurrence of Mr. Dundas, who said "it was notorious that at no period had the capital or commercial powers of the East India Company been able to embrace the whole, or near the whole, of the wealth of India, exported thence by trade to England, and he was anxious to authorise the Government of India to licence the appropriation of India-built shipping for the purpose of bringing home that India trade which the means and capital of the East India Company was unable to embrace." Far different, however, was the feeling at the India House. The great dread of interlopers, which had haunted it for two centuries, was still in full vigour. Though the cream of the India trade was still to be assured to the Company, the Directors could not

Feelings of the Court on the Private Trade, 1802.

brook that others should be permitted to taste even the lees. The proceedings of Lord Wellesley were arraigned with the greatest virulence. That " our Governor-General," as he was usually addressed in the public despatches, should give the slightest countenance to free trade, was not to be endured. He lost caste at once and irretrievably in Leadenhall-street. Every effort was made to thwart his administration and weaken his authority, and, during the last three years of his Indian career, the treatment he experienced from the India House was scarcely less rancorous than that which had embittered the life of his illustrious predecessor, Warren Hastings. The Court of Directors passed a vote, in the teeth of the Prime Minister, Mr. Addington, condemning the liberal commercial policy of Lord Wellesley, and the Court of Proprietors cordially adopted it. A farther period of ten years was required to break up the monopoly of two centuries, and open the gates of India to British enterprize and capital.

Resignation of Lord Wellesley. As soon as the arrangements in Oude were completed, Lord Wellesley sent in his resignation to the Court of Directors, assigning no other reason for this step but the completion of the plans he had devised for the security of the empire, and the general prosperity of the country. To Mr. Addington, however, he unburdened his mind, and explained the real motives of his retirement—the hostile disposition of the Court, and the withdrawal of their confidence. They had peremptorily ordered him to reduce the military establishments in the Peninsula, leaving him no option between an act of direct disobedience and the execution of measures which he considered fatal to the vital interests of the Government. The total disregard of the strong opinion he had expressed on the subject appeared clearly to intimate that they considered him no longer competent to govern the empire which he endeavoured to consolidate. They had issued the most positive injunctions to reduce many of the stipends which he had considered advisable at the close of the war. They had selected for especial censure the additional allowances granted by the Madras Government,

with his concurrence, to his brother, General Wellesley, to de-
fray the charges of his important and expensive command in
Mysore. He considered this reduction as "the most direct,
marked, and disgusting indignity which could be devised."
The Act of 1793 had invested the Governor-General in Council
with the power of enforcing his orders on the minor Presidencies, though they might happen to supersede the injunctions
of the Court of Directors. But the Court had now thought fit
to issue orders to those Presidencies to carry certain measures
into effect, notwithstanding any directions they might have received to the contrary from Calcutta. The authority of the
Supreme Government over the subordinate Presidencies was
thus neutralized.

The Court had not only taken upon themselves
to displace officers who enjoyed the full confidence
of the Governor-General, but to nominate others in
opposition to his judgment. For example, he had
placed Colonel Kirkpatrick, one of the ablest and most experienced officers in the service, in the important post of political
secretary. The Court cancelled the appointment, to the great
detriment of the public interests, and the injury of the Governor-
General's character and influence. They had likewise forced
on him the nomination of Mr. Speke, an ex-member of Council,
as officiating president of the Board of Trade, though he
had no higher recommendation than the favour of the Prince of
Wales. At Madras, the Court had removed from the office of
chief secretary Mr. Webbe, the most eminent statesman of that
Presidency, and the unflinching enemy of that system of intrigue and corruption which had for more than thirty years
disgraced the public service. This removal was the more
offensive as it was to be traced to the base insinuation of
some informer that Mr. Webbe exercised a strong influence on
the mind of Lord Clive, which, if true, was equally honourable
to both. Mr. Cockburn, the ablest financial officer at the
Madras Presidency, was likewise displaced to make room for
some nominee of Leadenhall-street. Lord Wellesley was well

*Court's inter-
ference in ap-
pointments,
1802.*

known to have approved of both these appointments, and indeed
of all the proceedings of Lord Clive, and he considered the
conduct of the Court of Directors in these instances as a reflection also on himself. This nomination to offices in India of
those who could secure the smiles of the Directors had been
checked by Lord Cornwallis, who threatened to throw up his
office if it were persisted in, " that he might preserve his own
character, and avoid witnessing the ruin of the national interests." By the subsequent Act of 1793, the power of appoint-
ing to official situations in India was vested in the local
Governments, subject only to the general control of the home
authorities. The interference with this patronage by the India
House was therefore not only highly injurious to the public
interests, but altogether unconstitutional. Lord Wellesley
justly remarked that if the Government of India was thus to
be thwarted in every subordinate department, deprived of all
local influence, and counteracted in every local detail by a
remote authority, interfering in the nomination of every public
servant, it would be impossible to conduct the government
under such disgraceful chains. It was a singular anomaly that
the Court of Directors should thus have grasped at appointments in India at the time when they themselves were de-
nouncing the appointment of Mr. Henry Wellesley, even for a
twelvemonth, as an invasion of their own rights. Lord Castlereagh, the President of the Board of Control, was anxious that
Lord Wellesley should remain another year in the government,
and he placed this letter to Mr. Addington, confidentially, in
the hands of the Chairman and Deputy Chairman of the Court.
They did not disguise from him that great dissatisfaction and
jealousy was felt by the Company with regard to certain measures of Lord Wellesley's government, which had been increased by the employment of Mr. Henry Wellesley. Lord
Wellesley had, in fact, touched the two privileges on which
the India House was most sensitive, its commercial monopoly
in the matter of the private trade, and its patronage in the appointment given to his brother, and the indignation of tho[

Directors rose to fever heat.   But the Chairs assured Lord
Castlereagh that they were not unmindful of his eminent services, and were alive to the importance of retaining them for
another year.   A despatch was sent out, officially
Lord Wellesley asked to remain 12 months, 1803. commending his zeal and ability, and requesting
him to postpone his departure to January, 1804.,
Little did they dream of the momentous results of this request,
and of the great revolution to which it would lead, in the irretrievable prostration of the Mahratta powers, to whose history
we now return.

CHAPTER XXI.

LORD WELLESLEY'S ADMINISTRATION—MAHRATTA AFFAIRS,
1800—1803.

Death of Nana Furnuvese, 1800. The destruction of Tippoo's power, and the complete ascendency established at Hyderabad, left the
Company with no antagonist but the Mahrattas,
and the two rival powers now stood front to front.   It was
the firm conviction of Lord Wellesley that the peace and tranquillity of India could be secured only by the extension of British
supremacy over all its princes, by means of defensive and subsidiary alliances, which recognized the British Government as
the arbiter in every dispute.   But nothing could be more un-
palatable to the Mahrattas chiefs than this policy.   The peace
and tranquillity of India implied the termination of that system
of plunder and aggression which was the foundation and
element of their power.   They believed, and not without reason,
that these subsidiary alliances would extinguish their independence, and deprive them of the respect of their subjects.
The offer of such an alliance, which was made in the first
instance to the Peshwa, in July, 1799, was therefore declined,

under the prudent advice of Nana Furnuvese. In March, 1800, that great statesman closed his long and chequered career. For more than a quarter of a century he had been the mainspring of every movement in the Mahratta empire. By the vigour of his character and the wisdom of his councils, he had controlled the disorders of the times, and he wanted only the addition of personal courage to render him supreme. He was distinguished by the rare, and among the Mahrattas of that age, the incredible qualities of humanity, veracity, and honesty of purpose. While he admired the English for their sincerity and their energy, he had a patriotic jealousy of the increase of their power, which it was his constant 'endeavour to restrain. " With him," wrote Colonel Palmer, the Resident, " has departed all the wisdom and moderation of the Mahratta government." He had been the only check on the growing ascendency of Sindia at Poona, who was left by his death without a rival and without control, and now ventured so far to indulge his spirit of domination, as on one occasion, when he feared that Bajee Rao meditated an escape, to surround his palace and place him temporarily under restraint. It was not, therefore, without secret delight that the Peshwa contemplated the rising power of Jeswunt Rao Holkar, by whose assistance he hoped to free himself from the tyranny of Sindia. In proportion as this hope increased, his inclination towards the alternative of a British alliance, which Lord Wellesley continued to press on him with great importunity, was slackened.

The Holkar family. To elucidate the rise of this celebrated chief, who played an important part in the transactions of the next five years, it is necessary to bring up the history of the Holkar family. Mulhar Rao Holkar, who raised himself from the condition of a shepherd to the dignity of a prince, died at the age of seventy-six, after a brilliant career of forty years. His only son died soon after the battle of Paniput, leaving his widow Aylah-bye, with a son and a daughter. The son died in 1766, and his widow, a woman of extraordinary powers, steadfastly resisted all the entreaties of the chiefs to adopt a

son and retire into obscurity, and resolved to undertake the
government of the state herself, in the capacity of regent.
With singular discernment she selected Tokajee Holkar, a
chief of the same tribe as Mulhar Rao, though not of his
kindred, to take the command of the army. It was scarcely
to be expected that in a country like India, and in a period of
unexampled turmoil, an arrangement which placed the military
power in the hands of a great soldier, while the civil government was administered by a female, would be of long continuance. But the gratitude and moderation of Tokajee, and
the commanding genius of the Bye combined to perpetuate it
for thirty years. He never failed in the homage due to her
position, and was never known to encroach on her authority.
She sat daily in open durbar, and gave public audiences without
a veil, and dispensed justice in person to all suitors. She laid
herself out to promote the prosperity of the country by the
encouragement of trade and agriculture. She acquired the
respect of foreign princes by the weight of her character, and
in an age of extreme violence succeeded in maintaining the
security of her own dominions. She raised Indore from a
mere village to the rank of a noble capital. Like all wealthy
Hindoo females, she fell under the dominion of the priesthood,
and expended large sums on religious edifices and establishments in every part of India, from Ramisseram to Hurdwar.
Relays of porters were daily employed at her expense in conveying the water of the Ganges to the sacred shrines in the
Deccan, however remote, and she was rewarded by the
brahmins with the title of an *avatar*, or incarnation of the deity.
Whatever opinion may be formed of these acts of superstitious
devotion, she was in other respects the purest and most exemplary of rulers, and added one more name to the roll of those
illustrious females who have adorned the native history of
India with their genius and virtues.

Death of Aylah-
bye and
Tokajee,
1795–97.

Aylah-bye died in 1795, and Tokajee in 1797,
and the reign of anarchy began, not to close but
in the entire submission of the state to British

authority, twenty years later. Tokajee left two sons by his wife, Kashee Rao and Mulhar Rao, and two by a concubine, Jeswunt Rao and Wittoojee. Kashee Rao was weak in mind and deformed in body, and his brother Mulhar Rao assumed the command of the army, and the government of the state. Kashee Rao repaired to Sindia at Poona, and he espoused his cause, and made a treacherous attack on the army of Mulhar Rao, who fell in the engagement. The house of Holkar, which had long been the rival of Sindia, was thus enfeebled and brought into complete subordination to his power, and another step was gained in his ambitious endeavours to obtain the universal control of the Mahratta commonwealth. Jeswunt Rao, who had taken part with Mulhar Rao, fled from the field of battle to Nagpore, but the raja, anxious to conciliate Sindia, placed him in confinement. He contrived, however, to make his escape, and sought refuge at the court of Anund Rao, the chief of the ancient principality of Dhar, to whom he was enabled to afford material assistance in coercing some of his refractory subjects. The enmity of Sindia still pursued him, and the raja was constrained to discard him, but, to compensate for this breach of Rajpoot hospitality, bestowed on him a parting gift of 10,000 rupees. He quitted Dhar with seven mounted followers, and about a hundred and twenty ragged, half-armed infantry, with the resolution to trust his future fortunes to his sword. Fully aware of the strong prejudice which existed against him on account of his illegitimacy, he announced himself as the champion and

Rise of Jeswunt Rao Holkar, 1795.

minister of his nephew, Khundeh Rao, the youthful son of Mulhar Rao, and called upon all the adherents of the house of Holkar to rally round him, and resist the encroachments of Sindia. The freebooters, who swarmed in Central India, Bheels and Pindarees, Afghans and Mahrattas, hastened to join his standard, and thus commenced the career of this predatory chieftain. Soon after, he was joined by Ameer Khan, a Rohilla adventurer, then about thirty-two years of age, who had just taken service

with the Chief of Bhopal, but quitted it in 1798 with a body
of free lances to traverse the country, and levy contributions
on his own account. For eighteen months the combined forces
of the two chiefs spread desolation through the districts on
the Nerbudda, but were obliged to separate when they were
completely exhausted. Ameer Khan proceeded eastward to
the opulent city of Sagor, belonging to the Peshwa, where he
subjected the inhabitants to every species of outrage, and
acquired incredible booty. Jeswunt Rao entered the province of Malwa, which had enjoyed repose and prosperity for
thirty years, and dispersed his predatory bands in every direction, and the country was half ruined before Sindia could take
measures to protect it. That chief was now obliged to quit
Poona, where he had continued to reside for eight years, ever
since his accession to the throne of his uncle, domineering
over the unfortunate Peshwa, from whom he extorted the sum
of forty-seven lacs of rupees on taking his departure. The
notorious Sirjee Rao Ghatkay was left as his representative
to maintain his authority with five battalions of foot, and
10,000 horse.

Holkar defeats
Sindia's army,
1801.

Nothing can give the mind a clearer idea of the
anarchy and misery which prevailed in Hindostan
at this period than the ease with which Jeswunt
Rao was able, by the allurement of plunder, to organise an
army of 70,000 men within two years. With this force he laid
waste the districts of Malwa, and then advanced against the
capital, Oojein. To this city the widows of the deceased
Mahdajee Sindia had fled with a large military force and their
treasures, to avoid the violence of Dowlut, Rao. Under the
pretence of espousing their cause, Holkar contrived to lull
them into security, and in the dead of night opened his guns
on their encampment, and constrained them to fly for their
lives, while he took possession of all their property, and of
their valuable park of artillery. Two bodies of Sindia's troops
were immediately pushed forward from the south to avenge
this insult, and expel Jeswunt Rao. One of these armies

though commanded by European officers, was constrained to
lay down its arms, and the other, under Colonel Hessing, was
attacked with such vigour as to lose a fourth of its number.
Of eleven European officers attached to it, seven fell in action,
and three were made prisoners. The city of Oojein was thus
placed at the mercy of Holkar, but so absolute was the control
which he had acquired over his troops that he was enabled to
restrain them from plundering it, even in the excitement of
victory; but he exacted the heavy ransom of fifteen lacs of
rupees, which he transferred to his own military chest. Meanwhile the Peshwa, liberated for the first time from the despotism of Sindia by his departure from the capital, gave full
scope to his natural disposition, and, instead of strengthening
his throne by conciliating his feudatories, subjected them to
the most wanton insult and plunder. His oppressive government became the object of universal hatred. Bands of
brigands sprung up in every direction, and laid the villages
under contribution. Wittoojee, the brother of Jeswunt Rao,
was driven by necessity to join one of these bodies, and was
taken prisoner. Bajee Rao sentenced him to be trampled to
death by an infuriated elephant, and seated himself in the
verandah of his palace to enjoy the revolting spectacle, and
the yells of the unfortunate youth. A universal feeling of
execration rose throughout the country at this atrocious
murder of a son of Tokajee, who had for thirty years
zealously maintained the interests of the Mahratta power.
Jeswunt Rao, who, with all his ferocity, was really attached to
his brother, vowed vengeance on his murderer, and it was not
not long before he had an opportunity of wreaking it.

Sindia defeats
Holkar, 14 Octo-
ber, 1801.
Sindia, alarmed by the defeat of his armies,
and the increasing power of Holkar, summoned
Sirjee Rao Ghatkay to join him with the troops
under his command. That miscreant, after the departure of
his master from Poona, proceeded to the Peshwa's southern
provinces, which he ravaged without mercy, and, when thus
called away, was encamped on his return within a mile of

the capital which he was on the point of giving up to plunder.
Sindia's army thus reinforced, and comprising fourteen of
De Boigne's battalions, met Holkar on the 14th October, 1801,
and totally routed him, capturing ninety-eight guns. This defeat was generally ascribed to the absence of Holkar's European
officers whom he had injudiciously left behind. Sirjee Rao
entered Indore in triumph, and gave it up to spoliation, to
avenge the plunder of Sindia's capital. His ruthless troops
were let loose on the city which Aylah Bye had spent a life in
embellishing, and the noblest edifices were sacked and reduced
to ashes. Those who were supposed to possess property were
tortured to disclose it, and the wells were choked up with
the bodies of females who destroyed themselves to escape
dishonour. If Sindia had followed up his victory with vigour,·
the career of Jeswunt Rao would probably have been
brought to a close; but, after expelling him from Malwa, he
thought fit to enter into negotiations with him, under the
impression that he was crushed beyond redemption. Holkar,
however, either from mistrust of Sindia, or under encouragement from the Peshwa, or perhaps from an overweening confidence in his own fortune, advanced the most extravagant
demands, and the negotiation fell to the ground. He was
not long recovering from the blow. His wild and daring spirit
was precisely suited to the character of the times and of the
country. His standard again became the rallying point of
the unquiet spirits who were hanging, loose on society in
Central India, and not a few even of Sindia's soldiers deserted to
it. With this force he proceeded northward, plundering every
village and town in his route, and, to the horror of his own
lawless but superstitious soldiery, not sparing the renowned
shrine of Nath-dowrah. He then crossed the Nerbudda, and
laid waste the province of Candesh, while one' of his commanders was sent to ravage the southern Mahratta provinces. General Wellesley soon after marched up through this
territory, and remarked that Holkar's troops had cut all the
forage, consumed the grain, and burnt the houses for fuel;

that the wretched villagers had taken to flight, with their cattle; and that, except in one village, not a human being was left between Meritch and Poona. Meanwhile, Jeswunt Rao, who had been encamped at Chandore, moved down upon Poona, with the object, as he asserted, of claiming the protection of the Peshwa from the hostility of Sindia.

Battle of Poona, 1802. The object of Holkar's march could not, however, be mistaken. The consternation at Poona may be readily conceived, and the Peshwa began to tremble for his own safety. Lord Wellesley had never abandoned the belief, that until we could obtain a footing and an influence at Poona, the peace of the peninsula would be periodically disturbed by Sindia and Holkar, and he had renewed his offer of an alliance with the Peshwa, whenever there appeared any chance of success. On the other hand, the vakeels of the raja of Berar and Sindia, constantly and earnestly dissuaded him from accepting it, and engaged to protect him from the designs of Holkar. The British negotiation fluctuated with the hopes and fears of Bajee Rao. Sindia sent his general, Sudaseeb Rao, with ten battalions of infantry, and a large body of cavalry to defend the capital from the threatened attack of Holkar; the Peshwa was thus encouraged to treat the advances of the Governor-General with indifference, and in the beginning of October, Colonel Close, the Resident, declared the negotiation at an end. As Holkar approached the neighbourhood of Poona, Bajee Rao made him the most humiliating offers, which he haughtily rejected, demanding the restoration of all the dominions belonging to his house, and the release of his nephew, and bitterly reproaching him with the murder of his brother, which he was now come to avenge. The troops of Sindia and the Peshwa were united under the walls of Poona on the 25th October. The combined force numbered about 84,000 horse and foot; and of Sindia's battalions ten were under the command of Colonel Dawes. Holkar also had fourteen battalions disciplined by European officers, together with 5,000 irregular infantry and 25,000

cavalry, and thus was exhibited the anomalous spectacle of
British officers arrayed against each other under the hostile
standards of native princes.   The battle was long and
obstinately contested.   Success at first inclined to Sindia and
his ally; the slaughter of Holkar's troops was prodigious,
and they had begun to give way, when he advanced from the
rear, and vaulting into his saddle, called out to them "now
or never to follow Jeswunt Rao."   He dealt about him like
a mad lion, and his foaming valour restored the fortune of
the day.   The victory was complete, and placed in his hands
the whole of the baggage, stores, and ammunition of his
opponents.   The Peshwa had come out to take part in the
engagement, but he was terrified by the first firing, and
hastened to place himself beyond the reach of it, on the hill
Parbutee, where he was surrounded by a considerable body
of his troops, who would have been more usefully employed
against Holkar.   As he perceived the scale of the battle
turn against him, he sent a messenger in haste to Colonel
Close, who was encamped in the neighbourhood, to accede to
all the conditions of the alliance which he had previously
objected to.   When he found the day lost he retired to Sun-
gumnere with about 7,000 men, and thence hastened to the
sea coast, and despatched letters to the Governor of Bombay,
requesting the accommodation of a vessel, in which he
embarked, and reached Bassein on the 6th December.

Holkar places
Umrit Rao in
power, 1802.

Jeswunt Rao, who entered the capital after the
battle, was anxious, above all things, to obtain
possession of the person of the Peshwa, and to
construct an administration in which he himself should possess
the same power and ascendency which Sindia had enjoyed for
eight years; but the Peshwa was too deeply incensed at his
conduct to listen to any overtures.   Finding at length that he
had no intention to return to his capital, Holkar sent for his
brother, Umrit Rao, and placed him at the head of affairs, and
seated his son on the musnud, bargaining for himself an immediate payment of two crores of rupees, and districts yielding

another crore, together with the command of the army and. the substantial power of the state. For two months after his victory, he exhibited a spirit of singular moderation, but in the end threw off the mask and gave up the city of Poona to indiscriminate plunder. Colonel Close was earnestly entreated by Holkar to continue as the British Resident at Poona, but he refused to countenance this usurpation by his presence, and retired to Bombay in the beginning of December. He was immediately placed in communication with Bajee Rao, who was now eager for the alliance which was to restore him to his throne. Accordingly, on the last day of December, 1802, the memorable treaty of "defensive alliance and reciprocal protection," was completed at Bassein. A British force of 6,000 infantry, with a suitable, complement of artillery, was to be stationed within the Peshwa's dominions, and districts in the Deccan yielding twenty-six lacs of rupees a-year were to be assigned for their support. The Peshwa agreed to entertain no European in his service belonging to any nation at war with the English, to engage in no hostilities or negotiations without their concurrence, and to refer all his claims on the Nizam and the Guickwar to the arbitration of the Governor-General. The treaty likewise guaranteed to the southern jageerdars, the great feudatories of the Peshwa, the full enjoyment of all their rights.

Treaty of Bassein, 1802.

The treaty of Bassein forms one of the most important epochs in the history of British India. It completely paralysed the head of the Mahratta commonwealth, and it inflicted a blow on the Mahratta power, from which it never recovered. Although the Peshwa's authority was often set at nought by the chiefs, they still continued to regard it as the centre of national unity, and a most important element in the existing struggle for the empire of India between the Mahrattas and the English. There has been no little diversity of opinion on the propriety of this treaty, but we have happily the views of two of the greatest statesmen of the age to assist us in judging of its merits. It was impugned

Remarks on the Treaty, 1802.

XXI.]   REMARKS ON THE TREATY.   141

by Lord Castlereagh, the President of the Board of Control, in a very able state paper, entitled "Observations on Mahratta affairs," and its policy was triumphantly vindicated in an elaborate memorandum by the Duke of Wellington, then General Wellesley. From his own personal experience of six years, which was superior to that of any one else in India, the General drew a very vivid sketch of the position and the policy of the various country powers, whose interests were affected by the treaty. He demonstrated that it was the inevitable corollary of the engagements which had been entered into with the Nizam. On that prince the Mahratta powers had interminable claims—the Asiatic claims of the strong on the weak—and they would have neglected no opportunity of enforcing them, which must have compromised the tranquillity of the Deccan. The subsidiary alliance which Lord Wellesley had entered into with the Nizam, identified his interests with those of the Company, and gave him the protection of the British arms against the claims and the aggression of the Mahrattas. The necessity which had thus arisen of supporting the Nizam against all his enemies must have involved the Company, sooner or later, in a war with the whole of the Mahratta nation, and this could be avoided only by forming an alliance with its recognised chief, on the basis of constituting the British Government the arbiter of these demands. Lord Wellesley considered the position of affairs at the end of 1802, as affording the best occasion for effecting this important object. The Peshwa was a fugitive, and both Sindia and Holkar, though with private and opposite intentions, had repeatedly urged him to interpose in the settlement of affairs at Poona. He had the wisdom to avail himself of this golden opportunity, which might never return, and to form a treaty with the Peshwa which placed the settlement of all claims on the Nizam in the hands of the British Government, and at the same time secured to it an absolute ascendency in the counsels of Poona. The great Duke placed it on record that, "the treaty of Bassein and the measures adopted in consequence of it, afforded the best prospect of preserving the peace of India, and that to have adopted any other measures would have rendered war with Holkar nearly certain, and war with the whole of the Mahratta nation more than probable," and his approbation has been ratified by the judgment of posterity. The war with Sindia and the raja of Nagpore in the following year arose ostensibly from the conclusion of the treaty, but a war with them was all but inevitable, and the only difference made by the treaty was to hasten its occurrence, and to deprive them of all the resources of the Peshwa.

Discontent of Sindia and the Bhonslay, 1803.   The establishment of the Company's paramount authority at the capital of the Mahratta empire by the treaty of Bassein gave great umbrage to the Mahratta powers. It thwarted the ambition of some, and the interests of all. Sindia had solicited the interposition of the Governor-General for the restoration of the Peshwa, only in the hope of regaining his power at Poona, and he was mortified to find that all his ambitious prospects in the Deccan were at once overturned. "The treaty," he said, "takes the turban from my head." Lord Wellesley had offered him the "benefit" of an arrangement similar to that which had been made with the Peshwa, but he could not fail to perceive that this new system of subsidiary alliances must sap the foundation of Mahratta power, as effectually as the invention of the system of the *chout* had enabled the Mahrattas to destroy the Mogul empire. He lost no time in deputing his prime minister to confer with the raja of Berar on the formation of a confederacy of Mahratta chiefs to oppose the common enemy. The raja, a collateral branch of Sevajee's family, had always cherished pretensions to the office of Peshwa, but the treaty of Bassein, by reinstating Bajee Rao under British protection, effectually destroyed all these expectations. He not only entered cordially into the views of Sindia, but became the life and soul of the hostile coalition. The Peshwa himself repented of the treaty as soon as he had affixed his seal to it, and commenced a series of intrigues to render it ineffectual. He

despatched a confidential agent to Sindia and the raja of
Nagpore, ostensibly to reconcile them to the alliance he had
formed with the British Government, but in reality to invite
them to Poona to assist him in frustrating it. Holkar, finding
all his plans thwarted by the policy of Lord Wellesley, and by
the advance of a British force to support it, quitted Poona and
retired to the -north. The raja of Nagpore made the most
strenuous efforts to induce him to join the league, and at
length succeeded in effecting a reconciliation between him and
Sindia, on the condition that all the dominions of the family
should be restored to him, and that his nephew, Khundeh
Rao, should be liberated. But although he signed the
engagement, and received possession of the family domains,
he evaded every solicitation to bring up his forces and join
the allies, alleging that he was unable to raise sufficient funds
for the payment of their arrears. But, no sooner did he find
Sindia actually involved in hostilities with the English, than
he let loose his famishing host on the possessions of that prince
in Malwa, while his confederate, Ameer Khan,• proceeded to
pillage his territories in another direction.

Lord Wellesley's military movements, 1803. Lord Wellesley had early intelligence of this
confederation, but he was anxious to maintain
peace, and caused a communication to be made to
Sindia and the Berar raja, that he was desirous of continuing his friendly relations with them unimpaired, but would
resist to the full extent of his power any attempt on their part
to interfere with the treaty of Bassein. To be prepared for
every contingency, he ordered the whole of the ·Hyderabad
subsidiary force under Colonel Stephenson, together with
6,000 of the Nizam's own infantry, and 9,000 horse to advance
to the north-western frontier of his kingdom; and they reached
Purinda, 116 miles from Bombay, on the 25th March. General Wellesley was likewise directed to march up from Mysore
in the same direction, a distance of 600 miles, with about
8,000 infantry, 1,700 cavalry, and 2,000 of the celebrated
Mysore horse, under an able native commandant. It was

important to the stability of the arrangements made with the Peshwa that the great southern jageerdars, who, in consequence of a long series of aggressions, mistrusted his intentions, and detested his person, should· be induced to·rally round his throne. For many years there had been constant struggles for power and plunder among the chiefs themselves; but the energy displayed by General Wellesley in the pursuit of Dhoondia Waug had spread his fame through the Deccan, and the strength of his character had inspired such general confidence that he was enabled to compose their mutual feuds, and to bring up with him six of the chief feudatories, with 10,000 of their troops. Holkar, on quitting Poona, had left it in the hands of Umrit Rao, with 1,500 troops; but that prince, on hearing of the advance of General Wellesley in the direction of the capital, resolved to give it up to the flames, and then to withdraw from it. This nefarious design could not be kept secret, and General Wellesley, on being apprized of it, made a rapid march of sixty miles in thirty-two hours, and ·reached Poona in time. to save it from destruction. Soon after, the Peshwa left Bassein, accompanied by Colonel Close, and on the

Restoration of the Peshwa, 1803.

13th May, a day selected by his astrologers as peculiarly fortunate, entered his capital, surrounded by British bayonets, and resumed his seat on the musnud under a British salute.

Development of the designs of the coalition, 1803.

Meanwhile, the hostile designs of the confederates became daily more apparent. Sindia was at Oojein when he heard of the battle of Poona and the defeat of his army by Holkar, and began to move to the south in November. He halted for some time at Boorhanpore on the Taptee, and despatched a letter to the Governor-General, asserting the Mahratta claim to the *chout* of the Nizam's dominions, and announcing his determination to proceed and enforce it. He then continued his march southward to form a junction with the raja of Nagpore, who entered his tents in the vicinity of that city on the 17th April, and advanced to meet Sindia with a large force. Both princes announced their intention to proceed to Poona, "to adjust the government of the Peshwa." The Resident informed Sindia that the Governor-General would not fail to consider any such movement on his part an act of hostility, involving the most serious consequences. Sindia asserted that as he was the guarantee of the treaty of Salbye, the Peshwa was not at liberty to sign a new treaty without his concurrence, or to act without consulting the great Mahratta princes. He stated, moreover, that they were proceeding to Poona on the express and repeated invitations of the Peshwa himself; whereas the Peshwa had invariably assured Colonel Close that he had forbidden their approach. Lord Wellesley likewise obtained possession of a letter addressed by the raja of Berar to the Nizam, which stated that after an interview with Sindia, and a satisfactory arrangement with Holkar, he should advance with the allies to Poona "to settle affairs." A letter was also intercepted from Sindia to the Peshwa's officers in Bundlekund, ordering them "to prepare for war." With these unequivocal tokens of hostility before him, the Governor-General directed Colonel Collins to demand from Sindia a categorical explanation of his intentions. The interview took place on the 28th May, when Sindia frankly admitted to the Resident that the treaty of Bassein contained nothing repugnant to his just rights. He disavowed any intention of invading the territories of the Company, or of their allies; but, in reference to the negotiations then on foot, he could give no decisive answer till he had seen the raja of Nagpore, then about forty miles

Sindia's fatal declaration, 1803.

distant; "when you shall be informed whether there is to be war or peace." These ominous words proved to be the knell of Mahratta power. That Sindia, encamped with a large army on the frontier of the British ally, the Nizam, should rest the question of war or peace simply upon a conference with an armed confederate, was considered by Lord Wellesley a public insult to the British Government, and so palpable a menace of hostility, that a conflict was no longer to be avoided. The complication of affairs at this juncture was increased by the arrival of the French squadron, already alluded to, at Pondicherry, which Sindia·did not fail to turn to account in his communications with the other Mahratta powers, as well as by the daily expectation of the death of the old Nizam, when the question of the succession to the throne of Hyderabad would open a wide door for the intrigues of the two Mahratta chiefs encamped on its frontier. But Sindia and the raja of Nagpore endeavoured to spin out the discussions with the Resident for two months longer, while they continued to press Holkar to cross the Taptee, and join their forces. During this period of suspense, the Peshwa was engaged in constant communications with Sindia, urging him to make no concession, but to advance at once to Poona. He was lavish in his promises to the Resident, but he took care to perform nothing. The contingent he was bound to furnish was withheld; supplies were prevented from reaching the English camp, and no opportunity was lost of embarrassing the operations of the British Government.

Full powers of General Wellesley—the result, 1803.
Early in May, General Wellesley had represented to the Governor-General that no reply to any reference could be received from Calcutta under six weeks, and that all the advantages of delay rested with the Mahrattas; he therefore suggested the propriety of deputing to some authority on the western coast the power of summarily deciding upon every question as it arose. Feeling the full·force of this advice, at this critical juncture, the Governor-General took on himself the responsibility—for which he was afterwards captiously censured—of vesting the full powers of government, civil, military, and political, in reference to Mahratta affairs, in General Wellesley, and after a clear and ample exposition of his own views, authorised him to commence hostilities, or to conclude treaties without any further application to Calcutta. This communication reached him on the 18th July, and he lost no time in announcing to Sindia and to the raja of Berar the plenary powers with which he had been invested, and called on them to demonstrate

by their conduct the sincerity of the pacific declarations which they continued to make. Their armies, he said, now occupied positions not necessary for the security of their own territories, but menacing both to the Company, the Nizam, and the Peshwa. He proposed that they should withdraw their forces respectively to Hindostan and to Nagpore, while he sent back the British armies to their usual stations. Then ensued another week of frivolous and fruitless discussion, in the course of which Sindia, with that mixture of simplicity and perfidy which is so often found together in the oriental character, said that he and his confederate could determine upon no movement, because the arrangements for Holkar's joining their camp were not as yet completed. Wearied with these studied delays, General Wellesley gave them twenty-four hours for their ultimatum, which they presented in this shape ; that he should dismiss his troops to their respective cantonments, and that they should fall back forty miles to Boorhanpore. To this the General replied, " You propose that I should withdraw to Seringapatam, Madras and Bombay, the troops collected to defend these territories against your designs, and that you and your confederate should be suffered to remain with your forces, to take advantage of their absence. I offered you peace on terms of equality, and honourable to all parties. You have chosen war, and are answerable for all consequences." On the 3rd August

Colonel Collins quitted Sindia's camp, and this circumstance became the immediate precursor of hostilities. Thus commenced the Mahratta war of 1803.

Colonel Collins quits Sindia's camp, 1803.

Preparations for war, 1803. Lord Wellesley, when he found that a war with Sindia and the raja of Nagpore was more than probable, determined to strike a decisive blow simultaneously at the possessions of both princes, in every quarter of India, though the field of operations was 700 miles apart in one direction, and 600 in another. In the grand combinations of the campaign he was his own war minister, and never had the resources of India been drawn forth on a scale of such magnitude, or applied with such efficiency. In the Deccan about 3,600 troops were left for the defence of Hyderabad and Poona, while a covering army of about 8,000 men protected the districts between the Kistna and the Toombudra. The advanced force under the command of General Wellesley of about 9,000, and of about 8,000 under Colonel Stephenson, was intended to operate against the main armies of the two allies. In the north of India, 10,500 troops were assembled under the Commander-in-chief, General Lake, to attack Sindia's disciplined battalions, and wrest from him his possessions in Hindostan. A force of 3,500 men was allotted for the occupation of Bundelkund. On the western coast of India an army of 7,300 men was organised to dispossess Sindia of his districts in Guzerat, and 5,200 men were prepared to take possession of the province of Cuttack, in the bay of Bengal. The whole force, amounting to about 55,000, was animated by that traditionary spirit of enterprize and enthusiasm which had created the British empire in the east, and which, on the present occasion, was heightened by a feeling of unbounded confidence in the master mind of the Governor-General. The armies of Sindia and the raja of Berar were computed at 100,000, of whom 50,000 were cavalry and 30,000 infantry, trained and commanded by European officers, together with a superb train of artillery of many hundred pieces.

Capture of Ahmednugur, Aug. 12, 1803.

As soon as Colonel Collins had left Sindia's camp, General Wellesley opened the campaign by an attack on Ahmednugur, Sindia's great arsenal and depôt south of the Nerbudda. This important fortress, though it had been considered impregnable since the memorable defence of it by Chánd Sultana in 1595, was surrendered after a brief resistance on the 12th August. The general then proceeded to take possession of all Sindia's territories south of the Godavery, and crossed that river on the 29th August, in the hope of bringing the contest to the issue of a general engagement. But the confederates spent three weeks in marching and counter-marching without skill, and without any apparent object except

that of avoiding the pursuit of the British armies. On the 21st
September General Wellesley found himself in the neighbourhood of Sindia's encampment, and, at a conference with Colonel
Stephenson, arranged that they should move on separate routes
to the attack of the enemy on the 24th. But the General was
misled by his scouts as to the actual position of the confederate
army, and after marching twenty-six miles on the 23rd, unexpectedly discovered that it was encamped at no greater distance than six miles, whereas he had been led to believe that it
was twice as remote from him. He was, likewise, assured
that the allied chiefs were on the point of retiring from their
present position, and under the apprehension that their infantry
might escape him, he resolved to bring on an action before the
close of the day, without waiting for the junction of Colonel
Stephenson. On ascending an eminence, he beheld the Mahratta
armies stretched out before him, consisting of 50,000 men, of
whom 10,000 were trained sepoys, and supported by a hundred
pieces of cannon.

Battle of Assye,   The handful of British troops which now moved
Sept. 23, 1803.   down to attack this formidable host did not exceed
4,500. The Mahrattas had taken up a strong position, as they
were always famous for doing, with their left resting on the
village of Assye, and their infantry entrenched behind formidable batteries. General Wellesley had given the most positive injunctions to the officer commanding the pickets to avoid
the cannon planted in the village, but he led his troops directly
up to the muzzle of the guns, which poured an incessant shower
on the assailants. The 74th, which supported them, was thus
exposed to a hotter fire than any troops had ever before encountered in India. To save that gallant regiment from utter
destruction, it was necessary to bring up additional corps ; but
so tremendous was the cannonade, that General Wellesley was
at one time doubtful whether he could prevail on any regiment
to advance and face it. The indomitable courage and energy
of British troops, however, bore down all resistance, and
Sindia's splendid infantry, who stood to their guns to the last

moment, were at length overpowered and dispersed. The victory was the most complete which had ever crowned British valour in India, but it was dearly purchased by the loss of one-third of the army. The slaughter would not have been half so severe but for the blunder of the officer commanding the pickets, for which the strategy of the General was not responsible. The raja of Nagpore fled at the first shot, and Sindia was not slow to follow his example. He lost all his guns, ammunition, and camp equipage. His army was completely and irretrievably disorganized, and he retreated with a small body of horse along the banks of the Taptee. He then made a rapid movement southward, vigorously followed

Capture of Boorhanpore, 16th, and Asseergur, 21st Oct., 1803. by General Wellesley, while Colonel Stephenson successively besieged and captured the flourishing town of Boorhanpore and the strong fortress of Asseergur. These were the last remaining possessions of Sindia in the Deccan, and General Wellesley was now at liberty to direct his undivided attention to the raja of Nagpore, who was the most determined enemy of the Company, and the prime mover in this war.

Capture of Cuttack, 1803. During the month of September, the army under Colonel Harcourt advanced into the maritime province of Cuttack, abutting on southern Bengal, of which the Nagpore family had held possession for more than half a century. It lay between the Bengal and the Madras Presidencies, and the Court of Directors had always cast a longing eye upon it, and pressed the acquisition of it, if necessary, by purchase, on successive Governors-General for twenty years. It was now to be added to their dominions by the fortune of war. The whole country was occupied without even the semblance of opposition. As the British army approached the temple of Jugunnath, which is considered to sanctify the whole province, and render it "the land of merit;" the brahmins hastened to the camp to inform the Colonel that on the preceding night they had inquired of the god whether he would rather live under the protection of the English than of the Mahrattas, and he had replied that he greatly preferred the English. This very sagacious and prudent determination was considered of such importance as to be communicated by express to , Calcutta.

Armistice with Sindia, 1803. Sindia, stripped of the last of his possessions in Candesh, by the capture of Asseergur, made overtures of peace to General Wellesley, which, after a wearisome negotiation, resulted in a provisional armistice on the 23rd November. It stipulated that he should keep his army to a position forty miles east of Elichpore, and that his camp should not approach within the same distance of either of the British armies, then operating against the raja of Nagpore. Colonel Stephenson was marching to the siege of Gawilgur, a strong and important fortress in the Nagpore territories, in which the royal treasures were said to be deposited. The raja and his troops who had been for some time moving about in the southern districts, closely followed by General Wellesley, now moved up to the defence of the fort. The General, who had been separated from Colonel Stephenson for two months, opportunely joined him in time to support and cover the siege. On the 28th November, the British force, after a long and fatiguing march, came up with the Nagpore army, on the plain of Argaom. Sindia, who was

Battle of Argaom, 28th Nov., 1803. waiting for the result of circumstances, had not ratified the armistice, or observed its conditions, but was encamped within four miles of his confederate, and, in the engagement which ensued, did not hesitate to send his cavalry to aid him in charging the British regiments. Though it was late in the day, General Wellesley resolved to engage the enemy, but his troops had no sooner come within range of their guns, than three entire battalions, who had behaved with distinguished gallantry on the field of Assye, under a far hotter fire, broke their ranks and fled. Fortunately, the General happened to be at no great distance, and succeeded in rallying them, and re-establishing the battle, or it would have been inevitably lost. The raja abandoned all his cannon and ammunition;

II.   M and few of his troops would have escaped if there had been an hour of daylight left. On the 15th December the fortress of Gawilgur surrendered to Colonel Stephenson, and General Wellesley prepared to march on the city of Nagpore. The raja, reduced to despair by these rapid reverses, and trembling for his capital and his throne, hastened to sue for peace. The negotiation was entrusted to Mr. Mount Stuart Elphinstone, a young civilian of great talent and promise, who subsequently rose to great eminence in the public service, and had the honour of twice declining the post of Governor-General, for which not even an English statesman could have been better qualified. The treaty, known as that of Deogaom, was completed in two days. The province of Cuttack was ceded to the Company, and a letter-post was established without a break between Calcutta and Madras. The districts of Berar west of the Wurda, had belonged in part to the Nizam, but the raja of Nagpore, who owned the other portion, had collected the revenues of the whole, and appropriated the lion's share to himself. This territory, which includes the " cotton field of the Deccan," was now entirely transferred to the Nizam. Half-a-century later he assigned it to the Company for the pay of his contingent, and they immediately endowed it with the inestimable blessing of a railway. The raja likewise engaged to refer all his differences with the Nizam and the Peshwa to the arbitration of the British Government, and to exclude all Frenchmen and all Europeans of any nation at war with England from his kingdom. The large cessions of territory which the raja was thus constrained to make comprised the most valuable of his possessions, and reduced him to a secondary rank among the princes of India; and the power of another member of the Mahratta pentarchy was effectually crippled.

Treaty of Deogaom, Dec. 18th, 1803.

General Wellesley had deprived Sindia of all his possessions in the Deccan. Colonel Murray at the same time, captured Broach, his only seaport, and occupied all his districts on the western coast in

Sindia's possessions in Hindostan, 1803.

Guzerat; but it was in Hindostan that he experienced the most overwhelming disasters. The valuable possessions of his crown in that quarter, which formed, in fact, an opulent kingdom, had been gradually enlarged and consolidated by the incessant labours of the late Mahdajee Sindia, and chiefly through the army raised and disciplined by De Boigne, on whose retirement to his native town in France, in 1796, the command devolved on General Perron. Dowlut Rao Sindia, from the period of his accession in 1792, had been continually encamped in the neighbourhood of Poona, coercing and fleecing the unfortunate Peshwa, and had never so much as visited his northern dominions. The governor of Delhi, emboldened by his master's absence, had the temerity to set his authority at defiance. General Perron was directed to invest the city, and it was surrendered under the threat of a bombardment. The aged and blind emperor, who had been treated by the native warden of the palace with great severity, and often left without the common necessaries of life, was now transferred, after ten years of suffering, to the charge of Perron, and as every effort was made to alleviate his wretched condition, he had good reason to congratulate himself on the change of masters. The continued absence of Sindia had thrown the whole administration of his dominions in Hindostan, both civil and fiscal, as well as the command of the army, into the hands of General Perron, who exercised this extensive power with great ability and moderation. He had succeeded in establishing the complete authority of Sindia throughout Rajpootana, and was gradually extending it over the Sikh states between the Jumna and the Sutlege. His advanced posts approached the Indus in one direction, and Allahabad in another, and throughout this wide expanse of country his power was paramount. The territory under his management yielded a revenue of two crores of rupees. The troops under his command consisted of 28,000 foot, not inferior in discipline or valour to the Company's Sepoy army, and 5,000 horse, with 140 pieces of artillery.

General Perron's power, 1803.

M 2

The jeopardy in which the Company's interests were placed
by the establishment of this powerful force—essentially French
in its tendencies—along the whole line of their western frontier, was self-evident, and Lord Wellesley naturally considered
the extinction of this danger an object of the highest importance. Happily for the accomplishment of his wishes, Sindia's
native officers entertained great jealousy of General Perron's
power, and Sirjee Rao represented to his master the indignation
felt by his great sirdars at the confidence which he thought fit to
repose in this foreigner. So strong was the adverse current
that in April, 1802, the General repaired to Sindia's camp,
and endeavoured to avert danger and to strengthen his
position by a _nuzur_ of fifteen lacs of rupees. But the incessant murmurs of his ministers at length induced Sindia to
divest Perron of the management of all the districts under
his charge, with the exception of those allotted for the maintenance of his troops. He was therefore contemplating a
retirement from Sindia's service at the time when General Lake
was preparing to take the field against him. The Governor-
General, anxious to take advantage of this feeling of disaffection, directed the Commander-in-chief to offer him a reasonable
consideration, if he would transfer his military power and
resources, together with the person of the emperor, to the
British Government. But, though he had received the greatest
provocations from Sindia, he honourably rejected every inducement to betray his trust.

Capture of Ally-
gur, 29th
August, 1803.

General Lake was invested with the same
civil, military, and political powers in Hindostan,
which had been conferred on General Wellesley
in the Deccan, and he took the field as soon as it was known
that Colonel Collins had quitted Sindia's camp. He advanced
towards General Perron's encampment on the 29th August,
but the enemy, though 15,000 strong, retreated without
firing a shot. The French General retired with his body
guard towards Agra, leaving Colonel Pedron in charge of
the important fortress of Allygur, the great military arsenal

and depôt of the army in Hindostan, with orders to defend
. it as long as one stone remained upon another. Every appli-
ance which science could suggest had been adopted in
strengthening the fort ; it was protected by ten bastions and
a ditch, a hundred feet wide, and thirty deep, containing
ten feet of water. Throughout Hindostan it was deemed
impregnable, and it was considered questionable whether any
amount of military strategy would have been sufficient to
secure its surrender. But it was captured at once by the
irresistible gallantry of the 76th Highlanders, commanded by
Major Macleod, who blew open the gate, and forced their way
in through the most intricate and loop-holed passages, raked
by a destructive fire of grape, wall-pieces, and matchlocks.
The number of guns captured amounted to 281. Our loss in
killed and wounded was 217, of whom 17 were officers. This
was one of those master strokes which served to confound
the native mind, and which essentially promoted the submission
of the native powers. General Wellesley, on hearing of it,
remarked, that he had often attempted to blow open a gate,
but had never succeeded, and that he considered the capture
of Allygur one of the most extraordinary feats he had ever
heard of: Yet, it was allowed to pass without any recognition for forty-eight years, and it was only in the reign of
Queen Victoria that a medal was struck to commemorate the
achievement, and presented to the few heroes who still survived. A week after, General Perron, having heard that his
enemies in Sindia's court had at length succeeded in procuring an order for his dismissal, informed General Lake
that he had resigned the Maharaja's service, and requested
permission to·retire with his family, his suite, and his property, through the British territories, to Lucknow. He was
received in the British camp with the distinction due to his
talents and position.

After the capture of Allygur, General Lake
Battle of Delhi,
11th September, advanced toward Delhi, and Bourquin, who had
1803.
          succeeded to· the command of ·Perron's army,

crossed the Jumna to oppose his progress. The British force, 4,500 strong, after a fatiguing march of eighteen miles, reached its encamping ground, within sight of the minarets of Delhi, and found the enemy posted in such force that the General, after a reconnaissance, deemed it advisable to begin the attack without delay. Bourquin's army, consisting of sixteen battalions of regular infantry and 6,000 cavalry, in all about 19,000 men, with a large train of artillery, was drawn up with its rear resting on the Jumna. The position appeared impregnable and General Lake ordered his cavalry, which was advancing in front, to feign a retreat; the enemy, deceived by the movement, immediately abandoned all the advantages of their position, and rushed forward with their guns, shouting and yelling after the peculiar fashion of native troops. The British infantry, led by the ever ready 76th Highlanders and by the Commander-in-chief in person, advanced steadily, amidst a storm of grape and chain shot, and after delivering one round charged with cold steel. The shock was irresistible, the ranks of the enemy reeled and then broke up in disorder, flying down to the river in which great numbers perished. The British loss was comparatively small, only 409, but one-third of the casualties fell on the noble Highlanders. Three days after, Bourquin and three of his officers surrendered to General Lake.

The release of the emperor, 16th September, 1803. The city of Delhi was immediately evacuated by the troops of Sindia, and the British standard was hoisted on its battlements, forty-seven years after the sack of Calcutta by Seraja Dowlah had extinguished the British power and name in Hindostan. The emperor, in a previous communication with General Lake, had expressed a strong desire to obtain the protection of the British Government; Lord Wellesley was no less desirous of granting it, and thus securing to the Company the advantage which was connected with the possession of his person. The Mogul throne had not lost all its prestige. The emperor, though a prisoner and sightless, was still considered the

fountain of honour throughout India, equally by the Hindoos
and Mahomedans, and a patent of nobility under his seal was
as highly prized in the remotest provinces of the Deccan, as
it had been in the days of Aurungzebe. Tippoo was the only
Mahomedan prince who had ventured to discontinue the
homage due to the royal house, and the day after his fall, the
Nizam's general solicited General Harris's permission to proceed in state to the great mosque, and resume the reading of
the *khootba* in the emperor's name. It was, therefore, considered important to the interests of the Company to be
identified with the house of Timur. It was arranged that
the heir apparent should arrive with his suite at the General's
tent at midday, but natives, and more especially native
princes, consider that punctuality lessens their dignity. The
General was kept waiting more than three hours, and it was
nearly sunset before the cavalcade reached the city, where, to
borrow the magniloquent diction of the Governor-General,
" in the magnificent palace built by Shah Jehan, the Commander-in-chief was ushered into the royal presence, and
found the unfortunate and venerable emperor, oppressed by
the accumulated calamities of old age, and degraded authority,
extreme poverty, and loss of sight, seated under a small
tattered canopy, the remnant of his royal state, with every
external appearance of the misery of his condition." The inhabitants of the city manifested great enthusiasm at the change
of masters, and the courtly news writers affirmed, that the
emperor not only shed tears, but had actually regained his
sight, in the excess of his joy. Lord Wellesley formed the
judicious resolution of removing him and the royal family
from the dangerous associations of Delhi, and proposed
Monghir for their future residence, but the emperor clung
with such tenacity to the spot which had been for six centuries the capital of Mahomedan greatness, that Lord Wellesley was reluctantly compelled to abandon this design.
But the wisdom of it was abundantly vindicated half a
century later, when the residence of the royal family at

Delhi, entailed a bloody tragedy, which terminated in
sweeping every vestige of the Mogul dynasty from the
soil of India.

Capture of   Leaving Colonel Ochterlony in command at Delhi,
Agra, Oct. 17,   General Lake marched down to Agra, which was
1803.   still held by Sindia's troops.   In the exercise of
the political powers with which he was invested, he concluded
a treaty with the raja of Bhurtpore, who sent a body of 5,000
horse to co-operate with his army.   He was the first to seek
an alliance with the British Government in the flood tide of its
success, and the first to repudiate it when the tide appeared to
be ebbing.   Agra capitulated, after a protracted siege, on the
17th October, and the treasure found in it, twenty-eight lacs of
rupees, was promptly and wisely distributed among the officers
and men, in " anticipation of the approval of the home authorities."

Battle of Las-   On the outbreak of the war Sindia sent fifteen of
waree, 1st Nov., his disciplined battalions across the Nerbudda to
1803.   protect his possessions in Hindostan.   They were
considered the flower of his army, and usually designated " the
Deccan Invincibles."   But before their arrival the battle of Delhi
had extinguished Sindia's army in the north, with the exception
of two battalions which joined the southern force, and raised
its strength to 9,000 foot, 4,000 cavalry, and 72 pieces of
artillery.   No attempt was made to relieve Agra, but it hung
on the skirts of the British army.   General Lake did not fail
to perceive that while so formidable a force continued unbroken
it would be impossible to obtain the general confidence of the
province, and he determined to attack it without delay.   He
had received an unfounded report that the Mahratta army was
endeavouring to avoid him, and, with his usual impetuosity,
started at midnight in search of it with his cavalry alone,
leaving orders for the infantry to follow.   He came up with the
encampment of the enemy at daybreak on the 1st November, at
the village of Laswaree, and found them, as usual, entrenched
in a formidable position, with their guns drawn up in the

front. The General led his cavalry up in person to the attack ; a fearful discharge of grape and double-headed shot mowed down column after column, and rendered the fiery valour of the troops useless. To prevent their utter extinction, the General was obliged to withdraw them from the conflict, to await the arrival of the infantry, who had marched sixty-five miles in the preceding forty-eight hours, and twenty-five miles since midnight. After a brief rest and a hasty meal, they were launched on the enemy's guns and battalions. The engagement was the severest in which the Company's troops had ever been engaged, not excepting that of Assye. Sindia's sepoys fought as natives had never fought before. They defended their position to the last extremity, contesting every point inch by inch, and refusing to give way while a single gun remained in their possession. But they were at length overpowered, and lost their ammunition and camp equipage, together with 71 pieces of cannon. It was even reported that one-half their number was left on the field, killed or wounded. On the British side the casualties amounted to 824, one-fourth of which belonged to the 76th Highlanders, who bore the brunt of the action. The General himself conducted every operation throughout the day, with more credit to his personal gallantry than to his military talent. Though a dashing soldier, and adored by his men, he was only a second-rate general ; but the flagrant defects of his arrangements were covered, as has frequently been the case in India, by the undaunted valour of his men, at the sacrifice of their own lives. The battle of Laswaree served to exhibit the high state of efficiency to which the French generals in the Mahratta service had brought their native troops. It does not appear that there was a single European officer with them during the engagement, yet so complete had been their training, that when left to themselves they exhibited a degree of skill and intrepidity which staggered General Lake himself, and constrained him to remark that if they had been led by their French officers the result of the day would have been exceedingly doubtful.

This defeat completed the humiliation of Sindia. In the course of twelve weeks the French battalions, the bulwark of his power, had been annihilated, and all his territories in the Deccan, in Guzerat, and in Hindostan, the rich patrimony bequeathed to him by his uncle, had been wrested from him. Seeing no alternative between the entire annihilation of his power and submission to the severe terms dictated by Lord Wellesley, he yielded to necessity, and within a fortnight after the raja of Nagpore had made his peace with the British Government, signed the treaty of Sirjee Anjengaom. It was negotiated on the one part by General Wellesley, on the other by Wittul Punt, Sindia's chief minister, who, though advanced in years, was still considered the first native diplomatist of the age, and was designated by General Wellesley the Talleyrand of the east. By this treaty Sindia ceded all his territories in Hindostan, lying in the Dooab between the Ganges and the Jumna, as well as those north of the Rajpoot principalities of Jeypore and Joudhpore; the fortress and territory of Ahmednugur in the Deccan, and Broach with its dependencies in Guzerat. He relinquished all claims on the Peshwa, the Nizam, the Guickwar, and the British Government, and agreed to recognize the independence of the rajas and feudatories in Hindostan with whom treaties had been concluded by General Lake, and a list of whom was to be delivered to him when the treaty was ratified by the Governor-General. Two districts to the north of the prescribed limits were, however, restored to him, and pensions granted to some of his officers and the members of his own family.

The engagement made with the Nizam at the commencement of hostilities stated that he should share equally with the Company the conquests made by their joint efforts, if he honourably fulfilled the conditions of the alliance. That aged prince, the son of the renowned Nizam-ool-moolk, who had been decorated with honours by Aurungzebe more than a century before, was at the time

on his deathbed, and expired four days after the war began.
IIis son, Secunder Jâh, was placed on the musnud by the
decision of Lord Wellesley. But though the Hyderabad forces
were sent to co-operate with Colonel Stephenson, the stipula-
tions of the treaty were scandalously violated by the Nizam's
civil and military officers, whose sympathies were entirely with
the confederates. Every obstacle was thrown in the way of
military operations. The provision of grain for the army was
purposely neglected, and permission was refused to purchase it
in the Nizam's dominions. The officers and men wounded at
Assye were denied an asylum in the fort of Dowlutabad, and
one of the Hyderabad commanders had the audacity to fire on
the British troops from the guns of his fort. The Nizam had
thus forfeited all claim to share in the spoils of war, but Lord
Wellesley generously bestowed on him the rich province of
Berar, lying to the west of the Wurda. The fortress and the
district of the Ahmednugur, acquired from Sindia, were transferred to the Peshwa, notwithstanding the perfidy of his conduct.
The province of Cuttack, the conquests in Guzerat, and the
valuable districts in Hindostan were incorporated with the
Company's dominions. These last, together with the province
ceded by the Nabob Vizier, were formed into the separate government of the north-west provinces, and now constitute the
Agra Presidency. The territory which Lord Wellesley had
annexed two years before to the Madras Presidency, and that
which he now added to Bengal, was estimated at the annual
value of six crores of rupees,—an amusing comment on the
Parliamentary denunciation of territorial aggrandisement.

Having thus reduced the power of the Mahrattas,
Treaties of alliance in the north, 1803. Lord Wellesley was anxious to prevent the revival
of their influence in Hindostan by establishing a
barrier between their possessions and those of the Company.
With this view, General Lake concluded treaties of alliance
and mutual defence with the Jaut prince of Bhurtpore, and
with the Rajpoot princes of Jeypore, Joudhpore, Machery
and Boondee, who were thereby absolved from all allegiance to

the Mahratta powers. Sindia had entrusted the fortress of Gwalior and some of his districts in that quarter to Ambajee Inglia, who, after the battle of Laswaree, in which he took an active part, offered to desert his master, and transfer the fort and half the territory to the British Government, on condition of being acknowledged the independent ruler of the remainder. A treaty was accordingly drawn up and signed, to which, however, he did not long adhere. His commandant refused to surrender Gwalior, which was besieged and captured by an English force. Ambajee returned soon after to Sindia's court, and was restored to favour. The rana of Gohud, whose dominions Sindia had appropriated to himself twenty years before, was reputed to possess great influence among the Jauts, and Lord Wellesley resolved to grant him the territory of which he had been dispossessed, together with the fort of Gwalior, on his engaging to subsidize three English battalions. The complications which arose out of this anomalous transaction we shall have occasion to notice hereafter. By the treaty of Bassein, the Peshwa had assigned for the maintenance of the subsidiary force districts in the Deccan yielding twenty-six lacs of rupees, but this arrangement was found inconvenient to both parties, and, upon the advice of General Wellesley, he was permitted to exchange them for territories in Bundelkund of the value of thirty-six lacs a-year; but as his authority in that province was merely nominal, the transaction was more advantageous to him than to the British Government, upon whom it entailed a long and harassing conflict. Lord Wellesley was, moreover, bent on establishing a subsidiary treaty with Sindia, and Major Malcolm was engaged for many months in a tedious negotiation, which, though eventually successful, produced no result, inasmuch as the quota of troops, 6,000 in number, was not to be stationed within his dominions, and their support was to be derived from the territories which he had already ceded unconditionally to the Company.

The Guickwar, 1800—1803.   It only remains to notice the progress of events in Guzerat, the greater portion of which was in-

cluded in the dominions of the Guickwar. It has already been
told how the Mogul authority in this province ceased in 1755,
when the capital Ahmedabad was captured by Damajee
Guickwar. He died in 1768, and was succeeded after a long
series of intrigues, by his son, Futteh Sing. On his death,
in 1792, his brother mounted the throne, and died in 1800,
leaving eleven children, and the country was immediately
distracted by their struggles for the supreme power. Anund
Rao, the eldest, though imbecile, was acknowledged as the
legitimate successor to the musnud, and, having taken an able
minister into his counsels, applied to the Bombay government
for aid against his brothers and rivals, and offered to enter into
a subsidiary alliance. This occurred at the time when Lord
Wellesley was intent on extending these political arrangements throughout India, as the most effectual mode of establishing British supremacy, and the offer was cordially accepted.
The subsidized force consisted of five battalions, and districts
yielding between eleven and twelve lacs of rupees a-year
were assigned for their support. The appearance of a British
army in the field extinguished all opposition, the authority of
Anund Rao was fully acknowledged, and Major Walker was
appointed Resident at the court, which was now transferred to
the new capital, Baroda. But the treasury was insolvent, and
the finances were in a state of apparently hopeless confusion.
The revenues amounted to fifty lacs of rupees a-year, and the
expenditure to eighty-two. The deficiency had been made up,
year after year, according to the fatal practice of native princes,
by loans at extravagant interest, and mortgages and assignments, which devoured the resources of the state, and
threatened the dissolution of all government. Major Walker
was one of those great men to whom the Company has been
indebted for the extension and the popularity of their rule. He
had acquired the confidence of the natives of Guzerat even to
a greater degree than that of his own Government, and with
the universal consent of nobles and people, assumed the entire
control of the administration. It was necessary in the first

instance to relieve the country from the native army, which
ceased to be necessary after the establishment of the subsidiary force, but it could not be disbanded without the payment
of arrears, which amounted to forty-one lacs of rupees. Major
Walker prevailed on the Governor-General to advance the
sum of twenty lacs, and by the extraordinary influence he had
acquired among the native bankers, obtained a loan of the
remainder from them, though not without a British guarantee.
The troops were at length paid up in full, and the country was
freed from the insolence of these Arab mercenaries. The maritime district of Kattiwar took advantage of the dissensions
of the time to refuse the payment of the tribute due to the
parent state, but Major Walker marched into the country and
constrained the insurgents to enter into an engagement for the
payment of nine lacs of tribute a-year. His expedition into
that province was rendered ever memorable by the moral results
Abolition of in- which it produced. The custom of infanticide
fanticide, 1804. was universally prevalent among its Rajpoot inhabitants, who preferred the death of their daughters to the
disgrace of an inferior alliance. By the influence of his official
position, but more particularly by the weight of his personal
character, Major Walker was enabled to obtain from all the
principal chiefs a pledge, both on their own part and that of
their fraternities, to abstain from the practice, to expel from the
community all who were found guilty of it, and to submit to
any penalty he might think fit to impose. The success of these
efforts in the cause of humanity has shed a brighter lustre on
his memory than all his political achievements, great as they
were. It was through his exertions that peace and tranquillity
were restored to the country, and the government of the
Guickwar consolidated. The connection of the state with the
British Government was closely cemented, and the resources
of another Mahratta prince were detached from the Mahratta
cause, and placed under the control of the Company.

Reflections.   The transcendent genius and energy of Lord
         Wellesley had thus, in the course of five years,

completely remodelled the whole policy of India, and placed the Company on the pinnacle of power. They had now become the masters of a great part of the continent, the protector of all the principal powers, and the acknowledged mediator in the disputes of all. Their sovereignty was greater, and their authority fixed on a firmer and more solid basis than that of Akbar or Aurungzebe. The administration of Lord Wellesley had reached its culminating point. The disasters which clouded the remaining period of his Indian career arose from the blunders of the Commander-in-chief, and not from any imperfection in his Government, though it was necessarily saddled with the obloquy they entailed.

CHAPTER XXII.

LORD WELLESLEY'S ADMINISTRATION CONTINUED, 1804-5.

Holkar's movements, 1804. WHILE Sindia and the raja of Nagpore were involved in hostilities with the Company, Holkar was employed in predatory expeditions in Hindostan, and on the conclusion of peace marched down to Muhesur, on the Nerbuddá, a great emporium of commerce, and plundered it of wealth estimated at a crore of rupees. With this treasure he was enabled not only to satisfy his own troops for the time, but to take into his pay those whom Sindia and the raja had discharged on the peace. His army was thus augmented to 60,000 horse and 15,000 foot, a force far exceeding his requirements or his resources, and which could be subsisted only by pillage. The Governor-General had sedulously avoided any collision with him during the five months of the war with the confederates; and General Wellesley had repeatedly assured him that as long as he refrained from attacking the dominions of the Company and its allies, the government would abstain from all interference with him. This assurance was also com-

municated to him by Lord Wellesley on the 10th February.
But repose was incompatible with his plans of ambition and
plunder. His fortune was in his saddle, and eighty thousand
of the lawless soldiery of Central India followed his stirrup.
By the humiliation of Sindia and Nagpore, he was the only
Mahratta chief left with an unbroken army; but, heedless of
the warning conveyed by their fate, he was impelled by his
own reckless disposition to hazard a conflict with the British
Government. He desired Ameer Khan to join him without
delay, "as he had made up his mind to meet General Lake in
the field." He sought an alliance with the brother of Zemaun
Shah, who had seized Cabul, and on a new seal which he had
engraved, styled himself, " the slave of Mahomed Shah, king
of kings." Letters were intercepted from him to the British
allies, exciting them to revolt. In the month of March he demanded of General Wellesley, then in the Deccan, the cession
of certain districts which he said had once belonged to his
family, adding that "if they were not restored, countries many
hundred miles in extent should be plundered and burnt, and the
English general should not have time to breathe, and calamities
should fall on lacs of human beings, by a continued war, in
which his armies would overwhelm them like waves of the
sea." He likewise despatched two envoys to General Lake,
with claims of a similar character. During their communications with the General some allusion happened to be made to
the friendly disposition now manifested by Sindia, when they
affirmed that Sindia had within a few days requested the co-
operation of their master in a war with the English, as a large
French force had arrived on the Coromandel coast, and was
about to come to his assistance. The envoys demanded with
studied arrogance the restoration of the chout, as the inalienable
right of the Mahrattas, and the restoration of twelve of the
finest districts in the Dooab, which they affirmed were part of
Holkar's family possessions. These insolent demands were
followed up by an inroad into the territories of our ally, the raja
of Jeypore. General Lake, in his embarrassment, wrote to

Lord Wellesley, "If Holkar should break into Hindostan, he will be joined by the Rohillas. I never was so plagued as I am with this devil. We are obliged to remain in the field at an enormous cost. If we retire, he will come down upon Jeypore, and exact a crore from the raja, and thus pay his own army and render it more formidable than ever. If I advance and leave an opening, he will give me the slip, and get into our territories with his horse, and burn and destroy."

War with Holkar, April, 1804. Lord Wellesley felt that there could be neither peace nor prosperity while this vast predatory horde continued to roam through Central India, and that an army of observation was more expensive than an army of action. On the 16th April, therefore, he directed Generals Wellesley and Lake to take the field against Holkar, whom he regarded as a mere chief of freebooters. General Wellesley, who commanded in the south, ordered Colonel Murray to advance with a force of about 5,800 men from Guzerat into Malwa, and take possession of Holkar's capital. General Lake moved with his army into the Jeypore territory, which Holkar was employed in plundering, on which he immediately withdrew his troops. Colonel Don was then sent with a large detachment against Rampoora, his stronghold in the north, and it fell on the 16th May. Holkar thus lost his footing in the country north of the Chumbul, and retreated in haste and confusion across that river. General Wellesley's clear military perceptions led him to urge General Lake to continue the pursuit with rapidity, even though there might be little hope of bringing Holkar to action. If, he remarked, he is pushed with vigour, the war will not last a fortnight; if not, God knows when it will be over. But, by an act of unaccountable imprudence, General Lake, instead of continuing the pursuit, broke up his encampment, and withdrew his army into cantonments in Hindostan, sending Colonel Monson with a single brigade to follow the steps of Holkar. This was the fatal blunder of the campaign, and it entailed a tremendous catastrophe. Lord Wellesley, it is true, approved the retirement of General Lake's

II. N

army, but it must not be forgotten that he also advised him, either to withdraw the force under Colonel Monson, or to strengthen it with a regiment of Europeans and two or three of cavalry. General Lake did neither. He had detached Colonel Monson, who was as remarkable for professional incompetence as for personal gallantry, into the heart of Holkar's territoreis, on the eve of the rains, with a small force, unaccompanied by a single European soldier, or any cavalry except 2,000 or 3,000 irregular horse recently raised, and utterly inefficient, to encounter a force ten times its number, and commanded by the most daring soldier of the day. As if in emulation of this error, Colonel Monson made no arrangements on his march for supplies, and no provision for crossing the various streams in his rear, which cease to be fordable after the rains commence. He still farther augmented the perils of his expedition by advancing through the Mokundra pass, and even fifty miles beyond it, for the idle object of capturing an unimportant fort, and thus put 200 miles between his force and its nearest support.

On the 7th July, Colonel Monson received the alarming intelligence that Holkar had called up all his battalions from the south, and was advancing against him with his entire force. It was likewise reported that the provisions in the camp were only equal to two day's consumption; and his troubles reached their climax by the intelligence that Colonel Murray, who was advancing from Guzerat to his aid, had retired with all his troops. The bewildered commander took council of Bappoo Sindia, the commandant of Sindia's contingent which accompanied the British force, but he was in league with Holkar, and advised Colonel Monson to fall back with his infantry and leave his irregular horse to follow. Acting upon this treacherous advice, he commenced his disastrous retreat. Holkar, who had the fullest intelligence of every movement in the British camp, immediately attacked the irregular horse and put it to flight. Bappoo Sindia fled on the first appearance of his troops, and

Colonel Monson's disastrous retreat, July, 1804.

after announcing the rout of the cavalry to Colonel Monson,
went over with all his troops to the enemy, not without his
master's concurrence. On the 10th July, Colonel Monson
reached the Mokundra pass, where he was attacked vigorously by the whole of Holkar's army, but obtained a signal
victory. The success of this conflict establishes the fact, confirmed by every succeeding encounter, that the disasters of the
army arose from no want of mettle in the troops, but from the
incapacity of their leader, and that under an abler commander
this little sepoy army would have baffled all the efforts of
Holkar. The next morning, Colonel Monson continued his
retreat, but on reaching Kotah, the regent, Zalim Sing, who
had assisted him on his advance—for which Holkar subsequently exacted a fine of ten lacs of rupees—refused admission to his troops on his retreat. His difficulties increased at
every step; all the rivulets were swollen, and it rained so incessantly that the guns sunk in the mud beyond recovery, and
were spiked and abandoned. The army was seventeen days
reaching Rampoora, though the distance from Kotah was only
sixty miles. There Colonel Monson was reinforced by two
battalions of sepoys and a corps of irregular cavalry, and supplied with provisions, sent to his aid by General Lake, on
hearing of the commencement of his retreat. At Rampoora
he remained twenty-four days, during the whole of which
period Holkar, with all his superiority of force, never ventured
to attack him. On the twenty-fifth day he most unaccountably
determined to fall back on Kooshalgur, where he expected to be
joined by Sudasheo Bhao, one of Sindia's generals, with six
battalions and twenty-one guns; but the Mahratta, seeing the
helplessness of the commander, and the miserable plight of
his army, not only went over to Holkar, but turned his guns
upon the British troops. The game was now up; and on the
26th August, the Colonel spiked his last gun; the enemy allowed him no rest; all order and all discipline was lost; the
retreat became a disorderly rout, and the last sepoy straggled
into Agra on the last day of August, fifty days after the

N 2

retreat had commenced. Colonel Monson attributed his disaster to the failure of Colonel Murray to join him from Guzerat. Colonel Murray attributed it to Colonel Monson himself. Both of them, as General Wellesley observed, were apparently afraid of Holkar, and fled from him in different directions. Colonel Monson advanced without reason and he retreated without cause. Twenty-three years before Colonel Camac had, with equal indiscretion, marched from the Jumna to Seronge in pursuit of Mahdajee Sindia, and found himself in the same predicament as Colonel Monson, in the heart of the enemy's country, destitute of supplies, harassed by an active foe, and abandoned by native allies in the hour of need. Yet, by the unfailing expedient of a bold and aggressive movement, suggested and carried out by Captain Bruce, he turned the tables on Sindia, captured his guns, ammunition, and camp, reduced him to extremity, and obliged him to sue for peace. But for the imbecility of the commander, the same triumph would doubtless have crowned the valour of the band of heroes under Colonel Monson, and Lord Wellesley would not have had to lament the annihilation of five battalions of infantry and six companies of artillery. This was the most signal disgrace inflicted on the British arms since the destruction of Colonel Baillie's force by Hyder, in 1780, and its effect on the prestige and influence of the Company was felt throughout India. The defeat was celebrated in ribald songs in every bazaar, and one couplet, describing the utter confusion of the rout has survived the lapse of more than half a century, "Placing the *houda* of the elephant on the horse, and the saddle of the horse on the elephant, did Colonel Monson fly away in haste." The raja of Bhurtpore, who had never been very steady in his fidelity, lost no time after this event in opening negotiations with Holkar.

Holkar besieges Delhi, 1804.   Flushed with success, Holkar advanced to Muttra with an army, estimated at 90,000 men. The British detachment stationed there retired upon Agra, and General Lake, with his accustomed energy, established his

head-quarters at that station, and lost no time in summoning
the various corps from their cantonments to repel this new and
unexpected eruption. Meanwhile, Holkar planned the daring
project of seizing the city of Delhi, and obtaining possession
of the person of the emperor. Leaving the greater portion of
his cavalry to engage the attention of General Lake, he started
in great secrecy, with his infantry and guns, and suddenly
appeared before the gates of the city on the 7th October. It
was ten miles in circumference, defended only by dilapidated
walls and ruined ramparts, and filled with a mixed population,
not as yet accustomed to British rule. The garrison was so
small as not to admit of reliefs, and provisions and sweetmeats
were therefore served to them on the battlements, but the
British Resident, Colonel Ochterlony, animated by the spirit of
Clive, and nobly seconded by the commandant, Colonel Burn,
defended the city for nine days, against the utmost efforts of
the enemy, 20,000 strong, with 100 pieces of cannon. At
length Holkar, despairing of success, drew off his army, and
sending back his infantry and guns into the territory of his
new ally, the raja of Bhurtpore, set out with his cavalry to lay
waste the British territories in the Dooab, in the ancient style
of Mahratta marauding. General Lake also divided his force ;
the main body was left under General Fraser to watch Holkar's
battalions of infantry, while he placed himself at the head of
six regiments of cavalry, European and Native, and his mounted
artillery, and started in pursuit of him. In this expedition
Holkar contrived invariably to keep twenty or thirty miles
a-head, ravaging and burning the defenceless villages as he
swept along. After a very harassing march of three hundred
and fifty miles in fourteen days, the General was
so fortunate as to come up with his encampment at Futtygur, on the 17th November, having
marched no less than fifty-six miles in the preceding twenty-
four hours. Holkar had been led to believe from the report of
his spies, that the British cavalry was a day's march behind him,
and had retired to rest. The horses were at picket, and the men

Pursued by Gen, Lake, 1804.

lay asleep by their side, wrapped in their blankets, when
several rounds of grape gave them the first intimation of the
arrival of their pursuers. Holkar mounted his horse and
galloped off with the few troopers around him, leaving the
rest of his troops to shift for themselves, and they were either
cut up or dispersed in all directions. He hastened back to
rejoin his infantry, but found on re-crossing the Jumna, that
Battle of Deeg, they had been subject during his absence to an
13th Nov. 1804. irreparable defeat. Four days before the action at
Futtygur, General Fraser had encountered Holkar's army, consisting of fourteen battalions of infantry, a large body of horse,
and a hundred and sixty guns, in the vicinity of Deeg. The
English force did not exceed 6,000, but contained in its ranks
the 76th Highlanders, the foremost in the path of honour and
danger, and they again bore the brunt of the battle. The
enemy was completely routed, and left eighty-seven pieces of
cannon on the field. But the victory was dearly purchased by
the loss of 643 killed and wounded, and more especially of
the noble general, who died three days after of his wounds.
On his removal from the field during the action, the command
devolved on Colonel Monson, who maintained the conflict with
the utmost gallantry, and had the satisfaction of recovering fourteen of the guns he had lost in his retreat. During the
engagement a destructive fire was opened on the British troops
from the fort of Deeg, which belonged to the raja of Bhurtpore. A battering train was immediately ordered up from
Agra, and the fortress was captured on the 23rd December.
Siege of Bhurt-
pore, 1805. The fortunes of Holkar were now at the lowest
ebb. He had lost all his forts in the Deccan.
General Jones, who, under the advice of General Wellesley,
had been appointed in the room of the incompetent Colonel
Murray to the Guzerat command, had taken all his fortresses
in Malwa, and marched up through the heart of the Mahratta
dominions, unmolested, and joined General Lake's camp. The
vast army with which Holkar had proudly crossed the Jumna
four months before, had dwindled away under repeated reverses,

and the entire destruction of his power appeared inevitable,
when every advantage which had been gained in the campaign
was thrown away by the fatal resolution of General Lake to
invest Bhurtpore. It was a town and fortress eight miles in circumference, surrounded by the invulnerable bulwark of a lofty
mud wall of great thickness, and protected by numerous
bastions, and a deep ditch, filled with water. It was garrisoned
by about. 8,000 of the raja's troops, and the remnant of
Holkar's infantry. General Lake refused to listen to any
argument, and without a sufficient siege train, without an
engineer officer of any experience, without even a reconnaissance, resolved, with breathless impetuosity, at once to
besiege the town. This memorable siege commenced on the 4th
January, 1805, and the army did not break up before the 21st
April. Four unsuccessful attacks were made which entailed
the unprecedented loss of 3,200 men in killed and wounded,
of whom 103 were officers. The raja was joined at his own
request during the siege by Ameer Khan, but the exorbitant
demands of that chief speedily dissolved the union, on which
he proceeded with his predatory horse into his native province
of Rohilcund, in the hope of raising it against the English.
General Smith was detached in pursuit of him, and after performing the extraordinary march of seven hundred miles in
forty-three days, overtook him at the foot of the Himalayu,
and chased him back across the Jumna. Though the siege of
Bhurtpore had not been successful, the raja severely felt the
loss of all his territorial revenues, and the exactions of Holkar,
and became anxious to bring the war to a close. He therefore
sent a vakeel to General Lake, ostensibly to congratulate him
on his advance to the peerage, of which intelligence had just
been received, but, in reality, to open negociations; and a
treaty was speedily concluded on condition that he
should pay twenty lacs of rupees towards the
expenses of the war, in four instalments. But the
submission of the raja, under such circumstances, could not
repair the loss of reputation which the British Government

Treaty with Bhurtpore, April, 1805.

sustained by the notorious failure of the siege. Nothing had
filled the princes of India with greater dismay than the easy
and rapid reduction of their strongest fortresses in positions
which appeared to be absolutely impregnable. But in the
present case, a British army, under the Commander-in-chief
in person, had been foiled for several months in every attempt.
to capture a mud fort, situated in a plain, and the Native
chiefs began to flatter themselves that our skill and our prowess
were on the wane. The remembrance of our disgrace was perpetuated even in remote districts by rude delineations on the
walls of British soldiers hurled from the battlements of Bhurtpore, nor was the impression created by this failure completely
removed till the capture of the fort by Lord Combermere,
twenty-one years afterwards.

Attitude of Sin-   This accommodation with Bhurtpore was has-
dia; Gohud, and tened by the menacing attitude of Sindia, to
Gwalior, 1805.   whose proceedings we now return. By the treaty
of Sirjee Angengaom, he had engaged in general terms to
relinquish all claim on the rajas and feudatories in the north,
with whom the Governor-General had concluded defensive
alliances. When the list of these chiefs was for the first time
presented to him, in April, 1804, with the ratified treaty, he
was mortified to find the name of the rana of Gohud, together
with the fort of Gwalior, included in it, and he urged the most
vehement objection to these alienations. Gwalior, on which he
set a high value, was, he said, the personal gift of the emperor
to him; and his servant, Ambajee Inglia, to whom it had been
entrusted, had no right whatever to dispose of it, when he
treacherously joined the English. As to the rana of Gohud,
he scouted the idea of acknowledging the existence of such a
being, whose power he had extinguished, and whose territories he had annexed to his own twenty years before. It
was an unfortunate circumstance that General Lake in the
north and General Wellesley in the south should have been
making arrangements and alliances affecting the interest
of Sindia, in total ignorance of the proceedings of each other.

When General Wellesley negotiated the treaty with Sindia
he was not aware that Lord Wellesley had determined to re-
establish 'the principality of Gohud, anñ to make the rana
independent. Sindia deprecated the revival of these ancient
and extinct claims, and justly observed that "it could not
fail to weaken the fundamental rights of actual possession, as
the greater portion of the Company's territories as well as his
own had no other foundation." General Wellesley affirmed
that Sindia had agreed to the treaty in the fullest confidence
that Gwalior was to remain with him, and that, for his ʼpart,
"he would sacrifice it and every other frontier town ten times
over to preserve our credit for scrupulous good faith, and that
the advantages and honour we had gained in the last war
and peace must not be frittered away in arguments drawn
from the overstrained principles of the law of nations, which
was not understood in India." Major Malcolm, the envoy at
the court of Sindia, entertained the same views, and anxiously
laboured for the restoration of these possessions to Sindia.
Lord Wellesley resented this opposition to his wishes, and
when the Major pleaded, in extenuation of his conduct, that
his sole object was to promote the public interests, remarked,
" Major Malcolm's business is to obey my orders and enforce
my instructions ; I will look after the public interests." The
Governor-General was all the more pertinacious on this occasion from being entirely in the wrong, and his conduct cannot
be more accurately described than by the expressive Indian
word, zid. Sindia was obliged to yield to his imperious demand, and submit to the alienation of Gohud and Gwalior, but
it continued to rankle in his bosom.

Hostility of   The disastrous retreat of Colonel Monson pro-
Sindia, 1804-5. duced a profound sensation throughout Hindostan; it created an impression that fortune was at .length
deserting the standard of the Company, and it strengthened the
hope that the Mahrattas might yet regain their former ascendency. 'Wittul Punt, Sindia's great minister, died in October,
1804, and was succeeded by Sirjee Rao Ghatkay, the invete-

rate enemy of the British power. Under his sinister advice, Sindia addressed a defiant letter to the Governor-General, impugning the good faith of the British Government in numerous instances. The letter, instead of being sent direct, was transmitted to his vakeel at Benares, who journeyed with it by slow stages to Calcutta, watching the progress of events, and it would never have been delivered at all but for our discomfiture before Bhurtpore. It reached the Governor-General four months after it was penned. Meanwhile, a secret alliance was formed against the Company, which included Sindia and Holkar, Ameer Khan, and the raja of Bhurtpore; and Sindia, emboldened by our reverses, ventured to attack the territories of our allies, and to invade Sagur. At the beginning of 1805, the encampment of Mr. Richard Jenkins, the British representative at his court, was assailed and plundered at the instigation of Sirjee Rao, in the hope of irretrievably compromising his master with the British Government. Sindia likewise put his army in motion, and announced his intention to march to Bhurtpore, and negotiate a peace between the raja and the Company, an insult which the Governor-General could not but feel acutely. But both he and General Wellesley were equally anxious to avoid a rupture with Sindia at this critical juncture. The army before Bhurtpore was disheartened by repeated failures; the British frontier, for several hundred miles, from Calpee to Midnapore was defenceless, and a combined attack of the allies might have been followed by disastrous results. Sindia continued to advance with 40,000 men, including Pindarees, and encamped eighteen miles beyond Subulgur, where he was joined by Ambajee Inglia. The Resident remonstrated against his crossing the Chumbul, as it would in all probability lead to a war, and urged him to return to his own capital. Sindia made the most amicable professions, but assured him that the embarrassment of his finances was so great as to prevent his retracing his steps; but if some arrangement could be made for relieving his pressing necessities, he would act in accordance with the Governor-General's desire. General

Wellesley, who was satisfied of the truth of this assertion, and who believed that Sindia was really impoverished, advised his brother to grant him some pecuniary aid, and he immediately made a retrograde movement of a few miles.

Progress of the settlement with Sindia, 1805. Five days after this retirement, Sirjee Rao, apparently without Sindia's concurrence, marched up to Bhurtpore with a part of his master's cavalry, and all his Pindarees ; but before his arrival the treaty with Lord Lake had been completed, though without the knowledge of the Mahrattas, and the raja refused to meet him. After the preliminaries of peace had been signed, a division of British troops attacked Holkar, who had been hovering about the fort during the siege, and completely defeated him, leaving under his standard only 3,000 or 4,000 exhausted cavalry. Sirjee Rao returned with Holkar to Sindia's encampment at Subulgur, where all the confederates, except the raja of Bhurtpore, were now assembled. Holkar and Ameer Khan soon intimated to Sindia that it would be impossible to keep their forces together without funds, and that all their projects against the Company must therefore be abandoned. He replied that his treasury was empty, and that although he had jewels enough, no money could be raised on them, but his general, Ambajee, was · possessed of boundless wealth, yet would not part with a rupee. Ambajee had been Sindia's lieutenant in Rajpootana and Hindostan for many years, and had amassed two crores of rupees, which he had deposited for safety in Kotah. With the full concurrence of Sindia, he was seized and confined, and Ameer Khan subjected him to the most exquisite tortures, till he consented to part with fifty-five lacs from his hoards, of which Sindia appropriated one-half to his own use. As Sindia and his confederates continued to encamp at Subulgur, General Lake moved down upon them as soon as the Bhurtpore treaty was signed, and the whole body retreated in haste and consternation towards Kotah. At the beginning of June the atrocities of Sirjee Rao constrained Sindia to displace him, and Ambajee was raised to the post of minister. With a lively recollection

of the injuries he had received from Holkar, he endeavoured
to sow dissension between him and Sindia, and at length succeeded in breaking up the alliance, which paved the way for an
amicable adjustment of all differences with the British Government. Soon after, Lord Lake addressed a letter to Sindia,
stating that if the Resident, who was still detained by him,
though treated with great respect, was not dismissed within ten
days, the relations subsisting between the two states would be
no longer considered binding. The day before the expiration
of this period, one of Sindia's principal ministers waited on the
Resident, and entreated him to waive the demand for his dis-
mission, "because it would give an appearance of enmity to
the relations of the two states." Sindia had nothing to gain
but everything to risk by a war, and he was sincerely desirous
of establishing a good understanding with the Company. He
had not forgotten how, in August, 1803, the departure of
Colonel Collins from his camp had been the signal of hostilities,
and he feared lest the retirement of Mr. Jenkins should produce the same disastrous result. On his part, Lord Wellesley
was equally desirous of peace. He had made up his mind to
restore Gohud and Gwalior, as a matter of policy, and was
ready to discuss any other concessions which might enable
him to place the army on a peace establishment and reduce the
burdens of the state. Another month or two would have
brought about an amicable adjustment of all differences, and placed the tranquillity of India upon
a solid basis. But on the 30th July, Lord Cornwallis landed in Calcutta, and assumed charge of
the Government and Lord Wellesley's whole scheme of policy
was at once subverted.

End of Lord
Wellesley's ad-
ministration,
1805.

The administration of Lord Wellesley is the
most memorable in the annals of British India.
He found the empire beset with the most imminent perils in every quarter, and he bequeathed it to his
successor in a state of complete security. He found a feeling
of contempt for our power gradually increasing at every court,

Remarks on
Lord Welles-
ley's adminis-
tration, 1805.

and threatening its existence, and he set himself with unexampled energy to restore our prestige. In rapid succession
he annihilated the French force at Hyderabad, and converted
all the resources of the Nizam to the use of the Company.
He extinguished the Mysore power and became master of the '
Deccan. He extirpated the French battalions of Sindia, and
turned his possessions in Hindostan into a British province. |
He paralysed the power of the great Mahratta princes so
effectually that, notwithstanding the timid and retrograde policy
of the next twelve years, they were never able to recover it.
He remodelled the map of India and introduced greater and
more important changes in all its political relations than had
been effected by any single prince, Hindoo or Mahomedan.
He doubled the territories and the resources of the Company.
He had a peculiar genius for creating and consolidating an
empire. He was the Akbar of the Company's dynasty. His
individual character was impressed on every branch of the
administration, and his inspiration animated every member of
the service in every department, and in every province. To
those around him, who were under his immediate influence, he
was the object of "hero worship," and the designation usually
applied to him was "the glorious little man." But his attention was chiefly directed to those great measures of state
which were required to secure and strengthen the Government.
The time had not arrived when the moral and intellectual improvement of the people was considered within the province
of the ruler. Lord Wellesley made no effort to promote the
education of the natives, and the erroneous policy initiated by
Lord Cornwallis of excluding them from all share in any
branch of the Government, and working it exclusively by
European agency, was approved and perpetuated. But he
constrained the civilians to acquire the language of the
people they were appointed to govern, which the Court of
Directors had neglected for thirty-five years ; and to his
administration belongs the distinguished honour of having,
under the influence of Mr. Udny and Dr. Carey, passed

the humane regulation prohibiting the sacrifice of children at Sagur.

· Lord Wellesley's great predecessor, Warren Hastings, was the first ruler who contemplated the necessity imposed by our position of extending British influence over every court, and making the Company the leading power in India. For the attempt to carry out this great conception, he was subjected to an impeachment and reduced to poverty. Twelve years after he had left India, Lord Wellesley felt the pressure of the same necessity, and resolved to pursue the same object, not by the simple exertion of influence, but by the exercise of authority. He was anxious to extinguish those internecine contests among the princes of India which for more than a century had turned its fairest provinces into a desert, encouraged a predatory and military spirit among the inhabitants, and formed an inexhaustible source for the supply of military adventurers, prepared to join the standard of any turbulent chieftain, for the purposes of ambition, plunder, and rebellion. He felt, as General Wellesley described it, that "no permanent system of policy could be adopted to preserve the weak against the strong, and to keep the princes for any length of time in their relative situations, and the whole body in peace, without the establishment of one power, which by the superiority of its strength, and its military system and resources, should obtain a preponderating influence for the protection of all." The Company was to be this preponderant power, but the Company was still a commercial body, and had an instinctive dread of all military operations which interrupted its investments and disturbed its balance-sheet. In the conflict between the merchant and the sovereign in Leadenhall-street, the influence and interest of the merchant prevailed, although Lord Wellesley maintained that "as long as the Company represented the sovereign executive authority in this vast empire, its duties of sovereignty must be paramount to mercantile interests." This irreconcileable difference of views created a strong feeling of

(marginal note) Lord Wellesley and the Court of Directors, 1803—5.

antipathy towards him at the India House, which, though
mitigated for a time by the influence of Lord Castlereagh,
broke out at length with irrepressible violence. His policy
was denounced, his measures were thwarted, and his government was humiliated and weakened. For a time he manifested,
as he said, "an invariable respect even for the errors of every
branch of their authority," but this respect was at length
extinguished by the virulence of their opposition, and in a
moment of exasperation, he designated them the "cheese-
mongers of Leadenhall-street," an expression never forgiven.
The India House accused him of "illegal appointments," of
"evasions of the law," of "contempt of Parliament," and
above all, of "a disdain of constituted authority," meaning
the Court of Directors. He charged them with "vindictive
profligacy," and "ignominious tyranny," and in writing to a
ministerial friend said that "no additional outrage, injury, or
insult which could issue from the most loathsome den in
the India House would accelerate his departure from India,
while the public interests seemed to require the aid of his
services,"

The impartiality of history requires that great
allowance should be made for the feelings of the
Court of Directors and the Court of Proprietors.
Parliament had thought fit to interdict all increase
of territory, and even to forbid all alliances with the native
princes, and the Directors fondly believed that under the
shadow of this wise and prudent injunction, as they deemed
it, they would be enabled to continue at peace with the native
powers, and to pursue their mercantile enterprises, which
they prized above all things, without interruption. But the
present Governor-General, in utter defiance of the authority of
Parliament, had been engaged in wars from Cape Comorin to
the Sutlege, had broken the power of prince after prince,
completed a gigantic revolution, and seated the Company on
the throne of the Great Mogul, and invested it with the
responsibility of governing one half and controlling the other

*Cause and
effect of alarm
at the India
House, 1805.*

half of India. It was impossible that a body constituted like the East India Company should not take alarm at the audacity of his aspirations, and the vastness of his schemes, and forbode the certain loss of the country, through the resentment excited against British ambition in every province. Even Lord Wellesley's friend, Lord Castlereagh, questioned whether, an empire founded on so broad a basis could be fed with its due proportion of British troops from England. He feared that the frame of the government had become too complicated and unwieldly for any other hands than those of Lord Wellesley, and, like the Directors, regarded with a feeling of consternation the vast extent of our dominions in India, and the ruinous consequences which seemed to be the inevitable result of it. The announcement of the war with Holkar filled up the measure of Lord Wellesley's delinquencies, and of the terror of the public authorities in England. Even before the news of Colonel Monson's retreat arrived, Mr. Charles Grant, the Corypheus of the Court of Directors, declared that he had "not only wantonly but criminally involved the Government in all the difficulties of another war with an able and powerful chieftain." Lord Castlereagh thought there could be no safety but in bringing back things to the state the Legislature had prescribed in 1793, in other words, in putting the clock back a dozen years. Sir George Barlow had been nominated provisional Governor-General at the special recommendation of Lord Wellesley, but at such a crisis it was deemed unsafe to entrust the destinies of the empire to one of his disciples. Lord Cornwallis was known to disapprove of Lord Wellesley's system of policy, and he was entreated to proceed to India and deliver the Company from its fatal effects, as he had been sent out twenty years before to rescue the British interests in India from the mischievous consequences of Hastings's plans. But before entering on his proceedings it is necessary to wind up the history of Lord Wellesley's career by a brief notice of the treatment he experienced on his return to England.

Prosecution of Mr. Paull, 1806.   The mode in which the great services of Lord Clive and Warren Hastings had been requited in England forbade the hope that the brilliant admi-nistration of Lord Wellesley would escape the homage of censure. A Mr. Paull, who, on the testimony of General Wellesley, was originally a tailor, had gone out as an adven-turer to India, and taken an investment of goods to Lucknow, where he was so fortunate as to obtain the countenance of the Nabob Vizier, and amassed a large fortune. On his return to India, after a short visit to England, the Nabob refused to admit him into the city, and it was only through the interces-sion of Lord Wellesley that the interdict was removed. Mr. Paull expressed unbounded gratitude to his benefactor, and professed the highest respect for his character. This feel-ing was not, however, of long duration. On his final return to England, in 1805, he bought a seat in Parliament, and on the 22nd May, 1806, brought forward "articles of charge of high crimes and misdemeanours committed by the Marquis of Welles-ley in his transactions with respect to the Nabob of Oude." In the course of his speech he assured the House that, "from the accursed day when Lord Wellesley set foot in India till the day of his departure, he had exhibited a constant scene of rapa-city, oppression, cruelty, and fraud, which goaded the whole country into a state of revolt." Mr. Paull then moved for papers relative to the transactions in Oude, in Furruckabad, and in Surat. The members of the Court of Directors who had seats in the House, while they disapproved of many of Lord Wellesley's measures, refused their support to so preposterous a charge; and Mr. Fox, then prime minister, declared that, since the trial of Mr. Hastings, he had shrunk from all Indian impeachments. The House, however, did not see fit to resist the production of evidence; but, after it had been taken on the first charge, a dissolution terminated all proceedings. At the ensuing election Mr. Paull stood for Westminster, and failed, and then put a period to his existence. Twenty months after, Lord Folkstone took up the thread of the prosecution, and

II.   O

moved twelve resolutions, which charged Lord Wellesley with
having, " under the impulse of unjustifiable ambition and love
of power, formed schemes of aggrandisement and acquisition
of territory, contravened two Acts of Parliament, violated every
principle of good faith, equity and justice, and the sacred obligations of a solemn treaty, and affixed a lasting stigma and
reproach on the British name." The resolutions were negatived
by 182 to 31, after which Sir John Anstruther, who had been
chief justice of Calcutta, moved a resolution to the effect that
Lord Wellesley, in the late arrangements in Oude, had been
actuated by an ardent zeal for the public service, and it was
carried by a triumphant majority.   Two months later, Sir
Thomas Turton brought the Carnatic question before the House,
and accused Lord Wellesley of atrocious delinquencies, and
went so far as to hint that he was accessory to the death of
the late Nabob.   The resolution was indignantly rejected by
the House, and a vote approving of Lord Wellesley's proceedings was carried, with only nineteen dissentient voices.

Far different was the conduct of the Directors
*Conduct of the
Directors and* and Proprietors, among whom the feeling of ani-
Proprietors, mosity towards Lord Wellesley was still unabated.
1807.
Towards the close of his administration, the Court
of Directors compiled a despatch, in which all the charges which
could be raked up were elaborately set forth.   It was the concentrated essence of the spirit of malignity which had been
fermenting in Leadenhall-street for several years.   The Board
of Control judiciously substituted for it a brief letter asking for
explanations in a tone of great moderation, and to it the Court
of Directors were obliged to affix their signature.   The Proprietors, however, ordered the original despatch to be printed,
and a motion was brought forward in their Court impugning
Lord Wellesley's policy, and applauding the Directors for
having " restrained a lavish expenditure of public money, and
opposed all schemes of conquest and extension of empire."   After
a long and acrimonious debate, 928 voted the condemnation of
Lord Wellesley, and only 195 his acquittal.   But, after the

lapse of thirty years, when passion and prejudice had given
way to the voice of reason, the Court of Directors availed themselves of the publication of his dispatches, in five volumes, to
assure him that in their judgment he had been animated
throughout his administration "by an ardent zeal to promote
the well-being of India, and to uphold the interest and honour
of the British empire," and that they looked back to the eventful
and brilliant period of his government with feelings common to
their countrymen.   They voted him a grant of £20,000, and
ordered his statue to be placed in the India House, as a recognition of the great services he had rendered to the Company.

CHAPTER XXIII.

ADMINISTRATION OF LORD CORNWALLIS AND SIR GEORGE
BARLOW, 1805—7.

Lord Corn-
wallis, 30th
July, 1805.

LORD Cornwallis landed in Calcutta on the 30th
July, 1805, and within twenty-four hours Lord
Wellesley had the mortification to learn that the
system of policy which he had pursued for five years with indefatigable zeal, was to be immediately and entirely subverted.
The incessant labours in which Lord Cornwallis had been
engaged for thirty years in America, in India, and in Ireland,
had exhausted his constitution, and those who had seen him
embark in the vigour of health twelve years before, could not
help remarking, with sorrow, that he now returned with
the hand of death upon him. It would have been well if,
at his advanced age, he had remained in England; but when
he was importuned by the Court of Directors and the Board of
Control to proceed to India and save the empire, he considered it
an imperative duty to obey the call, at the sacrifice of his ease
and comfort, and, probably, of his life. He came out to India,
therefore, pledged to the public authorities in England to over-

o 2

turn the existing policy of Government, as far as related to the princes of India, and he affirmed that he could not consider himself at liberty to pursue any other course. It was his primary object, he said, to remove the impression universally entertained of a systematic design to establish British control over every power in India. He was anxious to restore the native Governments which had been subverted by the progress of our arms, and the ascendency of our influence, to a condition of "vigour, efficiency, and independent interest." He was desirous of abandoning the position in upper India which had been secured by Lord Wellesley's successes, and

His view of the state of affairs, 1805.

to be quit of all our alliances and territories west of the Jumna. He lamented the almost universal phrenzy for victory and conquest which had, he said, seized even some of the heads which he thought the soundest, as repugnant to the interests as it was to the laws of their country,—yet Lord Wellesley and the public functionaries were equally ardent for an honourable peace. On the 1st August Lord Cornwallis wrote to the Court of Directors that finding we were still at war with Holkar, and could hardly be said to be at peace with Sindia, he had determined to proceed to the upper provinces, and avail himself of the interval of the rains, when military operations were suspended, "to endeavour, if it could be effected without a sacrifice of our honour, to terminate by negotiation a contest in which the most brilliant success could afford no solid benefit, and which, if it continued, would entail pecuniary difficulties we should hardly be able to surmount." He described the state of the finances as most deplorable, a fact which admitted of no denial. Two years of war had exhausted the treasury, and increased the public debt. Lord Lake's army was five months in arrears. The large body of "irregulars" who had been induced to forsake the native princes, and to take service with the Company, and who had thus contributed in no small degree to our successes, were no longer required, and the six lacs of rupees a-month they cost was felt to be a dead weight. Lord Wellesley had already made some progress in disbanding them, but Lord Cornwallis declared that he would rather fight them than pay them. They could not, however, be discharged without their arrears, and he adopted a second time the expedient, the most unpalatable to the Company, of robbing their investments to supply the wants of the state. A sum of twenty-five lacs of rupees was, accordingly, taken out of the hold of the China ships at Madras, and sent on to Calcutta, "to give him the chance of getting rid of this force."

Lord Corn-
wallis's policy,
1805.
During his progress to the north-west provinces Lord Cornwallis defined the line of policy he intended to pursue in a despatch to Lord Lake, dated on the 19th of September. He proposed to restore to Holkar all the dominions of the family as soon as he should manifest a disposition to accede to reasonable terms of accommodation. He was prepared to conciliate Sindia by resigning Gohud and Gwalior, after a suitable provision had been made for the rana, as well as Dholpore and two other districts, accounting to him likewise for the revenues which had been collected during their occupancy by the Company's officers. If the demand for the release of the Resident was likely to prove any obstacle to a reconciliation, he was prepared, as a mere point of honour, to waive it. He was disposed to abrogate the treaty with Jeypore, and leave Sindia at liberty to exact whatever contributions he chose from the raja. He considered the possession of the city of Delhi and the person of the emperor a very unfortunate circumstance, as we could only secure him from the danger of being carried off by the maintenance of a large and expensive army. He proposed, therefore, to remove him, if practicable, to some town nearer Calcutta, and to restore the old capital of India to Sindia, with liberty again to establish the power of the Mahrattas in Hindostan. Lord Wellesley had fixed the Chumbul as their future boundary ; and to guard against their encroachments had entered into defensive alliances with the princes to the north of that river. Lord Cornwallis resolved to

dissolve these alliances, and to compensate the princes for the loss of our protection by distributing among them the lands we had obtained to the west of the Jumna, which he considered a useless acquisition. He likewise addressed a letter to Sindia, with a sketch of the proposed arrangements, including a demand for the liberation of the Resident, and enclosed it to Lord Lake to be forwarded to his camp.

Lord Lake justly dreaded the effect of mani-
Lord Lake's remonstrance, 1805. festing so eager a desire for peace, and took upon himself the responsibility of withholding the letter to Sindia, more especially as the Resident had in the meantime been unconditionally released. In his reply to the communication of the Governor-General he advanced the most cogent arguments against this new course of policy. It would, he argued, be highly detrimental to the interests of the Company to allow the influence and the armies of the Mahrattas to be again introduced into Hindostan. If the princes to whom we had promised our protection were abandoned, they would fall a prey to Sindia, Holkar, and Ameer Khan, and large bodies of irregular troops thirsting for plunder would be planted on the frontier of our most fertile and opulent districts. Neither could we withdraw our protection from these princes, except on their own requisition, without a breach of public faith, and no offer of territory would induce them to relinquish this blessing, least of all, at a time when we were about to let loose the elements of anarchy and destruction in Central India. He observed that the Jumna, which the Governor-General proposed to make the boundary of the British dominions, was not a barrier of any importance, as, above its junction with the Chumbul, it was fordable in a variety of places except during a few weeks in the year, and would afford little protection from the incursions of an enemy.

Death of Lord Cornwallis, Oct. 5, 1805. Before this letter could reach its destination Lord Cornwallis was in his grave. As he proceeded up the river his strength rapidly declined,

and in the last month of his existence he lay in a state of
weakness approaching insensibility during the day, but rallied
towards the evening, when he listened to the despatches and
dictated replies. It was in this state of mental and physical
debility that the memorable despatch of the 19th September,
ordering a sudden revolution of policy in the Government of a
great empire, was composed and signed. It may reasonably
be doubted whether Lord Cornwallis was in a condition to
comprehend the scope and consequences of the measures to
which he gave the stamp of his authority. A week after, he
was unconscious of what was passing around him. He was
landed at Ghazeepore, where he expired on the 5th October.
His merits as a Governor-General have, doubtless, been over-
rated, but it would be difficult to name a public character who
more richly earned the esteem and confidence of society by
his sterling integrity, his straightforward and manly character,
and the spirit of justice and moderation which regulated all his
actions. If he had been in the full vigour of his faculties, and
had enjoyed an opportunity of intercourse with Lord Lake,
he would have been able to form an estimate of the change
which had taken place since he left the Government, and would
have perceived the impossibility of steering the vessel of the
state in 1805 by the almanack of 1793; and there is every
reason to believe that he would have modified the measures he
was now imprudently urging forward, under the impulse of the
alarm which brought him to India. As the public authorities
in England had sent out an old man of sixty-seven to govern
India without making any provision for the contingency of his
death, Sir George Barlow, of whom Mr. Pitt, Mr. Dundas
—now Lord Melville—and Lord Castlereagh, had said a few
months before that he was altogether "out of the question,"
succeeded to the office of Governor-General, and proceeded to
the upper provinces.

Sir George Barlow, Governor-General, 1805. Sir George Barlow was a civil servant on the
Bengal establishment, who had risen through the
gradations of office by a meritorious service of

twenty-eight years, to a seat in Council. For many years he had been at the head of some of the most important departments of state and had acquired a fund of knowledge and experience superior to that of any other officer. He had been extolled for his official aptitude and industry by three successive Governors-General, and although the Ministry in England had wisely resolved never again to place any local official at the head of the Government, Lord Wellesley, with all his discernment, had actually obtained the reversion of the Governor-Generalship for him. But Sir George was simply a respectable, plodding, first-rate civilian, whose natural abilities eminently qualified him for a subordinate situation, but who possessed none of that patrician elevation of mind which was needed for the management of an empire. While he continued under the influence of Lord Wellesley's genius he cordially adopted and assisted in carrying out his comprehensive views, and became so closely identified with his policy that he lost the prospect of succeeding him when that policy was condemned. This significant fact was communicated to him by his earliest patron, Lord Cornwallis, and it may possibly have exercised some influence on his opinions, and led him, on the arrival of that nobleman, to become the unflinching advocate of the new and opposite policy which was now in the ascendant at the India House.

On the death of Lord Cornwallis it devolved on Sir George Barlow to reply to the letter of Lord Lake, and to notify the course which the Government, now in his hands, intended to adopt. He announced his resolution to follow the footsteps of his deceased predecessor, and to dissolve the alliances with the native princes, which he had assisted Lord Wellesley in establishing. His policy, as he described it, was " directed to the divesting ourselves of all right to the exercise of interference in the affairs of the native princes where we possessed it almost to an unlimited extent by treaty, and to the withdrawing from all concern whatever in the affairs of every state beyond the Jumna."

Sir George's policy, 1805.

This course, he remarked, was "in conformity with the principles laid down by Parliament, with the orders of their honourable masters, and with his own convictions of expediency." As to the security of our territories, which Lord Wellesley intended to rest on the establishment of general tranquillity, under British supremacy, Sir George considered that it would be as effectually promoted by the prevalence of general anarchy beyond our frontier; and the revival of the mutual conflicts of the native princes, which had desolated the country for thirty years, but were now happily brought under control, was thus regarded as an object of complacency. It is difficult to believe that the British Government in India, even under the most timid administration, did ever deliberately·contemplate the idea of allowing the native chiefs to tear one another to pieces that they might find no leisure to invade our territories; but the voice of honour and humanity is never heard in the delirium of a panic. This despicable policy was aptly described by Mr. Metcalfe, subsequently Governor-General himself, as "disgrace without compensation, treaties without security, and peace without tranquillity."

Negotiations with Sindia, 1805. In the month of July, Lord Lake, with the full concurrence of Lord Wellesley, had addressed a letter to Sindia demanding the release of the Resident by a fixed day, on pain of hostilities. The requisition came at a very favourable season. The atrocities of Sirjee Rao Ghatkay, the inveterate enemy of the English, had constrained Sindia to discard him from the post of minister, and it was bestowed on Ambajee Inglia. He was favourable to a British alliance; and incensed against Holkar and Ameer Khan, who had recently tortured and plundered him, and he endeavoured, and not without success, to sow dissensions between them and Sindia. Sindia himself saw no farther benefit to be derived from any connection with these extortionate and predatory chiefs. He had a painful recollection of the field of Assye, and was anxious to avoid a second war with the Company; and to Lord Lake's requisition he replied

that the *rooksut*, or friendly departure of the Resident was
only delayed, according to usage, till the arrival of his successor. A fair opening was thus presented for negotiations;
but the question of taking the initiative, on which, more
especially in India, their success mainly depends, was the
point of difficulty. Happily, it was discovered that the moonshee Kavil-nyne, an old and favourite servant of Sindia, who
had assisted in concluding the treaty of Sirjee Angengaom,
but had been obliged to fly from the oppressions of Sirjee Rao,
was at this time residing at Delhi. Colonel Malcolm invited
him to the English camp, and it was concerted between them
that one of his relatives who happened to be in the service of
Sindia, should intimate to him the ease with which a negotiation could be opened with the General through Kavil-nyne.
Sindia eagerly embraced the proposal, and was the first to
make advances. Lord Lake thus occupied the vantage ground
of receiving an overture, and replied that no proposal could
be entertained while the Resident continued under restraint.
He was accordingly permitted at once to take his departure,
with suitable honours.

Equipment of
the army, Oct.
1805.

The negotiations were commenced without delay,
but it was felt that any adverse turn of circumstances might interrupt their progress, and possibly
throw Sindia back into opposition. Colonel Malcolm judged
rightly that nothing would tend so much to facilitate such
transactions as a display of military enterprize. Lord Lake
had a noble army under his command, but his military chest
was empty, and the financiers in Calcutta were very lukewarm
about supplying it with funds. Colonel Malcolm was mortified
to find "that they could not send Holkar to the devil for want
of seven or eight lacs of rupees," and he set himself to raise
the sum with all his natural ardour. He plied the native
bankers, but we had lost ground in the money-market, and he
could only raise a lac of rupees from them. He besieged the
collectors' treasuries for bills on Calcutta. He prevailed on
Government to sell the fortress of Deeg to the raja of Bhurt-

pore, from whom it was temporarily withheld, for the immediate payment of three lacs of rupees. By the beginning of October, the requisite sum was raised, and Lord Lake was enabled to take the field " in grand style," and to start in pursuit of Holkar. Colonel Malcolm felt that no place could be more advantageous for the discussion of a treaty than the encampment of a pursuing and successful general. The moonshee was, therefore, hurried along with the army, and resumed the thread of the negotiation, day by day, when the tents were pitched. The terms were at length adjusted, and sent to Sindia for his ratification. All the provisions of the treaty of Sirjee Angengaom, which were not modified by the new arrangement, were to remain in force. Gohud and Gwalior were restored to him as a matter of friendship, on his engaging to assign three lacs of rupees from the revenues to the rana. Pensions, which had been granted to different officers of his court, were relinquished, and annuities were settled on himself, his wife, and his daughter. The Chumbul was to form the boundary of the two states, but the British Government engaged to enter into no treaties with the rajas of Oodypore, Joudhpore, and other chiefs, the tributaries of Sindia, in Malwa, Mewar, or Marwar, and Sindia agreed never to admit Sirjee Rao into his counsels.

Holkar and Ameer Khan quitted the encampment of Sindia, when they perceived a change in his policy favourable to the English alliance, and proceeded to Ajmere. Holkar, notwithstanding his reverses, still exhibited a vigorous and daring spirit. Northern India swarmed with military adventurers, the fragments of the armies which had been broken up by our victories, and the " irregulars" whom the British Government was discharging. Holkar was thus enabled to collect together a body of about 12,000 horse and 3,000 foot, with thirty not very serviceable guns, and he would speedily have become as formidable as at any former period if time had been allowed him to complete his levies. He solicited the raja of Jeypore to join his standard, but meeting with a stern refusal, pushed on to the north of

Pursuit of Holkar, 1805.

Delhi, giving out that he had been invited into that region by the Sikh chiefs of Sirhind. But the heavy contributions which his necessities obliged him to levy on his route, and the remonstrances of the Resident at Delhi deterred them from joining him. Lord Lake now started in pursuit of him, at the head of his cavalry, and a small body of light infantry; and a British army was for the first time conducted to the banks of the Sutlege by the same general who had been the first to cross the Jumna. But its progress was suddenly arrested by the repugnance which the sepoys, from some superstitious feeling, manifested to cross it. Colonel Malcolm, on hearing of their hesitation, galloped into their ranks, and with that singular tact which gave him the mastery of the native mind, exclaimed ". the city and the shrine of Umritsir, with the water of immortality, is before you, and will you shrink from such a pilgrimage?" The words produced a magic effect, and the sepoys hasted across the stream and entered the Punjab, where Runjeet Sing, a young Sikh chieftain, of twenty-five, was laying the foundation of a great kingdom. Holkar fled as Lord Lake advanced, and had reached Umritsir, but Runjeet Sing was evidently averse to the further progress of a British army in his newly-conquered territories, and Lord Lake encamped on the banks of the Beeas, the ancient Hyphasis, in the neighbourhood of the spot where Alexander the Great had erected altars to commemorate the extent of his conquests. In that classical region the ratification of the treaty by Sindia was received on the 25th December, and a double salute was fired in honour of the day and of the peace. Runjeet Sing is said to have visited the English camp in disguise, to examine the military organisation of the foreigners who in the course of fifty years had become masters of India. After a brief nego-tiation, he concluded an agreement with Lord Lake, engaging to hold no farther communication with Holkar, and to constrain him to evacuate the Punjab. Holkar, now a helpless fugi-tive, sent an envoy humbly to sue for peace, and Lord Lake presented him with the draft of a treaty drawn up under the instructions of Sir George Barlow. All the family domains south of the Chumbul were to be restored to him; that river was to be his fixed boundary, and the British Government agreed not to interfere with any of the rajas or dependents of the Holkar family south of it. He was required to relinquish all right to Rampoora, and all claims on the state of Boondee; to entertain no Europeans in his service without the permission of Government, and to banish Sirjee Rao for ever from his presence. He was likewise to return to Hindostan by a prescribed route, and to abstain from injuring the territories either of the Company or of their allies.

To Holkar, whose fortunes were now desperate,

Treaty with
Holkar, Jan.
1806. and who had no alternative but to submit to any terms Lord Lake might choose to dictate, these proposals appeared a god-send. But the incredible lenity of the conditions, which confounded the minds of the native princes, only served to create a feeling of presumption in his breast, and to inflate him with the notion that the British Government could have been influenced only by a dread of his military prowess. His vakeels returned with a demand for eighteen districts in Hindostan, and additional jaygeers for his family in the Deccan, and liberty to levy contributions on Jeypore. But Colonel Malcolm replied that the British Government had already pledged its faith to the protection of the raja, and would not abandon him. "You have good reason for supporting him," retorted the envoys, "for he violated the sacred laws of hospitality in surrendering Vizier Ali, on your demand." Colonel Malcolm rejected all the demands and rebuked the impertinent taunt, which, however, served to show in what light that transaction was still viewed at the native courts. New difficulties and delays were studiously interposed, till Lord Lake's patience was exhausted, and he threatened to break up his camp and commence the pursuit of Holkar, when his vakeels at once produced the ratified treaty, and confessed that they were only endeavouring to gain credit with their master for their diplomatic tact.

Sir George Barlow, however, was not satisfied with the terms of either treaty. He considered that to fix the Chumbul as the boundary of the Mahratta dominions might be construed as a pledge to protect the native principalities lying to the north of it, and he was resolved, in obedience to the authorities in England, to dissolve all connection with them. While ratifying the treaties, therefore, he added declaratory articles, the effect of which was to withdraw our protection entirely from those states west of the Jumna, with whom alliances had been formed two years before. Rampoora, which Colonel Malcolm had positively refused to relinquish, was restored to Holkar, and he fired a royal salute on the occasion, declaring at the same time that the English were, nevertheless, "great rascals, and never to be trusted." The raja of Boondee was likewise left to his fate. Lord Lake made the most strenuous efforts to save that unfortunate prince. He had the strongest claims on the consideration, if not also on the gratitude of the Government. He had never failed in his attachment to the Company; regardless of the denunciations of Holkar, he had afforded shelter and aid to Colonel Monson during his retreat. His country, moreover, contained one of the most important passes into our northern provinces. Sir George turned a deaf ear to every remonstrance, and the raja was abandoned to the revenge and rapacity of Holkar.

Jeypore, 1800.   The course pursued with regard to Jeypore was yet more disgraceful. The raja was among the foremost to enter the system of defensive alliances concluded by Lord Wellesley. But his fidelity was shaken by the apparent decay of our power, when Holkar was chasing Colonel Monson before him, and Lord Wellesley informed Lord Cornwallis that his defection on that occasion had cancelled his claims to our alliance. In the following year, Holkar entered his territories and demanded his aid against the Company, but Lord Lake informed him that he had now an opportunity of making atonement for his former disloyalty, and that the

Declaratory articles, 1806.

boon of our protection would be restored to him if he resisted the advances of the Mahratta chief. Upon the strength of this promise, the raja not only obliged Holkar to quit his dominions, but afforded cordial and important aid to our de- tachments while passing through his districts in pursuit of him. Lord Cornwallis, who was the soul of honour, assured Lord Lake that any pledge which he had given to the raja should be considered sacred. But Sir George Barlow refused to recognise the obligation, and, at the time when Holkar was returning from the Punjab and entering the Jeypore territory, bent on plunder and revenge, caused it to be notified to the raja, that the British protection was withdrawn from him, in consequence of the breach of his engagements during Monson's retreat. We thus incurred the odium of having availed our- selves of the raja's services when they were of the highest value to us, and of abandoning him to destruction when we no longer needed them. It was in vain to attempt to reason with Sir George, and Lord Lake was subjected to the reproaches —the keener for their truth—of the raja's vakeels, who upbraided the British Government with having made its good faith subservient to its interests, and asserted that this was the first time it had abandoned an ally to suit its convenience. Indignant at the contempt with which his expostulations were treated, and the degradation of the national honour, and con- vinced, moreover, that he could not be a fit instrument for the execution of measures which he entirely disapproved of, Lord Lake, in the beginning of 1806, resigned the political powers which had been entrusted to him, and resolved to con- fine his attention to his military duties.

Aggressions   The treaty with Holkar had stipulated that he
of Holkar,   should return to Hindostan by the route pre-
1806.   scribed for him, and abstain from all aggression
on the territories of the Company or its allies. But Lord Lake was in haste to return, and save Government the field expenses of his army, and, instead of directing Holkar to pre- cede or accompany him, permitted him to remain behind. No

sooner did he find that the British army was fairly across the Sutlege, than he let loose his predatory bands on the Punjab and plundered the country without mercy. He proved himself, as Runjeet Sing said indignantly to the British envoy who visited his court four years later, a *pucka(hurāmzada)*— a determined (rascal.) Holkar was fully aware that he had no longer Lord Wellesley to deal with, and there was no article of the treaty which he did not violate with the greatest effrontery. Passing through the province of Hurriana, which had been granted to Abdul Sumud as a reward for the eminent services he rendered to the Company, Holkar laid waste the lands and levied heavy contributions on the people. Abdul implored the interposition of the British Government, which Sir George Barlow refused, but promised to make him a pecuniary compensation for his losses. Holkar then halted for a month at Jeypore, and finding that the Governor-General had withdrawn his protection from the raja, extorted eighteen lacs of rupees from him. He then proceeded to wreak his vengeance on the raja of Boondee for the assistance which he had given Colonel Monson during his retreat.

Remarks on these transactions, 1806.

This disastrous termination of the Mahratta war planted the seeds of another and more momentous contest. The difference between the policy of Lord Wellesley and of his two immediate successors, was not the restoration of peace or the prosecution of war and conquest. When the career of Lord Wellesley was terminated by the arrival of Lord Cornwallis, nothing remained to secure the pacification of India but to complete the accommodation with Sindia, which was in rapid progress, and to extinguish the power of Holkar and Ameer Khan, who were then reduced to extremity. If Lord Wellesley had continued five months longer in power, India would have been blessed with peace and tranquillity. The policy of the Court of Directors brought peace to the Company, but distraction to India, and the wisdom of Lord Wellesley's measures was lamentably vindicated by the twelve years of anarchy which followed the rejection of it. By abandoning all the defensive alliances which had been made, and enjoining a neutral and isolated policy, the Directors endeavoured to check * the advance of the British Government to supreme authority in India. But this attempt to control the inevitable progress of events proved not only abortive, but disastrous. It afforded an opportunity for the growth and maturity of a new predatory power, that of the Pindarees, who, after having exhausted the provinces of Central India, poured down on the British territories, and rendered it necessary, in self-defence, to assemble an army of more than 100,000 men to extirpate them. That which it fell to the lot of Lord Hastings to accomplish for the settlement of India in 1817, might have been effected with greater ease, and at a less cost, by Lord Wellesley's plans in 1805.

Career of Holkar, 1806-11. To continue the brief career of Holkar to its close. After his return to his own dominions he addressed letters to the other Mahratta princes exhorting them to form a national league against the common enemy, but Lord Wellesley had so effectually paralyzed their power as to leave them little inclination to respond to the call. Holkar determined to reorganise his army, to reduce its numbers, and improve its discipline. But the cavalry he had enlisted in the south, whom he proposed in the first instance to discharge, broke into open mutiny, and he was obliged to deliver his nephew, Khundeh Rao, into their hands as a hostage for their arrears. They immediately hoisted the standard of revolt, threw off their allegiance to Jeswunt Rao Holkar, and proclaimed the lad their sovereign. To appease them, he delivered up the sums he had extorted from Jeypore, on the receipt of which they marched back to their homes. Within a week, the unfortunate child, in whose name the government had hitherto been carried on, was removed by poison, under the instigation of Holkar's *gooroo*, or spiritual guide, the infamous Chimna Bhao, who soon after became the instrument of murdering Kashee Rao, the brother of his prince, and the only re-

II.   P

maining member of the royal house. The remorse of this double murder preyed on the spirits of Holkar, and he began to exhibit a degree of excitement in his conduct bordering on insanity. He had determined to increase and improve his artillery, and he laboured in person at the furnaces casting cannon with a wild impetuosity. He gave himself up to un-bounded indulgence. The shops at Bombay were ransacked for cherry brandy, and intemperance began to undermine his reason. His phrenzy rose eventually to such a pitch as to endanger the lives of his attendants, and his own officers seized him and confined him with ropes in a separate tent, under a guard, where he uttered the loudest objurgations, and tore his flesh with his nails. The most skilful doctors and the most renowned magicians were called in, but their prescrip-tions and incantations were equally without avail. After a

Death of Jes-wunt Rao Hol-kar, 1811. year of raging insanity he sunk into a state of fatuity, and expired on the 20th October, 1811. During the period of his incapacity the govern-ment of the state was carried on by his favourite concubine, Toolsee bye, and his minister, Buluram Sett, whom we now leave in charge of the administration.

Rajpootana—contest for a princess, 1806. The withdrawal of British protection from the territory west of the Jumna, left the fertile pro-vinces of Rajpootana at the mercy of the Mahrattas and the Patans. The princes, instead of uniting their strength against the enemies of their peace, wasted it for several years against each other in a conflict, which, though tinged with a ray of romance, entailed incalculable misery on their people. The contest was for the hand of Krishnu Koomaree, the beau-tiful daughter of the rana of Oodypore. An alliance with that ancient and illustrious house—"the sun of Hindoo glory"—was considered the highest honour to which a Rajpoot prince could aspire, and the princess was considered the "flower" of Rajpootana. She had been betrothed to Bheem Sing, the raja of Joudhpore, but his death broke off the match, upon which Juggut Sing, the raja of Jeypore, solicited her hand,

and being accepted as her bridegroom sent a splendid escort to conduct her to his capital. But Maun Sing, who had succeeded Bheem Sing as the raja of Joudhpore, was advised to demand the princess, on the ground that the alliance was contracted with the throne rather than with its occupant, and attacked and routed the convoy. The raja of Jeypore was incensed at the insult thus offered him, and collected an army of more than 100,000 men to avenge it. It was a motley assembly of Patans, Rajpoots, and Mahrattas. Ameer Khan, whose fortunes were reduced to so low an ebb when the treaty was made with Holkar in the Punjab that he was on the point of flying to Afganistan, had returned to Hindostan, and collected a large force, with which he joined the raja of Jeypore. Two of Sindia's commanders were likewise sent to espouse his cause; and Sevae Sing, a powerful Joudhpore noble, who had proclaimed a posthumous child of Bheem Sing the rightful heir of the throne, in opposition to Maun Sing whom he held in detestation, likewise joined his enemies. There were few of the Rajpoot chiefs who were not ranged under either flag. In the great battle which ensued, in February, 1807, Maun Sing was deserted by his nobles and sustained a total defeat. He fled from the field to the citadel of his capital, which he defended with great gallantry for many months, while his country was devastated by the enemy. To relieve himself from this scourge, he made overtures to Ameer Khan, who had no interest in reducing any of the Rajpoot states to destruction, and thus depriving himself of the prospect of plundering them in succession. The Patan, therefore, on the promise of fifty lacs of rupees a-year and a jaygeer of four lacs for his kitchen expenses, deserted the cause of the Jeypore raja, and that prince, in addition to the loss of a hundred and twenty lacs of rupees, which the war and his allies had cost him, now found his territories ravaged without mercy by his own ally. The fortunes of Maun Sing were thus retrieved; but he could not consider himself secure while Sevae Sing lived, and Ameer Khan agreed to effect his do-

P 2

struction for an additional sum of ten lacs. He paid him a visit at Nagore, his chief town, pretending to have deserted the cause of Maun Sing, and took an oath on the Koran as a pledge of his sincerity. Sevae Sing, suspecting no treachery, accepted an invitation to an entertainment; but while he was amused with dancing girls, the ropes of the tent were cut, he and his followers were entangled in its folds, and indiscriminately slaughtered by musketry and grape shot.

The raja of Oodypore had taken no part in the war of which his daughter was the innocent cause, but he was, nevertheless, subjected to plunder by Sindia and Ameer Khan, who were constrained to resort to rapine to subsist the armies which they persisted in maintaining on a scale beyond their resources. Wherever the Mahratta or the Patan encamped, a single day was sufficient to give the most flourishing spot the aspect of a desert, and their march was traced by the blaze of villages and the havoc of cultivation. In his extremity the rana applied to the British Government for protection, offering to make over one-half his territories for the defence of the other. Zalim Sing, the renowned regent of Kotah, together with the rival princes of Jeypore and Joudhpore, earnestly joined in this solicitation. There had always, they said, been in India some supreme power to which the weak looked for protection against the ambition and the rapacity of the strong. The Company had now succeeded to this paramount sovereignty, and were bound to fulfil the duties attached to it. The Mahrattas and the Patans, who were now spreading desolation from the Sutlege to the Nerbudda, were utterly unable to offer any opposition to the British arms, and the Governor-General had only to speak the word and peace and tranquillity would be restored. These facts could not be controverted, but such interference was known to be foreign to the existing policy of the India House. The Court of Directors, however, when reviewing the conduct of Sir George Barlow towards Jeypore, appeared to experience some slight touch

Rajpoot Princes and the British Government, 1809.

of compunction for the desertion of the raja, but they satisfied
their consciences with an idle lecture on " the necessity of
taking care, in all the transactions of Government with the
native princes, to preserve its character for fidelity to its
allies from falling into disrepute, and to evince a strict regard
to the principles of justice and generosity." The sincerity of
these professions would have been less liable to mistrust if
they had been accompanied by a change of policy; but the
Court distinctly repudiated the idea of taking the raja under
their protection at the risk of a war. From the British Government there was, therefore, no prospect of relief for the
wretched states of Rajpootana, and the raja of Oodypore was
obliged to come to a compromise with Ameer Khan, and to assign him one-fourth of his dominions to preserve the remainder
from rapine. He was likewise subjected to the indignity,
which no prince in India could feel so acutely as he did, of
exchanging turbans, as a token of friendship and equality,
with the Patan freebooter. That unscrupulous chief took
advantage of the ascendency he had thus acquired at Oodypore to perpetrate one of the foulest murders ever known,
even in that land of violence. He suggested to the rana that
the only means of quenching the feuds which distracted Rajpootana on account of his daughter, was to put her to death,
and he threatened to carry her off by force to Maun Sing if his
advice was not followed. Under the influence of an infamous
favourite, Ajit Sing, one of his nobles, the father consented
to become the executioner of his child. His own sister,
Chand bye, presented the poisoned bowl with her own hands
to the young and lovely princess, then in her sixteenth year,
and urged her in the name of her father to save the honour
of the house of Oodypore by the sacrifice of her life. She

meekly bowed her head, and exclaimed, " This is
Death of the
princess of   the marriage to which I was foredoomed," and
Oodypore,   drank off three successive doses, sending up a
1810.
                 prayer to heaven with her last breath for the life
and prosperity of her father. The news of this tragedy was

no sooner spread through the capital than loud lamentations burst from every quarter, mingled with execrations on the wretched father and his atrocious adviser. One of the great nobles, on hearing that the deed was in contemplation, galloped to the capital in haste to prevent it, but finding that he was too late, unbuckled his sword and shield, and placing them at the feet of the rana, said, "My ancestors have served yours for thirty generations, but never more shall these arms be used in your service."

Affairs of Hyderabad, 1806-7.　This narrative has carried us beyond the period of Sir George Barlow's administration, to which we now return. The greatest blot in his policy was the abandonment of Malwa and Rajpootana to anarchy and desolation. On the other hand, he deserves great credit for the resolution with which he maintained the peace of the Deccan, in opposition to the principle of non-intervention. Meer Allum, the able minister of the Nizam, had become obnoxious to his weak master by his steady support of the British alliance, and was threatened with assassination, and obliged to take refuge in the British residency. The Nizam then proceeded to open negotiations with Holkar and Sindia, and to assemble troops on his frontier, and manifested every disposition to dissolve his connection with the Company. Sir George felt that "there was no alternative but either to abandon the alliance altogether, or to make an effort to replace it on a just and proper foundation by a direct and decided interposition . . . but, the dissolution of the alliance would subvert the very foundations of British power and ascendency in the political scale in India, and become the signal and the instrument of the downfall of the remaining fabric of our political relations." He felt that we could not abandon our influence or our power at Hyderabad without finding the ground occupied by our enemies, the result of which would be universal "agitation, and distrust, and turbulence and expense." He did not therefore hesitate to discard the doctrine of neutrality. The Nizam was ordered to restore Meer Allum to the office of minister, to banish from his counsels all who were hostile to the British alliance, and to submit to the more direct interference of the Resident in the management of his affairs.

Affairs at Poona, 1806. The Court of Directors continued to view the treaty of Bassein on the same narrow grounds on which they were at first led to object to it, as the source of multiplied embarrassments. They considered that their government might be relieved from these difficulties if they could withdraw from all interference in Mahratta politics, and leave the Peshwa to resume his position as the head of the Mahratta commonwealth. Sir George Barlow resisted with equal steadiness every proposal to modify the treaty, and had the courage to state that, while he desired to manifest every attention to their wishes, he felt that there was a higher obligation imposed on him, that of maintaining the supremacy of the British rule, which would be compromised by any alteration of the policy established at Poona. It had been affirmed that such a course would be most agreeable to the Mahratta powers, to which he replied with truth that to withdraw from the position we occupied there would be gratifying to the Mahrattas in exact proportion as it afforded them the hope of subverting our authority and supplied the means of prosecuting designs hostile to British interests. The Peshwa advanced claims on the independent chiefs of Bundlekund, from many of whom he claimed chout; as the head of the Mahratta empire, he insisted on his share of the contributions which Holkar and Sindia were levying in Rajpootana, and he requested permission to appoint a representative in Hindostan; in other words, to revive the influence and power of which he had been deprived by the treaty of Bassein. But Sir George Barlow refused to admit any of these pretensions, and determined to maintain, in undiminished vigour, the ascendency which Lord Wellesley had established in the counsels of Poona.

State of the finances, 1806. The state of the finances called for Sir George Barlow's early attention. From the first establishment of the British Government in India, all its financial difficulties had arisen out of the wars in which it was involved. There was no elasticity in a revenue derived almost exclusively from the land, and it became necessary to have recourse to loans whenever the expenditure was found to exceed the income. On the return of peace and the removal of the military pressure, the finances had always, with one exception, resumed their spring. The extensive military operations of Lord Wellesley's administration had necessarily augmented the public debt, but this pecuniary strain, though manifestly of a temporary character, brought on one of the intermittent fevers of alarm at the India House, and large and comprehensive views of policy were needlessly sacrificed to obtain immediate relief, It appears to have been entirely overlooked that our wars in India had always been marked by this peculiarity, that they terminated in an accession of territory and revenue, which served to balance whatever incumbrance they had entailed. Thus, the increase to the debt during Lord Wellesley's administration was eight crores and a half of rupees, while the permanent increase of annual revenue was not less than seven crores. The Indian debt has seldom exceeded the income of two years; and this rule of proportion appears indeed to be the normal condition of Indian finance. In the year preceding the arrival of Lord Wellesley the revenue was eight crores, the debt seventeen. At the close of his administration the former had increased to fifteen crores and a half, and the latter to thirty-one. After the lapse of sixty years, the relative proportion remains without alteration. In the present year the revenues of the empire are forty-five crores, and the debt is ninety-two crores. By the cessation of the war and the reduction of the military charges, Sir George was enabled to reduce the annual expenditure, and within two years the deficit was converted into a surplus, which remained steady, with occasional variations, for twenty years, till the first Burmese war again depressed the scale.

Supersession of Sir George Barlow, 1806.   The great zeal manifested by Sir George Barlow in carrying out the views of the India House, re-

commended him to the Directors as the fittest successor of Lord
Cornwallis, the news of whose death reached England at
the end of January, 1806. The death of Mr. Pitt, and the
dissolution of his ministry had just introduced the Whigs to
power, after an exclusion of more than twenty years. Within
twenty-four hours of their accession to office they were called
on to make provision for the exercise of the full powers of the
Governor-General, and Lord Minto, the President of the Board
of Control, agreed, as a temporary measure, to the nomination
of Sir George Barlow. His commission was accordingly made
out and signed in February, 1806, but only ten days after, the
Ministry informed the Court of Directors that they had selected
Lord Lauderdale for that office. They passed a high encomium
on Sir George Barlow, but his policy was not in accordance
with the views of some of the leading members of the new
Cabinet. Lord Grenville, more especially, considered the administration of Lord Wellesley the most splendid and glorious
that India had ever seen, and he vigorously opposed the appointment, as his successor, of one whose chief merit, in the
opinion of the Court of Directors, consisted in a determination
to reverse his measures. The Directors strenuously resisted the
appointment of Lord Lauderdale, not only as an abrupt and
contemptuous rejection of their favourite, but also on personal
grounds. He had been a warm admirer of the French revolution, and during the height of its mania had dropped his
ancient and noble title, and assumed a costume symbolical of
Jacobinism. These follies had passed, but the Court did not
forget that he had also been a zealous advocate of Mr. Fox's
India Bill, and, more recently, of Lord Wellesley's doctrine of
free trade with India, which was considered a pestilent heresy
in Leadenhall-street. The Act of 1784 had vested in the
Crown the right of vacating any appointment in India under
the sign manual, and without the consent of the Court of
Directors. The Ministry now, for the first time, brought it
into exercise, and retaliated on them by a warrant cancelling
the commission of Sir George Barlow. The discussion between

the Board of Control and the India House was carried on for
many weeks, with great warmth, inasmuch as it not only involved the immediate question of Lord Lauderdale's appointment, but the more important point connected with the
interpretation of the Act of 1784, of the general right of
nomination to the office of Governor-General. In such a contest
the ministers of the Crown, being the stronger party, could not
fail to triumph, and the difference was accommodated by the
appointment of Lord Minto.

The Vellore   In the month of July, the Government was
Mutiny, 1806. astounded by a portentous event, unprecedented
in its annals—the massacre of European officers and soldiers by
the sepoys at Vellore. This fortress, situated eighty-eight miles
west of Madras,* and only forty miles from the frontier of
Mysore, had been selected, contrary to the wiser judgment of
the Court of Directors, for the residence of Tippoo's family,
and was speedily filled with eighteen hundred of their adherents and three thousand Mysoreans. The princes were
treated with the usual liberality of the British Government,
and were subjected to little personal restraint. The European
troops in the garrison consisted of about 370, and the sepoys
amounted to 1,500. One of the native regiments was composed of Mysore Mahomedans, many of whom had been in
the service of Tippoo. At three in the morning of the 10th
July, the sepoys rose in rebellion, and having secured the
main guard and the powder magazine, suddenly assaulted the
European barracks. They had not the courage to encounter
the bayonets of the soldiers, but poured in upon them volley
after volley through the venetians, till eighty-two had been
killed and ninety-one wounded. Parties of sepoys then proceeded to the residences of the officers, of whom thirteen fell
victims to their treachery. During the massacre, an active
communication was kept up between the mutineers and the
palace of the Mysore princes, many of whose followers were
conspicuous in the assault. Provisions were also sent out to
the sepoys, and the royal ensign of Mysore was hoisted on

the flag-staff amidst the shouts of a large crowd. The remaining Europeans, though destitute of ammunition, maintained their position under cover of a gateway and a bastion, till they were rescued by Colonel Gellispie. He was in garrison at Arcot, eight miles distant, and, on hearing of the outbreak, started without a moment's delay with a portion of the 19th Dragoons, and arrived in time to save the survivors. The gate was blown open with his galloper guns, and his men rushed in and obtained possession of the fort. Between three and four hundred of the mutineers were put to death, many were taken prisoners, and the remainder escaped by dropping from the walls.

Cause of the Mutiny, 1806. The searching investigation which was immediately made, clearly revealed the cause of the mutiny. The new Commander-in-chief, Sir John Cradock, soon after his arrival, had obtained permission from the Governor in Council, Lord William Bentinck, to codify the voluminous regulations of the military department, on the condition that no rules should be added to those in force without the express sanction of Government. The code on its completion was submitted to the Governor, and received his sanction, as a matter of form, but several innovations had been introduced by the Adjutant-General, of which no intimation was given to him. The sepoys, for instance, were forbidden to appear on parade with earrings, or any distinctive marks of caste, and they were required to shave the chin, and to trim the moustache after a particular model. These unnecessary orders were sufficiently vexatious, but it was the new form prescribed for the turban, which gave the sepoys the greatest offence, because it was said to bear a resemblance to a European hat. Orientals consider the head dress an object of particular importance, and cling to the national fashion with great tenacity. The Turk, who does not object to a European coat, trousers, and boots, will not relinquish the cap of his nation. The Parsee readily adopts a European costume, but retains his own distinguishing head-dress. Even the Hindoo, who apes European fashions, shrinks from the use of the hat, which among Asiatics is an object of instinctive abhorrence. In the present case, this feeling was aggravated by a report industriously circulated in the native army by the Mahomedans who led the movement, that it was the precursor of an attempt to force Christianity on the sepoys. Of all the Presidencies that of Madras had been the most officious in patronising the religions of the country. Forgetting the duty due to their own creed, and to the consistency of their own characters, the Madras functionaries had been in the habit of firing royal salutes on the birthdays of the gods, of constraining their own Christian servants to make offerings at different shrines in the name of the Company, and of employing the police to impress the poor ryots to drag the cars of the idols. At the same time, the ministrations of Christianity were so completely neglected, as to lead the natives to believe that their European conquerors were without a religion. But all these humiliating concessions to native prejudices did not secure the Government from the suspicion of a design to destroy the religion of the people, and to force a foreign faith upon them. A spirit of deep disaffection was diffused through the army, which was diligently fomented by the intrigues of the Tippoo family, who upbraided the sepoys with the badge of the infidel creed, which they were already obliged to wear. It was this family, to whom we had generously, but unwisely, given the large pecuniary resources now turned against us, which applied the torch to the mine which the Government had unconsciously laid. The exasperated sepoys were thus led on to rebellion and massacre. The same feeling of dissatisfaction was also manifested by the troops at Hyderabad, but it was extinguished by the judicious proceedings of the Resident and Colonel Montresor. The members of Tippoo's family were removed without loss of time to Calcutta, and their pensions were not curtailed, notwithstanding their complicity in these treasons and murders.

Recal of Lord William Bentinck, 1806. The Court of Directors were overwhelmed by the news of this mutiny, and in that spirit of vindictiveness which the excess of terror inspires recalled Lord William Bentinck and the Commander-in-chief within a week after the intelligence reached them, before they had received a single line of explanation from either of them. On his return to England, Lord William presented a memorial to the Honourable Court in vindication of his character and proceedings. "I have," he said, "been removed from my situation, and condemned as an accomplice in measures with which I had no farther concern than to obviate their evil consequences. My dismissal was effected in a manner harsh and mortifying; and the form which custom has prescribed to soften the severity of a misfortune, at all times sufficiently severe, have in this single instance been violated as if for the express purpose of deepening my disgrace . . . . I have been severely injured in my character and my feelings. For these injuries I ask reparation, if, indeed, any reparation can atone for feelings so deeply aggrieved, and a character so unjustly compromised in the eyes of the world." The Court endeavoured to soothe his feelings while they attempted to vindicate the propriety of his recal. They bore testimony to "the uprightness, disinterestedness, zeal, respect for the system of the Company, and, in many instances, success, with which he had acted in the Government—but, as the misfortunes which happened under his administration placed his fate under the government of public events and opinions which the Court could not control, so it was not in their power to alter the effect of them." The Court little dreamt that in this vain attempt to apologize for their conduct towards him, they were unwittingly shadowing forth their own doom, and the occasion of it. Half a century later, another, and a far more appalling, mutiny broke out in India, for which the East India Company was no more to blame than Lord William Bentinck was for the Vellore mutiny, but—to use the language of the Court,—" as the misfortune happened under their administration, and placed their fate under the government of public events and opinions which the Ministry could not control,"

they were deposed from the Government of the great empire
they had built up, and of their magnificent house in Leadenhall-street not one stone was left upon another.

Temple of   The province of Cuttack acquired in 1803, was
Jugunnath,   attached to the Presidency of Bengal, and the
1806.   question of dealing with the temple of Jugunnath
was forced upon the Supreme Council. Lord Wellesley
refused to connect it with his government, but Sir George
Barlow determined to assume the management of the establishment to the minutest item, not excluding the three hundred
dancing girls, and an army of pilgrim hunters. The pilgrim
tax was revived to cover these charges, and the balance was
carried to the credit of the Company, as Sir George deemed
such a tax a legitimate source of revenue. It is due to the
Court of Directors to state that they were opposed to this
anomalous and degrading job, but they were overruled by
the Board of Control. It was for many years the subject of
a bitter contention between the Government of India and
those who were anxious to maintain the consistency of our
religious character. Under the pressure of public opinion, the
tax was at length repealed; and some time after, Lord Dalhousie
had the courage to restore the management of the temple, and
of the lands which had once belonged to it, to its legitimate
guardians, the priesthood of Pooree.

Propagation of   Far different, however, was the course pursued
Christianity in by Sir George Barlow regarding the diffusion
India, 1806.   of Christian truth in India, to which we now turn.
The first Portuguese settlers had no sooner acquired a political
footing in India than they began, in the spirit of the sixteenth
century, to persecute the Pagans. They sent to India some
of the most able and zealous of their ecclesiastics, of whom
St. Francis Xavier was the most illustrious, under whose
instructions, though not without some degree of compulsion, a
large Roman Catholic community was formed on the Malabar
and Coromandel coasts. At the beginning of the eighteenth
century several German Protestant missionaries proceeded to

the Danish settlement of Tranquebar, a hundred and sixty miles south of Madras, under the patronage of the King of Denmark. They were followed by a succession of earnest men, and, among others, by the celebrated Swartz, who was held in honour both by Christians and Hindoos. By their zealous exertions a numerous body of converts was collected on the Coromandel coast. In 1793 Mr. William Carey proceeded to Bengal to establish a Christian mission, and laboured with much devotedness, but little success, for seven years in the district of Malda. In 1799 two other missionaries, Mr. Marshman and Mr. Ward, went out to his assistance. As they were, however, without a licence from the India House, they were ordered to quit the country the day after their arrival, but obtained an asylum at the Danish settlement of Serampore, in the neighbourhood of Calcutta, and were received under the protection of the Danish

The Serampore
Missionaries,
1800.

crown. Mr. Carey then removed to Serampore, and he and his colleagues established a fraternity which, under the title of the Serampore Missionaries, has attained a historical importance. They opened the first schools for the gratuitous education of native children. They set up printing presses, and prepared founts of types in various Indian languages. They compiled grammars of the Bengalee, Sanscrit, and other languages, into which they likewise translated the Sacred Scriptures. They cultivated the Bengalee language with great assiduity, and published the first works which had ever appeared in it, and thus laid the foundation of a vernacular literature. Their names will long continue to be held in grateful remembrance as the pioneers of civilization in Hindostan, to which they devoted their resources and their lives, at a time when the moral and intellectual improvement of the people was an object of profound indifference to the British Government. They, and the converted natives who had joined their establishment, itinerated through the districts of Bengal, and met with no small measure of success in preaching the doctrines of Christianity.

Opposition of Government, 1806?

Their missionary labours were, however, viewed by the Company in England and the Company's servants in India with great mistrust and jealousy. All previous conquerors, the Hindoos, the Boodhists, and the Mahomedans, had identified their religion with their policy, and supported it with the whole weight of their political and military power, and subjected those who professed a different creed to severe persecution. The English were the first conquerors who left their native subjects the unrestricted exercise of their own religion; partly, from that principle of religious toleration which had always distinguished the East India Company, but, chiefly, from the apprehension that an opposite course might rouse a fanatic opposition to their rule, and expose it to danger. It was under the impulse of this morbid feeling of dread that the Court of Directors set their faces sternly against all missionary efforts. They were thus placed in the false position of hostility to their own creed, which, among a people of strong religious sensibilities like the Hindoos, was calculated to create a feeling of contempt, or, what was worse, a dangerous suspicion that so unnatural a procedure must be intended to conceal some sinister design. The mutiny at Vellore was traced to an interference with the religious prejudices of the sepoys, and under the panic which it created, Sir George Barlow considered it necessary for the security of the Company's interests in Bengal, to put a stop to the labours of the Serampore Missionaries, lest the natives should regard them as an interference with their religion. He was not in a mood to reflect that it is only when the agency of the state is employed to enforce a change of religion that there is either disaffection or danger; that the natives of the country had been accustomed for centuries to religious discussions and conversions, and that during the seven years in which the Serampore Missionaries had been labouring in Bengal, the Hindoos who had become Musulmans greatly outnumbered those who had embraced Christianity, and, without creating any alarm. The missionaries themselves were convinced that

the truths of the Gospel would only be embraced in sincerity
when they were placed before the country separate from all
political influences. They, therefore, repudiated all aid from
the state, and deprecated the intrusion of the public authorities into their province. But their labours were at once and
peremptorily interdicted. They prudently bent to the storm,
the Vellore panic died out, and the restrictions laid on them
were quietly removed.

CHAPTER XXIV.

LORD MINTO'S ADMINISTRATION, 1807–1810.

Lord Minto's   LORD Minto, who was appointed Governor-Ge-
administration,   neral in 1806, was a well-trained politician, and
1807.
                    had been engaged for many years in the manage-
ment of public affairs. He was one of the managers appointed
by the House of Commons to conduct the impeachment of
Warren Hastings; and the prosecution of Sir Elijah Impey
was especially committed to his charge. The interest he had
taken in India pointed him out to his Whig colleagues when
they came into power, as the fittest member of their body for
the post of President of the Board of Control, and the twelve
months he passed at the head of that office gave him an
enlarged comprehension of Indian questions. He was an
accomplished scholar, distinguished above his predecessors by
his urbanity, a statesman of clear perceptions and sound judgment, mild and moderate in his views, yet without any deficiency of firmness. He was accepted by the Court of
Directors as their Governor-General on the understanding
that he should eschew the policy of Lord Wellesley, which
was still the great object of terror in Leadenhall-street, and
tread in the footsteps of Lord Cornwallis. After his arrival
in Calcutta he facetiously observed that when taking leave of

II.   Q the Chairman and his deputy at the India House and asking their final instructions, there seemed to be only two points on which they felt any anxiety—the importance of adhering most scrupulously to the policy of non-interference, and of controlling the consumption of penknives, which appeared by the latest indent to be growing extravagant. On reaching Madras he found himself called upon, as his first act of government, to determine the fate of the Vellore mutineers. Seventeen of the ringleaders had been executed by sentence of court-martial, but six hundred yet awaited their doom. Great difficulty had been felt in obtaining evidence of individual guilt. The excitement and animosity created by the mutiny had, moreover, subsided; the confidence of the army had been restored, and the officers ceased to sleep with pistols under their pillows. Lord William Bentinck advised the adoption of a mild course; the Commander-in-chief advocated a severe example. The Supreme Government, to whom the matter was referred, ordered the whole party to be transported beyond sea, which, to Hindoos, would have been a penalty worse than death. Lord Minto adopted the more generous and lenient counsel of Lord William Bentinck, and ordered that they should be dismissed the service, and declared incapable of ever re-entering it.

On his arrival in Calcutta, the early attention of Lord Minto was drawn to the state of anarchy into which the feeble policy of his predecessor had plunged the province of Bundlekund. By the treaty of Bassein the Peshwa had ceded to the Company for the support of the subsidiary force districts in the southern Mahratta country and near Surat, yielding twenty-six lacs of rupees a-year. A twelvemonth after they were exchanged for districts in Bundlekund, and the transfer was considered mutually beneficial. The lands in the Deccan were isolated from the Company's dominions, and the defence and management of them would have proved both troublesome and expensive, while they abutted on the Peshwa's territories. The

*Bundlekund—
Anarchy of
the province,
1807–1812.*

districts, in Bundlekund were more handy for the British
Government, while the Peshwa's authority in them was
nominal, and they yielded him no revenue. The exchange,
which received the high sanction of General Wellesley,
was effected in a supplementary treaty of December, 1803.
The province, however, was a prey to anarchy. It was over-
run with innumerable military adventurers, who gained a
subsistence by plunder, and who were necessarily opposed
to any form of settled government. A hundred and fifty
castles were held by as many chieftains, and they were incessantly at feud with each other. The inhabitants, a bold
and independent race, were disgusted with the stringency of
our judicial and fiscal system, and deserted their villages, and
too often joined the banditti. Two forts, Calinger and Ajygur,
universally considered impregnable, were held by chiefs
who owed all their power to rapine and violence, and headed
the opposition to the British authorities. Lord Lake assured
the Government in Calcutta that the peace of the province
could never be maintained without obtaining possession of
these fortresses, which might be effected by a vigorous effort
in a single campaign; but Sir George Barlow replied that " a'
certain extent of dominion, local power, and revenue, would
be cheaply sacrificed for tranquillity and security within a
more contracted circle." The sacrifice was made, but the
tranquillity and security were more distant than ever. The
chiefs who had seized the forts were left in possession of
them, and sunnuds, or deeds, were granted to them and to
some of the most notorious leaders of the freebooters, recog-
nizing their right to the lands they had usurped, upon a
vague promise of allegiance. Due respect was likewise paid
to the principle of non-interference, by allowing them to
decide their disputes by the sword, and this fair province, endowed with the richest gifts of nature, was turned into a
desert.

Lord Minto's
vigorous policy,
1807.
Within five weeks after Lord Minto had assumed the Government, he adopted the resolution

Q 2·

that "it was essential, not only to the preservation of
political influence over the chiefs of Bundlekund, but to
the dignity and reputation of the British Government to
interfere for the suppression of intestine disorder." The
whole policy of the state was at once changed, and it was
announced throughout the province that Government was
determined to enforce obedience to its authority.   The
numerous rajas, who had hitherto treated with contempt the
maudlin advice of the commissioner, hastened to make their
submission when they found the Governor-General in earnest,
and agreed at once to refer their disputes to the decision of
British officers.   But it was found impossible to extirpate the
banditti which infested the country, while they could obtain
shelter in the great fortresses ; a military force was, therefore,
sent to reduce them, and Ajygur was surrendered after a
breach had been made in the walls.   But one military adventurer, Gopal Sing, by his astonishing skill, activity, and resolution, aided by the natural advantages of a country filled with
fastnesses, contrived to evade the British troops in a series
of desultory and harassing movements, for a period of four
years.   He offered his submission at length, on condition of
receiving a full pardon and a provision for his family, and the
Government, weary of a conflict which appeared to be interminable, granted him a jaygeer of eighteen villages.   The last
fortress to submit was the renowned Calinger, which had
baffled the efforts of Mahmood of Ghizni, eight centuries
before.   It was likewise in the siege of this fort that Shere
Shah was killed, in 1545, and the Peshwa's representative,
Ali Bahadoor, had recently besieged it in vain for two years.
It was surrendered after an arduous siege, in which the
British force was, on one occasion, repulsed with the loss of
150 in killed and wounded.   The peace and happiness of
Bundlekund were restored, to be soon, alas; destroyed again
by one of the Company's *pucka*, or unscrupulous collectors,
who rack-rented the province, and blighted its prosperity as
effectively as the freebooters had done before him.

Career of
Runjeet Sing,
1780—1808.
The difficulty of maintaining the practice of non-intervention was still more clearly demonstrated before Lord Minto had been a twelvemonth in office, in reference to the proceedings of Runjeet Sing, whose career now claims attention. On the retirement of the Abdalee from India after the battle of Paniput, the affairs of the Punjab fell into confusion, and the half military half religious community of the Sikhs, who had been oppressed by all the successive rulers of the country, had an opportunity of gradually enlarging and consolidating their power. This country, lying in the track of every invader, from Alexander the Great to Ahmed Shah Abdalee, and which had been subject to greater vicissitudes and a more frequent change of masters than any other Indian province, was now in the hands of the Sikhs. Their commonwealth was divided into fraternities, termed *misils*, the chief of each of which was the leader in war, and the arbiter in time of peace. Of these clans, twelve were deemed the foremost in rank. Churut Sing, the head of one of the least considerable, had commenced a course of encroachments on his neighbours, which was carried on by his son, Maha Sing. He died in 1792, leaving an only son, Runject Sing, who at the early age of seventeen entered upon that career of ambition and aggrandisement, which, by a rare combination of cunning and audacity, resulted in the establishment of a power as great as that of Sevajee or Hyder. He acquired great credit for his prowess when, in 1799, Zemaun Shah entered the Punjab, which was still considered as an appendage of the crown of Cabul. Runject Sing had the discretion to aid him in moving his guns across the Jhelum, and was rewarded by the important grant of the town of Lahore, which was the capital of the country even before the Mahomedans crossed the Indus, and had always been associated with the supreme authority in the province. From 1803 to 1806, Runject Sing was diligently employed in extending his authority over the different fraternities and chiefs in the Punjab. In 1806, the

course of his conquests brought him down to the banks of the Sutlege, and he cast a wishful eye on the plains beyond it.

The Sikh States of Sirhind, 1807.
Between the Sutlege and the Jumna lay the province of Sirhind, occupied by about twenty independent Sikh principalities, of greater or less extent, the most considerable of which was Putteeala, with a revenue of about twenty lacs of rupees a-year, and a population of a million and a quarter. The chiefs had been obliged to bend to the authority of Sindia, which General Perron had extended to the vicinity of the Sutlege, but two of them, Kythul and Jheend, had rendered important services to Lord Lake in the campaigns of 1803 and 1805, and were recompensed with large grants of land. As the British power had now superseded that of the Mahrattas in this region, these petty princes offered their submission and fealty to it, and, although there were no mutual engagements in writing, considered themselves under the suzerainty of the Company, and entitled to their protection. The ambition of Runjeet Sing, which had as yet received no check, led him to contemplate the annexation of these states, and the extension of his dominions to the banks of the Jumna. He proceeded with his usual caution. A sharp dispute had arisen between the chiefs of Putteeala and Naba, and the raja of Naba invoked the interposition of Runjeet Sing, who crossed the Sutlege with a large body of horse, and dictated terms of reconciliation. No notice was taken of this encroachment by the Resident at Delhi, and Runjeet Sing flattered himself that he had no opposition to apprehend from the Company's officers. In 1807, the raja of Putteeala and his wife were again at variance regarding a settlement for her son ; Runjeet Sing was called in, and crossed the Sutlege a second time. He decreed an allowance of 50,000 rupees a-year to the boy, and received as a token of gratitude a valuable diamond necklace, and, what he valued still more, a celebrated brass gun. On his way home, he levied contributions on some of the petty chiefs, seized their forts and lands, and carried off all their cannon to augment his own artillery, which

was at this time the great object of his desire. These successive inroads filled the Sikh chiefs of Sirhind with alarm, and a
formal deputation proceeded to Delhi, in March, 1808, to implore the protection of the British Government, whose vassals,
they said, they had always considered themselves since the
extinction of Sindia's power; but the encouragement they
received was not so decisive as they expected. Runjeet Sing,
anxious to discover the views of the British Government in
reference to this appeal, addressed a letter to the Governor-
General, stating his wish to remain on friendly terms with the
Company, but adding, "the country on this side the Jumna,
excepting the stations occupied by the English, is subject to my
authority; let it remain so." This bold demand of the province
of Sirhind by Runjeet Sing, as a matter of right, brought
directly before Lord Minto, the important question whether,
in obedience to the non-interference policy of the Court of
Directors, an energetic and aspiring chief, who had, in the
course of ten years, erected a large kingdom upon the ruin
of a dozen princes, should be allowed to plant his army, composed of the finest soldiery in India, within a few miles of our
own frontier. The solution of this point could not brook
delay; there was no time for consulting the Court, and Lord
Minto boldly determined to take on himself the responsibility
of extending British protection to the Sikh chiefs, and shutting
up Runjeet Sing in the Punjab.

Forogn Alli-
ance, 1808.   It had been the policy of the Court of Directors
for many years to discourage all alliances with the
princes of India, but, at this juncture, they were driven by the
irresistible current of circumstances to seek alliances beyond
its frontier, for the protection of their interests. The treaty
of Tilsit, concluded between the emperor of Russia and Napoleon, was supposed to include certain secret articles which had
reference to extensive schemes of conquest in the east. More
especially was it believed to provide facilities for the gratification of Napoleon's views on the British power in India. To
anticipate these designs, it was resolved to block up his path

to India by endeavouring to contract defensive alliances with
the princes whose territories lay on the route, and to dispatch
missions to Persia, Afghanistan, and Lahore.
Mr. Charles Metcalfe, a young civilian, who had
been trained up in the school of Lord Wellesley,
and, indeed, under his own eye, was selected for the Punjab
embassy. The task assigned him was one of no ordinary
difficulty: on the one hand, he was to frustrate Runjeet Sing's
favourite project of extending his dominion across the Sutlege,
on the other, to conciliate his co-operation in opposing the
approach of a French army from the west. Runjeet Sing
received the mission with coldness and suspicion. His personal bearing towards the envoy was discourteous, all intercourse between the camps was interdicted, supplies were
refused, and the bankers were incited to refuse to cash his
bills, while his messengers were waylaid and his letters
opened. But he was resolved to allow no hostile conduct on
the part of Runjeet Sing to damp his ardour, or turn him
aside from his object. When at length he had obtained an
opportunity of explaining the object of his mission, the Sikh
cabinet intimated that the alliance appeared to be one in which
the British rather than the Punjab Government was interested, and that as it was intended to benefit the Company, it
ought also to include some advantage for the Punjab. They
did not object to the proposed treaty, but it must recognise
the sovereignty of Runjeet Sing over all the Sikh states on both
sides the Sutlege. Mr. Metcalfe replied that he had no instructions to make this concession; but, while the negotiation was
in progress, Runjeet Sing broke up his encampment at Kusoor,
and crossed the Sutlege a third time, and for three months
swept through the districts of Sirhind, plundering the chiefs
and compelling them, with the exception only of Putteeala and
Thanesur, to acknowledge his authority. The British mission
was dragged in his train, but Mr. Metcalfe felt that his presence seemed to give countenance to these aggressions, as
Runjeet Sing intended it should, and after proceeding several

(margin note) Embassy to Runjeet Sing, 1808.

stages, refused to advance farther, and eventually encamped at Umritsir, to await the return of the Lahore ruler.

Runject ordered Lord Minto, finding Runject Sing still bent on to retire, 1808. the subjugation of Sirhind, determined to lose no further time in arresting his progress, if necessary, by force of arms. By this time, moreover, Napoleon was entangled in the affairs of Spain, and the idea of an invasion of India, if it had ever ripened into a design, was abandoned. All anxiety for these foreign alliances was removed, and Lord Minto, having no longer anything to ask of Runject Sing, was enabled to assume a higher and more authoritative tone. The Commander-in-chief, then in the north-west, was directed to hold an army in readiness to march down to the Sutlege, and a letter was addressed to Runjeet Sing, telling him in firm and dignified language that by the issue of the war with the Mahrattas, the Company had succeeded to the power and the rights they had exercised in the north of Hindostan. The Sikh states of Sirhind were now, therefore, under the protection of the British Government, and would be maintained in all their integrity; the Maharaja must consequently restore all the districts of which he had taken possession during his late incursion, and confine his military operations in future to the right bank of the .Sutlege. Runjeet Sing, on the termination of his expedition to Sirhind, hastened back to Umritsir to exchange the toils of the camp for the enjoyments of the harem. Like Hyder Ali, he was the slave of sensual indulgence when his mind was not absorbed in the excitement of war. On the evening of his arrival, Mr. Metcalfe waited on him to present the letter of the Governor-General, but he exclaimed that " the evening was to be devoted to mirth and pleasure," and called for the dancing girls, and then for the strong potations to which he was accustomed, and before midnight was totally incapacitated for business. The communication from Calcutta remained for several days without acknowledgment, and, as it afterwards appeared, even without perusal. On the 12th December, Mr. Metcalfe transmitted him a note, repeating the statements contained in the Governor-General's letter, pressing the demands of Government on his attention, and pointing out the danger of refusing to accede to them, stating, however, that the British Government was anxious to maintain the most amicable relations with him. This letter, which seems to have given him the first monition of the hazard he was incurring of a serious collision with British power, staggered his mind, and brought him to reflection. Other perils had also beset him. At Umritsir, his favourite Mahomedan mistress had caused a Hindoo to be circumcised. ·That holy city, the Benares of. the Punjab, was thrown into a state of religious frenzy; all the shops were closed, and the priests threatened to excommunicate any who should venture to open them. Runjeet Sing, terrified by this storm of fanaticism, escaped to Lahore, but was pursued by the devotees and brahmins, who sat *dhurna* at his palace gate. This practice consisted in sitting night and day, fasting and praying, at the gate of the victim, till the demand was granted. If persisted in, it might involve the death of a brahmin, and it was therefore generally successful. So effective is this mode of intimidation, that it has been found necessary to prohibit it, under severe penalties by a special Regulation.

Mr. Metcalfe's firmness, 1809. Runjeet Sing contrived to pacify the priesthood and laity of Umritsir, but continued from day to day to evade any explanation with Mr. Metcalfe, who peremptorily demanded an audience on the 22nd December, and announced to him that a British force was on the point of advancing to the Sutlege, which would sweep his garrisons from Sirhind. He bore the communication for some moments with apparent composure, but· unable, at length, to control his feelings any longer, rushed out of the room, mounted his horse, and galloped about the courtyard for some time with frantic vehemence, followed by his body guard, while his ministers continued the conference with Mr. Metcalfe. It would be tedious to detail the various interviews which took place between them and Mr. Metcalfe for two months, or the constant

attempts which ,were made to overbear or to overreach him, or
the endless postponements and delays of this oriental court.
Mr. Metcalfe was proof against all cajolery, and continued with
invincible firmness to insist on the restoration of all the conquests
which Runjeet Sing had made on his late incursion. It was a
bitter pill for him to swallow, but he was constrained in the
end to submit. In all the range of British Indian history
there are few incidents to be found more remarkable than the
arrest of this young and haughty prince, in the full career of
ambition and victory, by the mandate of a youth of twenty-
four. Runject's lingering reluctance to relinquish his conquests was effectually .removed by the arrival of Colonel
Ochterlony with a British army on the banks of the Sutlege,
and the issue of a proclamation declaring the states lying
between that river and the Jumna under British protection.

Treaty with   On the 25th April, 1809, a treaty was concluded
Runjeet, 1809.   at Umritsir to " establish perpetual amity between
the British Government and the State of Lahore." It provided
that the British Government should have no concern with the
territories and subjects of the raja north of the Sutlege; and
that the raja should not commit any encroachments, or suffer
any to be committed on the possessions or rights of the chiefs
under British protection south of it. The treaty, which con-
sists of only fifteen lines, is one of the shortest on our records, and
is, perhaps, the only one which was never infringed. Runject
Sing subsequently became the most formidable native power
in India, and organised an army under European officers,
which, after his decease, shook the British empire to its
foundation, but for thirty years, up to the period of his death,
he maintained the " perpetual amity " with scrupulous fidelity.
Colonel Ochterlony, on withdrawing the army from the province left a garrison in Loodiana, and that fort became our
frontier station in the north-west; and thus the British
standard, which Lord Wellesley had planted on the Jumna,
was six years after erected by Lord Minto on the banks of
the Sutlege.

Embassy to   The embassy sent to Cabul to form a defensive
Cabul, 1808.   alliance against a French invasion, was fitted out
on a scale of magnificence intended to impress the Afghans
with·an idea of the power and majesty of the Company, and
it was entrusted to Mr. Mount Stuart Elphinstone, one of the
Wellesley school of Indian statesmen. The ruler of Afghanistan, Shah Soojah, the brother of Zemaun Shah, held his court
at Peshawur, which the envoy reached on the 5th March, 1809.
His reception was marked with the greatest courtesy, but the
ministers did not fail to observe that the object of the mission
was to promote the interests of the Company rather than those
of Afghanistan. They had nothing to dread from the arrival
of the French, and desired to know what benefit the Governor-
General intended to bestow on them for preventing the passage
of a French army through their passes; they were anxious, moreover, to ascertain what arguments or allurements the French
had to offer, before they committed themselves. It appears
unaccountable that the members of the Supreme Council in
Calcutta, thoroughly acquainted as they were with the oriental
character, should have fitted out a costly and pompous embassy
to a native court to solicit an alliance, without proposing any
reciprocal benefit. But, while the negociations were pending,
the expedition which Shah Soojah had imprudently sent to
Cashmere to regain possession of that province, was entirely
defeated. His brother Mahmood took advantage of this
disaster to seize Cabul and Candahar, and to threaten Peshawur. Shah Soojah,· whose army was annihilated, and whose
treasury was empty, earnestly solicited pecuniary aid from the
British Government, and Mr. Elphinstone strongly recommended a grant of ten lacs of rupees. As all Afghan soldiers
are mercenaries, this sum would have brought a sufficient
number of adherents to his standard to restore and consolidate
his power. But the dread of a French invasion had died out,
and it was no longer deemed important to conciliate the ruler
who held the "gate of India," as Cabul was then deemed.
The request was refused, and the embassy recalled. It is no

improbable conclusion that if this aid of ten lacs of rupees had been granted to Shah Soojah in this emergency, and he had thereby been enabled to maintain himself in Afghanistan, the Company would have been spared the fifteen hundred lacs of rupees which were wasted, thirty years after, in the abortive attempt to restore him permanently to his throne, and enable him to keep the "gate" shut against the Russians, who were supposed to be knocking at it. Shah Soojah, however, gave his consent to a treaty stipulating that any attempt of the French to advance through Afghanistan should be opposed, at the cost of the Company's treasury; but when it arrived with the ratification of the Governor-General on the 9th June, 1810, there was neither king nor ambassador to receive it. Shah Soojah was totally defeated by his rival, and fled across the Indus, and Mr. Elphinstone was returning to Hindostan; and of this expensive embassy there remained no other result but the noble history of it compiled by the envoy, which gave Europe the first authentic description of the region rendered memorable by the achievements of Alexander the Great.

Affairs of Persia, 1808.   The third embassy to counteract the supposed projects of Napoleon was sent to the court of Persia. At the commencement of 1806, the king of Persia wantonly involved himself in a war with Russia, which proved highly disastrous, and ended in depriving him of several of his valuable provinces. In his exigency he applied to the government of Calcutta, and, on the strength of the treaty concluded by Colonel Malcolm in 1800, demanded aid against the encroachments of Russia. But England was in alliance with the emperor, and the assistance was necessarily refused, on which the king made application to Napoleon, who eagerly embraced the proposal, and sent General Gardanne as his envoy

French embassy, 1807.   to Tehran, which he reached in December, 1807, with a large military suite. He was also accompanied by a body of engineer and artillery officers, some of whom were dispersed over the country, to investigate its resources and to make professional surveys, while others were employed in drilling the Persian levies, and introducing the system of European tactics and discipline. A treaty was speedily concluded, which provided that the Emperor should regain from Russia, and restore to Persia, Georgia and other frontier provinces which had been alienated; that any French army marching through Persia towards India should be supplied with provisions and joined by a Persian force; that the island of Karrack should be ceded to France; and that, if the emperor desired it, all Englishmen should be excluded from the king's dominions. The English Ministry, who considered the French embassy the advanced guard of a French army, determined to counteract these hostile designs, and to plant an ambassador at Teheran as the representative of the Crown, the Company, however, bearing all the expense of the mission. Sir Arthur Wellesley and Lord Minto, before he left England, earnestly recommended Colonel Malcolm for this duty, for which he was preeminently qualified by his skill in oriental diplomacy, his knowledge of the Asiatic character, and, more, especially, by the popularity he had formerly acquired at the Persian court. But the Court of Directors could not forget the lavish expenditure of his mission in 1800, amounting to seventeen lacs of rupees, and there were little minds among them who could not forgive his being a disciple of Lord Wellesley.

Sir Harford Jones's mission to Persia, 1807. Mr. Harford Jones, who had resided forty years at Bushire, first as a merchant, and then as the British consul, was selected for the post, created a baronet, and directed to proceed to Persia by way of Petersburg, where he was to concert measures of co-operation with the emperor of Russia. Meanwhile, came the defeat of the Russians at Friedland, the peace of Tilsit, and the alliance of the two emperors. Sir Harford was therefore directed to proceed direct to Bombay, where he arrived in April, 1808.

Col. Malcolm's mission and its failure, 1808. This appointment was made by the Ministry of which Lord Minto was a member, and while he himself presided at the Board of Control. He was not ignorant that after the despatch of a French minister by the emperor Napoleon, the Cabinet considered it necessary, that the British minister should appear at the Persian court as the representative of the Crown, and not of the Company. But, on his arrival in Calcutta, Lord Minto considered that " the separation which there was reason to apprehend between Great Britain and Russia" released him from the restrictions' thus imposed on him by the policy which the Cabinet had adopted regarding the Persian, mission. He resolved therefore to despatch Colonel Malcolm to the court of Persia to repre-sent the Indian Government, and directed Sir Harford Jones to remain at Bombay till the result of the, new mission could be known. On landing in Persia, Colonel Malcolm determined to approach the throne " with the language, not of supplication, but of temperate remonstrance and offended friendship." For-getting that the influence of the French at Teheran was supreme, and that they were feeding the king with hopes of deliverance from the grasp of Russia, presuming, also, on the ascendency he had acquired in his former mission, Colonel Malcolm assumed a dictatorial tone in his communications with the court. He despatched one of his assistants to the capital, but on his arrival at Shiraz he was forbidden to advance farther, and Colonel Malcolm was directed to place himself in commu-nication with the viceroy of the province, the king's son. Considering the authority then exercised by the French embassy at the Persian court, the king might have been expected to order the English minister peremptorily to quit his dominions, rather than permit him to enter into negotiations with his son. But Colonel Malcolm, instead of making any allowance for the king's position, or waiting for a turn in the tide of events, took umbrage at this message, precipitately abandoned the mission, and embarked with his suite for Cal-cutta. The intelligence of this disappointment reached Lord Minto on the 12th August, and he immediately wrote to Sir Harford Jones, removing the interdict on his movements, and leaving him at liberty to prosecute the mission which the Crown had entrusted to him.

Military expedi-
tion to Persia,
August, 1808. Ten days after the despatch of this letter, Colonel Malcolm landed in Calcutta, breathing vengeance against the Persian court for the fancied indignity inflicted on him. He readily persuaded Lord Minto and the Council that the only effectual mode of defeating the influence, or, as he called it, the intrigue, of the French at Teheran, was to make a military demonstration. Arrangements were immediately made for the despatch of a large force under the direction of Colonel Malcolm, to the Persian coast to occupy Karrack, an island in the Persian Gulf, thirty-three miles from the port of Bushire, which, in the glowing anticipations of Colonel Malcolm, was to become the emporium of commerce—though it contained no port— the seat of political negotiations, and the pivot from which we were to overawe Persia, Arabia, and Turkey. At the same time, a second letter was sent to Sir Harford Jones, dated seventeen days after the first, forbidding him to quit . Bombay, but he had embarked for Persia two days before it arrived. Lord Minto then despatched a third letter to him in Persia, announcing the military expedition, and commanding him to return forthwith to India. This communication did not, however, reach him before he had commenced negotiations with the Persian ministers at Shiraz, and their minds were filled with such indignation and alarm, on learning its con- tents, that Sir Harford deemed it necessary to appease them by assuming, as the representative of the Crown, an authority independent of the Governor-General, and giving them the solemn pledge that no aggression whatever should be com- mitted on the Persian territories, as long as the king mani- fested a disposition to cultivate friendly relations with England. He then prosecuted his journey to the capital which he reached in February, 1809. As soon as the report of these transactions reached Calcutta, Lord Minto addressed a letter to the king of Persia, disavowing the authority and

the proceeding's of Sir Harford ; and he likewise directed the
envoy peremptorily to leave the country, threatening to, dishonour his bills if he disobeyed the order. But in the meantime the object of the mission had been successfully accomplished. The union of interests which had been established
between Russia and France deprived the Persian monarch of
all hope of any aid from Napoleon for the recovery of the provinces he had lost. The proposals of the British
minister were readily accepted ; the French embassy was dismissed, the Persian envoy at Paris
was recalled, and a Persian ambassador was sent to London
in company with Mr. Morier. A preliminary treaty was concluded, the salient points of which were that any treaty made
with other European powers should be considered as void,
that no force commanded by Europeans should be permitted
to march through Persia towards India, and that if any
European army invaded the Persian territory, the British
Government should afford the aid of a military force, or, in
lieu of it, a subsidy, which, after long discussions, was
eventually fixed at twelve lacs of rupees a-year. Lord Minto
felt that Sir Harford had authentic credentials for his mission,
and that the national faith was pledged by his engagements ;
the treaty was accordingly ratified by the Government of
India. The unwise project of a military expedition adopted
under the influence of Colonel Malcolm's irritated feelings,
and which, if it had been carried out, would have entailed an
intolerable expenditure, and wounded the pride of the king
and his people, was discreetly abandoned. The Persian mission was thus brought to a conclusion, and Colonel Malcolm
returned to Madras.

Sir Harford Jones's treaty, 1810.

Lord Minto, however, felt that the rank and
estimation of the Government of India had been
compromised, within the sphere of its influence,
by the mission of Sir Harford Jones from the Crown, and
that it was necessary to restore it to the eminence it had
previously enjoyed. He considered it among the first of

Second mission of Colonel Malcolm; 1809.

II.   R his duties "to transmit to his successor the powers, prerogatives, and dignities of the Indian empire, in its relations with surrounding nations, as entire and unsullied as they were confided to his hands." Under this impression he entreated Colonel Malcolm "to go and lift the Company's Government once more to its own height, and to the station that belonged to it." Another embassy was fitted out in the most costly style to eclipse that of the Crown, with no other object than to establish the prestige of the East India Company in Asia, which the Crown was deemed to have impaired by taking the conduct of Persian diplomacy into its own hands. It was a most extraordinary mission for a most extraordinary purpose. Colonel Malcolm, whose genial humour and princely presents had made a very agreeable impression on the court eight years before, was welcomed with enthusiasm as he passed through the country to the royal presence. But in that presence was the ambassador of the Crown, whom the Government of India had thought fit to treat with the greatest contumely, disavowing his authority, dishonouring his bills, and sparing no pains to "blacken his face in the eyes of the Persian court." If he manifested any personal feeling at the unworthy treatment he had received, there are few who will not be prepared to condone it; and no one with a touch of loyal sentiment will censure him for the effort he made, at this difficult crisis, to uphold the dignity of the sovereign he was deputed to represent, against the pretensions of one who was only the delegate of an inferior authority, and who had no business at all at Teheran. There was every prospect of an unseemly and dangerous collision. The Persian courtiers were by no means distressed to find two rival ambassadors of the same nation contending for their favours, and they were preparing to play off the one against the other, in the hope of a golden shower of presents. But the good sense of Sir Harford and Colonel Malcolm gradually smoothed down all asperities, and it was not long before they agreed to unite their efforts to baffle the intrigues and the cupidity of the court. Colonel

Malcolm was received with open arms by the king, who considered him the first of Englishmen. "What induced you," said he at the first interview, "to hasten away from Shiraz, without seeing my son?" "How could I," replied the Colonel, with his ever ready tact, "after having been warmed with the sunshine of your majesty's favour, be satisfied with the mere reflection of that refulgence in the person of your son?" "Mahsalla!" exclaimed the monarch, "Malcolm sahib is himself again." But this agreeable communion was speedily interrupted by despatches from England, announcing the determination of the Ministry to supersede both Sir Harford Jones and Colonel Malcolm by an ambassador from England. Sir Gore Ouseley had acquired the confidence of Lord Wellesley by the great talents he exhibited when in a private station at the court of Lucknow, and upon his recommendation was appointed to Teheran as the representative of the king of England. The relations with the Persian court have from that period been retained by the ministers of the Crown in their own hands—a measure, which if judged by its general results, has not been successful, except, perhaps, when they have selected officers from the Indian service for the post. To manifest his esteem for Colonel Malcolm, the king instituted a new order of knighthood, that of the Lion and the Sun, and bestowed the first decoration on him. His mission, which cost twenty-two lacs of rupees, was beneficial only in. developing the talents of. the able assistants who accompanied him, Pottinger, Ellis, Briggs, Lindsay, and Macdonald, all of whom rose to distinction. The expenses of Sir Harford Jones were also imposed on the Company's treasury, and the two embassies did not cost them less than thirty-eight lacs.

Ameer Khan's attack on Nag- poro, 1809. To return to events in India. It has been already noted that Lord Minto had felt it necessary to repudiate the policy of non-interference in the case of the Sikh chiefs of Sirhind, and to take them under the protection of the British Government against the encroachments of Runjeet Sing. Within four months of the signature

R 2

of the treaty with that prince, another occasion arose to test
the propriety of maintaining this principle.   In 1809, the
adventurer Ameer Khan had reached the zenith of his power.
In the course of ten years he had gradually created a principality, which yielded a revenue of about fifteen lacs of rupees
a-year.   He was the recognised chief of the Patans, who had
for several centuries played an important part in the revolutions of Hindostan, and his adherents were anxiously looking
forward to the fulfilment of the prediction of a holy mendi-
cant that he was destined to found a new Patan dynasty at
Delhi.   But he had not the genius of Sevajee, or Hyder, or
Runjeet Sing, or indeed any aspirations beyond those of a
predatory chief.   His army was too great for his resources,
and, having drained the chiefs of Rajpootana, he was obliged
to seek for plunder in more remote provinces.   He determined
to select the raja of Nagpore for his victim, and a pretext was
not long to seek.   Holkar, for whom he professed to act during
his insanity, had been despoiled, as he stated, of some valuable
jewels twelve years before, when, on seeking refuge with the
raja, he was thrown into confinement at the instigation of
Sindia.   These jewels were now claimed, but the raja treated
the demand with the contempt it deserved.   Ameer Khan was,
however, resolved to enforce it, and poured down across the
Nerbudda with an army of 40,000 horse and 24,000 Pindarees, and on his march to Nagpore sacked the town of Jub-
bulpore.   The raja was only an ally of the Company, and not
entitled to claim its protection, but Lord Minto did not hesitate to affirm that " there could be but one solution of the question, whether an interfering and ambitious Mussulman chief, at
the head of a numerous army, irresistible by any power except
that of the Company, should be permitted to establish his authority on the ruins of the raja's dominions, over territories contigu-
ous to those of the Nizam—likewise a Mahomedan—with whom
projects might be formed . . . inimical to our interests."   The
raja had not so much as solicited our aid, though he was happy
to welcome it when he found that he was not expected to pay

for it, but two armies were ordered into the field for the defence of his territories, from which Ameer Khan was required to withdraw. In the name of Holkar he protested against the injustice of this interference, and appealed to the treaty concluded by Sir George Barlow, which bound the British Government not to interfere in his affairs. The argument might be unanswerable, but it no longer carried any weight.

Defeat of Ameer Khan, 1809.
But while the British troops were on their march, Sadik Ali, the commander of the Nagpore army, repulsed Ameer Khan and obliged him to retreat to Bhopal. There he recruited his force, and re-assembled the Pindarees, whom he had been obliged to dismiss during the rains, and advanced into the Nagpore territories, but was a second time defeated by the troops of the raja, a considerable body of whom is said to have consisted of Sikhs. He returned a third time to the conflict, and blockaded the Nagpore army in Chouragur, while his Pindarees spread desolation through the surrounding districts. But the British divisions were now closing upon him, and, under the pretence of an earnest request for his services by Toolsee-bye, the regent of the Holkar state, he withdrew with his army to Indore. Colonel Close took possession of his capital and his territories, and the extinction of his power appeared inevitable, when the British troops were unexpectedly recalled. He was allowed to recover his strength, and Central India was left for seven years longer at his mercy, because Lord Minto was apprehensive that the further prosecution of hostilities, after Nagpore had been effectually protected from his aggressions, might lead to complications displeasing to the Court of Directors. But the tide was beginning to turn at the India House against this neutral policy. In reviewing these transactions, the Court of Directors expressed

New policy at the India House, 1811.
their approbation of the conduct of Lord Minto, but veiled it under the sophism that " as it was a measure of defensive policy, it could not be deemed a violation of the law, or a disobedience of the orders prohibiting interference in the disputes of foreign states ;" as if interference for

the protection of Jeypore and Boondee did not equally come within the category of a "defensive policy." The Court went further, and questioned the propriety of the moderation which Lord Minto had exhibited towards Ameer Khan. "We are not satisfied," they said, "with the expediency of abstaining from disabling any power against whom we may have been compelled to take up arms from renewing his aggressions;" at the same time, they strongly advised the conclusion of a subsidiary treaty with the raja of Nagpore, though it would have involved the necessity of protecting him against all opponents, and extended the circle of those defensive alliances which had been reprobated six years before. But when this despatch reached Calcutta Lord Minto was in Java, and when he returned he found himself superseded in the Government.

Sir George Barlow at Madras, 1807—10. Sir George Barlow, who had been appointed to succeed Lord William Bentinck in the Government of Madras, proceeded to that Presidency on the arrival of Lord Minto. During the twenty months in which he filled the office of Governor-General he had disgusted society by his cold and repulsive manners, and the absence of all genial and generous feeling in the intercourse of life. He was never able to obtain that deference and respect, or to exercise that personal influence which is so important to the efficient administration of public affairs. The duties of retrenchment, at all times invidious, which devolved on him, were performed in the most ungracious manner. He manifested on all occasions a lofty sense of his official dignity, and exacted a stern and implicit obedience to his will. But that which was regarded in the case of Lord Wellesley as the natural absolutism of a great mind, was in Sir George Barlow resented as the vulgar despotism of power. The feeling of personal aversion which pervaded the community was heightened by a contempt of his abilities. At Madras, he became unpopular by isolating himself in a small circle of officials and confidants, and his administration has been described, and not unjustly, as a "season of unprecedented private misery, and unexampled peril and alarm."

Case of
Mr. Sherson,
1808.
The first occasion of offence arose from his unjust proceedings against Mr. Sherson, a civil servant deservedly held in high estimation. He was superintendent of the stores of rice laid in by the Government of Madras against the periodical famines on that coast. A charge of fraud had been brought against him, which was under investigation when Sir George Barlow entered on the Government. His accounts were submitted to the scrutiny of the civil auditor and pronounced correct, but as they did not happen to tally with the native accounts kept in the office, the new Governor removed both the auditor and Mr. Sherson from their situations. A prosecution was likewise commenced against Mr. Sherson in the Supreme Court, which ended in his honourable acquittal. The Court of Directors condemned these proceedings without reserve, restored Mr. Sherson to the service, and compensated him for his loss by a donation of 70,000 rupees.

The Carnatic
Commission,
1808.
Sir George Barlow incurred still greater obloquy by his proceedings in reference to the Carnatic Commission, appointed by Act of Parliament to investigate the debts of the nabob, for which the Company became responsible when they took over the Carnatic. The claims on the nabob amounted to the gigantic sum of thirty crores of rupees, of which the validity of less than a tenth was eventually substantiated. But the bonds were considered negotiable securities, and many of them, though originally fraudulent, had been honestly purchased, and the whole community of Madras, not excepting the officers of Government, was deeply interested in the enquiry. To secure impartiality, the Commissioners were selected from the Bengal Civil Service, and they had just opened their court when Sir George Barlow took his seat at the Council board. They appointed one Reddy Rao, who had been an accountant in the finance office of the late nabob, as their confidential adviser. A bond which he held came up for examination; its validity was impeached by a native, named Papia, but the Commissioners pronounced it genuine, and resolved to prosecute Papia's witnesses for

perjury. He anticipated this movement by charging Reddy Rao before a magistrate with forgery, and he was committed for trial. The Commissioners appealed to the Governor for support, and he ordered the Advocate-General to defend the case. The legitimacy of such a proceeding cannot be controverted; but the mere appearance of a public officer, in his official capacity, in connection with the investigation of claims which Government was interested in disallowing, created a feeling of indignation and dismay among the creditors, European and native, inasmuch as it could scarcely fail to deter timid natives from coming forward to give evidence. This feeling was intensely aggravated when the Governor, in a spirit which was considered vindictive, dismissed the magistrate who had committed Reddy Rao, expelled from the country Mr. Parry, a merchant, who had manifested opposition to the Commissioners, and banished Mr. Roebuck, a civilian of long standing, for his share in the proceedings, to a remote post of inferior rank and emolument, where he died soon after. Three actions were brought in the Supreme Court in reference to this transaction; and Reddy Rao was, convicted by the jury of forgery, but recommended to the favourable notice of the Crown by the judge of the Supreme Court, on the ground of his innocence. He received a pardon, as a matter of course, but before it could reach India he had terminated his existence by swallowing poison; and it was discovered after his death that the bond was spurious, and that he was deeply implicated in all the villanies of the Carnatic bonds.

The Madras Mutiny, 1809.   These undignified proceedings affected the reputation and the strength of the Madras Government, but the mutiny of the European officers of the army which was to be attributed in a great measure to the same violent and arbitrary spirit, threatened its very existence. Thrice in the course of less than half a century had the Company's Government been shaken to its foundation by the sedition of its European officers. The mutiny of 1765 was overcome by the undaunted firmness of Lord Clive. That of 1796 and

'97 was fostered by the feebleness of Sir John Shore, and extinguished by the simple mandate of Lord Wellesley, who, seeing a number of malcontent commanders congregated at his first levée, peremptorily ordered them to rejoin their regiments within twenty-four hours. The glance of his very remarkable eye had, it was said, quenched the mutiny. In the present instance a feeling of dissatisfaction had been for some time fermenting in the Madras army, and not without cause. There was an invidious distinction between the pay of the European officers in Bengal and Madras, and all posts of command and dignity were monopolised by the officers of the royal army. This spirit of discontent was unhappily promoted rather than repressed by the demeanour of the Commander-in-chief. A seat in council, with an additional allowance, had always been attached to the office, but on the dismissal of Sir John Cradock after the Vellore mutiny, the Court of Directors had refused it to his successor, on some technical ground, and filled up the vacancy with a civilian. The General considered this a personal grievance and affront, and he did not care to conceal the exasperation of his feelings from the officers of the army, who were the more disposed to sympathise with him as they were thereby deprived of a representative of their interests at the Council board. Since the close of the Mahratta war the

Abolition of
the tent contract, 1809.

Court of Directors had been fierce for retrenchment, and had threatened "to take the pruning-knife into their own hands," if they found any hesitation on the part of the Madras Government to use it. Among the plans suggested for · reducing the military charges was the abolition of the tent contract, which furnished the officers in command of regiments with a fixed monthly allowance to provide the men with camp equipage, whether they were in the field or in cantonments. The system was essentially vicious, but not more so than all the other devices in the King's and Company's army for eking out the allowances of commanding officers by anomalous perquisites. The Quartermaster-general, Colonel John Munro, had been requested to draw up a report

on the subject, and both Sir John Cradock and Lord William
Bentinck had come to the determination to abolish the contract,
when they were suddenly recalled. It fell to the unhappy lot
of Sir George Barlow, already sufficiently unpopular, to carry
this resolution into effect.

Charges against   This retrenchment increased the resentment
Col. Munro,   of the officers, and they determined to wreak
1809.
their vengeance on the Quartermaster-general,
who had stated in his report that the result of granting the
same allowance in peace and in war for the tentage of the
native regiments, while the expenses incidental to it varied
with circumstances, had been found, by experience, to place
the interest and the duty of commanding officers in opposition
to each other. This was a harmless truism, but when the
body is in a state of inflammation, the least puncture will
fester. The officers called on the Commander-in-chief, to
bring Colonel Munro to a court-martial, for aspersions on their
character as officers and gentlemen. The Judge Advocate-
general, to whom the question was officially referred, considered that the officers had neither right nor reason on their
side ; but General Macdowall, then on the eve of retiring from
the service, yielded to their wishes, and at once placed him
under arrest. He appealed to the Governor in Council, under
whose authority he had acted, and the Commander-in-chief
was ordered to release him. With this mandate he was
constrained to comply, but he gave vent to his feelings in a
general order of extraordinary violence, in which he protested
against the interference of the Government, and stated that
nothing but his approaching departure for Europe prevented
his bringing Colonel Munro to trial for disrespect to the Commander-in-chief, and contempt of military authority, in having
resorted to the power of the civil government in defiance of
the judgment of the officer at the head of the army. Colonel
Munro's conduct was likewise stigmatised as destructive of
military subordination, a violation of the sacred rights of the
Commander-in-chief, and a dangerous example to the service.

Sir George Barlow had up to this point acted with great forbearance and dignity, but he now lost his balance, and, instead
of treating the order with contempt as an ebullition of passion
from an intemperate officer, who was already on board the
vessel which· was to convey him to Europe, or directing it to
be erased from the order-book of each regiment, issued a
counter order, couched in language equally tempestuous and
objectionable, charging him with violent and inflammatory
proceedings and acts of outrage.   The resignation of the
service in India is always sent in by the last boat which leaves
the ship, and the officer thus enjoys the benefit of his pay and
allowances to the latest moment.   Sir George took advantage of the circumstance that the Commander-in-chief's
resignation had not been received, to inflict on him the indignity of deposition from his office.   He proceeded still further
to commit his Government by suspending Major Boles, the
deputy adjutant-general, who had signed the order.   The
Major pleaded, that by the rules of the service he was bound
to obey the orders of his superior officer, and that he had acted
in a ministerial capacity.   He had as unquestionable a right
to the same protection in this case as Sir George had considered Colonel Munro entitled to, when he was arraigned for
obeying the orders of the Governor in council, in reference to
the report on the tent contract.   The consequence of this
rash act was precisely what might have been expected in the
excited state of the army.   Major Boles was regarded as a
martyr, and addresses ·poured in upon him from every division and every station, commending his conduct, reprobating
the proceedings against him, and proposing to raise subscriptions to compensate the loss of his salary.

Sir George sus-
pends the
officers, 1809.   Three months passed on after the departure of
General Macdowall,—who was not destined to
reach home as the vessel foundered at sea,—and
the ferment created by these proceedings had begun to subside,
when Sir George blew the dying embers into a flame.   In the
height of the excitement a memorial had been drawn up to

the Governor-General, reciting the grievances of the Madras army, but all idea of transmitting it was dropped, as the agitation moderated. The reports which Sir George received from the officers commanding stations, relative to the feeling of their subordinates, was, as he acknowledged, very satisfactory; but, on the 1st of May, in a spirit of infatuation, he issued an order suspending four officers of rank and distinguished reputation, and removing eight others from their commands, on the ground of their having promoted the memorial, which had been clandestinely communicated to the Government. The whole army was immediately in a blaze of mutiny. The officers at Hyderabad were found to have taken no part in the memorial, and Sir George had the imprudence to compliment them officially for their fidelity, but they indignantly repudiated the distinction, and announced to the rest of the army their entire disapproval of the order of the 1st of May, and their resolution to make common cause in contributing to the support of the suspended officers. A hundred and fifty-eight officers of the Jaulna and Hyderabad divi-
Outburst of the sions, signed a flagitious address to Government,
Mutiny, 1809. demanding the repeal of the obnoxious order, and the restoration of the officers, in order "to prevent the horrors of civil war, and the ultimate loss of a large portion of the British possessions in India, and the dreadful blow it would inflict on the mother country." The Company's European regiment at Mausulipatam broke out into open mutiny, placed the commanding officer under arrest, and concerted a plan for joining the Jaulna and Hyderabad divisions and marching to Madras to seize on the Government.

Firmness of   Sir George Barlow had thus, by his want of tem-
Sir George   per and discretion, goaded the Madras army into
Barlow, 1810.   revolt, and brought on a portentous crisis. Colonel Malcolm, Colonel Montresor, and other officers of high standing and great experience, advised him to bend to the storm, and recal the obnoxious order of the 1st May. But while secretary to Government in Calcutta, he had seen the disastrous

effects of Sir John Shore's timidity in similar circumstances, and in the true spirit of Clive, he exhibited undaunted resolution in dealing with the mutiny, such as almost to make amends for the folly which had caused it. He resolved to vindicate the authority of Government at all hazards. He could command the resources of Bengal, Bombay, and Ceylon. The new Commander-in-chief, as well as the officers of high position and rank, were ready to support him. The King's regiments adhered firmly to their duty, and he determined, if necessary, to march the loyal portion of the army, against the disaffected. To test the feelings of the officers, he demanded the signature of all, without distinction, to a pledge to obey the orders, and support the authority of the Governor in council at Fort St. George, on pain of removal from their regiments to stations on the coast, though without the forfeiture of either rank or pay; but the majority of the officers, even . among the faithful, declined to affix their signatures to the pledge, and it is said to have been signed by less than a tenth of the whole body. The commanders of native regiments were likewise directed to assemble the sepoys and assure them that the discontent of the European officers was a personal affair, and that the Government had no intention to diminish the advantages which they enjoyed, but were rather anxious to improve them. This appeal to the native soldiery against their European officers was a hazardous policy, calculated to sap the foundations of military discipline. But the sepoys and their native officers resolved to remain faithful to their salt, and there was no collision except at the single station of Seringapatam, where the native regiments commanded by disaffected officers refused to submit, and were fired upon by the King's troops, and a hundred and fifty killed and wounded.

The energetic proceedings of Sir George Barlow
The mutiny quelled, 1810.   staggered the officers, and induced them to pause on the verge of a rebellion against the constituted authorities of their King and country, which must for ever have blasted their reputation and their prospects. Lord Minto had,

moreover, announced his intention of repairing forthwith to
Madras, and the general confidence which was felt in his
justice and moderation contributed to bring the officers round
to a sense of duty. The Hyderabad brigade, which had been
the foremost in the mutiny, was also the foremost in repent-
ance. On the 11th August, the officers addressed a penitent
letter to Lord Minto—not to Sir George Barlow—signed the
pledge, and advised their brother officers to follow their
example. The defection of the Hyderabad force from the
common cause broke the strength of the combination. The
Jaulna brigade, which had made two marches towards Hyderabad, returned to its cantonments and submitted to Government.
On the 16th, the European regiment at Mausulipatam sent in
its adhesion to the test; the seditious garrison of Seringapatam
surrendered that fortress, and a profound calm succeeded the
storm which had so lately threatened to uproot the Government.
On reaching Madras, Lord Minto issued a general order reprobating the conduct of the mutineers, and announcing his determination to inflict punishment where it was due. But he also
expressed his anxiety for the character and welfare of the
Coast army, in kind and conciliatory language, which produced
the happiest impression on the minds of men who had been
accustomed only to the harsh and haughty communications of
Sir George Barlow. All the Hyderabad officers were pardoned
in consideration of the valuable example they had set to the
army. A general amnesty was granted to all but twenty-one
officers, of whom four were cashiered and one acquitted; the
others accepted the alternative of dismissal; but all who had
been cashiered or dismissed were subsequently restored to the
service. The mutiny was the subject of long and acrimonious
debates at the India House, which terminated, after many
protests, in the recal of Sir George Barlow, and he, whose
nomination to the office of Governor-General had been twice
cancelled, and who had enjoyed that honour provisionally for
a period of twenty months, was deposed from the inferior post
which had been conferred on him, and consigned to oblivion. It

Recal of Sir
George Barlow,
1811.
was in connection with the administration of Sir George Barlow and of Lord Minto, respectively, as Governors-General, that Mr. Edmonstone, who had served under both as public secretary, and who was one of the most eminent and sagacious of the Company's servants in India, and subsequently the Nestor of Leadenhall-street, affirmed that " he was averse to selecting Governors from among those who had belonged to the service . . . and that a person of eminence and distinction proceeding from England to fill that office, if duly qualified by talent and character, carried with him a greater degree of influence, and inspired more respect than an individual who had been known in a subordinate capacity."

Suppression of
piracy, 1809.
The suppression of piracy is the especial vocation of the British nation in the east, and the attention of Lord Minto was at this time imperatively called to the performance of this duty. On the Malabar coast, at no great distance from Bombay, the chiefs of Kolapore and Sawuntwaroe were required to surrender their piratical ports, and to enter into an engagement to renounce and to punish piracy, to which they had been addicted from time immemorial. A more important enterprize was the suppression of this crime on the coast of Arabia, known from the most ancient times as the pirate coast, where it was practised chiefly by the Joasmis. The Arabs were the bravest soldiers and the boldest seamen in the east. The Joasmis had recently embraced the tenets of the Mahomedan reformer Wahab, and thus added the ferocity of fanaticism to the courage of the national character. The only alternative which they offered to their captives was the profession of the faith of the prophet, or instant death. Their single-masted vessels, called dows or bugalas, ranging from 150 to 350 tons, and manned with 150 or 200 men, according to the size, carried only a few guns, but they sailed in company, and it was rarely that any native craft was able to escape their pursuit. They had long been the terror of native merchant sloops, but had wisely avoided molesting English vessels. At length they became emboldened by the inactivity

of the English cruisers, which were not authorized to interfere with them, and in 1808 attacked and captured the "Sylph," with Sir Harford Jones's native secretary on board. The next year the "Minerva," a large English merchantman, fell in with the pirate squadron, and after a running fight of two days was carried by boarding. The pirates brought all the Europeans, one by one, to the gangway, and cut their throats, with the pious ejaculation, Alla Akbar! Great is God! Lord Minto was resolved to exterminate the whole litter of pirates, and a large armament was sent against their chief stronghold, Ras-al-kaima, on the coast of Arabia. It was defended with Arab obstinacy and carried by British valour. The whole town, with all the valuable merchandize which had been accumulated in many piratical expeditions, and an entire fleet of bugalas was delivered to the flames. Several other towns of inferior note on the coast were attacked and captured, and in one of them four hundred Arabs perished before it was surrendered. The blow was effectual, and for the time piracy was suspended in these waters, but the inveterate habits, the boldness, and the fanaticism of these Arab corsairs, led at length to the revival of it with greater audacity, and to a more signal chastisement.

CHAPTER XXV.

ADMINISTRATION OF LORD MINTO, CONTINUED, 1809—1813.

Occupation of Macao, 1809.   IN the year 1809, an expedition upon a small scale was sent to the coast of China. The occupation of Portugal by Napoleon, and the flight of the Prince Regent to Brazil, induced the British Ministry to determine on taking possession of the Portuguese settlements in the east. Goa was occupied by a British detachment, and an armament was sent to Macao, in the vicinity of Canton, on the coast of

China, which the Portuguese had held for more than two
hundred years. The governor had no means of resistance, and
,the settlement was at once occupied by the expeditionary force.
But the imperial viceroy at Canton announced that the unlicensed entry of foreign soldiers into the Chinese territory
was a violation of the laws of the empire, and ordered them
to be immediately withdrawn. The admiral alleged that
Macao had been long since absolutely ceded to the Portuguese
by the Chinese Government, and that he had come as their
ally, simply to defend the settlement against the French. The
viceroy replied that Macao was in every respect an integral
portion of the empire, and that it was disrespectful as well as
absurd to imagine that the aid of the English was required to
defend any portion of the dominions of the celestial dynasty from
foreign aggression. Finding that the troops still continued at
Macao after his remonstrance, he put a stop to the trade of the
Company, and prohibited all supplies of provisions, while he
made a reference on the subject to Pekin. Expel the barbarians, was the short and simple reply of the emperor. Chinese
troops were accordingly collected, and preparations made for
an assault, when the naval and military commanders wisely
judged that their instructions would not justify them in violating the orders of the emperor in his own dominions, at the
risk of involving their country in a war with the Chinese.
The troops were therefore withdrawn, and the Chinese Government exhibited no less moderation after the evacuation
than firmness before it, and allowed the trade to be resumed
without requiring any indemnity.

Depredations   The injury inflicted on British commerce in the
from the Mauri- eastern seas by privateers fitted out at the French
tius, 1800—1809. islands has been noticed in a previous chapter.
Lord Wellesley, who was checked in his design to conquer
them, was obliged to content himself with pressing the great
importance of this object on the public authorities in England.
But, by an act of unaccountable folly, the Ministry not only
neglected to send an expedition against the Mauritius and

II.   S

Bourbon, although they considered it important to subjugate every French island in the West Indies, but positively interdicted any attempt on the part of the Indian Government to reduce them, though an adequate force might at any time have been fitted out in India without any expense to the English treasury. The French cruizers and privateers accordingly continued to prey on British trade, and to sweep the sea from Madagascar to Java. The naval squadron on the Indian station, consisting of six ships of the line, sixteen frigates, and six sloops, was unable to protect the national interests, and six vessels from Calcutta, valued at thirty lacs of rupees, had been captured by the French in the course of as many weeks. The losses which the merchants of Calcutta had sustained since the recommencement of the war were moderately estimated at two crores of rupees, a sum far in excess of any expenditure which the reduction of the islands could possibly have entailed. A memorial was at length transmitted by the merchants to the Ministry, complaining of the insecurity of commerce and the supineness of the royal navy. It produced a salutary effect, and the Governor-General and the naval Commander-in-chief received authority to adopt the most decisive measures for the protection of trade. It was determined at first to seek the accomplishment of this object by a blockade of the Mauritius, but it proved utterly inefficient. Six of the Company's magnificent Indiamen, valued at more than half a crore of rupees, were captured by French frigates, who sailed out of the port with perfect impunity, and returned in triumph with their prizes in the teeth of the blockading squadron.

Naval disasters, 1810.

Upon the failure of this plan, the Government resolved, in the first instance, to take possession of the lesser island of Bourbon, and it was captured with little loss in 1810. But this gallant achievement was counterbalanced by a series of naval disasters, which could be attributed only to ignorance and mismanagement. Three French frigates, returning from a successful cruize, found their way, in spite of the blockade, into the Grand port, on the south-eastern side of the

Mauritius. Four English frigates were sent to cut them out, but the French vessels, reinforced by seamen and sailors from the town, and supported by powerful batteries on shore, baffled every effort. Two of the English frigates, after a gallant but unavailing defence, were set on fire, and the third struck her flag when not a man was left unwounded. A fourth was surrounded by a superior force, and obliged to surrender when all her provisions were exhausted. Soon after, a fifth frigate was captured by the French fleet, which thus maintained the national honour in these seas as nobly as Suffrein had done twenty-eight years before. Meanwhile, Lord Minto *Capture of the Mauritius, Nov., 1810.* was assembling at the three Presidencies an armament of overwhelming strength for the conquest of the island. The naval expedition consisted of one seventy-four and thirteen frigates, besides sloops and gunboats. The land force contained no fewer than nine European regiments, numbering 6,300 bayonets, and 2,000 seamen and marines, together with four volunteer regiments of sepoys and Madras pioneers : in all, about 11,300 men. To meet this force, the French general could only muster 2,000 Europeans and a body of undisciplined African slaves. The English army disembarked at Grand Baye on the 29th November, and the next day marched towards <u>Port Louis</u>, the capital of the island. The French could expect to offer only a partial resistance to this overwhelming force, and the general, unwilling to sacrifice the lives of brave men in a hopeless contest, surrendered the island on fair and honourable terms.

Expedition to Java, 1811. The subjugation of Holland by Napoleon placed the Dutch settlements in the east under his control, and it was deemed important to the interests of British commerce to occupy them. An expedition was accordingly sent to the spice islands, in 1809, and the chief of the group, Amboyna, rendered memorable in the annals of the Company by the massacre of their agents in 1612, was occupied after a feeble resistance. Banda and Ternate were surrendered soon after, and of the great colonial empire which the Dutch had

s 2

been two centuries in erecting, nothing remained to them but the island of Java. Lord Minto had received the sanction of the Court of Directors to proceed against it, and had summoned to his counsels Mr., afterwards Sir Stamford, Raffles, a member of the Government of Penang, who had acquired a knowledge of the languages, the condition and the interests of the various tribes in the Eastern archipelago superior to that of any other European. No time was lost, after the reduction of the Mauritius, in fitting out an expedition for the conquest of the island, and Lord Minto determined to accompany it, though in the capacity of a volunteer. It consisted of ninety sail, on which were embarked about 6,000 European troops, and the same number of sepoys. It was the largest European armament which had ever traversed the eastern seas. Its departure was delayed by various causes, and it did not reach the rendezvous at Malacca before the 1st June, 1811. The monsoon had already set in, and both the usual routes to Java were deemed inexpedient, if not impracticable. Captain Greigh, the commander of a brig, strongly recommended the passage along the south-west coast of Borneo, which he had recently surveyed, in which the fleet would be sheltered from the fury of the monsoon, and assisted by the breezes from the land. This opinion was strongly supported by Mr. Raffles, and as strenuously opposed by the naval commanders. The question was referred to Lord Minto, who decided on adopting Captain Greigh's suggestion, instead of yielding to advice which would have obliged him to defer the attempt to the next year, and entailed boundless confusion, and a prodigious expenditure. He led the way in the "Modeste" frigate, commanded by his son; the whole fleet cleared the intricate channels without a single accident, and anchored in the bay of Batavia, on the 4th August.

Strength of the enemy, 1811. Since the occupation of the island by the French, Napoleon had been indefatigable in his efforts to complete its defences. He sent out large reinforcements, and munitions of war, and, above all, an officer in whom he had confidence, General Daendels, who levied heavy contributions, and paid little attention to the convenience of the colonists, in his anxiety to construct new and formidable works in the vicinity of the capital. The entire body of troops under his command was reckoned at 17,000, of whom 13,000 were concentrated for the defence of Fort Cornelis, eight miles inland from Batavia. The capital of the island was occupied without resistance, and the military post at Weltevreden, with its stores and ammunition, and three hundred pieces of cannon, was surrendered, after a sharp action, and the English force advanced against Cornelis. For some unexplained cause, General Daendels had been recalled, and his post given to General Jaensens, the officer who had surrendered the Cape of Good Hope to the English squadron four years before. The emperor, at his final audience, reminded him of this disaster, and said " Sir, remember that a French general does not allow himself to be captured a second time." Jaensens, after assuming the command, made the most strenuous efforts to render the position of Cornelis, which was strong by nature, impregnable by art, well knowing that as soon as the rains set in, the malaria of the Batavian marshes would constrain the English to raise the siege and retire. Cornelis was an entrenched camp between two rivers, one of which was not fordable, and the other was defended by formidable redoubts and batteries. The entire circumference of the camp was five miles, and it was protected by 300 pieces of cannon.

The British Commander-in-chief, Sir Samuel Ahmuty, decided at first to assail it by regular approaches, but the attempt was soon found to demand such laborious exertions as the men were unequal to under a tropical sun. It was resolved, therefore, to carry it by a *coup de main*, and this brought into play the daring spirit of Colonel Gellespie; of Vellore renown, to whom the enterprise was committed. His column marched soon after midnight on the 26th August, and came upon the redoubt as the day began to dawn. His rear division had not come up, but he felt that

The attack and capture of Cornelis, 1811.

the smallest delay would prove fatal to his plans, and he was confident that the missing troops would be made aware of his position and hasten to join him, by the report of the firing. The redoubt was immediately attacked, and carried at the point of the bayonet. Colonel Gellespie then took possession of the frail bridge, which the enemy had unaccountably left standing, and the demolition of which would have been a serious, if not fatal, impediment, and, with the aid of the rear division, which had by this time joined him, carried a second redoubt. The overwhelming impetuosity of his troops captured all the others in succession, till he found himself in the foreground of the enemy's reserve, and of a large body of cavalry, posted with powerful artillery in front of the barracks and lesser fort. They were vigorously attacked, chiefly by the 59th, and driven from their position, when the Colonel, placing himself at the head of the dragoons and horse artillery, pursued the fugitives for ten miles, and completed the defeat and disorganisation of the whole French army. Thus was Java won in a single morning, and by the efforts of a single officer. The loss of the French was severe, and 6,000 of their troops, chiefly Europeans, were made prisoners, but the victory cost the British 900 in killed and wounded, of whom 85 were officers. General Jacnsens retired to Samarang, with about 8,000 native soldiers, but after several skirmishes with the detachments sent in pursuit of him, he found that no dependence was to be placed on his Javanese and Malay sepoys, and, notwithstanding the warning of his master, was constrained to give himself up a second time, and surrender Java and all its dependencies.

Revolt of Native Chiefs, 1811.   Some of the native chiefs of the island manifested a disposition to take advantage of the confusion of the times to throw off the European yoke; and the Sultan of Djojekarta declared war against the English and called upon the Javanese to rise and recover their independence. Colonel Gellespie conducted a force against his capital, which was protected by a high rampart and batteries, mounted with a hundred pieces of cannon, and manned by 17,000 troops, independently of an armed population calculated at 100,000. It was carried by storm, and another wreath was added to the laurels of that gallant officer. The Court of Directors had granted their sanction to the expedition with no other object than to extinguish the power of the French, and to obtain security for their own ships and commerce in the eastern seas. Hence, they gave instructions that if it proved successful, the fortifications should be levelled with the ground, the arms and ammunition distributed among the natives, and the island evacuated. It is difficult to conceive that so bar-barous a policy, which must inevitably have consigned every European on the island to destruction, could ever have been seriously entertained by an association of civilised men in the nineteenth century. But Lord Minto was not disposed to put weapons into the hands of the natives, and abandon the Dutch colonists, without arms or fortresses, to their vindictive passions,—to undo the work of two centuries, and resign that noble island to the reign of barbarism. He determined to retain it, and committed the command of the army to Colonel Gellespie, and the government to Mr. Raffles, under whose wise and liberal administration it continued to flourish for several years.

Supersession of Lord Minto, 1812.
Having thus established the power of Britain in the eastern archipelago, and given security to her commerce by expelling the French from every harbour in the east, Lord Minto returned to Calcutta early in 1812, and soon after learned that he had been superseded in the Government. The usual term of office was considered to extend to seven years, and Lord Minto had intimated to the Directors his wish to be relieved from the Government early in 1814. But the Prince Regent was impatient to bestow this lucrative appointment on the favourite of the day, the Earl of Moira, who had recently been employed, though without success, in attempting to form a new ministry. Under the dictation of the Board of Control, the chairman of the Court

of Directors was reluctantly obliged to move a resolution for
the immediate recal of Lord Minto. Circumstances detained
Lord Moira in England longer than he expected; he did not
reach Calcutta before October, 1813, and Lord Minto, who had
been intermediately honoured with a step in the peerage, did
not embark till within a few months of the period which he
had himself fixed for his departure, but the determination to
inflict on him the indignity of removal, in the midst of an
administration in which there had been no failure and no cause
of dissatisfaction, was dishonourable equally to the Ministry
and to their royal master.

The Pindarees —their origin, 1690—1800.   On the return of Lord Minto from Java, it
became necessary, for the first time, to order
troops into the field to repel the Pindarees, who
had burst into the province of Bundlekund, and threatened
the great commercial mart of Mirzapore. The earliest trace
of the Pindarees, as a body of mounted freebooters, is found
in the struggles of the Mahrattas with Aurungzebe towards
the close of the seventeenth century; but they come more
distinctly into notice under the Peshwa, the first Bajee Rao.
A large detachment of them accompanied the Mahratta expedition against Ahmed Shah Abdalee, and shared in the
disaster of Paniput. After the Peshwa had delegated the
charge of maintaining the Mahratta power in Hindostan to
his lieutenants, Sindia and Holkar, the Pindarees were ranged
under their standards and designated, respectively, the Sindia
Shahee and the Holkar Shahee Pindarees; but they were not
allowed to pitch their tents within the encampment of the
Mahratta princes, nor were their leaders at first permitted to
sit in their presence. A body of these freebooters accompanied Tokajee Holkar into Hindostan in 1769, and he
bestowed on the leader the *zuree putun*, or golden flag of distinction, which served to keep his band generally faithful to
the house of Holkar. Two other hordes followed the fortunes
of Mahdajee and Dowlut Rao Sindia in their expeditions to the
Deccan and Hindostan. But the connection of the Pindaree

leaders with the Mahratta princes was always loose and uncertain, and regulated more by the principle of convenience than of fealty. The princes found it useful to attach to their camp a large body of freebooters, who received no pay, and were content with an unlimited licence to plunder, and were always ready to complete the work of destruction in the districts which the Mahrattas invaded. The Pindaree leaders, on their part, found it advantageous to enjoy a connection, however indirect, with established governments, to whom they might look for protection in case of emergency. But this relationship did not restrain the Pindarees from plundering the districts of their patrons when it suited their interests, nor did it prevent the Mahratta princes from seizing the leaders after any of their successful expeditions, and obliging them to surrender the best part of their plunder.

Pindaree leaders, 1808. Two of the leaders, Heerun and Burrun, in the suite of Sindia, offered their services, soon after the death of Mahdajee, to the raja of Bhopal to plunder the territories of the raja of Nagpore, with whom he was at war. Their offer was prudently declined, on which they proceeded to Nagpore in quest of professional employment, and were readily engaged by the raja to lay waste the lands of Bhopal, which they accomplished so effectively that it was a quarter of a century before the country recovered from the effect of their ravages. On their return to Nagpore, the raja did not scruple to attack their encampment and completely despoil them of the rich booty they had collected in this expedition. Burrun was thrown into confinement, which he did not survive. Heerun took refuge with Sindia, and died soon after, when his two sons, Dost Mahomed and Wassil Mahomed, collected his scattered followers and reorganized the band. The leadership of Burrun's Pindarees devolved on Cheetoo, by birth a Jaut, who was purchased when a child, during a famine, by a Pindaree, and trained up to the profession. His superior abilities and his daring spirit of enterprize gave him the foremost rank in the troop, and recommended him to the notice of

Dowlut Rao Sindia, who took a large body of his followers
with him in the expedition to Hindostan in 1805, which has
been already alluded to. He was rewarded with a jageer, and
the title of nabob, which he engraved on his seal, in the pompous style of an oriental prince. He fixed his head-quarters
at Nimar, amidst the rugged hills and wild fastnesses which
lie between the Nerbudda and the Vindya range. From this
point, his Pindarees were dispatched in every direction on
plundering expeditions, from which even the territories of
Sindia were not always exempted. His armies were consequently sent in succession to reduce the Pindaree bands,
but were as constantly baffled as the Mogul armies had been
by the Mahrattas, at the beginning of their career. Sindia,
at length deemed it convenient to patch up a peace with
Cheetoo, and to cede five districts to him to preserve the rest
of his dominions from plunder.

Kureem Khan, another Pindaree leader of note,
Kureem Khan,
1811. was a Rohilla, or Patan, who entered the service
of Sindia at an early age, and at the battle of
Kurdla acquired a rich harvest of plunder in the Nizam's
camp, which enabled him to increase the strength of his predatory band. In the course of time, he obtained an assignment of lands from Sindia, together with a title, and married
into the noble family of Bhopal. He was bold, active, and
ambitious, and by the gradual encroachments which the distraction of the times enabled him to make on the dominions both
of Sindia and Holkar, he had, by 1806, acquired possession of
a little principality, yielding sixteen lacs of rupees a-year. He
enlisted infantry, cast cannon, formed a body of household
troops, and increased his Pindarees to 10,000 and for the first
time a Pindaree chief appeared likely to become a territorial
prince. But Sindia had no idea of permitting this development, and resolved to crush his rising power. He accordingly
proceeded to his capital on the pretence of a friendly visit, and
Kureem Khan advanced to meet him with a state little inferior
to his own, and presented him with a throne composed of a lac

and a quarter of rupees. Sindia treated him with the utmost condescension and engaged to grant all his requests. The Pindaree was completely thrown off his guard, and was persuaded to pay his parting visit to Sindia for the confirmation of these promises with a very slender retinue. He was received with distinction, but after the first compliments had passed, Sindia withdrew from the tent, under some excuse, when a body of armed men rushed in and secured Kureem Khan, who was hurried off to Gwalior, where he was detained in confinement for four years. Meanwhile, Sindia's territories were devastated without mercy by his Pindaree adherents, under the command of his nephew. An offer of six lacs of rupees was at length made for the release of Kureem Khan, which was, after much discussion, accepted, and the freebooter obtained his liberty. But it was not long before Sindia had cause to repent of an act dictated only by avarice. The Pindarees flocked to Kureem Khan's standard in such numbers that he speedily acquired more extensive territories and power than he had enjoyed before his captivity. Cheetoo was induced to join him with the whole of his force, and an alliance was likewise formed with Ameer Khan, then in the spring-tide of his career. Their united force did not fall short of 60,000 horse, and from the palace to the cottage, every one in Central India was filled with consternation at this portentous association of men whose only vocation was plunder. Happily, the union was short lived. Cheetoo, who had always cherished the hostility of a rival towards Kureem Khan, was prevailed on to desert him, and Sindia, whose territories he was laying waste with fire and sword, sent one of his ablest generals against him. His camp was assaulted and broken up, and he sought an asylum with Ameer Khan, who made him over to his nephew, Guffoor Khan, and Toolsee-bye, at Indore, by whom he was detained three years.

Their system
of plunder,
1812.
These were the acknowledged leaders of the Pindaree association, to whose encampment the minor chiefs flocked with their adherents when the season

arrived for their annual forays. The ranks of the Pindarees were constantly replenished by horsemen discharged from the service of regular Governments, or in want of employment and subsistence; by miscreants expelled from the community for their crimes, or men pursued by the importunity of their creditors, or who were weary of a peaceable life and of regular occupation. The Pindaree system thus afforded to every criminal not only a safe asylum, but active employment of the most exciting character, to the utter destruction of all the wholesome restraints of society. The predatory standard was generally raised at the Dussera festival, towards the end of October, when the rains ceased and the rivers became fordable. A leader of experience and acknowledged courage was selected, under whom a body of four or five thousand was ranged for the expedition. They were all mounted, two-fifths of them on good horses, armed with a spear from twelve to eighteen feet in length, and the remainder with a variety of weapons of inferior quality. Each horseman was provided with a few cakes for himself and a bag of grain for his horse, and these supplies were replenished as they proceeded, plundering from village to village. They were not encumbered with tents or baggage, and moved often at a speed of forty or fifty miles a-day, and even of sixty in case of emergency, and were thus enabled to baffle all pursuit. Neither were they fettered by any prejudices of caste, or any compunctions of tenderness, or any scruples of conscience. Their vocation was to plunder, and not to fight, and they fled whenever they encountered any resistance. They were the most dastardly brigands on record, and the history of their career is not relieved by a single humane, or even romantic action. The atrocities they committed on man and woman almost exceed belief. Unable to remain long in any one spot, the greatest despatch was required to complete the plunder of the village, and the most horrible tortures were inflicted to hasten the discovery of property. On their arrival in any locality terror and dismay at once seized upon the helpless inhabitants; villages were to be seen in a blaze, wounded and houseless peasants flying in every direction, fortified places shutting their gates, and keeping up a perpetual fire from their walls. Their progress through the country was a stream of desolation, for what they could not carry off they invariably destroyed. Their numbers, moreover, were swelled by the very miseries they inflicted, inasmuch as those who were thus reduced to destitution by their extortion were in too many cases obliged to join their ranks for a mere subsistence.

Attack of British territory, 1812.

Their depredations were for several years confined to the neighbourhood of the Nerbudda and the frontiers of the Peshwa, the Nizam and the raja of Nagpore. As these districts became exhausted they were obliged to enlarge the sphere of their expeditions, and, in one instance, swept through four hundred miles of country south of the Nerbudda, to the extremity of the Peshwa's and Nizam's territories, and returned laden with booty, which served to attract additional numbers to their body. In 1811, the Dussera was celebrated by an assemblage of 25,000 Pindaree horse, besides some battalions of foot ; and a detachment of 5,000 plundered up to the gates of Nagpore, and burnt down one of the suburbs of the city. The next year, a large body under Dost Mahomed penetrated through the native principality of Rewah, and plundered the Company's district of Mirzapore. They then proceeded towards Gya, within seventy miles of Patna, and having realized an extraordinary amount of spoil in this new and untrodden field, disappeared up the sources of the Soane before a British soldier could overtake them. This was their first aggression on British territory, and, coupled with the periodical devastation of the countries north and south of the Nerbudda, constrained Lord Minto to bring the subject before the Court of Directors, and entreat them to consider whether it was expedient " to observe a strict

Lord Minto's representations, 1812.

neutrality amidst these scenes of disorder and outrage, or to listen to the calls of suffering humanity, and interfere for the protection of the weak and defenceless states who implored our assistance against the ravages of the Pindarees and the Patans." Before he quitted the Government he again addressed the Court, pointing out that the augmented numbers, the improved organization, and the increased boldness of the Pindarees, arising from the success of their inroads, rendered the adoption of an extensive system of measures for their suppression a matter of pressing importance. If Lord Wellesley's purpose of establishing the paramount influence of the British Government throughout India had not been thwarted in England, the growth of this predatory confederacy would have been effectually checked, but the fatal policy adopted by the Court of Directors fostered it into a formidable power, the suppression of which, after eight years of impunity, as Lord Minto observed, would require much "laborious arrangement and combination, both political and military." It was the misfortune of his administration to be cast between the vigorous administrations of Lord Wellesley and Lord Hastings, one of whom organized, and the other consummated, the system of maintaining the tranquillity of India through British supremacy. It fell unhappily to his lot to act upon the neutral policy of the home authorities, of which he entirely disapproved, though he had to bear the odium of it. The boldness with which he repressed the ambition of Runjeet Sing, and the irruption of Ameer Khan into Nagpore, when he had an opportunity of acting on his own impulse, shows that, notwithstanding his constitutional caution, he would have dealt vigorously with the Pindarees if he had not been restrained by the India House. But his Government was, nevertheless, of essential service to the interests of India by demonstrating to the authorities in England the impracticability of their system of non-interference, and by preparing them to abandon it under his successor.

Review of the Permanent Settlement, 1813. At the close of Lord Minto's administration twenty years had elapsed since the introduction of Lord Cornwallis's permanent settlement and judicial institutions, which formed an important era in the history

of India, and it becomes necessary to review the effect they
produced on the welfare of the country. After twenty-five
years of unsatisfactory experiments in revenue settlements,
the Government in England, and Lord Cornwallis in India, by
a generous and noble inspiration, resolved at once to constitute
the zemindars who had to this time been the simple collectors
of the revenue, or rather the " hereditary administrators of
the revenue, with a beneficial interest in the land;" the actual
proprietors of every estate in Bengal and Behar, and to make
a permanent and irrevocable settlement with them, when only
two-thirds of the land were under culture. But the great boon
thus conferred was saddled with one condition, which proved
fatal to the great majority of them. Under the Mahomedan
government the zemindar, when he fell into arrears, was
summoned either to Dacca, or Moorshedabad, and subjected
to great indignities, and sometimes even to torture, till he
made provision for paying them up; but he was rarely deprived of his zemindaree. This system of coercion was
repugnant to the British character, and the penalty of eviction
was adopted in its stead. The zemindar was required to
discharge every instalment of revenue on the day on which it
fell due, and, on the first failure, his estate was put up to sale
by auction, and knocked down to the highest bidder; but
punctuality is not, in any circumstances, an oriental virtue,
least of all in pecuniary matters. The zemindars had been
brought up in prodigality and improvidence; they fell rapidly
into arrears, and were inexorably sold up. In the course of
seven years, dating from 1793, most of the great zemindars
who had survived the commotions of more than a century,
were ejected from the estates of which they had been recently
declared the sole proprietors. It was a great social revolution,
affecting more than a third of the tenures of land in a country
the size of England. In some respects this eviction was injurious to the people, for the old zemindars had lived in the
bosom of their tenantry for generations, and being almost exclusively Hindoos, had laid themselves out to promote their social

and religious festivities. They maintained large households, and expended with a lavish hand, in their circle, the sums which had been drawn, probably by extortion, from the ryots. The estates thus brought to the hammer were bought by the new aristocracy of wealth, which had grown up in the political, the commercial, and the judicial service of the Company, and with the growth of trade and the security of property. They were often absentees, and in every case strangers to the ryots, and all the beneficial ties which had associated the agricultural population with the old zemindars were thus dissolved. But the breaking up of these unwieldy zemindarees, equal in some cases to entire districts, was by no means unfavourable to the extension of cultivation, and the general improvement of the country.

Condition of the ryots, 1793— 1813.
The settlement of 1793, however, made no adequate provision for protecting the rights and interests of the ryot. After a century of discussion, it is now admitted that the ryot was the ancient and hereditary proprietor of the soil, possessing all the privileges of ownership, but bound to pay a certain proportion of the produce of every field, generally three-fifths, to the Government. This principle is enshrined in the ancient Hindoo maxim, " whose is the sweat, his is the land." In some parts of India the right of the ryot to his land is designated by a word which signifies indestructible. Tenant right, indeed, appears to have been from time immemorial the basis of all revenue systems. The Mogul settlement of Akbar, in 1582, was made with the ryots. After a minute survey and a careful valuation of the lands, field by field, his great financial minister, Toder Mull, fixed the proportion of the produce calculated in money, which was to be paid by each cultivator to the state; and this scale remained without alteration till the days of Lord Cornwallis, who acknowledged it to be the *asul*, or fundamental rent. The Mogul government appointed revenue officers, subsequently called zemindars, to collect the public dues from each village, granting them a commission of about

ten per cent., or its equivalent in land. The office was necessarily invested with large powers, and gradually became hereditary, and the zemindar came to occupy the position of the
fiscal representative of government within his circle. Whenever the nabob was anxious to augment his revenues, he
levied an additional impost on the gross payments of the
zemindars, and they distributed the assessment on the ryots,
generally in proportion to their rents, which thus became the
standard of supplementary taxation. These cesses were
usually legalised by the nabob's Government, but the zemindar
often abused his power and levied arbitrary and unauthorized
benevolences on the helpless ryot for his own exclusive
benefit, the *jumma,* or rent all the while remaining the same.
The settlement of Lord Cornwallis provided that all these
cesses should be consolidated with the rent, and embodied
in a *pottah,* or written lease ; and it peremptorily prohibited the
exaction of any additional imposts. For the protection of the
ryot it was ordained that the ancient and hereditary *khoodcast*
ryot, who had been in possession of his fields twelve years
before the settlement, should be liable to no enhancement of
his rent, and that from ryots with the right of occupancy of a
later date, the demand should not exceed the *pergunna* or customary rate, as recorded in the register of the village accountant. The zemindar did not therefore, at the period of the
settlement, receive an absolute estate, with all the English
adjuncts of ownership, nor was he at liberty to let the lands
by competition. The ancient and still recognised rights of the
ryots imposed an effectual limitation on his movements, and he
was amenable to the civil courts if he infringed those rights.
A large field was still left for improving his income ; first, by
planting new men on his waste lands, which he was at liberty
to let for whatever sum he could obtain ; and, secondly, by in-
ducing the old ryots to cultivate the more valuable articles of
produce, inasmuch as he was entitled, according to the custom
of the country, to demand higher rents from the fields on which
they were raised. The rule of proportion is the ancient and

II.   .T

prescriptive standard of assessment in the land of Munoo.   It
is the Indian solution of one of the most intricate and important of social questions.   It is equally applicable to every
stage of improvement, and it gives the zemindar, since he has
been endowed with the rights of the Government, an equitable
share of the increased value of his estate, while it prevents
his grasping the whole of it, and crushing the ryot.   These
restrictions on the zemindar at the time when he received the
boon of proprietorship were in accordance with the usages of
the country, and were intended, as the Court of Directors said,
" to protect the ryot from being improperly disturbed in his possessions, or subjected to unwarrantable exactions."   The Government likewise reserved the power of enacting regulations
at any future time for the welfare and protection of the ryots.
But this protection, instead of being steadily and honourably
maintained, has been gradually weakened.   By the 5th Regulation of 1812, the zemindars were allowed, except in the case
of hereditary *khoodcast* ryots, to form engagements on any
conditions which suited them, and they immediately inter-
preted it to signify that they had authority to dispossess even
ryots with a right of occupancy if they refused to submit to
their demands.   From that time the course of legislation
has invariably been adverse to the interests and rights of the
ryots, till, in 1859, an Act was passed to " prevent illegal exactions and extortions in connection with demands for rent," and
to restore the ryot to the condition in which the Government
pledged itself to sustain him by the sacred compact of 1793.

Distraint and sub-letting, 1813.   The condition of the ryot was further deteriorated
by the power of summary and unlimited distraint
with which the landlord was armed by Regulation
7 of 1799.   It afforded him the most ample means of oppression,
and was regarded throughout the country with feelings of
intense horror.   The wretchedness of the ryot was consummated
by the system of sub-letting which came in with the permanent
settlement.   The zemindar, having now obtained a distinct property in his estate, parcelled it out at enhanced rates, on leases

of two or three years to farmers, who in their turn sub-let it to
others at a still higher rate. The sub-letting often descended
to the fourth grade. The accumulated demand was extorted
from the cultivator by every ingenuity of oppression, and by
threatening him with the awful penalties of the law of distraint.
The rapid succession of these hungry adventurers was fatal to
the interests of the ryot, who lamented his unhappy fate, in his
own homely language, in having "three bellies to fill" in addition to those of his own family. He paid the extortionate
demand while there was anything left in his hut, or as long as
his *muhajun*, or money-lender, would supply him with money or
grain, and then deserted his village, and too often joined the
dacoits. The country thus became impoverished and depopulated; and five years of sub-letting was found sufficient
to reduce the number of houses in a village from a hundred to
forty, and the cultivation in the same proportion. As the
peasant moved off the land, the wild hogs took possession of
it, and the increase of the one was an unerring index of the
decay of the other. Under the operation of this system of
sub-letting, and the exactions to which it gave rise, the district
of Nuddea, within forty miles of Calcutta, was pronounced in
1810 to be the finest hog-hunting field in Bengal.

Ceded and con-
quered pro-
vinces, 1809.
On the acquisition of the ceded and conquered
provinces, which now constitute the Agra Presidency, Lord Wellesley, who considered a permanent
settlement indispensable to agricultural improvement, engaged,
in 1803, to bestow it on them after the expiration of the
decennial leases. The promise was confirmed in 1805. But
Sir George Barlow and Lord Minto were so anxious to confer
this blessing, as they deemed it, on the provinces, that commissioners were appointed to carry the new system into effect
before the termination of the old arrangements. But they
found the revenue department a mass of confusion; they could
obtain no reliable information regarding the tenures of land, or
the rights of property, or the resources of the districts, or the
means and prospects of improving them. There were exten-

sive waste lands without a proprietor, and a fourth of the
arable land was untilled.   Mr. Tucker, a member of the commission, and the highest financial authority in India, stated,
· in spite of his attachment to the principles of a permanent settlement, that he did not consider these provinces prepared for it,
and that it would entail a heavy and irretrievable sacrifice of
revenue, without any corresponding benefit to those connected
with· the land.   Lord Minto and his colleagues, however, con-
·troverted Mr. Tucker's opinions and conclusions, and continued
to maintain the necessity of an immediate and permanent settle-
·ment.   But the Court of Directors, whose sanction was necessary to confirm the arrangement, suddenly changed their
opinions in 1813, and prohibited the formation of any such
settlement at any future time.   This repudiation had all the
appearance of a breach of faith with the zemindars of the north-
west ; but under the periodical settlements which were made,
the revenues were increased fifty per cent., by a crore and a
quarter of rupees a-year, leaving the ryot a rag and a hovel.

Settlement of   The Madras Presidency consisted of the five
the Madras   northern sircars acquired by Lord Clive in 1765,
Presidency,   the conquests made by Lord Cornwallis in 1793,
1803—1813.
and the acquisitions of Lord Wellesley seven years
later. The Supreme Government, enamoured of the zemindaree
system, determined to extend it to the Madras territories.   No
zemindars, however, were to be found, but, under orders from
Calcutta, some who appeared to answer ·the description were
at length discovered, or created, in the older provinces, and a
settlement was commenced with them.   Soon after an attempt
to make village settlements was advocated by the Board of
Revenue, and sanctioned by the Court of Directors.   But, after
repeated vacillations, it was resolved to abandon both plans,
and to adopt the ryotwary system, which was created and
matured by a little band of soldiers, of whom Sir Thomas
Munro, with whose name it is identified, was the most eminent.
He assumed that the Government was the absolute proprietor
of the land, to the entire exclusion of all individual rights.

The settlement was to be made from year to year with each ryot, and the assessment was to be equal to one-third of the produce. After the lands had been surveyed and classified and assessed, the potail, or head man of the village, when the ploughing season began, distributed the fields among the villagers, who were not permitted to select their own lands, but constrained to take the good and the inferior in due pro-portion. When the season was so far advanced that a judg-ment could be formed of the crop, the rent of the year was fixed, nominally, by the European officer, but, in practice, by a native, called a *tehsildar*, who was generally imported from another village to prevent loss to the revenue from local influences. If the crop of particular fields failed, the deficiency was assessed on the whole village to the extent of ten per cent., which was often as much as the ryot himself received for the labour of the year. But the cultivator, though debarred from choosing his fields, was responsible for the rent of those arbitrarily allotted to him, and the collector had power to confine, punish, and flog him if he obstinately refused to cultivate them. If these oppressions drove him from his village, the collector followed him wherever he might go, and caused him to make good the assessment. The system was aptly described by the Board of Revenue as one which "bound the ryot by force to the plough, compelled him to till land acknowledged to be over-assessed, dragged him back if he absconded, deferred the demand upon him till the crop came to maturity and then took from him all that could be obtained, and left him nothing but his bullocks and his seed grain," and even these he was often obliged to dispose of. Successful efforts have been made during the last sixty years to mitigate the more flagrant evils of this system, but it is inherently and incurably vicious. It operates as a check on industry; it perpetuates a state of poverty throughout the country; it prevents the growth of capital and the accumulation of landed property, and it deprives the Government of the powerful support of a landed aristocracy.

A brief review of the working of the Cornwallis institutions of civil and criminal jurisprudence and police during this period of twenty years will be found interesting. Under the native Governments, all the functions connected with revenue, justice, and police were concentrated in the same individual,—nabob, zemindar, or village agent. Even where the Government did little to give justice, to the people, it left them at liberty to procure it for themselves. For some time before the introduction of British rule, the judicial machinery appears to have become deranged; but those who administered the rough forms of justice then in use had still the advantage of belonging to the country, of being assimilated to the people in language and religion, conversant with their usages, and not altogether indifferent to their good opinion. Their proceedings were simple and their decisions summary and final, and generally conformable to equity and good sense. The British Government, as a foreign power legislating for a conquered people, might have been expected to adopt a simple and intelligible system of jurisprudence, which could be easily worked. But Lord Cornwallis lived in an age when English law was considered the perfection of reason, and he took it for his model. His code was an intricate and perplexing network of law, and the machinery he constructed for administering it was clogged with technical rules and complicated forms. The business of the court was conducted in a language foreign to the judge, the suitors, and the witnesses. The judges who presided in it, and who regulated all its proceedings, were imperfectly acquainted with the language, feelings, opinions, prejudices, and moral habits of the people, and some of them were pronounced by their own brethren to be unfit for any branch of the service. The novelty of a court established for the exclusive cognisance of civil suits, attracted crowds of suitors. Every man who had a claim, or could manufacture one, hastened to the new court, and unbounded scope was given to the national passion for litigation. The demand for justice, or law, soon began to exceed the

Civil jurisprudence 1793— 1813

means of supply. In the year 1797, the number of suits instituted amounted to 330,000, and such was the pressure of business that some of the judges were known to conduct two or three cases at the same time. To secure perfect justice, appeal was allowed on appeal, but as the privilege was resorted to only to gain time, or to evade immediate payment, or to harass an opponent, it only served to impede the course of justice, and to defeat its own object. The judicial system speedily became so cumbrous and unwieldy, that serious apprehensions were entertained of its breaking down altogether. To reduce the files, legal fees were multiplied, in the hope of discouraging litigation. During Lord Minto's administration, various expedients were adopted in the courts in which the European judges presided, to expedite the progress of justice, but with only partial success. Some additional courts were established, but the cost of the judicial establishments which had risen in fifteen years, from thirty to eighty lacs of rupees a-year, began to excite alarm. The only real improvement of the time, consisted in increasing the number and the pay of the moonsiffs, who decided half the cases in the country. Their allowances were actually raised to fifty rupees a-month, but the most violent prejudices against the employment of native agency in the department of civil justice still continued to reign among the civilian judges, who considered that the want of integrity rendered it impossible for them to decide justly. Yet the existing system combined both the evils of European inefficiency and native venality. The helpless and bewildered European who sat on the bench, and whom it was the object of all parties to mystify, in most cases placed confidence in his able and astute *shristadar*, or head ministerial officer, who thus acquired such influence in the court, as to be able to boast, and with perfect truth, that it was "he who decreed, and he who dismissed." Hence the object of the suitor was,—using the homely phrase of the day,—"to make the crooked mouth of the *shristadar* straight." His evening levée was crowded; justice was sold to the highest bidder, and that office became one of greater power and emolument than that of the judge himself.

The provisions for criminal jurisprudence and the police resulted, in the same disappointment. The zemindars were formerly entrusted with the responsibility of the police, but as they had in some cases abused the power—in India all power is in all places abused—they were divested of it in 1793; and the duty was committed to an officer styled a *daroga*. The districts were unwieldy;—that of Midnapore was fifty miles in breadth, and a hundred and thirty in length;—and some of them contained a million of inhabitants. It was impossible for the magistrate, weighed down as he was with duties at the station, to visit his jurisdiction and check abuses. The daroga became a prince in his own circle. He was usually selected from the servants and dependants of the magistrate; he was inadequately paid by the state, but indemnified himself by extortion, and reaped a harvest from every crime. He inflicted unheard-of tortures on the people, beating and binding and starving them at his pleasure, and often scorching them with torches. It was this officer who apprehended accused or suspected persons, and sent them in to the magistrate with a train of witnesses. The magistrate, who was also loaded with the charge of civil justice, was often unable for months to take up the case, and to decide whether the party should be released or committed for trial to the court of circuit when it arrived. During this period the *accused or suspected person was kept in confinement, at his own expense, amidst the contamination of the gaol, and in one district there were at one time no fewer than fifteen hundred individuals awaiting the leisure of the magistrate to investigate the charges against them.

Dacoity, 1813. The period under review was marked by a great increase in the crime of dacoity, or gang robbery. It had been the curse of Bengal throughout British rule, and probably, long before; but it received a fresh stimulus from the oppression of the sub-letting system and the vices of the police arrangements. The great body of the dacoits followed their occupation of agriculturists and mechanics by day, and the vocation of dacoity by night, under the guidance of professional leaders. They were generally assembled in gangs of forty or fifty by one of the acknowledged chiefs, who organised the expedition against some wealthy shopkeeper or moneylender, or some one who had given information against them. On reaching the rendezvous, a priest performed a religious service to propitiate Doorga, the goddess of thieves, to whom a portion of their spoil was devoted. They then lighted their torches and proceeded to the village, often letting off a gun to warn the villagers to remain within doors. The house marked for plunder was surrounded, and the inmates tortured to reveal their property. The gang then departed with their plunder, and resumed their usual occupations the next morning. The great object of the villagers was to conceal the robbery, in order to avoid a visit from the daroga, whom they dreaded more than the dacoits. When he was able to obtain information of such an occurrence, he came down on the village, seized the most respectable householders, and exacted all they would pay to escape being sent up, either as suspected accomplices or as witnesses, to the magistrate's court, forty or fifty miles distant, to be indefinitely detained, or fleeced by his native officers. The dread of being obliged to give evidence also operated powerfully in keeping the crime concealed. Under the established judicial system, the chances of the dacoit's escape greatly exceeded those of his conviction, and, if liberated, he never failed to wreak his vengeance on the witnesses, sometimes to the extent to putting them and their families to death. Hence, when a requisition for evidence reached a village, it was no uncommon thing to find it at once emptied of all its inhabitants. To remedy this "monstrous and disorganised state of society," as it was aptly described in a minute of Lord Minto, the zemindar was invested with the office of commissioner of police, but as he was expected to bear all the expenses connected with it, and was to act in subordination to the detested daroga, the scheme fell to the ground. Special magistrates were then appointed to repress dacoity, one of whom was the farfamed 'linguist and poet, John Leyden; but they acted with a vigour beyond the laws, and apprehended men by thousands, of whom not one in forty was convicted. Their agency was speedily dispensed with, but the rigour of their proceedings served for a time to diminish the crime.

Remarks on the Cornwallis system, 1813.   It is a painful task to record the defects of the Cornwallis system, which was once pronounced "the noblest monument of a just and liberal policy that was ever erected in a conquered country." It was, undoubtedly, distinguished by a complete absence of selfishness and an earnest feeling of benevolence, and the sterling purity of motive which dictated it was a legitimate object of national pride. But it aimed at too much, and established judicial institutions unsuited to the native character and habits. The permanent settlement was a generous and self-denying act, and it developed the resources of Bengal and Behar, beyond all expectation; but it inflicted poverty and wretchedness on the great body of the cultivators. A singular fatality, indeed, seems to have attended all our revenue settlements in every province throughout an entire century, as we shall repeatedly have occasion to remark hereafter, and though devised with the best intentions, they have never been successful in promoting the welfare of the agricultural community. The failure of Lord Cornwallis's institutions was for the first time disclosed in the celebrated Fifth Report of the House of Commons, drawn up by Mr. Cumming, one of the ablest officers of the Board of Control. It took the public, who reposed entire confidence in the perfection of the system, completely by surprise; but it produced a salutary effect. It dissolved the dream of optimism in which the public authorities had indulged, and directed their attention to those reforms which have now been zealously and successfully prosecuted for half a century.

CHAPTER XXVI.

Negotiations for the Charter, 1809–1812. THE period was now approaching when the question of the exclusive privileges of the East India Company, which had been extended for twenty years in 1793, was to be submitted to Parliament, and the President of the Board of Control placed himself in communication with the India House several years before the expiration of the Act. The Chairman assumed a lofty tone, and had the presumption to assert the right of the Company to all the territories acquired in India by their armies, but was ready to pay due attention to any modifications of the existing system which were not incompatible with the principle of leaving the commerce and the government of India in their hands. He proposed, moreover, that the Proprietors of India stock should receive enhanced dividends in proportion to the improvement of the revenues of India; that the British public should contribute towards the liquidation of their debt, and that their privileges should be renewed for a further period of twenty years. The President of the Board replied that the Ministry were not prepared to encourage any arrangement which should preclude the merchants of England from embarking in the trade of India, from their own ports, and in their own ships. The negotiation then came to a pause, and before it was renewed the finances of the Company had become totally deranged. Drafts had been drawn from Calcutta to the extent of five crores of rupees towards the discharge of the debt in India. A crore of rupees had been lost by vessels which had perished at sea, or had been captured by French privateers. The Directors were, therefore, obliged to resort to Parliament for relief, and in June, 1810, a loan of a crore and a half of rupees was granted to them. In the following year they obtained permission to raise two crores on their own bonds, and in 1812 a further loan of two crores and a half of rupees was sanctioned by the House of Commons. These embarrassments did not, however, abate the resolution of the Directors to insist on what they represented as their right—a renewal of the charter on its existing basis; and they refused to recommend to their constituents to accept it on any conditions which would despoil them of their "most valuable privileges." Lord Melville, the President of the Board of Control, proposed, by way of compromise, to restrict the import trade of private merchants to London, and to subject it to the system of the Company's sales and management, on condition that the Directors should throw open the export trade to the nation. The Court refused to accede to this arrangement, and time was thus afforded to the out-ports to survey their interests and to urge their claim to a participation in the entire trade with increased energy.

Opening of the out-ports to import trade, 1813. The questions at issue between the Ministry and the India House were at length reduced to the single point of opening the out-ports to the admission of cargoes from India, but upon this both the Directors and the Proprietors determined to make a peremptory stand. On the 5th May, 1812, a series of resolutions was passed at the India House, which asserted that the removal of this trade from the port of London to the out-ports would break up large and important establishments, and throw thousands out of bread; that it would increase smuggling beyond the possibility of control, and entail the ruin of the China trade; that it would reduce the Company's dividends, depreciate their stock, and paralyze their power to govern India; that the tranquillity and happiness of the people of India would thus be compromised; that the interests of Great Britain in Asia would be impaired, and even the British constitution itself imperilled. The Ministry were not, however, appalled by this phantom of calamities which the genius of monopoly had conjured up, and informed the Court that if they still thought the extension of commercial privileges to the nation incompatible with the government of India in their hands, some other agency might be provided for administering it upon principles consistent with the interests of the public, and the integrity of the British constitution; but the Court of Directors refused to give way, and they were vigorously supported by the great body of the Proprietors, who regarded the admission of the out-ports to a share in the import trade a vital question, on which there could be no concession. They expressed their confidence that the wisdom of Parliament would never consent to gratify a few interested speculators by abolishing a commercial system which had existed for two centuries, and was fortified by a dozen Acts. In conformity with this resolution, a petition was presented to Parliament on the 22nd February, 1813, praying for a renewal of the privileges granted to the Company in 1793, and deprecating any interference with the China trade, or any extension of the import trade to the out-ports. Another petition was at the same time, unseasonably, submitted to the House soliciting the payment of a bill of two crores and thirty lacs of rupees, which the Company asserted was still due to them from the nation.

Growth of manufactures and commerce, 1793-1813. The claim advanced by the Company to a renewal of their exclusive privileges for another generation encountered a very strenuous opposition throughout the country. During the twenty years which had elapsed since 1793, the commercial and manufacturing industry of England had been developed beyond all former example, and new interests of extraordinary magnitude and power had grown up. The cotton manufacturers of Manchester, in the infancy of their enterprize, had solicited the Government to foster their exertions by imposing a protecting duty on the importation of piece goods from India. In the intermediate period, however, their textile fabrics had been brought to such a state both of perfection and cheapness as in a great measure to supersede the Indian manufacture, the imports of which had fallen from three crores and a half of rupees a-year to half a crore. They had, moreover, invaded the Indian market, where the import of Manchester cottons had increased from about seven thousand rupees a-year to ten lacs. The mill-owners now came forward and claimed the right of an unrestricted traffic with India, both export and import, from their respective ports, and in their own vessels. They maintained that however important the monopoly might have been in the early stages of our connection with India, it had now ceased to be either necessary or profitable, and only served to cramp the spirit of national enterprize. Indeed, the Company had themselves furnished the strongest argument for its cessation by the confession that their trade to India had for many years been carried on at a loss. The Ministers, on their part, had long since made up their minds to emancipate this trade from the fetters of the monopoly. The Emperor Napoleon, by his Berlin and Milan decrees, had closed all the ports of the continent against English commerce, and the public interests required that other channels of trade should, if possible, be opened out. The nation was passing through the most gigantic struggle in which it had ever been involved; the national resources were strained to an unprecedented degree, and it was necessary to spare no effort to sustain the energies of the country.

India Bill, 1813.   On the 22nd of March the ministerial plan for conducting the trade and administration of India was introduced by Lord Castlereagh into the House of Commons. He proposed to continue the government of the country in the hands of the Company for a further period of twenty years with liberty to pursue their trade, but, at the same time, to admit the whole nation both to the import and export trade, without any other restriction than that no private vessel should be of larger dimensions than four hundred tons. The exclusive trade to China, which alone yielded any profit, was to be confirmed to them. The restriction on the resort of

Europeans to India was to be virtually removed, though they were still required to take out a licence from the Court of Directors, or, if refused by them, from the Board of Control, but the local authorities were at liberty at any time to cancel it at their own discretion.

Opposition of the India House, 1813. These propositions were vigorously opposed by the Court of Directors, who petitioned the House for leave to be heard by counsel, and to bring forward witnesses to substantiate their claims. The first witness introduced was the venerable Warren Hastings, then in his eightieth year. Twenty-six years before he had been arraigned by the House of Commons at the bar of the Lords for high crimes and misdemeanours. He had outlived the prejudices and the passions of that age, and the whole House rose as he entered, and paid a spontaneous homage to his exalted character and his pre-eminent services. But his views of Indian policy belonged, for the most part, to that remote and normal period when he was employed in giving form and consistency to our rising power. He was opposed to all innovations, however necessary they had become by the progress of time and circumstances. When reminded that as Governor-General he had denounced the "contracted views of monopolists," and insisted upon it "as a fixed and incontrovertible principle that commerce could only flourish when free and equal," he had the moral courage to say that he had altered his opinions, and did not come there to defend his own inconsistencies. The evidence of Lord Teignmouth, of Mr. Charles Grant, of Colonel Malcolm, of Colonel Munro, and, indeed of all the witnesses, more than fifty in number, marshalled by the India House on this occasion, ran in the same groove. They affirmed that the climate of India and the habits and prejudices of the natives presented an insuperable barrier to the increased consumption of British manufactures. The trade of India had already reached its utmost limit, and it could be conducted with advantage only through the agency of the Company. The free admission of Europeans would lead to colonization; the weak and timid natives would become the victims of European oppression, and India would eventually be lost to England. These opinions were advocated, generally, in the spirit of a sincere conviction, and not of mere partizanship; and although, with our larger experience, we cannot fail to regret that so many great and eminent men should have clung to an erroneous creed, we are constrained to respect the benevolence of their motives when we find that they deprecated the proposed changes chiefly because they dreaded their injurious consequences on the well-being of the natives. But all the authorities and all the evidence the Court of Directors could muster proved unavailing. The House yielded to the voice of the nation, which had been unequivocally expressed in the petitions with which it was overwhelmed, and opened the gates of Indian commerce to the capital and enterprise of England.

Speeches of Lord Wellesley and Lord Grenville, 1813. The charter discussions in the House of Lords were rendered memorable by the speeches of Lord Wellesley and Lord Grenville. Lord Wellesley, when Governor-General, had incurred the wrath of the India House by advocating and encouraging the enlargement of the private trade, and asserting that it was not likely to lead to a large influx of Europeans, and that if it did, they could be kept under due control by the local authorities. On the present occasion, however, he abandoned his former opinions, and advocated with equal vigour the claims of the Company to the exclusive trade, not only of China, but also of India. He resisted the proposal to allow Europeans to settle in India, because they would outrage the prejudices of the natives, and endanger the security of the Government. He likewise passed a high encomium on the East India Company, affirming that no Government had ever fulfilled its duties with more exemplary fidelity and success. The sentiments expressed by Lord Grenville were the boldest and the most enlightened which had ever been heard within the walls of Parliament on the subject of Indian policy. He considered that twenty years was too long a period for farming out the commerce of half the globe and the government of sixty millions of people. The sovereignty of India belonged to the Crown and not to its subjects. The blended character of merchant and sovereign was an anomaly. No ruler had ever ⸗traded to advantage; no trading company had ever administered government for the happiness of its subjects. The Company had lost four crores of rupees by their trade to India in nineteen years, notwithstanding their monopoly; and they had traded with profit only to China, where they had neither sovereignty nor monopoly. The Government of India ought to be vested in the Crown. If, as he admitted, the transfer of the patronage to the Ministry would weigh down the balance of the constitution, appointments to the civil service should be given by competition, and cadetships distributed among the families of those who had fallen in the service of their country. That the trade of India was susceptible of no extension was a mere idle assumption; commerce increased by commerce, and trade begat trade in all countries, and India would furnish no exception to this universal law. These sound opinions, which were far in advance of the spirit and the courage of the age, carried no weight at the time, and the Bill passed as it came up from the Commons, without any modification. But the seeds of truth once planted in the fertile soil of England never fail to germinate and bring forth fruit in due season. It was a great stride for one age to break up the monopoly. It devolved on a succeeding age to make fresh advances in the career of progress. We find, accordingly, that at the next renewal of the Charter in 1833 the Company were entirely divested of their mercantile character, and confined to the duties of government, while the Charter of 1853 threw open the civil service to competition, and the government itself was transferred from the Company to the Crown five years later.

The missionary question, 1813. Reference has been made in a previous chapter to the restrictions which were imposed on the Serampore Missionaries by Sir George Barlow, in 1806, during the panic

created by the Vellore mutiny. Lord Minto, immediately on his
arrival, when new to the country, was led by their adversaries
to interfere with their proceedings; but their satisfactory explanations, and the discreet course they pursued, induced him
to desist from all opposition, and they were enabled for five
years to prosecute their labours without molestation. But in
the year 1812 Lord Minto's Government, without any apparent
motive, thought fit to adopt the most truculent measures
against the missionary enterprize, and to order eight missionaries, the majority of whom had recently arrived in the country,
to quit it. The alleged ground of this arbitrary proceeding
was, that they were without a licence from the Court of Directors; but as hundreds of Europeans, equally unlicensed,
had been allowed freely to enter and settle in the country, it
was felt to be a mere pretext for the indulgence of that feeling
of hostility to the cause, which was equally strong at that period
in the Council chamber in Calcutta and at the India House.
The feelings of the Court of Directors on this subject had all the
strength of traditional prejudices. They had violently opposed
and ultimately defeated the proposal made during the charter
discussions of 1793, to permit missionaries and schoolmasters
to resort to India, and their aversion to the introduction of
secular or religious knowledge had experienced no abatement.
It became necessary for the friends of missions to take advantage of the present opportunity, and appeal to Parliament for
its interposition. The question was entrusted to Mr. Wilberforce, who, in a speech distinguished for its eloquence, pointed
out the injustice and impolicy of the impediments imposed on
the resort of missionaries to India, and entreated the House to
remove them. He repudiated the remotest intention of forcing
Christianity on the country, and only sought permission to
place the truths of the Bible before the native mind for its
voluntary acceptance. But the India House and its witnesses,
with a few honourable exceptions, were as rigidly opposed to
this concession as to that of free trade, and reprobated the admission of missionary and mercantile agents with equal vehe-

mence. Of this powerful phalanx, Mr. Marsh, who had amassed a fortune at the Madras bar, and obtained a seat in Parliament, became the champion, and delivered a speech of extraordinary power and virulence against the missionary clause. Mr. Wilberforce had supported his argument by a reference to the proceedings and the success of the missionaries at Serampore; but Mr. Marsh assailed their characters with inordinate bitterness, denounced them as fanatics and incendiaries, and applied to them such gross epithets as the House had not been accustomed to tolerate. He asserted, moreover, that the safety of the British empire in India depended on the exclusion of all missionaries. But the voice of the country, which the House implicitly obeys, was raised with more than ordinary unanimity against the monstrous doctrine that the only religion to be proscribed in India should be that of its Christian rulers. The clause was passed by a large majority, and the same liberty was given to the introduction of Christianity which had been enjoyed by the Mahomedans and by the various Hindoo sectaries for the propagation of their respective tenets. At the same time a Bishop was appointed to Calcutta and an Archdeacon to Madras and Bombay, to superintend the chaplains; and a clause was added to the Bill at the last moment, and on the motion of a private member, to appropriate the sum of one lac of rupees a-year, out of a revenue of seventeen hundred lacs, to the object of public instruction.

Remarks on the charter, 1813. — The Charter Act of 1813 inflicted the first blow on the monopoly of the East India Company. For more than a hundred and fifty years that monopoly had been not only beneficial, but essential to the interests of British commerce in India. It gave a character of energy and perseverance to the national enterprize which enabled it to encounter opposition with success, and to survive reverses. Without it neither the commerce nor the dominion of England would have been established in India. The venality and oppression of the officers of the native powers, which a powerful

U 2

corporation was able to withstand, would have been fatal to
the private adventurer. But the monopoly became a positive
evil after the Company had become sovereigns. As rulers of
the country they owed it to the interests of their subjects to
grant the fullest scope for the expansion of their commerce,
instead of fettering it by the bonds of a state monopoly. The
extinction of the exclusive privileges of the Company was,
therefore, not less beneficial to India than to England. The
reasons advanced against it showed little judgment and still
less foresight; and it may serve to rebuke the dogmatism
with which official men are prone to enforce their opinions, to
note that all the gloomy predictions of the Court of Directors,
and even of the most renowned of their servants, who were regarded as the great authorities of the time on Indian questions, have turned out to be utterly fallacious, without a
single exception. The trade, which they assured the House
of Commons admitted of no expansion, has risen from thirteen
millions to one hundred millions in 1865, and still presents the
prospect of an indefinite increase. In 1813 India was reckoned
among the smallest of the customers of England, but fifty
years later she had attained the highest rank. The export of
British cotton manufactures to India at the renewal of the
charter in 1813 was only ten lacs, but in spite of the inveterate habits and prejudices of the natives, it has increased fifty
fold. The Europeans who have been admitted into India
have contributed in the highest degree to its improvement and
prosperity by their capital and enterprize, and so far from
being a source of danger to Government, it is certain that if
there had been a body of only five thousand European settlers
in the North West provinces during the last mutiny in 1857, it
would have been nipped in the bud. If the hand-looms of
India have been in many cases silenced by the power-looms of
Lancashire, the loss has been more than compensated by the
hundred crores of silver and gold which free trade has poured
into her bosom during the last fifteen years.

Lord Hastings,   The Earl of Moira, subsequently created Marquis

Governor-General, 1813.   of Hastings—by which title we shall begin to designate him—was appointed Governor-General in succession to Lord Minto, and took the oaths and his seat in Council on the 4th October, 1813. He was of the mature age of fifty-nine, a nobleman of Norman lineage, with a tall and commanding figure, and distinguished above all his predecessors by his chivalrous bearing. He had entered the army at seventeen, served for seven years in the war of American independence, and was, rewarded for his services with an English peerage. His life was subsequently passed in connection with great public and political affairs, and he brought with him to his high office a large fund of experience, a clear and sound judgment, and great decision of character, together with the equivocal merit of being the personal friend of the Prince Regent. It is worthy of note that the responsibilities of the Government of India produced the same change of views in him as in his illustrious predecessor. Lord Wellesley was so thoroughly convinced of the criminality of Warren Hastings that he had offered to assist in conducting the prosecution, and he came to Calcutta, as he admitted, with the strongest prejudices against him. But as he grew familiar, on the spot, with the policy and character of his administration, he expressed his unqualified admiration of it; and in 1802, when the Nabob of Oude, hearing that Mr. Hastings had been impoverished by his trial, offered to settle an annuity of twenty thousand rupees on him, the information was conveyed by Lord Wellesley in one of the most flattering letters the impeached Governor-General had ever received. In like manner Lord Hastings, in his place in Parliament, had denounced the spirit of Lord Wellesley's administration, and his ambitious policy of establishing British supremacy throughout India. He had now an opportunity of testing the value of that opinion, and he speedily saw cause to recant it. He had no sooner completed his survey of the position and prospects of the empire than he recorded his impression "that our object in India ought to be to render the British Government paramount in effect, if not declaredly so, to hold the other states as vassals, though not in name, and to oblige them, in return for our guarantee and protection, to perform the two great feudatory duties of supporting our rule with all their forces, and submitting their mutual differences to our arbitration." Before he quitted India he had waged war on a more gigantic scale than even Lord Wellesley; he had made the Company supreme throughout India, and declared that the Indus was, to all intents and purposes, the boundary of our empire.

State of India, 1813. In the autumn of 1813, Lord Minto quitted India with the firm belief that, with the exception of the Pindaree cloud, it was in a state of the most perfect security. "On my taking the reins of Government," wrote Lord Hastings, " seven different quarrels, likely to demand the decision of arms, were transferred to me." In fact, the non-intervention policy, which, during the preceding eight years the home authorities had considered the perfection of political wisdom, and the native princes the result of sheer pusillanimity, had produced the same result of fermentation and even anarchy, as the faint-hearted policy of Sir John Shore's days. The total withdrawal of our influence from Central India had brought on a contempt of our power, and sown the seeds of a more general war than we had as yet been exposed to. The government of Holkar was virtually dissolved when he became insane, and there ceased to be any authority to control the excesses of the soldiery, while Ameer Khan, with his free lances, was at once the prop and the burden of the throne. The troops of Sindia had been incessantly employed in operations tending to promote the aggrandisement of his power by usurpations. The Peshwa, who had recovered his throne in 1802 by the aid of the Company, had been husbanding his resources for the first opportunity of shaking off the yoke of this connection. Rajpootana was a prey to the rapacity of Ameer Khan, and the insatiable battalions of Sindia and Holkar. The Pindaree freebooters were spreading desolation through a region five hundred miles in length, and four hun-

dred in breadth, and a new power on the northern frontier of
the Bengal Presidency had matured its strength, invaded the
border districts, and bid defiance to the British Government.
The Company's army, which had been subjected to large
reductions, in a spirit of unwise economy, was found to be
inadequate to the defence of our extensive frontier. The
treasury was empty. The island of Java was an expensive·
acquisition. The Mauritius and Ceylon had been permitted to
draw on Calcutta, and had not allowed the privilege to remain
idle. The supercargoes at Canton were pouring their bills for
the Company's China investment on the Indian treasury, and
the Court of Directors were importunate for cash remittances.
Lord Hastings, at length, succeeded in overcoming the reluctance of his colleagues in Council to the transmission of thirty
lacs in gold, which, at the premium of the day, gave relief to
the India House to the extent of forty-five lacs, but it left the
cash balances in India so low as to be barely sufficient for the
current expenditure.

Description of Nepal, 1813. The first and immediate difficulty of Lord
Hastings arose out of the encroachments of the
Nepalese, or Goorkhas. The war into which he was forced
with them was bequeathed to him by his predecessor, who left
him no option but to draw the sword, or compromise the character of the Government by abandoning the interests of its
subjects. ↳ The valley of Nepal is embosomed in the Himalaya
mountains, and bounded on the north by some of its loftiest
and most majestic elevations, and on the south by the first and
lowest range. That range is skirted by a magnificent forest,
from eight to ten miles in depth, which presents an unvaried
aspect of gigantic trees; no breath of wind reaches the inte-
rior, which is littered with rank and decayed vegetation; no
animals inhabit it, and no sound of a bird is heard in its
recesses. An open plain, called the *teraee*, stretches to the
south of the forest, five hundred miles in length, and about
twenty in breath. The soil is watered by the various streams
which descend from the mountains, and, when cultivated, pro-

duces the most luxuriant crops, but during the greater portion of the year it is as pestilential as the Pontine marshes. It is dotted at considerable intervals with little hamlets, but the population, which is chiefly migratory, is composed of herdsmen, who annually bring their flocks and herds, in some cases from the distance of many hundred miles, to graze on its rich pasturage.

Rise and progress of Goorkha power, 1813. About the middle of the fourteenth century, various colonists of Rajpoots entered the country and subdued the aborigines, the Newars, a Mongolian race, professing the creed of Boodh. The principalities which the Rajpoots established in these hills generally included a strip of the adjacent forest and of the low lands. In the course of time, the weaker chiefs were absorbed by the stronger, and the country came to be partitioned among three families. In the middle of the last century, Prithee-Narayun, the chief of the mountain tribe of Goorkha, gradually raised himself to power, and having subdued the other rajas, founded a new dynasty, about ten years after the battle of Plassy. He was succeeded by his son in 1771, and his grandson, an odious tyrant, was put to death in open durbar by his half brother, in 1805. His infant son was proclaimed raja by Bheem-sen, who assumed the office of chief minister, and formed a council of regency of the principal military officers. The strength of the Goorkha dynasty consisted in its military organization, and the impulse of conquest which the founder communicated to it, was maintained with increasing vigour after his death. An expedition was sent across the northern mountains to Llassa, and the living type of Boodh was subjected to the humiliation of paying tribute to his Hindoo conqueror. But the Emperor of China, the secular head of Boodhism, resolved to avenge the insult, and invaded Nepal with a large army. The Goorkhas were signally defeated, and obliged to acknowledge the supremacy of China by submitting to the deputation of a mission to Pekin, with tribute, once every three years. Foiled in their projects in the north, they pushed their conquests four hundred miles, on the east, to Sikkim, and on the west to the Kalee river. Their most renowned general Umur Sing, who acted to a great extent independent of the regency, carried his arms beyond that river, which brought him in contact with the rising power of Runjeet Sing, and the two ambitious chiefs confronted each other in the mountainous region of the higher Sutlege. Umur Sing entered the Punjab, and invested Kote Kangra, a fortress in a position so strong by nature, that in the opinion of the ablest French engineers, it might be rendered impregnable by science and art. After an unsuccessful siege of four years, he was obliged, in 1813, to retire, with no little damage to his military reputation. He made several attempts to engage the British Government in a crusade against Runjeet Sing, but was, soon after, obliged to look to the defence of his own country against an invasion from Hindostan.

Goorkha en-croachments on British territory, 1809-1813. The Goorkhas, not content with the possessions they had acquired in the hills, pushed their encroachments into the low lands, and during the twenty-five years preceding the war we are about to describe, had usurped more than two hundred British villages. The subjects of the Company were thus exposed to perpetual aggression along the whole line of frontier, and there ceased to be any security for life or property. At length, the Goorkhas had the presumption to lay claim to the two districts of Boot-wul and Seoraj which they had seized in Goruckpore, though they had been ceded to Lord Wellesley by the Nabob Vizier in 1801. Lord Minto was anxious to avoid a war with the Nepalese, and suggested that delegates should be sent from the capital, Catmandoo, to meet the British representative, and investigate the merits of the question. The inquiry occu-pied more than a twelvemonth; the Goorkha envoys were unable to establish their claim, and Lord Minto forwarded a demand to the Nepal regency in June, 1813, for the immediate restitution of the districts, and intimated that in case of refusal they would be occupied by force. The Government in Calcutta was thus bound to support the demand, even at the hazard of hostilities. The Goorkha cabinet distinctly refused to resign the districts, and again asserted their right to them. Their reply did not, however, reach Calcutta till after Lord Hastings had assumed the government, when, on a careful examination of all the documents, he deemed it indispensable categorically to demand their surrender within twenty-five days. The period expired without any communication from the regent, and the magistrate of Goruckpore was directed to expel the Goorkha officers, and establish police stations in the two districts.

The Goorkhas determine on war, 1814.   Lord Hastings's letter created a profound sensation at Catmandoo, and convinced the regent that the local dispute regarding these border lands was rapidly merging into a question of peace or war with the British power. A national council, composed of twenty-two chiefs, was held at the capital, in which the subject of their future policy was discussed with great animation. Umur Sing said his life had been passed amid the hardships of war, and he was not ignorant of its risks. He deprecated a collision with the British power, and maintained that the lands in dispute were not worth the hazard. "We have hitherto," he said, "been hunting deer, but, if we engage in this war, we must be prepared to fight tigers." Several other chiefs offered similar advice; but the regent and his party, filled with an overweening conceit of their national prowess, treated it with scorn. "Hitherto," they said, "no power has been able to cope with us. The small fort of Bhurtpore was the work of man, yet the English were worsted before it, and desisted from the attempt; our hills and fastnesses are the work of the Deity, and are impregnable. Even the mighty Secunder, Alexander the Great, who overthrew many empires, failed to establish his authority in these mountains." They talked of the futility of debating about a few square miles, since there could be no real peace between the two states until the Company resigned the provinces north of the Ganges, and made that river their boundary. The council resolved on war, and, as if to render it inevitable, sent down a large force to Bootwul; the police officer was murdered in cold blood on the 29th May, and eighteen of his men were put to death. The Goorkhas had thrown down the gauntlet, and no course was left to the Government but to take it up promptly, without waiting a twelvemonth by a reference to the Court in Leadenhall-street. The whole Goorkha army did not exceed 12,000 men, and it was scattered over an extensive frontier; their largest gun was only a four-pounder, and it appeared an act of infatuation in the Nepal regency to defy the British power, but the uninterrupted successes of a quarter of a century had turned the hardy little mountaineers into an army of skilful and courageous veterans, confident in their own strength, and animated with a strong feeling of national pride. Their troops were equipped and disciplined like the Company's sepoys, and their officers adopted the English military titles. They moved about without the encumbrance of tents. They had no sooner taken up a position than they set to work to fortify it; every soldier worked at the entrenchment, and a strong stockade of double palisades, filled up with earth or stones, was completed in almost as little time as the English soldier required to erect his tent. But the chief strength of the Nepalese consisted in the impracticable nature of their country, and our entire ignorance of its localities.

Loan from Lucknow, 1814. Lord Hastings found himself dragged into a difficult war with an empty exchequer. On previous occasions the usual resource was to open a loan, but this was now out of the question, the Government notes being at a discount of nine or ten per cent., and the merchants in Calcutta paying twelve per cent. for money. In this dilemma he cast his eyes on the hoards of the Nabob Vizier, who had amassed a private fund of eight crores of rupees. The treaty of 1801 contained a loose engagement on the part of the Vizier to attend to the advice of the Resident regarding the amelioration of his system of government, which was vicious in the extreme. Various remonstrances had been made to him during Lord Minto's administration, but he had no mind for reforms which would embarrass his arrangements, and curtail his savings. These representations were rendered still more unpalatable by the bearing of the 'Resident, who assumed a dictatorial tone, which lowered the Nabob in the eyes of his Court and his subjects, and broke in upon him at all hours when he had anything to prescribe. He interfered in the private, and even personal, arrangements of the Nabob, and went so far as to raise objections to the beating of the *nobut*, the great drum, the exclusive and most cherished privilege of royalty, because it disturbed his morning slumbers. Lord Hastings, who had resolved to treat the native princes with every consideration, ordered these irritating demands for reform to be discontinued, and the Vizier, who had been informed of the embarrassment of the treasury in Calcutta, offered the Company a gift of a crore of rupees, "to mark his gratitude," as Lord Hastings said, "for my having treated him as a gentleman." Lord Hastings left Calcutta early in 1814, on a tour through the provinces, and a visit to Lucknow. The Nabob died during the journey, but his son renewed the offer, not without a latent hope that it might conduce to the appointment of another Resident, which was the supreme wish of his heart. Lord Hastings was unable to receive the money as a gratuity, but agreed to accept it as a loan. He was now furnished with the sinews of war, but he was destined to a severe disappointment. Of the old eight per cent. loan which the Government in Calcutta had been endeavouring to convert into six per cents., a sum of fifty-four lacs was still unredeemed, and the members of Council, without giving a hint of their design to Lord Hastings, took upon themselves to advertise the payment of this sum, which absorbed more than half the Lucknow loan. This was regarded in Calcutta as a clever stroke of economy, but it was an act of supreme political folly. It completely deranged the plans of the Governor-General, and

would have produced the most disastrous effect on the campaign if he had not submitted'to the humiliation of soliciting
a second crore, which was granted with no little reluctance.

With regard to the plan of the campaign,
Plan of the Goorkha cam-paign, 1814. Lord Hastings considered it highly impolitic to
confine our operations to the defence of an im-
mense length of frontier, which it would be found impossible
to guard effectually against the inroads of a hostile, vigorous,
and rapacious neighbour. He felt confident that our military
character could be sustained only by a bold and successful
assault on the strongest of the enemy's positions in the hills.
With a view to distract the attention of the regency, he
planned four simultaneous attacks on four points—the western
on the Sutlege, the eastern on the capital, and two others on
intermediate positions. Of the Goorkha army, one-third, under
Umur Sing, guarded the fortresses on the Sutlege; two thousand were distributed between the Jumna and the Kalee
rivers, and the remainder protected the capital and its neighbourhood. Four British armies were accordingly assembled
in the field, comprising in all about thirty thousand men with
sixty guns.

The division under General Gillespie, who had
General Gil-lespie's division, 1814. acquired a brilliant reputation in quelling the
mutiny at Vellore and in Java, was the first in the
field. He advanced at the head of 3,500 men into the Dhoon
valley to lay siege to the fortress of Nahun. On the route he
came upon the fortified position of Kalunga, defended by six
hundred Goorkhas, under the command of Captain Bulbuddur
Sing. On receiving the summons to surrender late in the day,
the Goorkha chief coolly replied that it was not customary to
carry on a correspondence at such an hour, but he would pay
his respects to the General the next morning. Lord Hastings
had repeatedly enjoined General Gillespie to avoid storming
works which required to be reduced by artillery, but this order
was totally disregarded, and in the impetuosity of his reckless
courage, he determined to carry the fort by assault. His

men were staggered by the murderous fire which the Goorkhas
skilfully directed against them as they advanced up to the
wicket, when the General, irritated by the repulse, placed
himself at the head of three companies of Europeans and
rushed up to the gate, but was shot through the heart as he
waved his hat to his men to follow him. A retreat was immediately sounded, but not before twenty officers

General Gil-
lespie killed,
Oct. 31, 1814. and two hundred and forty men lay killed and
wounded. A month was lost in waiting for heavy
ordnance from Delhi. On the 27th November a breach was
reported practicable, and a second attempt was made to storm
the fort, but after two hours' exposure to a galling fire the
troops were withdrawn, with a loss of six hundred and eighty
in killed and wounded. The sacrifice of men in these two
futile assaults exceeded the whole number of the garrison,
and it was at length resolved to bring the mortars into play.
The place was little more than an open space surrounded by a
stone wall. Three days of incessant shelling rendered it un-
tenable, and reduced the garrison from six hundred to seventy,
when the brave Goorkha commander sallied forth at the head
of the survivors and escaped. If the positive orders of Lord
Hastings had been obeyed in the first instance, the Government would have been spared a lamentable loss of life and
the disgrace of two failures, which, at the opening of the campaign, disheartened their own troops as much as it emboldened the enemy. The reputation of this division was
not retrieved by General Martindell, who succeeded to the
command, and laid siege to Jytuk at the end of December.
It was situated on a lofty and almost inaccessible mountain,
and strengthened by extensive and substantial stockades and
breastworks. The whole district was under the command of
Colonel Runjoor Sing, the son of Umur Sing. Two powerful
detachments were sent to occupy two important positions,
but owing to the blunders of the General, they were both
overpowered and cut up. With a force of 1,000 Europeans
and 5,000 natives he allowed himself to be held at bay

by 2,300 natives. Then, despairing of success he turned the siege into a blockade, in which the rest of the campaign was entirely wasted.

Division of General J. S. Wood, 1814: The division under General J. S. Wood was appointed to re-take Bootwul, and penetrate Nepal through Palpa, but its efforts were paralyzed by similar imbecility. After much unnecessary delay the General took the field in the middle of December, and, without making any reconnoissance, allowed himself to be brought unexpectedly on the stockade of Jeetpore by the treachery of a brahmin guide, on the 14th January, 1814. It might have been expected, however, that a British army of 4,500 men, fully equipped, would have been a match for 1,200 Goorkhas, but the General, after fighting his way to a position which commanded the entrenchment, and placed it within his grasp, sounded a retreat just as the enemy had begun to abandon it. The opposition he had encountered, although insignificant, made so deep an impression on his feeble mind that he retired within the British frontier, and confined his exertions to an attempt to defend it; but the Goorkhas, emboldened by his pusillanimity, penetrated it in every quarter, and scarcely a day passed in which some village was not pillaged and burnt. Reinforcements were sent to him without delay, but he had neither the spirit nor the skill to employ them, and his division was rendered worse than useless throughout the season. The chief reliance of Lord Hastings for the successful issue of the campaign was placed

General Marley's division, 1815. on the army entrusted to General Marley, 8,000 strong, which was destined to march directly on the capital, only a hundred miles from our frontier, but he proved to be more incompetent than even Wood and Martindell. After reaching Puchroutee on the 20th December, he lost a month in, devising the best mode of advancing to Catmandoo. Two detachments were sent to two points, east and west, twenty miles distant from head-quarters, without any support. No military precautions were adopted in these isolated positions, and the Goorkhas simultaneously surprised both corps on the 1st January. The officers were deserted by the sepoys, but fell fighting with their usual valour, and all the guns, stores, and magazines fell into the hands of the enemy. The skill and audacity manifested by the Goorkhas in these encounters confounded the wretched General, and he made a retrograde movement to guard the frontier against an enemy, magnified by his fears to 12,000 men, but who never exceeded even a tenth of that number. As he declared that his army was inadequate to the object assigned to it, Lord Hastings strained every nerve to reinforce him, and, including two European regiments, raised its strength to 13,000—a force sufficient to have disposed completely of the whole army of Nepal. But General Marley could not be persuaded to enter the forest, and on the 10th February mounted his horse before day light, and rode back to the cantonment of Dinapore, without delegating the command to any other officer, or giving any intimation of his intentions. General George Wood was then sent to assume the command. An encounter was accidentally brought on with the Goorkhas, in which four hundred of their number perished, and their comrades, dismayed by this reverse, abandoned all their positions in the neighbourhood, and left the road to the capital open; but General Wood had as little spirit as his predecessor, and this division was likewise lost to the object of the war.

Effect of these reverses in India, 1815.

This was the first campaign since the Company took up arms in India in which their own troops outnumbered those of the enemy, and in the proportion of three to one. The plan of operations appears to have been skilfully and judiciously adapted to the novel character of this mountain warfare. It was the unexampled incompetence of four out of five of the generals which rendered it abortive, and enabled the enemy to hold our armies in check outside the forest from the frontier of Oude to the frontier of Bengal. "We have met," wrote Mr. Metcalfe, the Resident at Delhi, "with an enemy who decidedly

shows greater bravery and steadiness than our own troops.
In some instances Europeans and natives have been repulsed
with sticks and stones, and driven for miles like a flock of
sheep." "The successes of the Goorkhas," wrote Lord
Hastings, " have intimidated our officers and troops, and
with a deeply anxious heart I am keeping up an air of indifference and confidence; but were we to be foiled in this
• struggle, it would be the first step to the subversion of our
power." The reverses which our arms had sustained were
published throughout India, and served to revive the dormant
hopes of the native princes. For several months the country
was filled with rumours of a general confederacy against us.
Mahrattas, Pindarees, and Patans appeared for a time to
suspend their mutual animosities, under the impression that
the time had come for a united effort to extinguish our supremacy. The Peshwa took the lead in these machinations, and
sent envoys to all the Mahratta courts, not overlooking the
Pindaree chiefs. A secret treaty of mutual support was concluded, the first article of which bound the princes to obey
and serve him in this crusade. The army of Sindia was
organized on our frontier to take advantage of our difficulties.
Ameer Khan, with a body of 25,000 horse and foot, thoroughly
organized and equipped, and one hundred and twenty-five
guns, took up a position within twelve marches of our own
districts, and insulted our distress by offering to march to
Agra, and assist us in combating the Goorkhas. Runjeet Sing
marched an army of 20,000 men to the fords of the Sutlege,
and 20,000 Pindarees stood prepared for any opportunity of
mischief. To meet the emergency Lord Hastings ordered
. the whole of the disposable force of the Madras Presidency
up to the frontier of the Deccan, and despatched a Bombay
force to Guzerat. The Court of Directors were importunate
for retrenchment and reductions, but he considered the public
safety paramount to obedience, and raised three additional
regiments of infantry, enlisted bodies of irregular horse,
remodelled the whole of the Bengal army, and by these and

II.   X

other arrangements increased its strength to 80,000 soldiers.
But, as the natives observed, the Company's *ikbal*—good
fortune—was still in the ascendant. The clouds began to
break. Runjeet Sing was recalled to his capital by a threatened irruption of Afghans; Sindia's two principal commanders,
after long discord, attacked each other; Ameer Khan found
more immediate employment for his bands in the plunder of
Joudhoore, and the Pindaree leaders quarrelled among themselves. The cloud was completely dispersed by the brilliant
success of General Ochterlony, to which we now turn.

Operations of
General Ochter-
lony, 1814-15.

The division of General Ochterlony was destined
to dislodge the Goorkhas from the territories they
had acquired on the higher Sutlege, the defence
of which was entrusted to the gallant Umur Sing, and the
ablest of the Goorkha commanders was thus pitted against
the ablest of the English generals. The scene of operations
was a wild and rugged region, presenting successive lines of
mountains, rising like steps one above another, to the loftiest
peaks of the Himalaya. It was broken up by deep glens,
and covered with thick forests, and still further protected
by six forts on points almost inaccessible, and by numerous
stockades. It would not have been easy to imagine a more
difficult field for military operations. The General had formed
a correct estimate of the bold character of his opponent, and
the advantages which he enjoyed in his positions, and in a
spirit of high enterprize, tempered with sound judgment, he
proceeded towards his object by cautious, yet sure, steps. He
did not disdain to copy the tactics of the Goorkhas, and erect
stockades to protect isolated detachments, which saved many
of them from being overpowered, though other generals were
disposed to condemn the device as a confession of weakness.
Having crossed the plain from Loodiana, he entered the hills
and encamped on the 1st November before the fort of Nala-
gur, where he received intelligence of the disaster at Kalunga
and the death of General Gillespie. But he had wisely
brought on the whole of his battering train, which he caused

to play on the fort for thirty hours, when the commander
surrendered it, and the campaign opened auspiciously by the
capture of an important fortress, with the loss of only one
European soldier. It would be wearisome to enter into any
detail of the operations of the next five months, during which
the gallantry of the British troops was matched.by the heroic
valour of the Goorkhas, and the strategy of British engineers
was repeatedly foiled by the tact and resolution of Umur
Sing. The service was the most arduous in which the Company's army had ever been engaged in India. At the elevation of more than five thousand feet above the level of the
sea, at the most inclement season of the year, amidst falls of
snow, sometimes of two days' continuance, the pioneers were
employed in blasting rocks and opening roads for the eighteen-
pounders, and men and elephants were employed day after
day in dragging them up those Alpine heights. The energy of
the General, and the sublime character of the warfare, kindled
the enthusiasm of the army. By a series of bold and skilful
manœuvres every height was at length surmounted, and
every fortress save one captured, and on the 15th April Umur
Sing found himself confined to the fort of Malown, situated
on a mountain ridge, with a steep declivity of two thousand
feet on two sides. The next day Umur Sing assaulted the
British works with his whole force, under the direct command
of his ablest general, who, on leaving the Goorkha camp
directed both his wives to prepare for suttee, as he had
determined to conquer or fall. He fell covered with wounds,
and General Ochterlony ordered his body to be wrapped in
shawls and delivered to his master. His wives sacrificed
themselves on the funeral pile the next day. The Goorkha
army was obliged to retire, with the loss of five hundred men.
But the feeling of exultation occasioned by this victory was
damped by the loss which the army soon after sustained in
the death of Lieutenant Lawtie, of the engineers, a young
officer of the highest professional zeal, penetration, and
promise, to whom, as field engineer, the General had been

x 2

more indebted for the success of his operations than to any other officer. The whole army went into mourning for him.

Fall of Almora —surrender of Malown, 1815. Information reached the General's camp soon after of the occupation of Almora. This province formed the centre of the Nepal conquests westward, and Lord Hastings considered that the reduction of it would greatly facilitate the operations against Umur Sing, by cutting off his communications with the capital. As no regular troops could be spared for this service, Colonel Gardner, an officer of great merit, who had been in the Mahratta service, was directed to raise some irregular corps in Bundlekund. These raw levies, under their enterprizing commander, entered the province, and speedily cleared it of the Goorkhas. The capital fell on the 27th April to Colonel Nicolls, an officer of the regular service, who was sent with a large force to complete the work which Colonel Gardner had begun. The Goorkha force at Malown was thus isolated, and deprived of all hope of reinforcement, which led the Goorkha officers to intreat Umur Sing to make terms with General Ochterlony, but the stern old chief spurned their advice, and the great body of his troops passed over to the English. He himself retired into the fort with about two hundred men; who still clung to his fortunes, but when the English batteries were about to open, he felt unwilling to sacrifice in a forlorn conflict the lives of the brave men who had generously adhered to him to the last, and accepted the terms offered to him, thus ceding the whole of the conquests which the Nepalese had made west of the Kalee. General Ochterlony allowed him to march out with his arms and accoutrements, his colours, two guns, and all his personal property, "in consideration of the skill, bravery, and fidelity with which he had defended the country committed to his charge." The same honourable terms were likewise granted by General Ochterlony to his son, who had defended Jytak for four months against General Martindell. The Goorkha soldiers did not hesitate to take service under the Company's colours. They were formed into three regiments, and no sepoys have ever manifested greater loyalty or valour.

The discomfiture of their ablest general and the loss of their most valuable conquests took away from the Council of regency at Catmandoo all confidence in their mountain fastnesses, and induced them to sue for peace. The conditions proposed by Lord Hastings were, that they should resign all claims on the hill rajas west of the Kalee; cede the belt of low lands denominated the *teraee*, restore the territory of Sikkim north of Bengal, and receive a British Resident. To the relinquishment of the *teraee* the Goorkhas manifested greater repugnance than even to the residence of a British representative at the court. The revenue derived from these lands, though small, was important to a poor state; some of the most valuable jageers in them were held by the members of the regency, and Lord Hastings therefore reduced his demand to a portion of this territory. The negotiations were at length brought to a close, and the Goorkha commissioners came down to Segowlee and signed the treaty on the 2nd December, under an engagement that the ratification of it by the regency should be delivered within fifteen days. The treaty was duly signed by the Governor-General in Calcutta, and a royal salute was fired in honour of the peace; but it was premature. Umur Sing and his sons had arrived at Catmandoo, and urged the chiefs still to confide their fortunes to their swords, to dispute every inch of mountain territory, and, if driven from it, to retire to the borders of China. Acting under this advice, the council determined to reject the treaty, and sent an envoy to announce their resolution to continue the war. At the same time they made every effort to collect their military resources, and to fortify the passes. Lord Hastings, on his part, spared no pains to strike a decisive blow at the capital before the rains commenced. An effective force of 20,000 men was rapidly assembled, and entrusted to the command of Sir David Ochterlony, who had intermediately been created a baronet. On emerging from the forest,

Margin note: Second Goorkha campaign, and peace, 1816.

and approaching the first pass, on the 10th February, 1816, he found that the works of the Goorkhas were altogether unassailable. But Captain Pickersgill, of the quartermaster-general's department, had discovered a route to the left which, though incomparably difficult, would enable the general to turn the flank of the enemy. The enterprize was the boldest effort in the whole course of this mountain warfare, but it proved completely successful, and at once decided the issue of the campaign. During the night of the 14th February General Ochterlony marched in dead silence through a narrow ravine, where twenty men might have arrested a whole army. By seven in the morning the Choorea heights, to the west of the enemy's position, were gained without any resistance. There the force bivouacked for two days without food or shelter, while the other detachments were brought up. The General then advanced to Mukwanpore, within fifty miles of Catmandoo, where the Goorkhas made a stand, but were completely defeated. This blow took away from the regency all conceit of fighting; the treaty was sent down in hot haste with the red seal attached to it, and peace was finally concluded on the 2nd March, 1816.

Remarks on the war, 1816.   The Nepal war, though waged in a difficult region, and prolonged for eighteen months, was managed with such singular economy as to add only fifty-four lacs of rupees to the public debt. The Goorkhas were not only the most valiant, but the most humane foes we had ever encountered in India, and they also proved to be the most faithful to their engagements. Unlike other Indian treaties, that which was made in 1816 has never been violated, and the Goorkhas, instead of taking advantage of our exigencies in the mutiny of 1857, sent a large force to assist in quelling it. The barren region which was the scene of this deadly conflict of 1815 has proved an invaluable acquisition to the empire. It has furnished sites for sanataria at Simla and Mussooree, at Landour and Nynee-thal, where the rulers of British India are enabled to recruit their strength during the heat of sum-

mer, as the Mogul emperors were wont periodically to exchange the feverish temperature of Agra and Delhi for the
delicious climate of Cashmere. The distance between Calcutta and Simla is abridged by a rail, and a thousand miles are
now traversed with greater speed than a hundred in the days
of Akbar and Jehangeer; while the electric telegraph, which
conveys messages to the extremities of the empire in a few
minutes, gives a character of ubiquity to the Government while
sojourning in the hills.

Insurrection at The Nepal war closed on the 5th March, 1816,
Bareilly, 1816. and the Pindaree war commenced on the 16th
October in the following year. The intermediate period was
not, however, a season of tranquillity. Two military operations
were forced on Government in the north-west provinces,
which, though of comparatively minor importance, enabled
Lord Hastings to assure the Court of Directors, who were
importunate for the reduction of the army, that "our own
possessions were not precisely as secure as an estate in York-
shire." To relieve the pressure on the finances, it was resolved
to impose a house-tax for the support of the municipal police
on certain of the great towns, and, among others, on Bareilly,
the capital of Rohilcund. The rate was to be assessed by
each ward, and the expenditure controlled by the towns-
men. It was by no means oppressive in amount, the highest
sum being only four rupees a-year, and the lowest class being
altogether exempted from it. But a house-tax was an innovation not sanctioned by custom or tradition, and a spirit of
opposition was roused against it among those who willingly
submitted to the anomalous but ancient system of town
duties. The Rohillas, the most turbulent of the Afghan
colonists in India, determined to resist it. The magistrate, on
entering Bareilly to arrange the details of the assessment with
the principal inhabitants, was assailed by a mob excited by
the *moofty*, or chief priest, and obliged to order his guard to
clear the way, when three of their number, together with six
or seven of the inhabitants, were killed and wounded. They

were regarded as martyrs by the populace, and the exasperation became intense. Messengers were despatched to the
neighbouring town of Rampoora, which was the general resort
of large bodies of Afghan adventurers, who streamed down
annually from their own barren mountains to seek military
service among the various princes of India. From Rampoora
and other towns reinforcements were drawn to Bareilly during
the night, and in the morning five or six thousand fanatics
were found to be assembled under the green flag of the prophet. Happily the military force of Government had also
been augmented at the same time, and in the severe conflict
which ensued no fewer than four hundred of the insurgents
were killed and a greater number wounded, but the whole body
was dispersed. Had the result been different the whole province of Rohilcund would have immediately risen in rebellion,
and Ameer Khan, a Rohilla by birth, who was encamped at
the time within a few marches of Agra with 12,000 Rohillas
under his standard, would not have allowed the opportunity
Hatras, 1817. to slip. This event evinced the impolicy of allowing the great landholders in the adjacent Dooab, or country
lying between the Jumna and the Ganges, to continue to
garrison their castles with a large body of military retainers,
as they had done when the province belonged to Sindia. One
of these zemindars, Dyaram, a Jaut, and a relative of the raja
of Bhurtpore, had been permitted to retain his estates and his
fortress of Hatras, on the borders of Rohilcund. He had
already presumed to levy contributions on the country, and
to give shelter to thieves and robbers ; and he now proceeded to
exclude every servant of the Government from his town, and
to interrupt the process of the courts. His fort, which was
considered one of the strongest in the country, was surrounded
by a ditch a hundred and twenty-five feet broad and eighty-
five feet deep. It had been placed in a state of complete
repair, and strengthened by the adoption of all the improve-
ments made by the Government engineers in the adjacent
fort of Allyghur. He and a neighbouring zemindar, equally

refractory, were able at any time to assemble a force of 10,000 men. Lord Hastings deemed it important that this baronial castle should no longer bid us defiance, and ●rdered up an overwhelming force, together with such an array of mortars —his favourite weapon—as nothing could possibly withstand. On the 1st March, 1817, forty-five mortars and three breaching batteries began to play on the fort, but the garrison gallantly stood this storm of shot and shell for fifteen hours. At length, however, the great magazine blew up with a concussion which was felt at Agra, thirty miles distant, and which destroyed half the garrison and nearly all the buildings. Dyaram made his escape with a few horsemen. The complete reduction of one of the strongest fortresses in Hindostan in a few hours, not only secured the ready submission of the contumacious zemindars in the Dooab, but created a salutary impression throughout India, and doubtless contributed to the success of the ensuing campaign. Hatras is now a peaceful railway station.

CHAPTER XXVII.

TRANSACTIONS WITH NATIVE PRINCES, 1814—1817. PINDAREE AND MAHRATTA WAR, 1817.

Patans and Pindarees, 1814—1817. THE policy of Lord Wellesley had been steadfastly repudiated by the Court of Directors, but the wisdom of it was amply vindicated by the desolation which followed its abandonment. It was under the operation of their principle of non-intervention that the power of the Patans and the Pindarees grew up to maturity, and became the scourge of Central India. Ameer Khan, the Patan freebooter, had gradually established a substantive power, but the predatory element was always predominant in it. His army was more efficient than that of any native prince of the time, and received a fixed rate of pay, which, however, was seldom disbursed with regularity. It was estimated at not less than 10,000 foot 'and 15,000 horse, with a powerful artillery. It was his game to levy contributions from princes and states, and he moved about with all the appliances for the siege of the towns which resisted his demands. The object of the Pindarees was universal and indiscriminate plunder, and they swept through the country with such rapidity as to make it impossible to calculate their movements, or to overtake their detachments. While a force, for example, was assembled in haste to protect Mirzapore and the towns on the Ganges from their approach, they had already effected their object, and turned off to Guzerat, and were ravaging the western coast. While preparations were made to expel them from Guzerat, they had crossed the peninsula and were laying waste the opposite coast. The selfish argument employed by Sir George Barlow in defence of his neutral policy, that the disorders it might engender would prove a safeguard for the Company's dominions, had proved utterly fallacious. It was found that when the cauldron, seething with the elements of anarchy, was ready to boil over, it was those who had the greatest stake in India who were exposed to the greatest risk.

Representations to the Court of Directors, 1813 —1815.   One of the latest acts of Lord Minto's administration, as already stated, was to impress on the Court of Directors the necessity of adopting an extensive and vigorous system of measures for the suppression of the Pindaree hordes. Lord Hastings, on his arrival in India, found 50,000 Pindarees and Patans in the heart of India, subsisting entirely by plunder, and extending their ravages over an area as large as England, and one of his earliest acts was to point out to the Court, in language stronger than that of his predecessor, the increasing danger of this predatory power. He even went so far as to advance the opinion that the affairs of the Company could not prosper until their Government became the head of a league embracing

every power in India, and was placed in a position to direct its
entire strength against the disturbers of the public peace. But
such a course of policy was systematically opposed by the two
members of his Council. The senior, Mr. Edmonstone, was one
of the most eminent of the Company's servants, and combined
talent of a very high order with an affluence of official experience, but he lacked the higher endowments of the statesman.
He had filled the office of political secretary during the administration of Lord Wellesley with great distinction, and was
generally understood to have given a cordial support to his
comprehensive views. During the government of Lord Minto
he was the oracle of the Council chamber; but, having now
taken his seat at the Board, and become responsible for the
measures of Government, his habitual caution induced him to
incline to the policy of Sir George Barlow, when he perceived
the intention of Lord Hastings to subvert it, and he reprobated the extension of our political alliances and relations.
His colleague, Mr. Dowdeswell, had all the narrow-minded
prejudices of Sir George Barlow, without a tithe of his abilities. The Court of Directors still clung to their cherished
policy of non-intervention, and in reply to the despatch of
Lord Hastings of the 29th September, prohibited him "from
engaging in plans of general confederacy, and of offensive
operations against the Pindarees, either with a view to their
utter extirpation, or in anticipation of expected danger."
They enjoined him to undertake nothing which might em-
broil them with Sindia ; they forbade any change in the existing system of political relations, and directed him to maintain,
with as little deviation as possible, the course of policy
prescribed at the close of the Mahratta war. They directed
him, moreover, to reduce the strength of the army, and make
every measure conducive to the promotion of economy. This
communication was more than six months on the way, and did
not reach India before April, 1816.

Proposed alli-   To prevent the irruption of the Pindarees into
ance with   the Deccan, Lord Hastings endeavoured to form a

Nagpore and Bhopal, 1814. subsidiary alliance with the raja of Nagpore, and thereby to establish a British force on the Nerbudda. To such an alliance the Court of Directors had given their sanction several years before, but the raja set his face sedulously against it, well knowing how irretrievably it would compromise his independence. Lord Hastings then contemplated a similar connection with Bhopal, and also with Saugor, in the hope of being able to hold the Pindarees in check by establishing a chain of posts from Bundlecund to the Nerbudda; but he considered it advisable to await the reply of the Court of Directors to his proposal of a general league. Bhopal was a small principality in Malwa, in the valley of the Nerbudda, lying between the British territories and the head-quarters of the Pindarees. It was founded by an Afghan favourite of Aurungzebe, who assumed independence soon after the death of his master. In 1778 the reigning prince was the only chief in Central India who afforded any support to General Goddard in his adventurous march across the peninsula. His kindness on that occasion exposed him to the vengeance of the Mahrattas, but it has never been forgotten by the British Government. The testimonials granted by the General of the important services rendered to him are carefully preserved as heirlooms in the royal archives of Bhopal. The state had been governed for many years by the celebrated Vizier Mahomed, a man of rare talent and resolution. In 1813 Sindia and the raja of Nagpore, impelled by the simple lust of acquisition, entered into an alliance for the partition of the territory, and a body of 60,000 troops laid siege to the capital. The noble defence of it for nine months by the Vizier has always been the subject of special admiration among the Mahomedan princes of India. But the garrison was at length reduced by casualties and desertions to about two hundred men; the stock of provisions was exhausted, and the destruction of the little state appeared inevitable, when it was arrested by the desertion of the Nagpore general. He pretended that he had been warned in a dream to relinquish the enterprize; but he was

himself a Mahomedan, and both he and the Afghans in the
Nagpore army had a strong feeling of sympathy for their
fellow-countrymen in Bhopal, and were unwilling to reduce
them to extremities. Sindia was happy of an excuse to retire
from an inglorious siege; but the confederates renewed it in
1814, and Vizier Mahomed applied with increased importunity
for the interference of the British Government. Lord Hastings
felt that it was important to preserve a principality situated
like that of Bhopal from subjugation, and scarcely less so to
prevent the growth of Sindia's influence at the court of Nagpore, and he directed the Resident at Delhi to grant the Nabob
the alliance he solicited without waiting for instructions from
Leadenhall-street. The two Mahratta princes were therefore informed that Bhopal was now under British protection,
and that their forces must be withdrawn forthwith. The raja
of Nagpore, after some hesitation, recalled his army, but
Sindia assumed a lofty bearing—it was at the time of our
disasters in Nepal—and declared that Bhopal was one of his
dependencies, with which the British Government was debarred from interfering by the treaty of 1805. Bhopal, it was
well known, though sometimes invaded, had continued to maintain its independence amidst the anarchy of the times; but the
Mahratta powers considered every province which they had
once laid under contribution as a perpetual dependency.
Sindia's claim was successfully met by a reference to documents; but the vigorous preparations which Lord Hastings
was making to enforce his demand, combined with the successes of General Ochterlony, proved a stronger argument, and
induced him to lower his tone. His two commanders, moreover, who had long been at variance, attacked each other
under the walls of Bhopal, and his army was soon after
recalled. But the projected alliance fell to the ground. Vizier
Mahomed never had any serious intention of encumbering
himself with it, and with genuine Afghan duplicity was treating with Sindia at the same time that he was negotiating with
the British Resident, in the hope of playing off one party

against the other. Lord Hastings, disgusted with this perfi-
dious conduct, ordered that his envoy should be dismissed
without an audience when he next made his appearance at
Delhi. The miscarriage of this project, however vexatious at
the time, saved the honour of the Company's Government, as
a despatch was soon after received from the India House
positively forbidding the Governor-General to contract the alliance, or indeed to adopt any measure which might give
umbrage to Sindia.

Affairs of Poona,   To turn to the progress of events at Poona.
1803—1814.   Bajee Rao, the last of the Peshwas, though not
deficient in a certain kind of ability, had none of the talents
for government which had more or less distinguished his ancestors. For the success of his schemes he always depended
on the spirit of intrigue, which was his ruling passion through
life, and no dependence could ever be placed on his most solemn
assurances. He was the slave of avarice and of superstition.
In the course of ten years he had succeeded, by incessant extortion and extreme parsimony, in amassing treasure to the extent
of five crores of rupees, but he was lavish to extravagance in
the support of brahmins and temples, and his time was spent
in constant pilgrimages. In these tours he was always accompanied by a golden image of Vishnoo in a state palankeen,
surrounded by a numerous and expensive staff of priests,
and escorted by a guard of his choicest troops. The violent
death of the Peshwa, Narayun Rao, a brahmin, was universally attributed to his father Raghoba; and to absolve his
family from the guilt of this impious deed, he fed a hundred
thousand brahmins, and planted a hundred thousand mango-
trees around Poona. After having absorbed the estates of
many minor chiefs, he turned his attention in 1812 to the
great feudatories of the Mahratta empire, denominated the
southern jageerdars,—most of them of greater antiquity than
his own house,—whom he had long regarded with a rapacious
eye. When united they were able to bring 20,000 men into
the field, and might at any time have created a revolution at

Poona, but for the presence of the subsidiary force. The eminent services which they rendered to General Wellesley in 1803 had given them a strong claim on the British Government, on which they presumed so far as to relax in their allegiance to the Peshwa, and refuse him their stipulated contingents when required to repel the Pindarees. The Resident was therefore obliged to interfere, but the settlement which he dictated was unsatisfactory to both parties, inasmuch as it bound the jageerdars to do homage to their liege lord, and guaranteed their possessions against his cupidity.

Trimbukjee,   About the year 1813, one, Trimbukjee, who
1813-1815.   eventually became the cause of the Peshwa's ruin, began to rise to notice at his court. He was originally a spy, but by his intelligence and energy, and not less by pandering to his master's vices, gained a complete ascendency over his mind. Trimbukjee, on his part, manifested such servile devotion to the Peshwa, as to assure Mr. Elphinstone, the Resident at Poona, that he was ready even to kill a cow at his bidding. He entertained an inveterate animosity towards the British, and was incessantly urging Bajee Rao to shake off their alliance, and re-assert the ancient power, and revive the policy, of the Mahratta empire. It was under his influence that the general confederacy against the Company's Government was organised in* 1815. His next device was to establish the ascendency of his master at the Guzerat court. The Peshwa had claims on that state, extending back for half a century, which, with the accumulation of interest, amounted to three crores of rupees. The lease of the district of Ahmedabad, which the Peshwa had given to the Guickwar for ten years, was about to expire, and he was anxious to renew it. The Guickwar, therefore, deputed his chief minister, Gungadhur Shastree, to Poona, to settle these perplexing questions, but such was the universal dread of Trimbukjee's violence, that the Shastree would not venture on the journey without a safe conduct from the Resident. His reception at Poona was ungracious, and he was baffled by perpetual

evasions and obstructions. The renewal of the 'lease of
Ahmedabad was peremptorily refused, and it was bestowed
on Trimbukjee, who was also introduced to Mr. Elphinstone
as the Peshwa's chief minister. The Shastree, seeing no
prospect of the success of his mission, determined, with the
concurrence of Mr. Elphinstone, to return to Baroda. The
Peshwa and his favourite, on hearing of this intention, immediately changed their tactics, and spared no pains to win him
over to their interests. Trimbukjee flattered him with the
assurance that Bajee Rao had conceived so high an opinion
of his talents, that he was about to confer on him an office of
great dignity at Poona, and as a proof of his sincerity, to offer
his own sister-in-law in marriage to the Shastree's son. The
Shastree was induced by this cozenage to agree to a compromise of all his master's claims for lands yielding seven lacs of
rupees a-year. This bargain might have been advantageous,
considering that the Peshwa, in addition to the arrear of
three crores, claimed an annual tribute of twenty-five lacs of
rupees, but it was made without the consent of Mr. Elphinstone or the Guickwar, both of whom at once repudiated it.

Murder of the An auspicious day had been selected by the
Shastree, 1815. astrologers, and the most splendid preparations had
been made for the nuptials, but the Shastree, on hearing that
his royal master rejected the settlement, requested that
they might be at once suspended. He had already given
great offence to the Peshwa by refusing to allow his wife
to visit the palace, where she must have been witness to
scenes of revolting debauchery, but the interruption of the
wedding, which humiliated the Peshwa in the eyes of his
subjects, was considered an unpardonable insult, which nothing
but the blood of the Shastree could expiate. The Peshwa
proceeded on pilgrimage to Punderpore, and the Shastree,
though warned of his danger, was so infatuated as to accompany him. To throw him off his guard, the most cordial
communications were maintained with him, and he was induced,
by the repeated importunity of Trimbukjee, to pay his devo-

tions after dusk at the shrine. On his return, he was over-
taken at a distance of three hundred yards from the temple,
by the assassins of the Minister and cut to pieces. The murder
of a brahmin of the highest caste, and, moreover, a Shastree,
renowned for his sacred learning, in a holy city, at the period
of a pilgrimage, and in the immediate precincts of the temple,
filled the Mahratta community with horror and dismay. But
the victim was also 'the minister of a British ally, and had
proceeded to the court of Poona, under the guarantee of the
British Resident, who determined to lose no time in vindicating
the honour of his Government. Mr. Elphinstone returned in
haste from the caves of Ellora, which he was at the time
employed in exploring, to Poona, and instituted a rigid
enquiry into all the circumstances connected with the assassination. The guilt of Trimbukjee was established beyond all
question, and Mr. Elphinstone called on the Peshwa to place him
under arrest, and eventually to give him up. The demand
was strenuously resisted by Bajee Rao, who began to levy
troops, and to sound the other Mahratta powers to ascertain
how far he could depend on their aid, if he broke with the
British Government. Sindia's reply was disguised under the
form of a banker's letter : "This banking house is the Naek's
(the Peshwa's), while your house is in want of cash (troops),
you must submit to the importunity of creditors (the Company).
The Naek ought to go about some time on pilgrimage, but let
him write a bill in his own hand, and whatever money is
required shall be sent." The Peshwa was half inclined to
make common cause with his favourite and minister, whom he
could not surrender without incurring obloquy, and to raise
the standard of the Mahratta empire. But Mr. Elphinstone
had taken the precaution of calling up troops to the capital ;
the Peshwa's natural cowardice overcame every other feeling, and Trimbukjee was made over to him on the 25th
September, 1815, on condition that his life should be spared.
He was conveyed to the fort of Tannah, where he freely
admitted the murder of the Shastree to the British officers,

but assured them that he had not acted without his master's orders.

Lord Hastings returned to Calcutta from the North West towards the close of 1815, and on the 1st December placed on record an elaborate minute, drawn up from the notes of Mr. Metcalfe, in which he pointed out in stronger language than he had before employed, the increasing dangers arising from the growth of the Pindaree power, and the urgent necessity of active measures to suppress it.   To effect this object he proposed a general system of alliances, under the guarantee of the British Government, a complete revision of our relations with the native powers, and a new settlement of the Mahratta dominions.   The chief objection of the Court of Directors to any vigorous effort to root out the Pindarees, was the dread of irritating the Mahrattas generally, and Sindia in particular.   But Lord Hastings did not hesitate to assure them that "if there was no choice left, he should prefer an immediate war with the Mahrattas, for which we should be fully prepared, to an expensive system of defence, against a consuming predatory warfare, carried on clandestinely by the Mahratta powers, wasting our resources, till they might see a practicable opportunity of coming to an open rupture."   Mr. Edmonstone and Mr. Dowdeswell questioned the existence of any such hostile feeling among the Mahratta princes, and opposed the formation of any new alliances; the plan was therefore submitted to the home authorities, without their concurrence.   While this minute was on its way to England, the necessity of some immediate effort to curb the Pindarees was rendered the more imperative by their increasing audacity.   The *dussera* festival, when the plan of the campaign was usually organised, was celebrated in 1815 at Nimaur, the head-quarters of the great Pindaree leader Cheetoo, by a larger assemblage than had ever been collected before.   The Company's territories had hitherto been unmolested, owing to the constant, vigorous, and active preparations of Government, but at the suggestion of the Mahratta princes,

Lord Hastings's second representation to the Court, 1815.

Pindaree irruption, 1815-16.

the depredations of the Pindarees were now to be especially
directed against them, and the dominions of the Nizam. On
the 14th October, a body of 8,000 predatory horse crossed the
Nerbudda, and swept through the Nizam's territories as far
south as the Kistna, and returned to Nimaur so richly laden
with booty, that it was found necessary to invite merchants
from all quarters to purchase it. This extraordinary success
brought additional crowds to their standard, and a second
and larger expedition, consisting of 23,000 Pindarees, crossed
the Nerbudda in February. One large division poured down
on the Northern Sircars, sacked the civil station of Guntoor
on the Coromandel coast, and for ten days plundered the
villages around with perfect impunity. Troops and arms were
despatched from Calcutta to Masulipatam by sea, in all haste,
but the Pindarees had disappeared before their arrival; indeed,
they moved with such rapidity, that it would have been as
impossible to overtake them as a flight of locusts. Officers
were subsequently appointed by Government to ascertain the
injury they had inflicted on the country, and it was found that
in the Company's territories alone three hundred and thirty-
nine villages had been plundered, and many of them burnt, one
hundred and eighty-two persons put to death, five hundred
wounded, and three thousand six hundred subjected to torture,
while the loss of property exceeded twenty-five lacs of rupees.
The inhabitants had not seen the smoke of an enemy's camp
for fifty years. Ever since Clive had annexed the Northern
Sircars to the Company's territories in 1765, the people had
felt that they were living under the protection of a power
whose name was a sufficient guarantee of safety; but all
confidence was now extinguished, and they began to desert
their villages. The atrocities committed by these marauders,
and the refinement of cruelty they practised on their victims,
were thus vividly, described by Mr. Canning :— " Rapine,
murder in all its shapes, torture, rape, and conflagration, were
not rare and accidental occurrences in their progress, but the
uniform object of every enterprize. There were instances

where the whole female population of a village precipitated themselves into the wells as the only refuge from these brutal and barbarous spoilers; where, at their approach, fathers of families surrounded their own dwellings with fuel, and perished with their children in the flames kindled by their own hands." No previous invasion of the Pindarees had been so systematically directed against the Company's dominions, or perpetrated with so much audacity.

Subsidiary
alliance with
Nagpore, 27th
May, 1816. The success of this expedition manifested the great importance of obtaining the co-operation of the raja of Nagpore, through whose territories the Pindarees passed on crossing the Nerbudda. The raja had steadily resisted every proposal of a subsidiary alliance, but his death on the 22nd March, 1816, opened a favourable opportunity of obtaining it. He was succeeded by his son Persajee, nearly forty years of age, blind, palsied, and sunk into a state of complete idiotcy. His nephew, known in the history of India as Appa Sahib, was recognised as regent, but was opposed by a powerful faction, both in the court and in the zenana. He found it impossible, therefore, to maintain his position without foreign assistance, but, instead of invoking the aid of Sindia or Holkar, or one of the Pindaree leaders, any of whom would have been happy to hasten to his relief, and thus to obtain a substantial footing at Nagpore, he applied to Mr. Jenkins, the Resident, and offered to conclude the subsidiary alliance his uncle had rejected, on condition of receiving the support of the British authorities. Lord Hastings eagerly embraced a proposal which would place the resources of Nagpore at his disposal, and enable him to plant a British force on the Nerbudda. A treaty was accordingly concluded on the 27th May, which provided that a force of 6,000 infantry, and a regiment of cavalry, together with a due proportion of artillery, should be subsidised by the Nagpore state, at an expense of seven lacs and a-half of rupees a-year. It was likewise stipulated that the raja should engage in no foreign negotiation without the concurrence of the British Government, to whom

likewise all differences with foreign princes were to be submitted. The Nagpore ministers earnestly pleaded for the
insertion of a clause prohibiting the slaughter of kine in the
Nagpore territories, but it was distinctly rejected, as a similar
request had been refused to Sindia's envoys twelve years
before. " Thus have I been enabled," wrote Lord Hastings,
" to effect what has been fruitlessly laboured at for twelve
years. Sindia's designs on Nagpore, as well as the Peshwa's,
are defeated, and the interception of the Pindarees is rendered
certain." Soon after, orders arrived from England, revoking
the permission which had been formerly given to conclude this
alliance ; but it arrived too late to do any mischief.

Attempted alliance with Jeypore, 1816.   In a former chapter it has been stated that in
1805 Sir George Barlow repudiated the engage-
ment of Lord Lake to afford protection to Jeypore,
and abandoned it to spoliation. The Court of Directors approved of this decision, but they appear subsequently to have
felt some degree of compunction at this sacrifice of British
honour and of the welfare of Jeypore, and in December, 1813,
gave their sanction to the renewal of the alliance with that
state. The Nepal war, which occurred soon after, rendered
it advisable to postpone the execution of these instructions.
Meanwhile, Ameer Khan and his freebooters, having drained
Joudhpore, entered Jeypore, and laid siege to the capital,
with the intention of completing the reduction of the state.
The raja despatched a vakeel to Mr. Metcalfe, at Delhi, to
implore his interposition, and Lord Hastings, availing himself
of the warrant of the Court of Directors, determined to conclude the alliance, and receive Jeypore under British protection. Mr. Edmonstone and Mr. Dowdeswell strenuously
opposed this measure, but Mr. Seton, the third member of
Council, concurred with Lord Hastings, and enabled him to
carry out his plans by his own casting vote. Mr. Metcalfe was
then instructed to entertain the raja's application. Two
armies, each 9,000 strong, were ordered to assemble in the
neighbourhood of Muttra to support this resolution, and to

expel the Patans from Jeypore. To be prepared for any
opposition which might be offered by Sindia or Holkar, who,
having repeatedly plundered Jeypore, had the usual Mahratta
claims upon it, the four subsidiary armies of the Nizam, the
Peshwa, the Guickwar, and the Bhonslay, were ordered to
take up strategic positions in the south. The force thus
assembled fell little short of 40,000 infantry and 12,000
cavalry, and was sufficient to crush whatever antagonism
might arise, but the raja of Jeypore dreaded the alliance with
the Company almost, if not altogether, as much as he dreaded
the exactions of Ameer Khan, and in the true spirit of Oriental
policy carried on negotiations simultaneously with both parties,
menacing the Patan with the weight of a British force, which,
he said, he had only to sign the treaty to bring down upon
him. The threat was effectual, and Ameer Khan, anxious
to avoid a collision with British troops, raised the siege.
As soon as his retirement had relieved the raja from his
terrors, he endeavoured to evade the alliance by advancing
new and preposterous terms. The negotiation was, therefore, broken off, and all the military movements counter-
manded.

Despatches
from the India
House, 1816.   Mr. George Canning, one of the most brilliant
of English statesmen, accepted the office of President of the Board of Control in June, 1816, and
was immediately required to investigate and decide on the
largest and the most momentous question which had ever
been submitted to the Board. This was the adoption or rejection of the plans proposed by Lord Hastings in the previous
month of December for a general system of alliances with the
native powers, under the guarantee of the Company, in order
to extinguish the Pindaree confederacy, to restore tranquillity
to Central India, and give security to the British possessions.
It was a bolder scheme of policy even than that of Lord
Wellesley which had been for ten years under the ban of the
Court of Directors; it was nothing less than the establishment of the universal supremacy of the Company throughout

the continent of India. Mr. Canning was new to the Government, and it is, therefore, no matter of surprise that he should have been unwilling to assume the responsibility of introducing so fundamental a change in the policy of the empire, and have resolved rather to adhere to the existing system, which was pronounced the safest, not only by the sage counsellors in Calcutta, but by those who might be considered his constitutional advisers in Leadenhall-street. He accordingly drew up a very elaborate and interesting minute, which reviewed the political condition of India, and laid down rules for the guidance of the local authorities. It exhibited the clearest tokens of his great talent and of his inexperience. The Secret Committee, who signed it officially, said they were unwilling to incur the risk of a general war for the uncertain purpose of extirpating the Pindarees. They would not sanction any extended political and military combinations for this object. It was probable that we might calculate on the aid of Sindia to protect the Company's dominions from their aggressions. Any attempt at this time to establish a new system of policy tending to an undue diffusion of our power must necessarily interfere with those economical considerations which it was more than ever incumbent to recommend. They even suggested the expediency of improving any opportunity which might be presented of treating with any of the Pindaree chiefs, or with the men for delivering up their leaders. Such advice kindled the indignation of Lord Hastings. "When the Honourable Committee," he replied, "suggest the expediency of engaging one portion of the Pindaree association to destroy another, I am roused by the fear that we have been culpably deficient in pointing out to the authorities at home the brutal and atrocious qualities of these wretches . . . and I am confident that nothing would have been more repugnant to the feelings of the Honourable Committee than the notion that the Government should be soiled by a procedure which was to bear the colour of a confidential intercourse in a common cause with any of these

Despatch of 26th September, 1816.

gangs." But immediately after the transmission of this despatch of the 5th September, Mr. Canning received intelligence of the irruption of the Pindarees on the Coromandel coast, and the desolation they had spread for ten days through the Company's districts, and his views underwent an immediate and auspicious change. Within three weeks another communication was sent out under his directions, which said : "The previous instructions discouraging plans of general confederacy and of offensive operations were not intended to restrain the exercise of your judgment and discretion upon any occasion when actual war on our territories might be commenced by any body of marauders. We think it due to your lordship not to lose an instant in conveying to you an explicit assurance of our approbation of any measures which you may have authorized or undertaken, not only for repelling invasion, but for pursuing and chastising the invaders. We can·no longer abstain from a vigorous exertion of military power in vindication of the British name and in defence of subjects who look to us for protection." The enormities of the Pindarees had overcome even the dread of irritating Sindia, the great bugbear of the India House : "Any connection of Sindia and Holkar with the Pindarees against us or our allies, known, though not avowed, would place them in a state of direct hostility to us."

Pindaree campaign, 1816-17.

The Pindaree expedition of 1815-16 was sufficient to convince Mr. Canning of the necessity of adopting energetic measures to eradicate this plague, but it required another season of desolation to convince Mr. Edmonstone and Mr. Dowdeswell of the same truth. Lord Hastings was confident that the establishment of the Nagpore subsidiary force at the fords of the Nerbudda would be sufficient to intercept the Pindarees. As the period of their annual swarming approached, Colonel Walker moved up to the ferries with a body of 6,000 horse and foot ; but this force was soon found to be utterly unequal to the protection of a line a hundred and fifty miles in extent. The Pindarees pushed across in detachments between his posts, one of which was ninety miles from its nearest support. A party of 5,000 men suddenly crossed the river on his extreme right, within sight of his infantry, while his cavalry was posted on the opposite flank, and rushed forward with such speed as to baffle all pursuit. They fell on the Company's district of Kimedy, and burnt a portion of the town of Ganjam, and, but for the presence of a large force which happened to be assembled in order to quell a local insurrection, would have laid Juggunnath and the district of Orissa under contribution. Another body laid waste the territories of Nagpore and Hyderabad. Such was the audacity which success had created in the minds of these freebooters that one of the leaders, with a band of only five hundred horse, swept through the Peshwa's dominions, and after having plundered two hundred miles of the Malabar coast, returned leisurely up the valley of the Taptee. Though attacked with some success during their progress homewards, the men brought back so rich a booty in their saddles as to give fresh vigour to the predatory spirit. The expedition of the season of 1816–17 was the boldest the Pindarees had ever undertaken, and it gave rise to the gravest considerations. With the Nagpore subsidiary force guarding the passages of the Nerbudda, 23,000 Pindarees had succeeded in crossing it with ease. Independently of the Nizam's reformed contingent and of the Poona brigade, no fewer than 32,000 men belonging to the Company's and King's force had been stationed to guard the country between the Kistna and the Toombuddra, but the Pindarees had nevertheless dashed through the Peninsula and across it, and plundered both coasts. It was true that they suffered severely on two occasions, when Major McDowell and Major Lushington succeeded in overtaking them, but the eminent success of these officers was a happy contingency, and not owing to the efficiency of the defensive measures which had been adopted, which, while they proved totally abortive, occasioned an amount of expenditure exceeding the largest calculations of the cost of a more energetic policy. These reflec-

Determination of the Council, 16th December, 1816. tions brought the Council round to the views of Lord Hastings; and on the 16th December, while the permissive despatch of the Court of Directors was coming round the Cape, it was unanimously resolved that "the resolution adopted of refraining from any system of offensive operations against the Pindarees till the sanction of the Court could be received should be abandoned, and that vigorous measures for the suppression of the Pindarees had become an indispensable object of public duty."

Sindia's determination, 1817. The season was too far advanced for any such operations, but preparations were silently commenced on a large scale to take the field in the cold season of 1817. Intimation was immediately conveyed to Sindia of the resolution which had been adopted to extirpate the Pindarees, and he was required to co-operate in carrying it out; but they had agents in his camp, and warm partizans among his ministers, who laboured to persuade him that with their powerful aid he might hope to bid defiance to the Company, and that his own security would be weakened if he allowed these bands, who were almost an integral part of his army, and ready at any time to flock to his standard, to be extinguished. The Pindaree vakeels boasted that they would out-do the exploits of Jeswunt Rao Holkar, and that fifty thousand of their body were ready to carry fire and sword to Calcutta; but Sindia was not to be misled by this gasconade. Assye was yet fresh in his memory. More recently he had seen the Company triumphant in Nepal; they had secured the resources of Nagpore; they had evidently abandoned their neutral policy, and the spirit of Lord Wellesley again animated their counsels. He was, therefore, induced to promise his co-operation, though not without great reluctance, and only on condition that the lands recovered from the Pindarees should be transferred to him. This perfunctory aid was not likely to be of much practical use, but it was important to deprive the cause of the Pindarees, if but ostensibly, of one of their most stáunch supporters.

Hostility of
Bajee Rao,
1816-17.

During these negotiations at Gwalior events of deep importance were in progress at Poona. Trimbukjee had been confined in the fort of Tannah, in the island of Salsette, which, for greater security, was garrisoned only by European troops ; but a plan was laid for his deliverance, and it was communicated to him in Mahratta songs, chaunted by a fellow-countryman who had taken service as a groom with one of the officers, while he walked his master's horse to♦ and fro under Trimbukjee's window. He effected his escape in September, 1816. For several months after this event Bajee Rao manifested a spirit of unusual cordiality towards the Resident, Mr. Elphinstone, but Lord Hastings had incontrovertible proof that he was all the while engaged in active and hostile negotiations with Sindia, Holkar, Ameer Khan, and the Pindarees. He received the intimation of the resolution to eradicate the Pindarees with every demonstration of delight, but Mr. Elphinstone heard at the same time of the assembly of seditious troops within fifty miles of the capital. At his earnest request a detachment was sent to disperse them, but the commandant, after having held several conferences with them, reported that no insurgents were to be found. Early in March, 1817, it was discovered that these movements were directed by Trimbukjee himself, who was actively employed in raising new levies, while the Peshwa was importuning Mr. Elphinstone to condone his offence and allow him to return to Poona, which was necessarily refused. Meanwhile, another and a more serious revolt broke out in Candesh, and a fortress was occupied by the insurgents. The attitude of the Peshwa became gradually more hostile. He hastened the enlisting of troops, collected guns and bullocks, provisioned his forts, and sent away his wardrobe, jewels, and treasures to his strongest fortress. To counteract these movements Mr. Elphinstone ordered a large British force to Poona, and sent several detachments against the insurrectionary bands, who were in every case signally routed. On the 1st April he presented a note to the Peshwa reproaching him with the hostile movements he was abetting, and declared that the good understanding between the two Governments was now at an end. Several weeks of fruitless discussion ensued, during which Bajee Rao repeatedly made preparations to quit the capital, which would have been the signal of a general insurrection, but was restrained by his fears. On the 6th May, Mr. Elphinstone brought the controversy to an issue by peremptorily demanding the surrender of Trimbukjee within a month, and the delivery of three of the Peshwa's fortresses to be held as security. To this request he refused to accede with unusual coolness of determination, and declined to make any effort to apprehend his favourite. Troops were ordered up to Poona, and twenty-four hours allowed the Peshwa for his decision. The brave Gokla and the commandant of artillery urged a bold appeal to arms, but he had not the spirit to adopt their advice. The fortresses were made over, and a proclamation issued offering two lacs and a half of rupees for the apprehension of Trimbukjee.

Treaty of June 5th, 1817.   Lord Hastings, however, deemed it necessary, on the eve of his great operations against the Pindarees, to exact greater securities from this faithless prince, and Mr. Elphinstone was instructed to submit to him the draft of a new treaty, binding him to renounce Trimbukjee for ever, to relinquish formally and substantially the character of supreme head of the Mahratta empire, to dismiss the agents of the foreign princes from his court, and to abstain from all further communication with them, referring all matters in dispute to the Company's Government. He was likewise required to resign all his rights feudal, pecuniary, and territorial, in Saugor and Bundlekund, and in lieu of the contingent of 5,000 horse and 3,000 foot, which he was under obligation by the treaty of Bassein to maintain as an auxiliary force, to cede territory yielding twenty-four lacs of rupees a-year. His ministers endeavoured to mitigate the severity of these demands, which their master's offences, whatever they might be, did not, in their opinion, merit, and which were peculiarly grating to his feelings; and they stated that we seemed to exact a greater degree of fidelity to engagements than any native prince was able from his habits to observe.   But Mr. Elphinstone was inflexible, and the treaty was signed without any modification on the 13th June.   The heavy penalty thus inflicted on the Peshwa for his delinquencies was doubtless the most rigorous, perhaps also the most questionable measure of Lord Hastings's administration, and could be justified only on the ground of inexorable necessity.   It is necessary, therefore, to refer to Lord Hastings' own vindication of his proceedings. "I exacted," he said, "cessions from him as the penalty of his base and profligate attempt to excite a general conspiracy against us.   These terms were in themselves severe.   When, however, they are measured by the magnitude of the injury aimed at us, they will not appear harsh, nor will the necessity of them be doubted, when it is considered that our experience has shown the impossibility of relying on his most solemn professions.   We had no choice, consistently with our security, but to cripple him, if we left him on the throne."   When the intelligence of these proceedings, as well as of the large additions which had thus been made to the Company's possessions, reached England, Mr. Canning bowed gracefully to the irresistible spirit of progress which, in spite of every effort to repress it, was inherent in the constitution of the Company's Government.   His despatch to Calcutta stated: "We feel all the objections which lie against measures tending to reduce or humiliate those native states which, from the extent of their dominions, and from their military talents, were formerly ranked as substantive states.   The course of these proceedings, however, sufficiently proves the almost irrepressible tendency of our Indian power to enlarge its bounds and to augment its preponderance, in spite of the most peremptory injunctions of forbearance from home, and the most scrupulous obedience of them in India; but, while expressing our approbation of these,

measures, political and military, we consider it particularly
important to declare that we consider any such case as forming
an unwelcome though justifiable exception to the general rule
of our policy. The occurrence of such exceptions has been
unfortunately much too frequent." Yet, so vain are human
wishes, that even before this dispatch had left the India
House, the whole of the Peshwa's kingdom had been incorporated with the dominions of the Company, with the exception
of the small section given to the raja of Sâtara.

Holkar's Court,   To revert to the progress of events at the
1811-17:   Court of Holkar. On the death of Jeswunt Rao
in 1811, Toolsee bye, the favourite of his harem, adopted a
son of his by another concubine, and determined to conduct the
government herself in the character of regent. The virtues
of Aylah bye, during her successful administration of thirty
years, had created a predilection for a female reign, which
was of no little service to the plans of Toolsee bye. She was
in the bloom of youth and beauty, and with the most fasci-
nating address combined great intelligence and invincible
resolution; but her spirit was vindictive, and her morals were
dissolute, and she speedily exhausted every feeling of respect.
Ameer Khan, who held large jageers from the state, and
exercised a preponderating influence in its councils, quitted
Indore soon after the death of Jeswunt Rao to pursue his
schemes of avarice and ambition in Rajpootana, leaving a
relative, Guffoor Khan, with a large body of troops, to maintain the Patan ascendency; but there was no regularity or
solidity in the government. The income of the state, under
the most economical management, was insufficient to maintain its overgrown army. When the troops became mutinous
for pay, districts were assigned for their support to the commanders, who used their power only to fleece the people.
Open villages were sacked, and walled towns cannonaded.
The inhabitants took to flight, the lands remained without
tillage, and the country presented a scene of desolation and
woe. The lawless soldiery did not spare the possessions of

Sindia, and at length threatened the Bye herself with their violence. She sought refuge for a time with Zalim Sing, the regent of Kotah, the only court in Central India which in that period of confusion afforded an asylum for the unfortunate, but she was nevertheless constrained to part with her jewels to appease their rapacity. Soon after, she became enamoured of Gunput Rao, the hereditary dewan of the state. The minister, Buluram sett, ventured to remonstrate with her on the scandal which her amours created, and she caused him to be cut down in her presence. To avenge this foul murder, Guffoor Khan laid siege to the town to which she had retired. She placed herself at the head of her Mahratta horse, and with undaunted courage led the assault till the elephant on which she was seated with the young prince was struck by a cannon ball and became unmanageable, when she mounted a horse, and placing the lad in her lap, fled from the field. Tantia Joge, a brahmin and a merchant, who had risen to distinction by his administrative talents, then accepted the post of minister, and was considered the head of the Mahratta party, while Guffoor Khan, with nine battalions of infantry, headed the Patans. Between these factions the government fell into a state of complete anarchy, and it was at this period, in the autumn of 1817, that the agents of Bajee Rao arrived in the camp to promote the confederacy he was forming against the British Government.

Distracted State of India, 1817. The disorganisation of Central India had now reached its climax. The commanders in Sindia's and Holkar's army were beyond the control of the Government, and employed their troops wherever there was any prospect of plunder. The smaller states were subject to constant spoliation. The Rajpoot principalities were prostrated by internal discord, and the periodical pillage to which they were subject. The soldiers in Central India who depended in a great measure on violence for their means of subsistence, and whom there was no native power with the disposition or the strength to control, fell little short of 100,000. The history of the previous eight centuries presents no period of such intense and general suffering, and there was every appearance of the approaching dissolution of the bonds of society. On the 8th July, Lord Hastings left Calcutta, and proceeded to the upper provinces to reduce this chaos to order. The plan of operations which he laid down was comprehensive, bold, and decisive. He was convinced that if the Pindarees were simply dispersed, they would speedily assemble again, and that the only mode of dealing effectually with them was to assault them in their haunts, and hunt them through the country, till their organisation was irretrievably annihilated. He felt, moreover, that to prevent the renewal of such confederacies, it was necessary to resettle Central India, which now exhibited only a general scramble for power and plunder, to define the boundaries of each prince, and prevent mutual encroachments by the ascendency of one paramount authority. Mr. Canning had sanctioned the adoption of vigorous measures, not only to resist the inroads of the Pindarees, but also to chastise them, but in the same despatch he alluded, without qualification, to the instructions of the previous year, which interdicted plans of general federation; and the standing orders to form no new treaties without the warrant of the India House, had never been revoked. Lord Hastings was however, convinced, that without a general combination of all the princes north of the Nerbudda, under the supremacy of the Company, there was no hope of permanent tranquillity; but this policy found little favour with the members of Council. On his progress to the north-west, therefore, he communicated to them his reasons for deviating from the views of the home authorities, and took on himself the sole responsibility of the general system of alliances he had determined to form. To the Court of Directors he wrote that unexpected events had presented a juncture which required to be dealt with according to its own peculiar features, and that he had construed their instructions as not applicable to circumstances so little analogous to what had been contemplated by them.

Lord Hastings proceeds up the country, 1817.

Extent of military operations, 1817.

The military operations on which Lord Hastings was now about to enter were on a grander scale than any in which the Company had as yet been engaged. They embraced the whole extent of country from the Kistna in the south, to the Ganges in the north; and from Cawnpore in the east, to Guzerat on the western coast, six hundred miles in one direction, and seven hundred in another. The army was, moreover, the largest which had ever taken the field in India under British colours. The battle of Plassy, which laid the foundation of British power, was won with 2,100 men. The army with which Lord Cornwallis struck down the power of Tippoo in 1793 did not exceed 31,000. The troops assembled by Lord Wellesley during the Mahratta war, independent of the irregular horse of the allies, amounted to 55,000. On the present occasion Lord Hastings called out the armies of the three Presidencies, and, including irregulars and the contingents of native princes, was enabled to assemble a force of 116,000 infantry and cavalry, with three hundred guns. The magnitude of this force was out of proportion to the simple object of extinguishing bands of marauders, who never stood an attack. But Lord Hastings knew that the Mahratta powers had an interest in common with the Pindarees, and were opposed to the extinction of an association which might be turned to account in any struggle with the British Government. He had every reason to believe that a general confederacy had been formed of the native powers against the interests of the Company. Sindia was known to have received twenty-five lacs of rupees from the Peshwa, as the price of his assistance, and to have given a direct assurance of support to the Pindarees and to Ameer Khan, in case they were attacked. Lord Hastings had determined that in this crusade against the Pindarees, no native prince should be allowed to remain neuter, and his preparations were intended to provide against every adverse contingency which might arise. Happily, the powers of Governor-General and Commander-in-chief were combined in his hands, and all arrangements, both military and political,

II.   Z were directed by the same mind, and regulated by the same undivided authority. A complete harmony of operations was thus secured, which eminently contributed to the success of the war. The veteran soldier of sixty-three took the field in person, and gave promptitude and energy to every movement. The plan which he drew out of the campaign, with its manifold combinations from points widely separated from each other, exhibited military talent of no ordinary standard. Four armies advanced from the Deccan under the direction of the Madras Commander-in-chief, Sir Thomas Hislop, and four from the north-west provinces, to converge on the haunts of the Pinda-rees, and prevent the possibility of their escape. The only event which was likely to disturb these well-devised plans was the support which they might obtain from the Mahratta powers, but Lord Hastings considered that after the treaties he had concluded with the Nagpore raja and the Peshwa, he was safe from any interference on their part, and the regent of Holkar's cabinet was negotiating for British protection.

Treaty with Sindia, 1817.   In the north, however, it was necessary to place an effectual curb on the hostile tendencies of Sindia and Ameer Khan. Sindia's army was at this period in a state of more than ordinary insubordination, and one division had placed its commander under arrest. But rumours had been spread through the camp that Bajee Rao was about to erect the national standard and attack the Company, and Sindia's troops became eager to join him in this warfare, while Sindia himself as it afterwards appeared, had pledged his faith to that prince. There could be little doubt that the whole of Sindia's military resources would be engaged against Government in the coming struggle, and it was necessary to meet this emergency with promptitude. A note was accordingly delivered to him by the Resident, on the 10th October, stating that the Governor-General considered the treaty of 1805 abrogated by his having excited the Pindarees against the British Government, and repeatedly granted them an asylum after they had been openly engaged in plundering the territories of the Company.

Government was therefore no longer fettered by that clause of the treaty which placed restrictions on the formation of any connection with the chiefs of Malwa and Rajpootana, with whom Lord Hastings had now determined to contract alliances for the security of the Company's territories.   It stated that the British Government was not seeking any private advantage, and that the sole object of the armaments then assembled was to extinguish all predatory associations and restore tranquillity.   Sindia was therefore requested to give his co-operation, and to place his troops at the disposal of the Governor-General, to be stationed according to his judgment, with a British officer attached to each division.   As a proof of his sincerity he was moreover required to admit a British garrison, temporarily, into the fortress of Hindia on the Nerbudda, and into Asseergur, reputed the strongest fort in India, and the key of the Deccan.   During these negotiations Sindia was detected in a correspondence with the raja of Nepal, whom he prompted to a simultaneous attack on the Company's dominions.   The letters were found on his messenger, inserted between the leaves of a Sanscrit manuscript of the Vedas, and, to his great confusion, were returned to him in open durbar. To hasten his determination and fix his wavering mind, Lord Hastings took the field on the 16th October, crossed the Jumna on a bridge of boats, and marched directly upon Gwalior, while General Donkin, with the left division, moved down at the same time towards the same point.   Sindia was confounded by the rapidity of these movements, which not only cut him off at once from all communication with the Peshwa and the Pindarees, but also with the bulk of his own army then encamped in his southern provinces, and left him isolated at Gwalior, with not more than 8,000 troops.   On the 5th November, the two British divisions were within two marches of his capital, when he signed the treaty, and thus saved his kingdom from the fate which overtook the other Mahratta powers.

The Cholera, 1817.   While Lord Hastings lay in the vicinity of Gwalior, his camp was desolated by a visitation of the cholera. This disease had made its appearance at intervals during the previous forty years in different parts of India, but never with such alarming violence as on the present occasion, and the year 1817 is marked as the period when this mysterious scourge. of the nineteenth century became permanently established as an epidemic in India. It broke out in the first instance in the district of Jessore, within fifty miles of Calcutta, and depopulated entire villages. It baffled the skill both of the European faculty and the native doctors, none of whom were able to discover the cause or the cure of the malady. The superstitious natives resorted to the expedient of making one more addition to the three hundred and thirty millions of their deities, and established rites to propitiate the malevolent goddess of the cholera. It gradually crept up the banks of the river, and about the 13th November entered Lord Hastings' camp, and for a time paralysed the army in mind as well as body. It was calculated that the strength of the force, including its camp followers, was diminished by deaths and desertions to the extent of nearly twenty thousand. Lord Hastings was apprehensive lest an exaggerated report of the prostration of the army might induce Sindia to violate the arrangements he had so recently made, and he called his staff together, and directed them, in case he should fall a victim to the disease, to bury him in his tent under the table, and to conceal his death till Sindia had fulfilled his engagements. Under the advice of the medical officers, the position of the camp was shifted to the banks of the Betwa, and the virulence of the disease subsided.

Ameer Khan, 1817.   Ameer Khan, at this conjuncture, was scarcely a less important chief than Sindia. The little band of freebooters with whom he begun his course, had grown up into an army of fifty-two battalions of well-trained infantry, and a powerful cavalry, and a hundred and fifty pieces of cannon. It was as essential to the peace of India to break up the Patan, as the Pindaree force. Lord Hastings did not therefore hesitate to offer to guarantee to him the territories he held in jageer from Holkar, if he engaged to disband his army and surrender his guns, for a valuation. A month was allowed him for the acceptance of the proposed treaty, and though he wavered at first, the defeat of Bajee Rao and of the raja of Nagpore, and the extinction of their power, to which we shall presently allude, convinced him that the star of the Company was still in the ascendant, and he at once accepted the alternative of the treaty, and became an independent feudatory prince, with an income of fifteen lacs of rupees a-year, a dignity to which a career of eleven years of violence and crime gave him little claim.

The intimation given to Sindia of the nullifica-
Treaties of alliance with the native princes, 1817-18. tion of that clause of Sir George Barlow's treaty, which barred all interference with the states of Malwa and Rajpootana, was followed up with vigour. The chiefs were informed that the neutral policy had ceased to exist, and that the British Government was prepared to admit them to alliances which would protect them from the oppressions to which they had been subjected. The intelligence diffused joy through the provinces, and the princes became eager to embrace the offer. There was at least this advantage connected with the reversal of Lord Wellesley's policy by the Court, that the incalculable misery thereby inflicted on the country prepared the princes to appreciate the restoration of it more highly than they might otherwise have done. The chief management of this series of alliances was entrusted to Mr. Metcalfe, and the residency at Delhi was speedily crowded with the agents of nineteen princes of Central India. The first to enter into the arrangement was the venerable Zalim Sing, who had for half a century managed the affairs of the Afghan principality of Kotah with extraordinary ability. So great was the reputation of his virtues that in that age of violence he became the general umpire in the disputes of the surrounding princes, and their treasures were deposited in his fort as in the safest of sanctuaries. He promoted the operations against the Pindarees with great zeal,

and was subsequently rewarded with the grant of four districts taken from Holkar's possessions. The raja was an imbecile cypher, unknown beyond the precincts of the palace, and Lord Hastings offered to conclude the treaty with Zalim Sing himself, but his own feeling of moderation, and a respect for public opinion, which would have condemned this assumption of royalty, induced him to decline the honour, and content himself with the office of hereditary minister. Then came the nabob of Bhopal, the virtuous and accomplished Nusser Mahomed, who cheerfully accepted the alliance which his father had rejected. The assistance he afforded in the Pindaree campaign, and the kindness of his ancestors to General Goddard, were acknowledged by the grant of five valuable districts taken from the Peshwa. Under the auspices of the British Government his revenues, which had been reduced by usurpation to little more than a lac of rupees a-year, were improved to the extent of ten lacs. The raja of Boondee had braved the threats of Holkar in 1805, and afforded succour to General Monson. He had been ungenerously abandoned by Sir George Barlow to the vengeance of that chief, and to the spoliation of Sindia, but was now taken under British protection, and his devotion requited by an accession of territory, and an entire exemption from the heavy tribute imposed on his state by Holkar. No events connected with this great settlement of Central India produced a more favourable impression on the native mind than this grateful recognition of ancient services in the hour of triumph. The raja of Joudhpore had been brought to the brink of ruin by the Mahrattas and the Patans, and he eagerly accepted the offer of an alliance which relieved him from all further dread of their exactions. No Rajpoot state had suffered so severely from rapine as Oodypore. To the rana who had lost the greater portion of his territories, and whose revenues had been reduced to two lacs of rupees a-year, the arrangement now proposed by Lord Hastings, which cleared his country at once of the swarm of plunderers which had fastened on it, was a godsend. It was

the proud boast of the house of Oodypore, with its claim of
unfathomable antiquity, that it had never given a daughter in
marriage to the throne of Delhi, in the height of its grandeur,
and had never acknowledged the sovereignty of Mogul or
Mahratta, though repeatedly overwhelmed by both; but the
sovereign now cheerfully submitted to the supremacy of the
foreigner, who, as he said, " had come in ships from a country
before unknown."   The last of the principal Rajpoot states to
accept the alliance was Jeypore, and it was not till the raja
saw every power prostrate before the British arms, and the
settlement of Central India on the eve of being completed without including him, that he consented to come into the system.
Treaties were also concluded in succession with the secondary
and minor principalities, upon the same basis of " subordinate
co-operation and acknowledged supremacy," and of the
reference of all international disputes to the arbitration of
the Company.   All these treaties, with the exception of two,
were negotiated and signed within the short period of four
months.

CHAPTER XXVIII.

THE PINDAREE AND MAHRATTA WAR—MISCELLANEOUS NOTICES, 1817—1822.

Outbreak of the
Peshwa, 1817.
THE head-quarters of the three Pindaree chiefs
were centrically situated in the south of Malwa,
and it was towards this position that the left division of the
Bengal force and two divisions of the Deccan army began to
advance about the middle of October.   This movement was
immediately followed by the explosion of the plot which the
Peshwa had been organising amongst the Mahratta powers
for the overthrow of the Company's power.   He himself
broke out on the 5th November; the raja of Nagpore on the
26th of that month, and Holkar on the 16th December.   The

Peshwa had left his capital immediately after signing the
Treaty of the 13th June, and proceeded first on a pilgrimage
to Punderpore, and then to the palace he had recently erected
at Maholy, seventy miles from Poona. There he was visited,
at his own request, by Sir John Malcolm who had been
appointed to the command of a division of the Madras army,
and was making the tour of the native courts as political
agent in the Deccan. The Peshwa, who affected to consider
him an ancient friend, complained with great animosity of the
humiliation the treaty had inflicted on him; but he manifested, notwithstanding, a feeling of so much cordiality
towards the British Government, and so great an anxiety to
assist in putting down the Pindarees that the kind and
credulous general was thrown off his guard, and encouraged
him to increase the strength and efficiency of his army.
Mr. Elphinstone, with a better knowledge of the duplicity of
the Peshwa, predicted a different destination for this force,
but was unwilling to check the generous sympathies of Sir
John. General Smith's division was, therefore, allowed to
quit Poona, and proceed to join the expedition against the
Pindarees, and the cautionary fortresses were restored.
Bajee Rao now redoubled his efforts to augment his army,
and advanced a crore of rupees from his private hoard to
Gokla, to whom he committed the entire management of his
political and military affairs. No pains were spared to conciliate the southern jageerdars, whom hitherto the Peshwa
had always regarded with the strongest aversion, and they
were ordered to attend his stirrup at the earliest moment
with their full contingent of troops. His forts were repaired,
stored and garrisoned, and orders were issued to equip the
Mahratta fleet. Special envoys were sent to the Mahratta
princes to enlist them in the confederacy. A plan was laid
for the assassination of Mr. Elphinstone, whom he feared and
hated, but the noble-minded Gokla refused to lend himself to
so base a scheme, and it was dropped. Great exertions were
made, under the immediate direction of the Peshwa, to

whose feelings such an effort was particularly congenial, to
seduce the sepoys from their loyalty, but though a large
number of them had been enlisted within his own provinces,
and their families were completely within his power, they
exhibited a noble example of fidelity to the Company, and
brought the sums which had been left with them by the
Bajee Rao's emissaries to their own officers.   The Peshwa
returned to Poona at the beginning of October.   At the last
interview with Mr. Elphinstone, he deplored the loss which
he had sustained of territory, revenue, and dignity, but
repeated the assurance that the troops he had assembled
were intended to co-operate against the Pindarees.   Towards
the close of the month, however, his cavalry gave unequivocal tokens of the hostile disposition of their master by
caracoling round the British encampment and insulting the
officers and men.   Mr. Elphinstone, seeing a conflict inevitable, called up a European regiment from Bombay, and
thus imparted to his little native force that confidence which
the presence of European soldiers always inspires.   The
camp was at the same time removed from Poona to a more
defensible position at Kirkee, about two miles distant, but
the whole British force did not exceed 3,000 while the
Mahratta army mustered 18,000 horse and 8,000 foot.

Battle of Kirkee,   The preparations of the Peshwa were now
5th Nov., 1817.   mature, and, in the full assurance that Sindia and
Ameer Khan were already in the field, and that their example
would soon be followed by the raja of Berar and Holkar, he
precipitately plunged into hostilities on the 5th November—
the very day on which Sindia signed the treaty which
detached him from the confederacy.   Towards noon he sent
one of his ministers to Mr. Elphinstone to propound the
terms on which he would consent to continue on terms of
friendship with the British Government.   They were sufficiently arrogant, and were rejected, as a matter of course.
While his messenger was on his way back, the plain
was covered with masses of cavalry, and an endless

stream of soldiers issued from every avenue of the city.
Mr. Elphinstone lost no time in joining the camp, but he
had no sooner quitted the Residency than the Mahrattas
rushed in and burnt it to the ground, together with all his
valuable papers. Considering the great disparity of force,
he believed it would be most judicious boldly to take the
offensive, and he advised Colonel Burr, the commander, to
assail' the Mahrattas instead of awaiting their attack. The
superstitious minds of the Peshwa's soldiers had been
depressed by the accidental fracture of the staff of the
national standard as they were leaving the city; but their
confidence was destroyed by the fearless advance of the British
troops, who they had been assured would take to flight on
the first appearance of the Mahratta army. The Peshwa
proceeded to the neighbouring hill Parbutee, to observe the
conflict which he had not the courage to engage in; while
Gokla, in the true spirit of a soldier, rode about from rank to
rank animating the troops. He opened the engagement from
a battery of nine guns and enveloped the British force with
his cavalry. The infantry was left in the rear with the
exception of one battalion, raised and commanded by a
Portuguese officer, de Pinto, which boldly advanced against a
regiment of sepoys. It was repulsed, but pursued with such
ardour, that a gap was created between it and the rest of the
British line. Gokla seized the opportunity, and launched a
select body of 6,000 cavalry against the regiment while in a
state of confusion. The veteran Colonel Burr, though
labouring under a violent and incurable disease, took his post
by the colours of the corps, which he himself had formed and
led for many years, and aided by the nature of the ground
succeeded in breaking the force of the charge. The
Mahrattas were disconcerted, and began to retire, and on
being charged by the British troops completely deserted the
field, which was won with ease, with the loss of only eighty-
six killed and wounded. General Smith, on hearing of these
transactions, hastened back to Poona, which he reached on

the 13th of the month. The Peshwa had received a large accession of strength from the southern jageerdars who brought up their troops with alacrity, but he declined another engagement and, leaving his camp standing, fled southward on the 17th, when the city of Poona surrendered to General Smith; ·and thus ingloriously fell the power of the Peshwa, one hundred years 'after it had been established through the concessions obtained from the Emperor of Delhi in 1717 by his great grandfather, Ballajee Vishwunath.

Events at Nag-pore 1816—1817. Appa Sahib, the regent of Nagpore, continued to maintain the most friendly relations with the Resident for several months after the conclusion of the subsidiary treaty in June, 1816. But on the 1st February, 1817, the imbecile raja Persajee was found dead in his bed, and subsequent inquiries established the fact that he had been strangled by order of Appa Sahib, who immediately mounted the throne and assumed the title of Mahdajee Bhonslay. From that time there was a marked change in his conduct. Having attained the supreme power in the state, he became anxious to be relieved from that state of dependence in which the alliance had placed him, and he entered cordially into the views of the Peshwa to whom he gave the strongest assurances of support. Early in September, an agent of the Pindaree Cheetoo was presented at his 'durbar, and received a dress of honour. An active correspondence was also carried on with Poona, and troops were enlisted in large numbers. The Resident demanded an explanation of these strange proceedings, but the raja continued to profess an inviolable attachment to the Company, and on hearing of the attack made on Mr. Elphinstone by Bajee Rao on the 5th November, enveighed against such perfidy in very strong terms; while, at the same time, he was collecting his resources for a treacherous assault on Mr. Jenkins. All his preparations appeared to him to be complete, and on the evening of the 24th November, he sent to inform the Resident that an agent had arrived from the Peshwa to invest him with a dress of honour,

and with the ancient title of *senaputtee,* or commander-in-
chief of the Mahratta empire, and that he intended to proceed
to his camp the next day to assume these honours. Mr. Jenkins
was impudently invited to be present on the occasion, but he
remonstrated on the danger of these proceedings, and cautioned
the raja against identifying himself with a prince who was
then in arms against the Company. Appa Sahib, however,
persisted in going to the camp, and assumed these decorations
with every demonstration of military pomp.

Battle of
Seetabuldee,
1817.

This ceremony was the signal for an attack on
the Residency. It lay to the west of the city
from which it was separated by a small ridge
running north and south, with two hills at the extremity
called the Seetabuldee hills, a name which has become as
celebrated in the annals of British India, as ever Thermopylæ
was in the annals of Greece. The raja's force amounted to
about 18,000 men, of whom 4,000 were Arabs, the bravest
soldiers in the Deccan, and at this time the sinews of the
Mahratta armies; he had likewise thirty-six guns. The
force at the Residency consisted of two battalions of Madras
infantry, considerably weakened by disease; two companies
of the Resident's escort, three troops of Bengal cavalry and
a detachment of Madras artillery, with four six-pounders.
Towards the evening the Nagpore guns were brought to bear
upon the British position, and a vigorous assault was made
on the lower hill, which, though slackened during the night,
was impetuously renewed in the morning, but repelled with
great gallantry. At length a tumbril exploded, and in the
confusion of the moment, the Arabs charged directly up the
hill and captured it, and immediately turned the gun they
found there, together with two of their own, on the larger
hill. Emboldened by this success, the enemy began to close
in upon the Residency in every direction, and to prepare for a
general assault. The Arabs likewise rushed into the huts of
the sepoys who became dispirited by the shrieks of their
women and children; the ammunition and supplies were

running short; one-fourth the little force, including fourteen officers, was either killed or wounded; the latter were tended throughout the engagement by the ladies. It was a most appalling crisis, and there was every reason to conclude that the impending assault would result in the entire annihilation of the force, when the fortunes of the day were at once changed by the gallantry of Captain Fitzgerald, who commanded the Bengal cavalry. He had repeatedly entreated permission to charge the enemy, but had been refused. Seeing the destruction of the whole force inevitable, he made a last attempt, and with increased importunity, to be allowed to advance. " Tell him," replied Colonel Scott, "to charge at his peril." " At my peril be it," replied Fitzgerald, and rushed upon the main body of the enemy's horse with irresistible fury, cut up the infantry, and captured two guns. This noble exploit was witnessed from the hill with ecstacy, and a spirit of the highest enthusiasm was kindled in the breasts of the troops. At this juncture one of the enemy's tumbrils exploded, the Arabs were seen to be disorganised, and officers and men plunged down the hill and chased the enemy before them like a flock of sheep. By noon, the conflict which had lasted eighteen hours terminated in the complete triumph of the British arms. It was, perhaps, the severest trial to which native troops had ever been exposed, and the result reflected the highest honour on their courage and constancy. But there can be little doubt that the great perils of the day might have been avoided if Colonel Scott had followed the example of Colonel Burr, and boldly charged the enemy at the outset. Lord Hastings bestowed the highest encomium on all who were engaged in this brilliant action, but it was not till the commencement of Queen Victoria's reign, twenty years later, that any mark of distinction was bestowed on the heroes of Seetabuldee. The order of the Bath was conferred on the survivors, Mr. Jenkins and Captain Lloyd. The 24th Madras Infantry occupied the place of the 1st Regiment which was struck off the roll for its share in the Vellore mutiny. The

sepoys now prayed that in lieu of any other recognition of
their services they might be permitted to resume the former
number and facings of the regiment, a request which was
most cordially acceded to.

Deposition of Appa Sahib, 1818. Reinforcements poured into Nagpore from all
quarters, and on the 15th December, Mr. Jenkins
was in a position to dictate terms to the raja.
He was required to dismiss his troops, to deliver up his guns,
to repair to the Residency and to admit that by this unprovoked
attack his kingdom was placed at the disposal of the British
Government. He was, however, given to understand that on
his acceptance of these terms, his throne would be restored
to him with no other reservation of territory than was sufficient for the support of the subsidiary force. These conditions were accepted, but on the morning of the 16th December
he sent to inform the Resident that his Arab troops would not
allow him to quit the camp. General Doveton, therefore,
moved up against it, when the raja, yielding to his fears,
mounted his horse and accompanied by two of his ministers
and a few attendants rode into the Residency. A portion of
his guns, thirty-six in number, was likewise surrendered, but
the remainder were not obtained till after a severe engagement which cost the British force a hundred and forty in
killed and wounded. After the Nagpore army was dispersed,
a body of about 5,000 Arabs and Hindostances threw themselves into the fortified palace of the raja, and defended it
with great resolution for a week. It became necessary to
order up a battering train, but the Arabs, believing that they
had done enough to save their honour, evacuated the place
on the easy terms offered them. Lord Hastings had resolved
to punish the wanton attack on the Residency by the deposition of Appa Sahib, but was unwilling to weaken the authority
of the Resident by refusing his assent to the more lenient
arrangement he had made, and the raja resumed his dignities
on the 8th January, 1818. His incurable spirit of intrigue,
however, hurried him to his destruction. He incited the forest

and mountain chiefs to resist the British troops: he impeded
the surrender of his forts, and went so far as to invite the
Peshwa, while pursued by the British divisions, to move into
his territories, and prepared to join his standard. The timely
discovery of this clandestine correspondence defeated his
schemes. Lord Hastings ordered him to be sent to honourable
confinement at Allahabad, and Persajee, the next heir, to be
raised to the throne. Appa Sahib set forward on his journey
on the 2nd May, 1818, but on the way succeeded in corrupting the fidelity of the guard, and made his escape from the
camp. After wandering about the country for several years
he proceeded to Joudhpore, but the raja refused to follow the
example of Jeypore in the case of Vizier Ali, and to sully.
his character by violating the laws of Rajpoot hospitality,
and surrendering him to the demand of Government. Appa
Sahib subsequently obtained shelter at Lahore, and died a
pensioner on the bounty of Runjeet Sing.

Progress of events in Holkar's camp. 1817.
Lord Hastings had made the offer of a treaty
to Toolsee bye, and she sent a secret communication to the Resident of Delhi proposing to
place the young prince and the Holkar state under
British protection. The administration was vested in her as
regent, but all real power was in the hands of the military
chiefs, Ramdeen, a Hindostanee brahmin, Roshun beg, who
commanded the cavalry, and more particularly, Guffoor Khan,
the head of the Patan faction. As soon as it became known
that the Peshwa had risen in arms, the various detached corps
of Holkar's army were recalled to head-quarters, and the resolution was unanimously adopted to march forward and support him. A large sum was distributed by his agent among
the troops, and a larger donation was promised when they
reached the Nerbudda. The army, consisting of 20,000 men,
and comprising a body of cavalry esteemed the finest in India,
marched from the cantonments at Rampoora towards the Deccan in a spirit of great enthusiasm. On approaching Mehidpore,
the commanders found that the British force under Sir Thomas

Hislop and Sir John Malcolm, had advanced to Augur, fifteen miles distant, in pursuit of the Pindaree Cheetoo, who had joined their encampment. Sir John opened a correspondence with the commanders, and' offered them the very liberal terms proposed by Lord Hastings ; but they felt that any connection' with the Company would extinguish their power and importance, and the troops dreaded the loss of all future prospects of plunder. The chiefs merged all their differences in the presence of a common danger, and in their anxiety to maintain the independence and the honour of the Holkar state, took an oath of mutual fidelity. The regency was suspected of a leaning towards the British alliance ; Tantia Joge was, therefore, placed under restraint; Gunput Rao was seized amidst the execrations of the troops, and on the evening of the 20th December, Toolsee bye was conducted to the banks of the Siprec, and her beautiful head struck off, and her mangled remains cast into the stream.

Battle of Mehidpore, 1817. Sir Thomas Hislop moved up to Mahidpore on the 21st December, to bring on the issue of a battle. Holkar's army was admirably posted on the opposite bank of the Sipree, its left flank defended by an angle of that stream, its right resting on a deep morass, and its front lined with a formidable battery of seventy guns. The main feature of the engagement was the bold, if not rash, device of crossing a difficult river by a single ferry in the face of an enemy strongly entrenched, and then rushing forward to seize his guns, which had rapidly silenced the light field pieces of the British army. The sepoys were mowed down by the enemy's artillery, but continued to advance with extraordinary steadiness. Holkar's artillerymen stood to their guns till they were bayonetted beside them. The batteries were at length stormed; the infantry fled; and the cavalry, which, with all its vaunting before the action, had kept aloof and given no assistance to the foot, galloped off the field when the fortune of the day seemed to be adverse. The victory was decisive, but it was not won without the sacrifice of 778 in killed and wounded. The movements of the day were directed by Sir John Malcolm, who had never commanded in a general action, and was less notable as a general than as a diplomatist. The same result might have been secured with less slaughter by better strategy, if he had eschewed the favourite but insane practice of hurling the men on the enemy's batteries and endeavouring to carry them by cold steel. The young Holkar, with the hereditary gallantry of his race, was actively engaged throughout the battle, and shed tears as he saw his troops retreating from the field. His sister Beema bye, a young widow of twenty, manifested equal spirit during this campaign, and rode at the head of 2,500 horse, on a fine charger, with a sword by her side and a lance in her hand, but was closely pursued, and seeing no chance of escape, surrendered to the British officer, and was conducted to her brother's court. Holkar's entire camp, with sixty-three guns, and a large magazine of military stores, fell to the victors, and the power of the state was irretrievably broken. Tantia Joge was immediately released and sent to the British camp with the most humble submissions. A treaty was soon after concluded at Mundesur, by which cessions of territory were made to the Company, to Zalim Sing, to Ameer Khan, and to Guffoor Khan, both of whom acquired independence at the expense of this kingdom, which was thus reduced to two-thirds of its former dimensions, and entirely lost its independence, after twenty-five years of anarchy.

Operations against the Pindarees, 1817-18.　It remains to narrate the operations against the Pindarees, who were encamped during the rains of 1817 in three divisions, to the number of about 23,000 horse, under Cheetoo, Kureem Khan, and Wassil Mahomed. They were not ignorant of the measures which were in progress to extirpate them, and they implored the aid of the Mahratta powers, but, under the dread inspired by Lord Hastings' preparations, none of them had the courage to stand up in their defence, or even to grant them a fortress of refuge for their families. As the British divisions closed upon their haunts in Malwa, from the north and the south, they were dispersed in every direction. Letters from Sindia inviting Kureem Khan and Wassil Mahomed to Gwalior, fell into the hands of Lord Hastings, and he immediately marched his division to a position within thirty miles of Sindia's camp, which effectually precluded all access to it by the Pindarees. They were obliged, therefore, to fly westward, but were intercepted by General Donkin, who captured Kureem Khan's elephants, kettle-drums, and standards, as well as his wife and family. The two chiefs burnt their tents, and, abandoning their baggage, fled with about 4,000 of their best horse to the south. The rest of their followers were cut up, partly by the British troops and partly by the villagers, whom they had exasperated by their former depredations. They were not without hope of sharing the protection which Jeswunt Rao Bhao had offered to the Pindarees, and particularly to Cheetoo at Jawud. He was one of Sindia's commandants in charge of a third of his army, but had virtually thrown off his allegiance, and despoiled the rana of Oodypore of many districts and forts, of which he gave no account to his master. He had the temerity to fire on the troops of General Brown as he passed under the ramparts of Jawud, and refused to surrender the Pindarees whom he harboured. Lord Hastings, without any reference to his connection with Sindia, ordered him to be treated as a public enemy, and the general attacked his camp and carried his fort by assault. The two Pindaree chiefs, deprived of all hope from Jawud, hastened down to the Nerbudda, but were so hotly pursued by the detachments which tracked them, that they were unable any longer to keep their men together. Their minds were now reduced to such a state of depression as to welcome the terms which Colonel Adams offered them through the mediation of the nabob of Bhopal. Kureem Khan was settled on a small estate beyond the Ganges, in the district of Goruckpore. Namdar Khan, his lieutenant, came in with no other stipulation than that he should not be sent to Europe or to Calcutta.

Wassil Mahomed was placed under supervision at Ghazeepore, but being detected in an attempt to escape, put a period to his existence by poison. Cheetoo, the most renowned of the Pindaree leaders, was pursued by Sir John Malcolm with his heavy guns, and easily managed to keep fifty miles a-head of him. His bivouac was, however, beaten up by Colonel Heath, on the night of the 25th January, after which he wandered through Malwa for more than a twelvemonth with about two hundred followers, but he was hunted out of all his old familiar haunts, and, being driven at length by hunger to separate from his son and his last companion, plunged into a jungle infested with tigers. After a diligent search, his horse was discovered grazing, saddled and bridled, and not far off the mangled remains of this renowned freebooter, who had recently ridden forth at the head of 20,000 men.

Result of the campaign, 1818. The political and military operations thus brought to a happy issue, were undertaken without the Supreme Council, and in excess of the instructions received from England, on the sole responsibility of Lord Hastings. The success of the campaign was remarkable, not less for its rapidity than for its completeness. In the middle of October, 1817, the Mahrattas, the Pindarees, and the Patans, presented an array of more than 150,000 horse and foot, with 500 pieces of cannon, prepared to offer a very strenuous resistance to the designs of the Governor-General. By an admirable combination of movements, and extraordinary promptitude of action, this formidable armament was scattered to the winds in the brief space of four months. The power of Sindia was paralysed; the power of Holkar irretrievably broken; the Patan armies of Ameer Khan and Guffoor Khan had ceased to exist; the raja of Nagpore was a captive in the English camp; the Peshwa was a fugitive, and the Pindarees, who had inspired terror in the minds of Mr. Canning and the Directors, had disappeared. The campaign finally extinguished the Mahratta empire, on which Lord Wellesley had struck the first blow. It broke up every military organisation within the

Sutlege, with the exception of that of Sindia. It subdued not only the native armies, but the native mind, and taught the princes and people of India to regard the supreme command in India as indisputably transferred to a foreign power. It placed the Company on the Mogul throne with a more absolute authority than Akbar or Aurungzebe had ever enjoyed. The great revolution which was thus consummated, just sixty years after it began at the battle of Plassy, was effected, not only without the concurrence but in opposition to the constant injunctions of the East India Company, and the Board of Control. Every fresh addition of influence or territory was reprobated by them as the offspring of a spirit of encroachment and ambition, and fresh injunctions of moderation were poured on the local Government. But, from the first appearance of the Company as a military and political power in India, it became the constant aim of its princes to expel the intruder, and one confederacy after another was formed to accomplish this object. The general progress of our Indian empire was thus epitomized by Lord Hastings :—" We have been wantonly assailed—we have conquered the unprovoked enemy—we have retained the possessions wrested from him, not only as a legitimate compensation for the peril and expense forced on us, but also on considerations of self-defence." The last and most extensive confederacy was swept away by Lord Hastings himself. India was prostrate before the power of Britain, and the drama of society under native sovereignty was closed.

Remarks on these events, 1818.   To the chiefs who lost their independence, and with it all that feeling of dignity, which was sometimes the parent of royal virtues, the change was doubtless a great calamity, but to the community at large it was an unequivocal blessing. For twelve years the whole of Central India had been left to the uncontrolled dominion of native princes, and the universal wretchedness and wild anarchy which ensued showed how utterly unfit they were, under the existing circumstances of the country, to maintain peace, order, or security. The extension of British authority was, therefore, a matter of necessity, and although a foreign rule was more galling to the national pride than even the excesses of a native prince, it brought the most substantial advantages to the country. A solid tranquillity was substituted for general violence, under the guarantee of a power both able and willing to restrain the passions of princes and states. A feeling of universal security was diffused through the country, and the people were led to seek wealth and distinction, not through wars and convulsion, but by cultivating the arts of peace. The settlement of India by Lord Hastings in 1818 was, moreover, erected on so sound and stable a basis that, after the lapse of half a century, it is found to have required fewer renovations than so great a political edifice might be expected to need. Having thus extinguished all opposition, and consolidated the rule of the Company, Lord Hastings proclaimed the universal sovereignty of Great Britain throughout the continent of India. The fortunes of the surrounding countries have always been affected more or less by the revolutions of India, and the establishment of a British empire in this central position could not fail to tell upon the Mahomedan principalities on the west, and the various Boodhist kingdoms on the east. It was, in fact, the establishment of European supremacy in Asia, and, considering how effete these Asiatic monarchies have been growing, while the power, the resources, and the confidence of the European family have been constantly on the increase, this supremacy becomes progressively firmer and more permanent, and none of the revolts which may be expected from time to time, will be of any avail to subvert it. Strange to say, this stupendous revolution in the destinies of Asia has been accomplished by the audacity of the servants of a peaceful and unambitious company of merchants in London.

Battle of Korygaum, 1818.	To bring the narrative of this war to a close, it only remains to notice the pursuit and surrender of the Peshwa, and the capture of the Mahratta forts. Bajee Rao began his retreat southward on the 28th November, 1817, and on his route caused the raja of Satara and his family to be brought from the old capital into his camp. Finding that he was closely pursued by General Smith, he turned northward and marched up the Beema to Joonere, sixty miles north of Poona, and then doubled down to the south, giving out that he intended to attack Poona. Colonel Burr, the commandant, therefore, deemed it advisable to call down to his support the detachment left at Seroor, under Captain Stanton, consisting of one battalion of infantry, three hundred irregular horse, and two six-pounders, manned by twenty-four European artillery-men. He commenced his march at eight in the evening, and at ten the next morning reached the high ground on the Beema, near the village of Korygaum, about sixteen miles from Poona, which was found to have no other defence than a dilapidated mud wall. To his surprise he perceived the whole of the Peshwa's army, 25,000 strong, encamped on the opposite bank of the river: The Mahratta troops were immediately sent across against this handful of soldiers, jaded with a fatiguing march through the night, and destitute of either provisions or water. The contest which ensued was one of the most arduous and brilliant in the history of British India. The Peshwa sat on a rising ground watching the attack, which was directed by Gokla and Trimbukjee. Every inch of ground in the village was disputed with desperate valour, and the streets were repeatedly taken and retaken. The sepoys were sinking from exhaustion, and frantic with thirst, but Captain Stanton refused to surrender on any terms. At length the officer commanding the artillery fell, and in the momentary confusion which ensued, the Peshwa's Arabs rushed forward and captured one of the guns, but Lieutenant Pattinson, the adjutant of the battalion, though lying on the ground mortally wounded, raised himself up, and led on the grenadiers, till a second ball prostrated him. Animated by his example, the sepoys repulsed the Arabs, and regained the gun. Throughout the day officers and men exhibited a spirit of inflexible resolution, and kept the whole Mahratta force at bay. If the contest had been renewed the next morning, it must have proved fatal to this little band of heroes, but happily the Peshwa heard of the approach of his enemy, General Smith, who had never relaxed the pursuit of him, and he retreated in haste southward, which enabled Captain Stanton to fall back on Seroor. The distinguishing character of this action, which rivalled that of Seetabuldee, was the extraordinary fortitude displayed by the sepoys when they were without any European support, save the twenty-four artillerymen, of whom twenty were killed and wounded. Of eight officers engaged, three were wounded, and two killed, and the total loss amounted to a hundred and eighty-seven; but Captain Stanton was only a Company's officer; his services were performed in India, and they received no recognition whatever from his country. The Peshwa, on leaving Korygaum, fled towards the Carnatic, but his progress was arrested by General, afterwards Sir Thomas, Munro, who had been appointed to the superintendence of the southern districts. His force was small and inadequate to its duties, but every deficiency was supplied by his talent and energy, which made him the complete master of whatever position he occupied. He organised a body of local horse to whom he entrusted the protection of the districts, while he himself advanced northward with his regular troops, arrested the progress of the Peshwa, and captured the strong fortresses of Badamee, Belgaum, and Solapore. The professional resources, vigour, and strategy which he exhibited in this short campaign served to augment in no ordinary degree the renown he had already acquired by his civil administration.

Restoration of the Satara family, 1818. On the 10th February, General Smith took possession of Satara, the capital of Sevajee, and hoisted the ancient standard upon its ramparts. Experience had proved that no engagement, however solemn, would prevent a Peshwa from claiming the allegiance of the other Mahratta powers, or restrain them from acknowledging it. The treaty of Bassein in 1803 bound the Peshwa " neither to commence nor to pursue any negotiations with any other power whatever, without giving previous notice, and entering into mutual consultation with the East India Company's Government;" but this did not impair his influence over the other chiefs, or prevent his combining them in a confederacy against the Company. By the treaty of the 5th June, 1817, he renounced all claim as the executive head of the Mahratta empire, to their fealty, and all their vakeels were dismissed from his court; but within a few weeks he organised another conspiracy, and brought the forces of Holkar and the raja of Nagpore into the field against the Company. Lord Hastings determined, therefore, that there should no longer be a Peshwa, and, in accordance with the example set by Lord Wellesley in the case of Mysore, he made over a portion of the Mahratta dominions to the family of Sevajee. A manifesto was issued, on hoisting the old Mahratta standard, in which Mr. Elphinstone, after dwelling on the misconduct of the Peshwa, announced that he and his family were for ever excluded from the public affairs of the Deccan. A small portion of his territories, yielding fifteen lacs of rupees a-year, was erected into a principality for the raja of Satara, and the rest incorporated with the Company's dominions. General

Battle of Ashtee, 1818: Smith then resumed the wearisome pursuit of the Peshwa, and on the morning of the 19th February had the satisfaction of hearing his kettle-drums beating for the march at the village of Ashtee, on the opposite side of a hill which separated them, and immediately prepared for the attack. Bajee Rao sharply upbraided Gokla for this surprise, and quitting his palankeen, mounted a horse and fled, leaving his general to cover his retreat. Gokla, stung with the unjust reproach of his dastardly master, determined not to survive the day, and placing himself at the head of three hundred horse, rushed on the sabres of the British cavalry. He received three pistol shots and three sabre cuts, and covering himself gracefully with his shawl, expired on the field of honour. He was the last, and one of the noblest, of the great Mahratta commanders. He had fought bravely by the side of General Wellesley in 1803, and had received many tokens of distinction from the British Government, but he sighed for the independence of his country, and on being appointed minister by the Peshwa, manifested an inveterate hostility to the subsidiary alliance. He was usually called " the sword of the empire," and his death hastened the destruction of his master, in whose camp there ceased to be any order or confidence. The raja of Satara was rescued at the battle of Ashtee, and conducted to the palace of his ancestors, and installed on the throne of Sevajee, amidst the acclamations of the Mahrattas.

Surrender of
Bajee Rao,
1818.
The discomfiture of the Peshwa's army at Ashtee satisfied many of the Mahratta chiefs of the hopelessness of his cause, and his army was daily dwindling away by desertions. But the raja of Nagpore, notwithstanding his engagements with the Resident, determined to make common cause with him, and Bajee Rao advanced to Chanda, expecting to be joined by him there, but the clandestine correspondence was discovered in time, and the design was frustrated. It would be tedious to detail the movements of the Peshwa after this, to the north, to the south, and to the east; they were regulated by the sole object of evading his pursuers, from whom, however, he seldom obtained more than a brief and accidental respite. Hunted out of the Deccan, he made a final move to the north, crossed the Taptee on the 5th May, and advanced to the Nerbudda, in the hope of reaching Hindostan, and benefiting from the power, or the mediation, of Sindia. But all the fords were guarded; the British armies were closing on him, and, seeing no chance of escape, he sent an agent on the 16th May to Sir John Malcolm at Mhow, with a letter, in which he appealed to the generosity of the British Government, and lavished his flatteries on " his oldest and best friend." Sir John was so greatly moved by this appeal that he deputed two of his assistants to the Mahratta camp to open a negotiation with the Peshwa. Lord Hastings condemned this imprudent step,

because it fostered the impression that he was in a condition to treat, whereas, according to his own confession, his fortunes were desperate, and his first encounter with any British division must have annihilated his force. Sir John even went so far as to admit the Peshwa to a personal conference, in which the wily Mahratta brought all his eloquence and blandishments into full play. The British General's sympathy with fallen greatness overcame his political prudence, and he made concessions far beyond the necessity of the case. He promised him a personal allowance of eight lacs of rupees a-year, as well as a provision for the jageerdars in his camp, and gave a most improvident guarantee of the vast endowments of temples and brahmins, on which this superstitious prince had for fourteen years squandered the resources of the state, and which a native successor would at once have resumed. Lord Hastings, who had destined the Peshwa an allowance of two lacs of rupees a-year, was mortified at the prodigality of these terms, and in his letter to the Court of Directors justly observed "that in the hopeless circumstances in which the Peshwa was placed any terms granted to him were purely gratuitous, and only referrible to that humanity which it was felt your honourable Court would be desirous should be granted to an exhausted foe." The policy of Sir John's arrangements with the Peshwa has been the subject of much discussion, and some censure, but it is due to his memory to state that it received the approbation of Sir David Ochterlony, Sir Thomas Munro, Mr. Elphinstone, and Mr. Jenkins. They considered that the Peshwa might have indefinitely prolonged the contest if he had thrown himself, with the body of eight thousand men who still adhered to his fortunes, into Asseergur, the commandant of which had received the most positive injunctions from Sindia to succour him, and that his surrender, which at once terminated the war, was cheaply purchased even by this large annuity. He was conducted to Bithoor, a place of religious sanctity, sixteen miles from Cawnpore, and lived long enough to receive an amount of two crores and fifty lacs of rupees,

the major part of which he bequeathed to his adopted son,
Nana Sahib, who, finding the British Government unwilling to
continue the pension, became the great demon of the mutiny
of 1857. The Peshwa's brother, Umrit Rao, had received a
pension of seven lacs of rupees a-year from Lord Wellesley,
under circumstances altogether exceptional, and removed to
Benares where he enjoyed the allowance for twenty-one
years. It is worthy of remark that the sum total received by
the two brothers amounted to more than four crores of rupees,
and it may fairly be questioned whether any instance of
similar fidelity to engagements is to be found in the native
history of India.

Capture of
forts, 1818.
The country which had been the scene of warfare was studded with forts, which continued to
hold out after the submission of the princes. Many of them
were of great strength, in positions almost impregnable, and
would have baffled all the engineering skill of native generals,
but they were reduced in a few months. The circumstances
connected with the capture of two of them deserve individual
record. The forts were garrisoned in many cases by Arab
mercenaries. While the native armies in Hindostan had been
supplied for several centuries by a constant stream of Afghans,
the armies of the native princes in the Deccan were constantly
recruited from Arabia and Abyssinia, through the various ports
on the Malabar coast. In both cases the recruits equally exchanged a condition of poverty for prospects of wealth and distinction. The Arabs were held in high estimation by the princes
for their resolution, courage, and fidelity, and received double
the pay of Hindostanee sepoys. They served also as a counterpoise to the native soldiery, and assisted to check that
spirit of mutiny which is indigenous in all Indian armies. The
fort of Talneir was garrisoned by Arabs. The commandant
was a member of a very distinguished Mahratta family, and
not only gave up the fort, but surrendered himself to the
General. The Arabs continued to hold the citadel, and a parley
was held with them by the English officers, but as they were

mutually ignorant of each other's language, a misunderstand-
ing arose which led to fatal consequences. The wicket was
opened, and two officers of high rank entered, but the Arabs,
who did not understand the movement, assailed them, and
they lost their lives. The British troops without, exasperated
at what they considered an act of treachery, rushed in and
put the garrison, three hundred in number, to the sword, and
the next morning Sir Thomas Hislop hung the unoffending
commandant. The execution doubtless struck terror into the
minds of the natives, and facilitated the surrender of other
forts, but it was an act of unrighteous severity, and roused a
feeling of just indignation in England. It was unworthy the
British character, and has always been considered to tarnish
the laurels of the General. The capture of Maligaum, on
the other hand, exhibited an example of scrupulous good faith
which served to elevate the British name. It was the chief
fortress of the unfortunate province of Candesh, once filled
with thriving towns and a flourishing population, but reduced
to unexampled wretchedness by Holkar's rapacious soldiery,
and the exactions of Bajee Rao's officers and his Arabs.
The only terms offered in every case to these mercenary
troops were the payment of their arrears and a free passage
back to their native land; but they had little disposition to
relinquish the enjoyments of India for the barren wastes of
Arabia. They concentrated their strength at Maligaum,
which they defended with the obstinacy of despair. After
three weeks had been lost before it, a sufficiently powerful
battery train was brought up; the chief magazine exploded;
and the Arabs, seeing their position hopeless, made an offer
to capitulate, but with the example of Talneir before them,
required a written assurance of safety. The Mahratta moonshee, who drew up the document, exceeded his orders, and
stipulated to do whatever might be beneficial to their interests,
to pay all their arrears, and to conduct them to any destination they might select. The General, on discovering the mistake, was anxious to limit the execution of the promise to his

own instructions, but Mr. Elphinstone determined to give the, most generous interpretation to the engagement, and treated them with exemplary kindness. At length, the only fort remaining to be occupied was Asseergur. Sindia had furnished Lord Hastings with an order on the commandant to surrender it, but sent him private instructions to retain it and to afford every assistance to the Mahratta cause. He therefore harboured the raja of Nagpore, took charge of Bajee Rao's most valuable property, and offered him an asylum. He distinctly refused to surrender the fort, and it became necessary to invest it. The eyes of India were fixed on the siege as the expiring struggle of the Mahratta empire. A battery of thirty-four mortars and howitzers, and twenty-eight heavy guns, played on it incessantly for a fortnight with little hope of success; but the powder in the fort was at length reduced to three maunds, or. two hundred weight, and the commandant felt himself obliged to capitulate. When he was told that his master would be not a little displeased by the neglect of his orders, he produced a letter from Sindia, ordering him to hold the fort, and give every assistance to Bajee Rao, with the significant remark,—"Should you not do so I shall be perjured." The only retribution inflicted on Sindia for this act of treachery was the retention of the fort. This was the last shot fired in the war, though it had virtually terminated within four months of its commencement.

Mr. Canning moved the usual vote of thanks to Lord Hastings and the army in the House of Commons, in April, 1819, in a speech which doubled the value of this national recognition of their services; but he did not attempt to conceal his objections to the policy of Lord Hastings. He stated that the House and the country were in the habit of appreciating the triumphs of our armies in India with great jealousy; that, almost uniformly successful as our military operations had been in that part of the world, they had almost as uniformly been considered questionable in point of justice; that the

Proceedings of the Home Authorities, 1818-20.

termination of a war in India, however glorious, was seldom
contemplated with unmixed satisfaction, and that the increase
of our territories was ascribed, by sober reflection and impartial philosophy, to a spirit of systematic encroachment and
ambition. These considerations, he said, were not necessarily applicable to the Pindaree and Mahratta war; but the
House was to understand that the vote was intended merely
as a tribute to the military conduct of the campaign, and not
in anywise as a sanction of the policy of the war.   The
Court of Directors, while " duly appreciating the foresight,
promptitude, and vigour with which Lord Hastings had dispersed the gathering elements of a hostile conspiracy," recorded their deep regret that any circumstance should have
led to an extension of territory.   Their official communications
still more decidedly indicated their hostility to the Governor-
General and his policy. The despatch written on receiving
information of the brilliant success of the campaign was
loaded with petulant and frivolous animadversions, and " not
mitigated by the slightest indication of satisfaction at the
fortunate issue of 'the military exertions." They censured
him for having disobeyed their orders regarding the reduction
of the army, though. they had incontestible evidence that,
under existing circumstances, a compliance with these orders
would have been fatal to the interests of the empire.   In
anticipation of the great struggle with the Mahratta power,
Lord Hastings had remodelled the Quartermaster-general's
department, in order. to increase its efficiency. The Court
reprobated this measure because it had not previously received
their sanction.   At the same time, they pressed on him the
appointment of one of their own nominees to the post of
Quartermaster-general, whereas Parliament had placed the
nomination to offices exclusively in the hands of the local
authorities, leaving with the Court of Directors the gift of
appointments to the service. A Government like that of
India, which is obliged to do almost everything itself, cannot
hope for success except by employing the ablest men in the

service. Hence, the most responsible offices in India are given, as a rule, to merit, and only exceptionally by favour. The interference of the India House in these appointments always proceeded on the opposite principle; and, in the present instance, Lord Hastings affirmed that it would "have been difficult to find in the whole army a field officer more signally unfit for the post."

The tranquillization and settlement of India would have been a sufficient distinction for any administration, but Lord Hastings established still higher claims to public gratitude. He was the first Governor-General to encourage the moral and intellectual improvement of the natives. The India House had hitherto assumed that any attempt to enlighten the people would create political aspirations, which must endanger the power of the Company, and might lead to its subversion. This illiberal sentiment was not confined to Leadenhall-street; it was the feeling of the age. In 1811 Sir John Anstruther, who had for many years enjoyed the dignity of chief justice in Calcutta, and obtained a seat in Parliament on his return, when the question of native education was incidentally introduced in it, inquired, with a feeling of surprise, "whether it was really intended to illuminate the people of India, and whether it was exactly desirable to do so." The same views were prevalent in India, and no effort had been made, or even contemplated, to impart to the natives that knowledge to which Europe owed its distinction. Lord Hastings utterly repudiated this policy, and embraced the earliest opportunity after the Nepal war of proclaiming that "this Government never will be influenced by the erroneous position that to spread information among men is to render them less tractable and less submissive to authority. . . . It would be treason against British sentiment to imagine that it ever could be the principle of this Government to perpetuate ignorance in order to secure paltry and dishonest advantages over the blindness of the multitude." The instruction of the people, which had hitherto

been avoided as an element of danger, was thus, for the first
time, recognised as a sacred duty, and a powerful impulse was
given to the cause of education. Lady Hastings established
a school in Barrackpore Park, and compiled treatises for the
use of the scholars. Numerous vernacular schools were
opened in the neighbourhood of Calcutta by Mr. May, the
missionary, and by Dr. Carey and his colleagues, which received liberal encouragement from the Government and the
public. Early in 1816 some of the most wealthy and influential native gentlemen in Calcutta formed an association for
the establishment of a college to impart a liberal education to
their children and relatives, by the cultivation of the English
language and European science, and Lord Hastings accepted
the office of patron. Emboldened by the liberal policy which
was now in the ascendant, the Serampore Missionaries, on the
31st May, 1818, issued the first newspaper ever printed in a
native language in India. It was styled the "Sumachar
Durpun," or mirror of news, and Dwarkenath Tagore, a name
respected equally in England and in India, was the first to
patronise it. This attempt to rouse the native mind from the
torpidity of centuries by the stimulus of a public journal
created great alarm among the leading men in the Government, but Lord Hastings determined to encourage the under-
taking by allowing the numbers to be circulated through the
country at one-fourth the ordinary rate of postage. He
manifested the same spirit of liberality towards the English
press, and notwithstanding the strenuous opposition of the
members of his Council, removed the censorship which
Lord Wellesley had imposed upon it seventeen years before,
amidst the anxieties of war. In deference, however, to the
despotic feeling which pervaded the governing class of Calcutta, he laid severe restrictions on the editors regarding the
subjects or personages they were allowed to touch, any infrac-
tion of which was to be visited by an indictment in the
Supreme Court, or by the penalty of deportation. But the
Supreme Court, on the occasion of the first application, re-

fused to grant a criminal information, and Lord Hastings was unwilling to inflict the odium of banishing an editor on his administration. The restrictions, therefore, fell into abeyance, and the press became practically free. In replying to an address from Madras, Lord Hastings embraced the opportunity of vindicating his policy by stating that he was "in the habit of regarding the freedom of publication as the natural right of his fellow-subjects, to be narrowed only by special and urgent cause assigned." . . . "Further," he said, "it is salutary for supreme authority, even when its intentions are most pure, to look to the control of public opinion." The announcement of this heterodox doctrine gave great offence at the India House, and a despatch was immediately drafted reprobating the abolition of the censorship, and directing it to be re-imposed. But Mr. Canning treated the proposal with silent contempt, and it has been said that the draft was never returned to the Directors.

Settlement of land revenue at Madras, 1818.

The final adjustment of the land revenue at Madras belongs to this period. The great advocate of the ryotwary system, General Munro, visited England in 1818, when he was invested with the ribbon of the Bath, and it was doubtless under the influence of his counsel that the Court of Directors issued orders to establish it generally throughout the Presidency. An annual settlement was accordingly completed, in 1820, for each field and with each renter. The more grievous evils of the system, as described in a previous chapter, were corrected, and, instead of justice being subordinate to revenue, revenue was made secondary to justice. The outrageous practice of forcing lands on the ryot against his interest, and holding him responsible for the rent, whether he cultivated them or not, and of subjecting him to corporal punishment, and sometimes to torture, when he was unable to make it good, was abrogated. Sir Thomas was anxious also to abolish altogether the absurd rule of consigning the defaulting ryot to gaol, where he lingered for years, without any benefit to the revenue, and

II.   2 B

often died; but he could only prevail on the Revenue Board
to mitigate it. It was the special order of the Court of
Directors that the rent should be fixed on so moderate a scale
as to afford encouragement to agricultural industry, but the
peculiar circumstances of the Madras Presidency were unfavourable to such lenity. In Bengal the Company came at
once into possession of rich and fertile provinces, yielding a
revenue beyond the wants of the state, and could afford to
indulge the luxury of moderation in assessing the zemindars.
The Madras Presidency grew up gradually amidst struggles
and embarrassments, and was never able to meet its expenses
without drawing on Bengal. Hence it was obliged to scruti-
nise the sources of revenue with great rigour, and to put
a heavy pressure on those who contributed it. The land was
found to have been over-assessed under the native princes,
but the exigencies of the British Government precluded much
relaxation. The litigation introduced by the Supreme Court,
which picked the suitors to the bone, speedily dispersed the
old accumulations of wealth, and the whole Presidency presented an aspect of pauperism and wretchedness. The ryotwary system perpetuated this state of things; however
plausible and even benevolent in theory, it has practically
failed to promote either the welfare of the ryot or the prosperity of the state, and while under the zemindary and
permanent settlement of Bengal, the area of cultivation has
been rapidly extended, that of Madras has been always
stationary. The number of renters paying revenue direct to
Government in 1823 was under a million; it stands now considerably above two millions; there can, therefore, be no
application of capital to the improvement of the soil, and the
Presidency remains in a state of stagnant inferiority.

This question of the tenure of land has been in
Fraudulent
sales of land in almost every province and at all periods the stum-
the North-West, bling-stone of British rule in India. The same
1821.
fatality as elsewhere, attended the settlement
of the ceded and conquered provinces obtained from Sindia and

the Nabob of Oude at the begining of the century. A folio volume of a thousand pages of civil, criminal, and fiscal regulations was immediately inflicted on them, with the most benevolent intentions but the most disastrous result. The astute natives of Bengal did not fail to follow the collector into those provinces. They monopolised every post of power and influence, and by their superior acquaintance with the mysteries of the new system of civil and fiscal law, were enabled to turn the inexperience of the Hindostanees to their own benefit. The zemindars who were now, for the first time, obliged to pay their rents with rigid punctuality, fell into arrears, and were ousted from their lands. The Bengalee officials devised manifold expedients, and often resorted to fraud, to embarrass and confound the simple land-holder and bring his estate to the hammer, when it was bought, at first, in some fictitious name, and eventually trans-ferred to the real purchaser. Many of the zemindars, more-over, had been arbitrarily entered as mere farmers in the first rent-roll, which was prepared in haste, and when it came to be subsequently revised found themselves deprived of their estates through the chicanery of the Bengalee officers, who contrived to secure the proprietorship of the lands to their creatures and eventually to themselves. This system of plunder was systematically carried on for many years, and inflicted greater misery on the landed proprietors than the occasional whirlwind of Mahratta desolation. The ease with which the natives of Bengal had acquired possession of property, in one case, of ninety villages, and in another, of even a whole pergunna, attracted others to the quarry, and the raja of Benares, and a wealthy banker of that city obtained property yielding eight lacs of rupees a-year. The estates of the country were gradually passing out of the hands of the ancient aristocracy who had survived many political revo-lutions, but were completely prostrated by this process of legal jugglery which was reducing them to the condition of paupers. " Yours," said a high spirited Rajpoot, " is a strange

2 B 2

rule; you flog a man for stealing a brass ewer, while you
reward him for stealing a whole pergunna." Mr. Campbell
Robertson had endeavoured to protect the rights of the
oppressed zemindars, but he was defeated by the stolid judges
of the Court of Appeal, and he boldly determined to bring
the subject to the notice of the Supreme Government. Lord
Hastings and the Council listened to his representations,
and a regulation was passed the preamble of which frankly
acknowledged the injustice, and a special commission was
appointed to enquire into the transfers of property which
had been made during the previous eight years. Some few
of the more egregious acts of iniquity were redressed, but
in the majority of cases there was no relief.

Disturbances
in Cuttack,
1818.
In the province of Cuttack, which was ceded
by the raja of Nagpore in 1803, the same cause
led to an open insurrection. The natives of
Orissa are proverbial for mental dulness, and the province
has always been considered the Bœotia of India. During the
native dynasties, the chief offices of the state were generally
occupied by natives from Telingana in the south, or Bengal
in the north. On the acquisition of the province by the
Company a swarm of Bengalee baboos flocked into it,
obtained possession of nearly every post of influence or
profit, and took an unfair advantage of the simplicity of the
people, and their ignorance of our institutions. The assessment of the lands, made at random, was thirty per cent.
above that of the Mahrattas. It was rigidly enforced, and,
combined with the improvidence of the zemindars, brought
half the estates in the province to the hammer in a dozen years,
when they were bought up by the Bengalee officials, often
at a nominal value. The raja of Khoorda, the descendant of
an ancient dynasty, who enjoyed the hereditary privilege of
sweeping the temple of Jugunnath, had paid the Mahrattas,
when they were able to squeeze anything out of him, about
15,000 rupees a-year. He was assessed by the collector at
eight times the sum, and dispossessed of his patrimonial

estates for default. To add to the wretchedness of the inhabitants; the Company's salt monopoly was introduced and the cost of that necessary of life was raised six-fold to the peasant, in a province where the sea furnished it. spontaneously. Under this accumulation of misery the people sold all they possessed, and then their wives and children, and eventually took to the jungle. The country being thus ripe for revolt, one Jugbundoo, the hereditary commander of the old Hindoo rajas, who had been dispossessed of his property, raised the standard of rebellion to which 3,000 of the disaffected immediately flocked. He plundered and burnt the civil station of Khoorda and repulsed two detachments of sepoys which were sent against him. This success served to increase his force, and he proceeded to take possession of the town of Jugunnath; the fort, buildings, and bungalows were set on fire, and the collector retreated with the treasure to Cuttack. No injury was inflicted on any but the tyrannical and odious native functionaries. But the triumph of the insurgents was short; reinforcements poured into the province and dispersed them. The people were assured that their grievances would be redressed if they were peaceably represented, and they at once submitted to the authority of Government. A special commissioner was appointed to the charge of the province; some who had been taken in arms were executed; the most notorious of the oppressive officials were punished, and the assessment was reduced forty per cent. The province has since enjoyed the services of a succession of able Bengal civilians, Wilkinson, Sterling, Packenham, and others, and its tranquillity has never been disturbed. Another proof has thus been afforded of the fact that with a mild assessment, congenial institutions, and an equitable administration, there is perhaps no country more easy to govern than India, even under foreigners.

Financial and territorial Increase; 1822.
In reviewing the pecuniary results of Lord Hastings' administration, it is pleasing to observe that, notwithstanding the expensive war which

lasted eighteen months in the mountains of Nepal, and the assembly of eight armies in the field during the Mahratta and Pindaree campaign, the finances of the Company were at no former period in so flourishing a condition as at the close of his administration. The Government bonds which at his arrival were at twelve per cent. discount, were at a premium of fourteen per cent. at his departure. The debt had indeed increased by four crores and a half during his administration; on the other hand, the cash balances in the various treasuries exceeded the sum in hand when he landed by five crores of rupees, but on grounds which every real Indian statesman will admit, he forebore to reduce those balances for the mere ostentation of paying off debt. The increase of annual receipts was equivalent to six crores of rupees, without the imposition of a single new tax; and the increase of expenditure about four crores, leaving a clear surplus revenue of two crores of rupees a-year; the year 1822 may, therefore, be considered as the brightest period of the finances of the Indian empire, when they exhibited such prosperity as they had never reached before, and have never reached since. If the military operations of this period resulted in an increase of territory, it will not be deemed matter of surprise or regret. Lord Hastings commenced the Pindaree war with the confident hope that the pacification of India would be accomplished without any defalcation from any native state, and without adding a rood to the Company's territories. But "the irrepressible tendency of our Indian power to enlarge its bounds," which Mr. Canning deplored, was fatal to this resolution. The unprovoked aggression and the complete overthrow of the Mahratta powers placed their territories at the absolute disposal of the Company. The larger portion of the dominions of Holkar and of the raja of Nagpore was restored to them, but Lord Hastings considered that the entire annexation of Bajee Rao's kingdom, the principality of Satara excepted, was forced on him by "the imperious necessity of guarding against the speedy renewal of a treachery so rooted in its nature as to admit of no other prevention."⋅ These provinces were, therefore, annexed to Bombay which had previously drained the Bengal treasury to the extent of a crore of rupees a-year, but was now enabled in some measure to support its own establishments.

Miscellaneous notices, 1814-22 —Singapore. By the peace of Paris in 1815 the settlements of the French, the Danes, and the Dutch were restored to them, with the exception of Ceylon; but during the war, trade had been diverted into new channels, and these settlements never recovered their former importance. The island of Java, to the mortification of those who understood its great value, was inconsiderately restored to the Dutch, and it is at present the only Asiatic dependency which contributes an annual revenue to. its European master. The influence of the Dutch was thus restored throughout the eastern archipelago, and their ancient spirit of monopoly and hostility to foreign intruders was developed to such an extent as to threaten the entire exclusion of British commerce from those seas. Lord Hastings was fully alive to the importance of this commerce, and, under the advice of Sir Stamford Raffles, who had governed Java while it was in our possession with great ability and success, authorized him to establish a new settlement in the centre of the Malay states. By an unperceived and prompt movement, he obtained the cession of the island of Singapore from the raja of Johore, and hoisted the British colours on the 5th September, 1819. It was, from its commanding position, the key of the gulf of Siam, if not also of the China seas. Such an acquisition did not fail to excite the indignation of the Dutch authorities in Java, who immediately laid claim to it as one of their own possessions. The most strenuous remonstrances were addressed to the English Ministry, and so little were British interests in the east understood in Downing Street, that it was, for a time, seriously contemplated to submit to the demands of the Dutch, to abandon the island, and to recall Sir Stamford for his temerity. After a long period of vacillation, however, the sanction of the

public authorities in England was fortunately obtained to the
retention of this possession, which has grown from a fishing
village to an entrepôt of trade amounting to five crores a-year.
Singapore is a noble monument of Sir Stamford Raffles' states-
manship, and will perpetuate the grateful remembrance of it in
the sphere in which his talents were so beneficially exhibited.
The Company's　Lord Hastings' administration may be consi-
fleet.　　　dered as the palmy period of the Company's commercial navy, then the largest in the world. Though, under
the influence of a sharp competition, the trade to India brought
no gain to Leadenhall-street, the captains suffered no abatement of their profits. The command of one of the Company's
vessels was always reckoned worth a lac of rupees a voyage,
chiefly from the high charge for passage-money. The customs of the period when the Company were simple traders
still continued in vogue. A special court was held when the
captains took their official leave of the Directors. On reaching
the Presidencies in India they were received with great distinction at Government House, and took rank with the
first class of the civil service. An officer of high standing
was always sent in a Government vessel down to the new
anchorage, a hundred miles below Calcutta, to dispatch the
fleet. The uniform of the commanders and of the various
grades of officers vied in splendour with that of the royal
navy, and both were exhibited, side by side, in the shop
windows of the London tailors, and the captains endeavoured,
likewise, to maintain on their own quarter-decks the same
etiquette which was observed in the king's ships. The China
trade, of which the Company still enjoyed the monopoly, was
managed by officers denominated supercargoes, who lived
like princes at Canton, and -amassed ambitious fortunes in a
few years. The patronage of the China service was deemed
the most valuable in the gift of the Directors, and was generally reserved for their immediate relatives. Their vessels
were manned and armed on the most liberal scale, after the
model of the royal navy, and such was the excellence of their

equipment that on one occasion the fleet under the command
of Captain Dance succeeded in beating off the French squadron
of Admiral Linois, who attacked them with one ship of eighty
guns, two heavy frigates, a corvette, and a brig. The Directors received no higher salary than two hundred and fifty
rupees a-month, but their individual patronage was calculated,
on an average, to be equivalent to two lacs and a half of
rupees a-year. The sale of appointments was strictly forbidden by Act of Parliament, and with some exceptions the
rule was honourably observed by them ; but as they formed the
most important and powerful commercial body in the first
commercial city in the world, they experienced little difficulty in obtaining seats in Parliament, and one-fourth their
number was generally found in the House of Commons.

Civil Service. At no previous period had the character of the
civil service for talent and efficiency stood so high as during
the administration of Lord Hastings, which might in most
cases be traced to the training it had enjoyed in the school of
Lord Wellesley. Many of the civilians, moreover, were connected with some of the best families in England, and served
to give a high tone of character to the service, while their
refinement of feeling and dignity of demeanour, combined
with that elevation of mind which the management of great
affairs has a tendency to create, fitted them to maintain the
honour of their country in negotiations with the princes and
nobles of the country. Their intercourse with the people
was uniformly marked by such kindness and consideration as
few, if any, conquerors have ever exhibited towards the conquered. The highest ambition of the civil and military officers
of Government, and of those who had amassed wealth at the
bar or in commerce, was to obtain a seat in Parliament. In
the year 1819, the number of members connected with India
amounted to forty-two, independent of the four commissioners
of the Board of Control. They entered the house chiefly
through the medium of the nomination boroughs, of which
the majority were swept away by the Reform Bill of 1832.

But Parliament had already become weary of Indian questions, which, thirty years before, attracted crowded houses. The Secretary of the Board of Control stated in Parliament that "the India budget was always considered a dull and disagreeable subject by the House; the practice of making budget speeches had therefore been discontinued. The time and attention of the House was quite enough occupied without throwing away a day in the discussion of a topic which would be sure to drive gentlemen away from it." During the five years of Mr. Canning's tenure of the office of Minister for India, the only occasion on which he touched on the subject of India in the House—except when moving thanks to Lord Hastings—was in reference to a bill for licensing Scotch marriages there. British interests in India did not, however, suffer from the indifference of Parliament, where every subject becomes the sport of party contention. It was during this period of neglect that the great revolution of Lord Hastings' administration was consummated, and twenty-eight actions were fought in the field, and a hundred and twenty forts captured, many scarcely accessible, and some deemed impregnable, and nineteen treaties made with native princes, and the sovereignty of Great Britain proclaimed throughout the continent.

Death of Warren Hastings and Francis, 1819.
In the year 1819, Warren Hastings died at the age of eighty-eight, thirty-four years after his return from India. Within four months also, his great opponent, Sir Philip Francis, paid the debt of nature. It was immediately proposed to place Hastings' statue at the India House, among those statesmen and heroes who had contributed to the creation and stability of the British empire in India, and it was carried with only four dissenting votes.

Hyderabad affairs—Chundoo Lall, the contingent, 1809-1818.
One of the last acts of Lord Hastings' administration had reference to the affairs of Hyderabad, and it is necessary therefore to bring up the arrears of its history. Meer Alum, who had managed the

Nizam's government with consummate ability for thirty years, died in 1808. The Nizam, who was devoted only to his pleasures, and eschewed all serious business, was anxious to appoint a Mahomedan noble, Moneer-ool-moolk, to the vacant office, but the Resident described him as both a coward and a fool, and the Government in Calcutta refused to sanction the nomination. After an irritating discussion of six months, a compromise was at length effected by giving him the ostensible post of minister, with the splendid emoluments attached to it, and entrusting Chundoo Lall, a Hindoo, with the power and the responsibilities of the office. He had been an efficient assistant to the late minister, and was better fitted for its duties than any other man at Hyderabad, by his talent, experience, and activity; but he was utterly unscrupulous in his dealings with the court or with the people. The Nizam, chagrined by the defeat of his wishes, abandoned all interest in public affairs, and retired to the privacy of the harem. The Court of Directors had interdicted all interference in the internal affairs of the state, and directed the Resident to confine his attention to the reform of the Hyderabad contingent. This was a body—distinct from the subsidiary force —of 6,000 foot and 9,000 horse, which the Nizam was bound by the treaty made with him in 1800 to keep up in time of war. By the strenuous efforts of the Resident, these cowardly levies of the Nizam, who had always avoided an enemy, were converted into a strong and valuable force of 10,000 men, horse, foot, and artillery. It was disciplined and commanded by European officers, drawn chiefly from the Company's army, with which it was soon enabled to vie in military spirit and efficiency. It was supported by the Nizam's treasury, at a cost of thirty lacs of rupees a-year. It was at the entire disposal of Chundoo Lall, and ministered to his power and dignity, and likewise afforded him material assistance in the collection of the revenue and the coercion of refractory zemindars; he was, therefore, unwilling to check its profuse expenditure. It was not only over-officered, but the officers

were overpaid. The appointments were eagerly coveted, and
became a source of valuable patronage to the Resident, the
Contingent being generally designated his plaything. As one
extravagant allowance was heaped on another, the officers
exclaimed "Poor Nizzy"—the nickname of the Nizam—"pays
for all." The contingent was doubtless an effective force, but
for a time of peace, and in a country which the British Government was engaged to defend, it was little better than a
magnificent job.

Administration
of Chundoo
Lall, 1808-20.
The administration of Chundoo Lall was, with
some intervals of relief, the scourge of the
country for thirty-five years. It was supported
by British influence, but not controlled by British honesty.
Nothing flourished but corruption. Every public office was
put up to sale, and the purchaser reimbursed himself by extortion. Justice, or rather judicial decrees, could be obtained
only for money. The land revenue was farmed out to those
who made the largest advances to the minister in anticipation
of their collections. The tenure was therefore insecure, and
it was a common remark that the farmers proceeded to their
districts looking over their shoulders all the way, to see
whether some other contractor, who had made a higher bid,
was not following to supplant them. The farmers, moreover,
had the power of life and death, and the under farmers,
through their local agents, wrung the last farthing from the
wretched peasantry. A peaceful and industrious population
was converted into bands of rebels and banditti. Life and
property were everywhere insecure. Hundreds of villages
were deserted, cultivation ceased, and provisions rose to
famine prices. The sums thus obtained by insatiable rapacity
were expended by Chundoo Lall in making his position secure.
He erected a noble palace for the Resident, and stocked it
with the most costly chandeliers and furniture from Bond
Street. He bribed with a lavish hand all who had any interest
at the court; he subsidized the zenana, and conciliated the
Nizam by indulging his passion for hoarding. The Resident

at length obtained the permission of the Governor-General to make some effort, by his advice and influence, to arrest the progress of desolation. His exertions had begun to produce some beneficial result, when he was succeeded in November, 1820, by Mr. Metcalfe, who, after a tour through the country, deemed it necessary to adopt more stringent measures of reform. Some of his political assistants and of the European officers of the contingent were placed in charge of districts to superintend a new settlement, to check oppression, and to control the police. The system which he introduced, and which remained in force .for several years, was equally un-palatable to Chundoo Lall, whose exactions it restrained, and to the native authorities, whose dignity it lowered. It was also censured by Lord Hastings, as greatly in excess of his instructions, and as being tantamount to taking the govern-ment of the Nizam's dominions out of his hands; but it was highly beneficial to the community. Security was at once re-established. Three hundred villages were repeopled in a short time, and cultivation was resumed and extended. No revenue had previously been obtained but at the point of the sword; under this new policy, not a trooper marched nor was a musket shouldered to enforce the public demand. No country is more blessed with the gifts of nature than the territory of Hyderabad. Under Chundoo Lall it was fast relapsing into jungle; under Mr. Metcalfe's management it was becoming a garden.

Messrs. Palmer and Co., 1816-20. Mr. Metcalfe had not, however, been long at Hyderabad without perceiving that every prospect of prosperity was impeded by the dealings of Palmer and Co. with the state. Mr. William Palmer had established a banking-house at Hyderabad in 1814, with the full concurrence of the Resident, and soon after became connected with Chundoo Lall, and began to make advances to the Nizam's Government. An Act of Parliament had prohibited all such transactions with native princes without the express sanction of the Governor-General, and for this an application was made

in June, 1816. It was acceded to with the full consent of the
Supreme Council, and in accordance with the legal opinion of
the Advocate-General, who drew up the deed. In April,
1818, when the Peshwa was in arms, and it became necessary
to pay up the arrears of the contingent to prevent the troops
from going over to the enemy, Palmer and Company came
forward and agreed to furnish the minister with two. lacs and
a half of rupees a month, at twenty-five per cent. interest, on
the security of assignments on the land revenues, to the
extent of thirty lacs a-year. This proceeding received the
unanimous approval of the Governor-General in Council. But,
about this period, the firm was joined by Sir William Rumbold, a connection of the Governor of Madras, whom the
Court of Directors had removed from that appointment in
1782. He came out to India in 1813, and, as testified by
Mr. Metcalfe, visited the various native courts where British
influence was predominant, in the hope of making a rapid
fortune as in the olden time, and at length fixed on Hyderabad,
and was admitted into partnership with Palmer and Co.
He had married a ward of Lord Hastings, who regarded her
with parental kindness, and, in an evil hour, wrote to
Sir William, " The partners speculate that your being one of
the firm will interest me in the welfare of the house. It is a
fair and honest conclusion. The amount of advantage which
the countenance of Government may bestow must be uncertain, as I apprehend it would flow principally from the opinion
the natives would entertain of the respect likely to be paid by
their own Government to an establishment known to stand
well with the Supreme Government." To this letter Sir
William gave the widest publicity, and it came to be currently
reported and believed that he was the son-in-law of the
Governor-General, and that the rents collected by Palmer and
Co. were, in fact, payments to the British Government.

Proceedings and   The house had now obtained a firm footing at
fall of Palmer Hyderabad, and there was a constant stream of
and Co.,
1820-22.   loans from the bank to the Nizam's treasury.

Funds were received in abundance from depositors at twelve per cent., and lent to the Nizam at twenty-four per cent., on the security of fresh assignments. Notwithstanding frequent repayments, the debt was continually on the increase by the process of compound interest. In 1820 Chundoo Lall was put up to solicit the sanction of Government to a new loan of sixty lacs for the professed design of paying up the public establishments, with a view to their reduction, of clearing off debts due to native bankers, and of making advances to the ryots. Lord Hastings considered that these were legitimate objects, of sufficient importance to justify the casting vote which he gave in favour of the proposal, but with the distinct understanding that it was not to be regarded as giving even an implied guarantee of the loan on the part of Government. But Mr. Metcalfe discovered, on his arrival, that only a portion of the sixty lacs had been actually paid into the Nizam's treasury, that eight lacs formed a bonus to the members of the firm, and that the remainder consisted of other sums lent, or said to have been lent, to the Nizam, without the knowledge of the Government of Calcutta, and consolidated in the new loan to which its sanction was thus surreptitiously obtained. But Mr. Metcalfe likewise felt that the house was gradually becoming a great political power in the state, chiefly through the influence which one of its members was said to possess with Lord Hastings. The authority of the Resident was thus superseded, and Chundoo Lall, believing that he held his place by the protection of the members of the firm, deemed it more for his interest to communicate with the Governor-General through them, than through his representative. The Government of the Nizam was prostrate before Palmer and Co., as that of the nabob of Arcot had been before his creditors, and the revenues of the country were gradually passing into the hands of the firm. Sir Charles Metcalfe—he had recently succeeded to the baronetcy—at length ventured to communicate his observations and views on the subject to Lord Hastings without reserve, but he found that his mind had been prepossessed, and his feelings worked upon by the correspondence of the Rumbold family, Lord Hastings went so far as to exhibit a feeling of resentment at the opposition which Mr. Metcalfe had manifested to the proceedings of the firm. But the transaction of the sixty lac loan, to which the sanction of Government had been obtained by false representations, was too gross to admit of any palliation. It was also discovered that other advances had been made without sanction, and that, as Chundoo Lall observed, "the exorbitant rates of interest charged by the house, and the overwhelming amount of their interest on interest, had raised their claim to more than a crore of rupees." Lord Hastings and his Council passed a severe condemnation on these transactions, and resolved to make arrangements for relieving the Nizam from the grasp of his inexorable creditors. Fifty years before, Lord Clive had obtained the Northern Sircars as a gift from the Emperor of Delhi, but had agreed to pay the Nizam, in consideration of their having formed a part of his province, a *peshcush*, or annual acknowledgment, of seven lacs of rupees. This payment was arranged when the Company was an insignificant power ; to the astonishment of the native princes, it was religiously continued after the Company had become supreme in India. It was now capitalised, and a crore of rupees was remitted from Calcutta, soon after Lord Hastings quitted India. The debt due to Palmer and Co., deducting the clandestine bonus, was paid off, and within a twelvemonth they were insolvent.

Thanks of the Directors and Proprietors to Lord Hastings, 1822.   The antipathy of the Court of Directors to Lord Hastings had been repeatedly manifested in captious criticisms, and in the reluctant praise and eager censure they bestowed on him. This feeling became more intense after Sir William Rumbold had joined the banking-house at Hyderabad, when they issued orders in the most peremptory and offensive terms to revoke the licence which had been granted to it by the Government of India, though it had been unnoticed in Leadenhall-street for three years. Their despatch implied a mistrust of Lord Hastings's motives, and shewed a disposition to identify him with whatever appeared objectionable in the transactions of Palmer and Co. Indignant at these insinuations, and at the tone of their communication, he sent home his resignation, on the ground that he had lost their confidence. The Court assured him that he was entirely mistaken, and, in May, 1822, voted the thanks they had hitherto steadily withheld from him, as Governor-General, "for the unremitting zeal and eminent ability with which, during a period of nine years, he had administered the Government of British India with such high credit to himself and advantage to the interests of the East India Company." The Proprietors concurred in this resolution, and requested the Directors to " convey to his Lordship the expression of their admiration, gratitude, and applause." He embarked for Europe on the 1st January, 1823.

Remarks on his administration, 1822. In political genius, Lord Hastings can scarcely be said to rank with Warren Hastings or Lord Wellesley, though in completing the work they had begun and consolidating the British empire in India, he exhibited talent of the highest order. His administration was rendered memorable by the benefits he conferred on the old capital of the Moguls and the new capital of the Company. Ali Merdun, as stated in a preceding chapter, had executed the grand design of conveying a large portion of the water of the Jumna, where it issues pure from the mountains, by means of a canal, to the city of Delhi. It had, however, been devoid of water for sixty years, and its banks were everywhere prostrated. Lord Hastings caused it to be completely restored, and bestowed on the inhabitants the inestimable boon of fresh and wholesome water—without the imposition of a water-rate. The improvement of Calcutta had been totally suspended since the departure of Lord Wellesley. Under the direction of Lord Hastings, the ventilation of the town was promoted by piercing it in the

II.   2 c

centre with a street sixty feet wide. Squares were laid out
with tanks, or reservoirs of water, in the centre, surrounded
by planted walks; and the foreshore of the river which was
lined with wretched huts and. rendered impassable by mire
and filth, was adorned with a noble strand road worthy of
the city of palaces, as Calcutta was justly designated. No
Governor-General has ever laboured with greater assiduity
in the performance of his duties. Between the age of sixty
.and seventy he was at his desk at four in the morning—and
always in full military uniform—examining the boxes of papers
from different departments which had been piled up in his
room over night. He made an effort to acquire some knowledge of the language of the country, but he was obliged to
relinquish it when he found that his moonshee was making a
fortune by the opportunity afforded him of private intercourse
with the Governor-General, when he attended him in his
study. In the fevered climate of India,—which, since the
facilities for visiting England have been multiplied, is considered insupportable,—he laboured for nine years at the
rate of seven and eight hours a-day, without a hill sanatarium to resort to, or the convenience of a sea-going steamer.
The only speck on his administration was the interest he
manifested in the Rumbolds. As the head of the state it
became him at once to withdraw his confidence from them
when he discovered the mischievous use to which they were
turning it, but the kindliness of his nature betrayed him into
political weakness, and led him to take too lenient a view of
the conduct of those who were bringing odium on his government, for which he suffered severely during the remaining
years of his life.

Debate at the
India House,
1826.

Within two years after his return from India,
his friend, Mr. Douglas Kinnaird, brought forward
a proposal in the Court of Proprietors for a
pecuniary grant befitting the greatness of his services and
the gratitude of the Company. If there had been any sincerity in the tribute of "admiration, gratitude, and applause"

which had been recently paid him by that body, it would
have been cordially welcomed, but it only served to disclose
the strong current of rancour which underlay the crust of
official compliment. The motion was met by an amendment,
calling, in the first instance, for all the papers connected with
• the Hyderabad transactions, and, eventually, with the whole
of Lord Hastings's administration. A twelvemonth was
employed in compiling and printing this mass of documents,
of which a folio volume of a thousand pages was devoted to
the Hyderabad loans. It was to this single point and not to
the general merits of Lord Hastings's administration that the
attention of the Court of Proprietors was especially directed.
If the question under discussion had referred to some grand
measure of imperial policy, involving the welfare of millions,
it would probably have been disposed of in a few hours ; but
it turned upon Lord Hastings's alleged delinquency in the
matter of Palmer and Co. ; it had all the zest of personality,
and the debate was prolonged for six days. Towards the
close of it Mr. Kinnaird submitted a resolution that "nothing
contained in the papers tended to affect in the slightest
degree the personal character or integrity of the late
Governor-General." But the Chairman, Mr. Astell, opposed
the motion by an amendment, stating that, "while admitting
that there was no ground for imputing corrupt motives to the
late Governor-General, the Court records its approbation of
all the despatches sent out by the Court of Directors."
These despatches, four in number, charged Lord Hastings
among other misdemeanors with " having lent the Company's
credit to the transactions at Hyderabad, not for the benefit
of the Nizam, but for the sole benefit of Palmer and Co.,
with having studiously suppressed important information,
with proceedings which were without parallel in the records
of the East India Company, and with assuming to elude all
check and control." The approbation of these despatches
was the severest condemnation which could be inflicted on
Lord Hastings; but Mr. Astell's motion was adopted by a

majority of two hundred and twelve. Thus did the East India Company, with all the documents connected with his brilliant administration before them, dismiss him from their Court with the verdict that he was simply not guilty of having acted from corrupt motives. It was an ungrateful return to the man who had raised them to the pinnacle of political power and invested their rule with a moral grandeur. The happy remark made in the case of Warren Hastings, that if there was a bald place on his head, it ought to be covered with laurel, was peculiarly applicable to him. But the East India Company, princely beyond all other rulers in their munificence, have not been able to rise above the influence of vulgar and invidious prejudices in dealing with the merits of their most illustrious men—Clive, Warren Hastings, Lord Wellesley, and Lord Hastings. Lord Hastings did not long survive the indignity thus cast on him. He died at Malta on the 24th August, 1827, and, in the succeeding year, the India House endeavoured to make some atonement for their vote of censure by placing the sum of two lacs of rupees in the hands of trustees for the benefit of his son.

CHAPTER XXIX.

ADMINISTRATION OF MR. ADAM AND LORD AMHERST.

On the receipt of Lord Hastings's resignation,
Lord Amherst appointed Governor-General, 1822. the Court of Directors, with the ready concurrence of the Ministry, nominated Mr. Canning, the late President of the Board of Control, Governor-General. A better appointment it would have been difficult to conceive, but India was not destined to enjoy the benefit of his transcendant talents. When on the point of embarking, the sudden death of the Marquis of Londonderry—with whose

name as Lord Castlereagh during Lord Wellesley's administration the reader is already familiar—led to his joining the
Cabinet at home. Two candidates then appeared for this
splendid office, Lord William Bentinck and Lord Amherst.
Lord William had the strongest claims on the Court of Directors ; they had hastily removed him from the Government
of Madras, in the height of the panic created by the Vellore
mutiny, but on a calm review of the case, had acknowledged
" the uprightness, zeal, and success of his services." He was
eminently qualified for the Governor-Generalship by his great
administrative ability, his intimate knowledge of the native
character and habits, and of the system of the Indian Governments, and not less by his intense fondness for the work.
Lord Amherst's claim rested on his embassy to China, and the
exemplary patience and fortitude with which he had maintained the dignity of the British crown against the arrogance
of the Pekin court. He had also suffered shipwreck on his
return. The preference was given to him, and he landed in
Calcutta on the 1st August, 1823.

During the interregnum, the government devolved on Mr. Adam, the senior member of
Council, an officer of ability and resolution, and
great political experience, but totally disqualified
for the highest post in the empire by the strength of his local
partialities and prejudices. Lord Hastings had left ten crores
of rupees in the treasuries, in addition to a surplus revenue of
two crores a-year, and the Government was bewildered with
this unexampled exuberance of wealth. Lord Hastings thought
that one-half the excess might be very appropriately allotted
to the Proprietors of India stock, and the other half to the
nation. But the Act of 1813 had ordained that, with the
exception of the lac of rupees to be applied to public instruction, all surplus revenue should be assigned to the reduction
of the debt. A portion of it was therefore employed in con-
verting the Company's six per cent. paper into five per cents.,
which produced a saving of thirty lacs of rupees a-year. With

Mr. Adam, Governor-General, ad interim, 1823.

a portion of the accumulation in the treasuries, it was at one time proposed to pay off the debts of the civilians. The proposal was by no means so preposterous as it may at first sight appear. They formed the official aristocracy of the British dynasty, and supported the honour of their position by a liberal expenditure, which was often, however, beyond their means. There was no lack of wealthy natives ready to furnish the means of extravagance to youths to whom the administration of large districts would be eventually committed. They were seldom importunate for a settlement ; the bond was readily renewed from time to time, with the addition of interest, but when the victim had risen to power, his native creditor demanded either the discharge of his debt, now swelled to a prodigious amount, or some influential appointment in his court, where he would of course exemplify the oriental rule of turning power into money. The office was often indignantly refused, but the knowledge of the civilian's indebtedness to the native, which could not be concealed, deprived him of the reputation of independence, which in popular estimation was essential to the impartial distribution of justice. To liberate the judge or collector from the thraldom of the native money-lender, and to make him the creditor of the state, was therefore as much a benefit to the district as to the individual himself. But the debts of the civilians were found to be so formidable, that the project was never carried out, and within a twelvemonth the Burmese war came and cleared out the treasury, and converted the surplus into a deficit.

Persecution of the Press, 1823. Mr. Adams's brief administration of seven months was marked by great energy, and not a few good measures; but it is now remembered only by his illiberal proceedings against the press, and his vindictive persecution of Mr. Buckingham, who had come out to Calcutta in 1818, and established the " Calcutta Journal." It was the ablest newspaper which had ever appeared in India, and gave a higher tone and a deeper interest to journalism. A knot of young men in the public service, of brilliant talents, headed by

Mr. Henry Meredith Parker, ranged themselves around the paper, and contributed by their poignant articles to its extraordinary success and popularity. The editor, availing himself of the liberty granted to the press by Lord Hastings, commented on public measures with great boldness, and some times with a degree of severity which was considered dangerous. But the great offence of the Journal consisted in the freedom of its remarks on some of the leading members of Government. They had been nursed in the lap of despotism, and their feelings of official complacency were rudely disturbed by the sarcasms inflicted on them. Madras, as a rule, has been unfortunate in its governors; no fewer than six have been recalled—one of them unjustly—and, with the exception of three or four, the rest have been very second-rate men. One of these, Mr. Hugh Elliott, then filled the chair, to the regret of the public, and the Journal affirmed that he had obtained an extension of his term of office, which was announced to the community in a circular with a black border. This innocent pleasantry was registered among the offences of the paper. The Calcutta secretaries had about this time taken to wear a green coat, and the Journal styled them the "gangrene of the state." Mr. Adam had systematically opposed the liberality shown towards the press by Lord Hastings, and only waited for his departure to impose fetters on it, and to make an example of the obnoxious Journal. A regulation was accordingly passed in April, 1823, which completely extinguished the "freedom of unlicensed printing," but the Calcutta Journal continued to write with the same spirit as before. The senior Presbyterian minister, a zealous partizan of Government, had set up a rival Tory paper, and indulged in invectives against Mr. Buckingham, which, when indicted in the Supreme Court, were pronounced to be libellous. Not only was no check imposed on him by the Government, but he was nominated to the well-paid office of clerk to the Stationery Office. The appointment, when announced at home, was condemned by his own church, and revoked by the Court of

Directors. The Calcutta Journal ridiculed the incongruity of this union of offices, which obliged the reverend gentleman to employ himself in counting bundles of tape and sticks of sealing wax, when he ought to be composing his sermons. For this venial offence, Mr. Adam came down at once on Mr. Buckingham, revoked his licence, banished him from India, and ruined his prospects. He appealed for compensation to the India House, but an overwhelming majority of Proprietors passed a resolution approving of the proceedings of the Governor-General. A petition to disallow the press regulation was presented to the Privy Council, and rejected without any hesitation. Mr. Adam died at sea on his way to England, after an honourable service of thirty years, leaving behind him, as the Directors justly remarked, " the reputation of exemplary integrity, distinguished ability, and indefatigable zeal."

Rise and pro-
gress of the
Burmese
power,
1753—1815.

Lord Amherst had no sooner assumed the government, than he found himself involved in hostile discussions with the Burmese, which terminated within five months in a declaration of war. The kingdom of Burmah lies to the east of Bengal, from which it is separated by hills and forests, inhabited by various tribes of barbarians. Alompra, a man of obscure birth, but cast in the same mould as Hyder Ali and Runjeet Sing, began his career with a hundred followers, and after liberating his country from the yoke of Pegu, succeeded, about the year 1753, four years before the battle of Plassy, in establishing a new dynasty at Ava. Conquest was, as usual, the vital principle of this new government, and the Burmese soon became a great aggressive power. They successively repelled four invasions of the Chinese, and in 1766 compelled the king of Siam to cede the Tenasserim provinces to them. The province of Aracan, which had long been an independent, and at one period a powerful kingdom—as repeated invasions of Bengal testify—was annexed to the Burmese dominions in 1787. This province stretched along the eastern shore of the

Bay of Bengal, and was separated by the river Naaf from the Company's territories, in which several Aracan chiefs took refuge six years after, and were pursued across the frontier. Sir John Shore, then Governor-General, surrendered the fugitives on condition that the Burmese should retire to their own side of the river. This concession, which he considered the dictate of justice as well as of prudence, was attributed by the Burmese to pusillanimity, and the deputation of Colonel Symes, soon after, on a mission to Ava, confirmed this impression. He was received with scanty honour, and much gasconade, and the Burmese monarch, on learning from him that the English were at war with Bonaparte, inquired why the Governor-General had not applied to him for 40,000 troops, who would have swept the French from the face of the earth. In 1798, the oppressions of the Burmese forced a body of more than 30,000 Aracanese to seek a refuge in the British district of Chittagong. In their flight through the wilds and forests, without food or shelter, they experienced the extremity of distress, and the paths were strewed with the bodies of the aged and the helpless, and of mothers with infants at the breast. To refuse them an asylum would have been an act of barbarity, and they were settled in the waste lands of the district. The Burmese governor of Aracan demanded the surrender of the whole body, under the threat of an invasion. A large force of sepoys was dispatched to protect the frontier, while Colonel Symes was sent on a second mission to Ava, where he was treated with more than the usual arrogance of the Burmese court. A third embassy was unwisely sent in 1809, and Lieutenant Canning, the envoy, was subjected to increased indignity. The Aracan refugees were animated with inextinguishable hatred of their Burmese oppressors, and made repeated inroads into Aracan. Every effort was made by the British Government to restrain them, but nothing could convince the Burmese that they were not acting under the instigation of the public authorities in Calcutta. The repeated refusal of the Governor-General to deliver up these helpless creatures to the Burmese executioner exasperated the Government of Ava, and in July, 1818, Lord Hastings received a rescript from the king demanding the surrender of eastern Bengal, including Moorshedabad. "The countries of Chittagong and Dacca, of Moorshedabad and Cossimbazar," he said, "do not belong to India. They are ours; if you continue to retain them, we will come and destroy your country." Lord Hastings treated the letter as a forgery, and returned it to the king.

Further conquests of the Burmese, 1815—23. For several years before the war we are about to describe, the Burmese had been engaged in extending their conquests to the north-west of Ava. The kingdom of Assam, abutting on the Company's district of Rungpore, stretches eastward through the valley of the Berhampooter to the mountains which separate it from China. It had maintained its independence against the repeated assaults of the Mogul emperors, and had defeated the most celebrated of Aurungzebe's generals. But disputes had now arisen in the royal family which gave the Burmese an opportunity of interfering, and they established a paramount influence in it in 1815. In 1822 Muha Bundoola, the great national hero, completed the reduction of it, and annexed it to the Burmese crown. Munipore, a valley lying to the east of Bengal and encircled with mountains, had once planted its standard on the walls of Ava, but the dissensions of the palace introduced Burmese influence, and it was absorbed in the kingdom of Ava. The Burmese also entered the little principality of Cachar, on the north-east corner of Bengal, but were checked by the Supreme Government, who considered it impolitic to allow them to plant their camps and stockades so near the border. The dynasty of Alompra had thus, in the course of seventy years, succeeded in establishing its authority over territories eight hundred miles in length, stretching from the confines of Bengal to those of China. The uniform success of every enterprize had filled the Burmese with an overweening conceit of their strength, and the evident indisposition of the Company's Government to go to war, combined with repeated embassies to Ava, and a profound ignorance of the resources of British power, inspired them with an irrepressible desire to try conclusions with the English in the field. "From the king to the beggar," as stated by Mr. Laird, an Englishman residing in the country, "the whole community was hot for war." Muha Bundoola, on his return from Assam, offered to drive the English from Bengal with no other troops than the strangers dependent on Ava. "The English"—such was the language of the royal council —"have conquered the black foreigners, the people of castes, who have puny frames, and no courage. They have never fought with so strong and brave a people as the Burmese, skilled in the use of the spear and the sword."

Origin of the Burmese war, 1823.

The Burmese lost no time in giving effect to this determination. At the southern boundary of the Chittagong district, at the estuary of the Naaf, lies the little island of Shahpooree, which had always been considered a part of the Company's territories. To defend it against the hostile disposition manifested by the Burmese, a small guard was posted on it in 1823. The Governor of Aracan claimed the island as Burmese territory, and insisted on the removal of the troops. The Governor-General proposed to appoint a joint commission to investigate the question of right, and the Burmese authorities answered the overture by sending over a thousand men, who hoisted the Burmese flag, put a part of the feeble detachment to death, and drove off the remainder. Lord Amherst immediately sent a force which dislodged the Burmese, and addressed a letter to the king, attributing the aggression to the presumption of the Governor of Aracan, and stating that his Government, however anxious to remain at peace, must resort to retaliation if such insults were repeated. The Court of Ava was thus confirmed in the conviction that the English dreaded an encounter with its troops, and Muha Bundoola was sent with a large army to Aracan with orders to expel the English from Bengal,

and to send the Governor-General to Ava, bound in the golden
fetters which he took with him. To the official letter no
direct reply was vouchsafed from Ava, but the Governor of
Pegu was directed to signify the "pleasure of the king of the
white elephant, the lord of the seas and of the land, that no
further communication should be sent to the golden feet, but
that the Governor-General should state his case in a petition
to Muha Bundoola, who was proceeding to Aracan with an
army to settle every question." Lord Amherst, finding that
every effort to maintain peace only rendered war more imminent, and that the Burmese were preparing to invade Bengal
simultaneously on the north-east and the south-east, issued a
declaration of war on the 24th February, 1824; and thus
began the first Burmese war. At a subsequent period, when
the Court of Directors became impatient under the boundless
cost and dilatory prosecution of the war, they condemned the
origin of it, as a dispute about a contemptible and uninhabited
island, a mere sand-bank; and Lord Amherst deemed it necessary to draw up an elaborate defence of his proceedings; but
the labour was altogether redundant. The war was universally acknowledged in India by the most experienced statesmen to be "not only just and necessary, but absolutely and
positively unavoidable." "The clearest case," said Sir Charles
Metcalfe, "of self-defence and violated territory." If it had
been conducted with the energy and promptitude of the
Mahratta war in the days of Lord Wellesley, or the more
recent Mahratta and Pindaree war, both of which were
brought to a successful issue, before the news of the first
shot reached Leadenhall-street, there would have been little
discussion as to its origin.

Arrangements
of the cam-
paign, 1824.

The Burmese were the most despicable enemy
the British arms had ever encountered in the east.
Their army was a miserable half-armed rabble,
without discipline or courage. They had few muskets, and
their swords and pikes were of a very inferior description.
Their chief defence lay in the admirable skill and rapidity

with which they constructed stockades, and which our commanders, with rare exceptions, committed the folly of endeavouring to carry by storm, instead of expelling the enemy
by shells and rockets. A hoe and a spade was a more essential part of the equipment of a Burmese soldier than a musket
or a sword. Each man as he advanced dug a hole in the
ground deep enough to afford him shelter, from which he fired
in security until he was unearthed by the impetuosity of the
British troops.   This information was acquired during the
course of the war, but at the commencement of it the Government in Calcutta was profoundly ignorant of the national
mode of warfare, of the military force and resources, the population and the geography of the country, or of the approaches
to it from our own provinces.   The Commander-in-chief, Sir
Edward Paget, then in the north-west, asserted that any
attempt to enter Burmah either through Cachar or Aracan,
would end in disaster, inasmuch as the troops, instead of
finding armies, fortresses, and cities, would meet with nothing
but jungle, pestilence, and famine.   The plan of the campaign
was drawn up by Captain John Canning, who had traversed
the country and visited the capital; and it was unhappily on his
knowledge that the Government placed its sole dependence.
He represented that the occupation of Rangoon, the great
port of the Irawaddy, would paralyse the Burmese Government, and that the means of constructing a flotilla for navi-
gating the river, as well as provisions and draught cattle,
might be procured in and around that town in abundance.
Though the river, like the Ganges, was an impetuous torrent
during the rains, the south-west monsoon which prevailed at
that season of the year, would, he affirmed, enable the expedition to stem the current and sail up to the capital. It was
resolved, therefore, to land the expedition at Rangoon as the
rains commenced.   The plan was visionary and preposterous,
as the military authorities in Calcutta, with their knowledge
of the rivers of India, ought to have foreseen; and the adoption of it was the first and most fatal error of the campaign.

The expedition was collected in the spacious harbour of Port
Cornwallis, in the largest of the Andaman islands, lying in
the Bay of Bengal, about three hundred miles south of Rangoon.   It consisted .of about 11,000 European and native
troops, the latter drawn exclusively from the Madras Presidency, and it was placed under the command of Sir Archibald
Campbell, who had served with distinction under the Duke in
Spain.   The fleet of transports was convoyed by three vessels
of war, and by the " Diana," a little steamer recently built in
Calcutta, and the first which ever floated in the waters of the
east.   The appearance of this vessel confounded the minds of
the Burmese, among whom there was an ancient prediction
current, that the kingdom would be invincible till a vessel
moved up the Irawaddy without sails or oars.

Disaster at   While the expedition was in course of equip-
Ramoo, May 17, ment, Bundoola entered Aracan for the invasion
1824.   of Bengal with an army variously estimated at
ten and twenty thousand men.   The defence of the frontier
had been left to a small and inadequate force stationed at
Chittagong; and a weak detachment of about three hundred
native infantry, with several hundred of the local levies and
two guns, had been imprudently pushed forward under Captain
Noton to hold a post on our extreme boundary, a hundred
miles from the nearest support.   The approach of Bundoola
was well known in Calcutta, and the public authorities were
repeatedly urged to reinforce the small body of troops which
was to sustain the first shock of the Burmese, but the request
was treated with indifference.   The consequence was deplorable.   The Burmese force advanced on the 17th May to
Captain Noton's pickets; and the untrained men of the local
corps fled.   The little band of sepoys was completely surrounded, but they maintained the struggle gallantly for three
days with little food or rest, and were then constrained to
retreat, when they fell into irretrievable confusion.   Captain
Noton and five officers were killed, and three wounded.   The
detachment was annihilated, and the eastern districts of

Bengal were seized with a panic, which extended even to Calcutta. But a large force was sent in haste to the frontier, which effectually checked the advance of the enemy, and Bundoola was soon after recalled to oppose the British force at Rangoon.

Arrival of the expedition at Rangoon, 1824.　The expedition arrived off that town on the 11th May, to the inexpressible surprise of. the Burmese, who had never dreamt that the English, whom they were about to expel from Bengal, would venture to attack them in their own territory. No preparations had been made to repel them, and the only defence of the town consisted in a quadrangular teak stockade, about twelve feet high, with a battery of indifferent guns, which were· silenced by the first broadside from the " Liffey." Happily, the discharge was so opportune as also to rescue from destruction the Europeans resident in Rangoon, eleven in number, who had been seized and condemned to death on the approach of the fleet. Their arms had been bound behind as they were made to squat on the ground, and the executioner stood before them sharpening his weapon, when the shot from the frigate battered the building, which the Burmese officers abandoned in great trepidation, and thus afforded the prisoners the means of escape. The troops landed without any opposition, but they found the town deserted. It appeared that the governor, seeing all resistance hopeless, had ordered the whole population, men, women, and children, to quit it, and retire to the jungles with all their provisions and flocks and herds. The mandate was implicitly obeyed, partly from a dread of the strangers, but more especially from the terror which the ferocity of their own government inspired in all breasts. By this unexpected stroke of policy the whole plan of the campaign was defeated. Every hope of obtaining the means of advancing to the capital by water or by land was extinguished, and Sir Archibald was obliged to confine his efforts to the shelter of his troops during the six months of inaction to which they were doomed. One entire regiment was quar-

tered in the Dagon Pagoda, the pride of Rangoon, a magnificent edifice, which is justly admired for the lightness of its
contour, the happy combination of its parts, and the vastness
of its dimensions, and which serves to give us a very high
opinion of the splendid Bouddist architecture with which India
was once filled.   The object of the Burmese commander was
to isolate the British encampment and intercept all supplies,
in which he completely succeeded, as well as to destroy the fleet
with the fire rafts which the Burmese constructed with singular
skill, but which was prevented by the vigilance of the British
officers.

Sickness and mortality of the troops, 1824.

Within a week after the occupation of Rangoon,
the rains set in with great violence ; the country
around became a swamp, and the miasma, combined
with the sultry heat, brought fever and dysentery
and death into the camp.   The condition of this noble army
was rendered the more deplorable by the want of wholesome
food.   There was no lack of cattle in the neighbourhood
which would have amply supplied all its necessities,
but the Government in Calcutta, by a stretch of folly unknown in India, had forbidden the commander to touch them
lest he should wound the prejudices of the natives, and the
European soldiers were allowed to perish that the cows might
live.   The troops were thus left to depend on the supplies
brought from Calcutta, which was proverbial for the dis-
honesty of its cured provisions ; the meat was found to be
putrescent, and the maggoty biscuits crumbled under the
touch.   Owing to the culpable neglect of the public authorities in Calcutta, and more especially of the commissariat, the
army at Rangoon was left for five months in this state of
destitution after its exigences had been completely revealed.
It was only through the prompt and indefatigable exertions
of Sir Thomas Munro, the governor of Madras, in forward-
ing supplies that the army was not altogether annihilated.
The unhealthiness of the season, and the unwholesomeness
of the food soon filled the hospitals, and of the whole force

scarcely three thousand men remained fit for duty. In the month of August an expedition was sent to the Tenasserim provinces, which stretched four hundred miles along the coast. The chief towns were occupied, and in the capital, Martaban, was found an immense arsenal filled with the munitions of war. These districts, remote from the stern influence of the Governor of Rangoon, furnished the troops to some extent with the supplies of vegetables and meat which were so greatly needed. In the beginning of October a large force was sent against Kaik-loo, fourteen miles from Rangoon, where the Burmese had erected a strong stockade. The troops who attempted to storm it were repulsed with considerable loss; but, on the appearance of a larger force, the Burmese were found to have evacuated it.

Actions of the 7th and 15th Dec., 1824. The King of Ava at length resolved to collect all his strength for one vigorous effort to expel the invaders from the country. The renowned Bundoola was sent down to Rangoon with an army of sixty thousand men, and arrived in front of the British encampment on the 1st December. The rapidity and precision with which corps after corps took up its station, and immediately threw up entrenchments, reflected great credit on Burmese skill and discipline. Within a few hours the British camp was completely surrounded with stockades, and the busy line of soldiers suddenly disappeared behind 'them, the men sinking in couples into the burrows they had dug, which were stocked with a sufficient supply of rice, water, and fuel. The works, which were watched with intense interest from the British encampment, appeared to rise by the wand of a magician. The first attack on them was made on the 6th December, when two columns supported by gunboats broke through the right of the Burmese entrenchments and dispersed the defenders. Instead, however, of quitting the field, Bundoola pushed his troops the next day up to the great pagoda, but the twenty guns which had been mounted on it, opened a brisk cannonade, and four British columns

II.

simultaneously attacked his force and routed it. But his
spirit of perseverance was not exhausted. He sent incendiaries into the town who burnt down one-half of it, and
he erected another series of stockades more formidable than
any the British army had yet encountered, but on the 15th
December, all his hopes were blasted by a total defeat, and
he withdrew the whole of his force to Donabew, forty miles
up the river.

Conquest of   Leaving Sir Archibald at Rangoon without an
Assam, 1825,   enemy, we turn to the operations of the war in
other quarters. At the beginning of 1825, the province of
Assam was wrested from the Burmese by Colonel Richards,
who met with no resistance in occupying the capital,
Rungpore, though it was mounted with two hundred pieces
of ordnance. The Commander-in-chief, as already stated,
Campaign in   had dissuaded Government from any attempt to
Cachar, 1824.   invade Burmah through Cachar or Aracan, but
when it became evident that the Rangoon expedition had failed
to achieve anything, he changed his opinion and encouraged
Lord Amherst to organise one army to advance through
Cachar and Munipore southward upon Ava, and another to
penetrate Aracan, cross the Yomadown hills, and debouch
in the valley of the Irawaddy and then turn up north to the
capital. Both expeditions proved abortive. The Cachar
force consisting of 7,000 men was entrusted to the command
of Colonel Shouldham. The Burmese had evacuated the
province, but a more formidable enemy was found in the
unexampled difficulties of the route. The army was enabled
to advance along a road which the pioneers had opened with
immense labour and perseverance to a point within ninety
miles of Munipore, but the country beyond it was found to
consist of an unbroken succession of abrupt hills and dales,
the hills clothed to the summit with impenetrable forests,
and the dells rendered impassable by deep quagmires. The
rains commenced in February, and continued without abatement throughout March. The troops were harassed beyond

endurance. Hundreds of bullocks and camels, and a large proportion of the elephants, sunk under fatigue, or were imbedded in the mire. To transport the stores, the artillery, the heavy baggage, and all the *impedimenta* of a civilised army through such a region and under such circumstances was impossible, and the Colonel prudently relinquished the attempt and returned to Bengal. The expedition to Aracan was still more unfortunate. It consisted of about 10,000 men, and proceeded on its march from Chittagong on the 1st January. The commander was General Morrison, a King's officer of good repute, but he imprudently rejected the advice of the experienced Company's officers on his staff, who were acquainted with the face and character of the country. There was a constant succession of blunders, and the army was three months marching down the coast, a distance of only two hundred and fifty miles, and did not reach the capital of the province, which was occupied with little resistance, till it was too late in the season to make any farther progress. The monsoon commenced early in May, the country was flooded and became a pestilential marsh. One-fourth of the troops perished by disease, and two-thirds of the remainder were in hospital. Few ever recovered their former health and vigour, and the Aracan fever was long remembered with feelings of horror. The army, as an organised body, had ceased to exist, and on one occasion, when a wing of a European regiment was mustered on parade, only one soldier, it was said, appeared to answer to his name. But it was not till the end of the year that the new Commander-in-chief, Lord Combermere, consented to withdraw the remains of the army from this lazaretto.

Conquest of Aracan, 1825.

Sir Archibald Campbell, after having been encamped nine months at Rangoon, and lost two months of the season for operations, at length moved up towards the capital, on the 13th February. The army was divided into three columns, one of which, by an unaccountable fancy, was sent down under Colonel Sale, to occupy the town

Second Campaign, 1825.

and district of .Bassein, on the southern coast, where there was no reason to apprehend any kind of danger. The small Burmese force fled at his approach, and he returned to Rangoon without any loss, save that of invaluable time. Another column moved up by land, under the personal command of Sir Archibald, without seeing the face of an enemy. The third proceeded by water up the Irawaddy, under Brigadier Cotton, and came abreast of Donabew on the 28th February. All the resources of Burmese engineering science had been employed by Bundoola in strengthening the fortifications of this post. The stockade extended a mile along a sloping bank of the river, and was composed of solid teak beams, fifteen feet in length, firmly driven into the earth. Behind this wooden wall the old brick ramparts afforded a firm footing for the defenders. Upwards of a hundred and fifty guns and swivels were mounted on the works, which were, moreover, protected by a wide and deep ditch, rendered formidable by spikes, nails, and holes. The garrison consisted of twelve thousand men, and was commanded by Bundoola himself, who maintained so stern a discipline that on one occasion when some of his artillery-men shrunk from their post on seeing their commander shot down, he descended to the spot, and ordered the heads of two of the recreants to be struck off and fixed to a pole, by way of example. The Brigadier succeeded in carrying the smaller works, but met with a signal defeat in his attempt to storm the larger entrenchment; and having indiscreetly left one of his regiments behind him on the route, pronounced his force unequal to the capture of the place. Sir Archibald had scarcely three months left for the campaign when he left Rangoon, and the capital was five hundred miles distant. But it was indispensable to retrieve the honour of the British arms, and to keep open his communications with the sea. Preferring, as he remarked, the sacrifice of time to the loss of men, he marched back to the succour of Brigadier Cotton with his whole force, and thus incurred the loss of an entire month. The attack began on the 1st

April, when a shower of shells and rockets was poured down
on the Burmese encampment. The next morning, the heavy
guns and mortars began to play on it, but no answer was
returned, and soon after the whole of the Burmese army was
observed to be in full retreat. Bundoola had, in fact, been
killed by the bursting of a shell the preceding night, and
with him expired all the courage and spirit of his troops. No
farther obstacle was offered to the advance of the General,
and Prome was occupied without firing a shot. But the rains
were approaching, and the second campaign was brought to
a close within ten weeks, during which the army had advanced
a hundred and fifty miles.

Negotiations for Peace, 1825. The war was found to be more expensive than
any in which the Company had ever been engaged.
The mere field expenses, together with the cost of the additional troops who had been enlisted without necessity at
the Bengal Presidency to fill up the gap temporarily created
by the Burmese expedition, were estimated at a lac of rupees
a-day. It was proposed to halt at Prome, and act on the
defensive, but Lord Amherst wisely rejected this advice, under
the conviction that the most effectual mode of bringing the
war to a termination was to push on rapidly towards the capital. At the same time he urged the General to welcome any
disposition on the part of the Burmese for peace, and that no
opportunity of negotiation might be lost, associated in a
commission with him, the naval Commander-in-chief, and
Mr. Thomas Campbell Robertson, a civilian of experience and
judgment, who had been the political agent at Chittagong.
Mr. Ross Mangles, a young civilian of great promise, was
appointed to act as secretary. Before the arrival of the
Commissioners, the General had intimated to the Burmese
Court that he was authorized to negotiate a peace. The overture was readily accepted; an armistice was concluded for a
month, and envoys were sent down from Ava to the British
encampment. They were informed that the King would be
required to abstain from all interference in Cachar and Assam,

to recognise the independence of Munipore, to cede the provinces of Aracan and Tenasserim, and pay two crores of rupees.
towards the expenses of the war. They stated that it was
beyond their power to accede to these severe terms, and the
armistice was prolonged to enable them to make a reference
to Ava. The reply of the King was brief and simple : " The
English must empty their hands of what they hold, and then
send a petition for the release of the European captives ; but
if they hint at the cession of territory or the payment of
money there must be an end of all friendship." In that spirit
of indomitable perseverance which the Burmese had manifested throughout the war, and which in some measure atoned
for the want of courage, another army of forty thousand men
was collected and sent to Prome, with orders to expel the
English. With this body there was an engagement at Watti-
gaum in which the British troops were repulsed from the
stockades with the loss of two hundred men, of whom ten
were officers. Emboldened by this success, the Burmese commander advanced against the British lines, but was signally
defeated and very closely pursued. On the 26th December
a boat with a flag of truce made its appearance with fresh
envoys from Ava to renew the negotiations. It was anchored
in the middle of the stream, and the plenipotentiaries entered
it from opposite directions, with a retinue of fifty men on each
side. The Burmese ministers waived every objection to the
territorial cessions, but withstood the pecuniary payment, on
the score of poverty, with so much earnestness that the
English Commissioners were induced to reduce it by one-half.
A treaty was accordingly signed on the 3rd January, and the
royal ratification was promised on the 18th of the month. A
little incident which occurred during the conference serves to
illustrate the character of Burmese officials. One of their
attendants, in lighting a cigar on the roof of the boat, happened to drop a spark on some loose gunpowder, which caused
a slight explosion, and startled the principal envoy. When
the offender was named to him, he exclaimed, " cut off his

hand," and a moment after added, "off with his head," and the sentence would have been executed at once, but for the earnest entreaty of Sir Archibald. But the ratification never arrived; the time was employed, as the Burmese had intended it should be, in strengthening the fortifications of Mellown, which lay opposite the British encampment on the Irawaddy. The British force attacked it with great vigour on the 19th January, captured all the guns, stores, and ammunition, and after delivering the encampment to the flames, pursued its march towards the capital.

The king began now to tremble for his throne,

Final engage-
ment and peace, and released Dr. Price, one of the American mis-
1826.   sionaries whom he had placed in confinement, and sent him down with another of the European captives to renew the negotiations. They were informed that no severer terms would be exacted in consequence of the victory at Mellown, but that one-fourth of the indemnity must be paid down within twenty days. The two European gentlemen returned to Ava, with the promise of appearing in the English camp on the 12th February, if the proposal was accepted by the king. But before that day he was induced to make one final effort to avert this humiliation. One of his military chiefs, in a burst of patriotism, engaged to expel the invaders if he were entrusted with an army. All the troops the Burmese were now able to muster did not exceed the number of 16,000, and with these the general marched down towards the English encampment, resolved to abandon the national mode of warfare, and, instead of digging holes and erecting stockades, to assail the British army boldly in the open field. Sir Archibald had only 1,300 men left out of his whole army to meet this force, but 900 of them were European veterans. The result of the engagement, which took place at Paghan-mew, may be easily imagined. The Burmese force was totally routed, and fled back to the capital in wild disorder, and the Burmese general expiated his patriotism by being trampled to death under the feet of an elephant. Sir Archibald advanced

to Yandaboo, within forty miles of the capital. The last
Burmese army had been extinguished, the strength of the
monarchy was completely exhausted, and the king hastened to
send Dr. Price, in company with Mr. Judson, the head of the
American mission, who had suffered a cruel captivity in Ava
for two years, and with two of his own ministers, to accept
whatever terms the English general might dictate. They
brought with them the first instalment of the money, and all
the European prisoners save one, who was detained for a
time, because the king had been informed that the Company
had married one of his relatives! The treaty of Yandaboo was
signed on the 24th February. The king ceded Assam, Aracan,
and Tenasserim to the Company, agreed to pay a crore of
rupees towards the expenses of the war, and to submit to the
admission of a British minister at Ava, although there is
nothing to which Eastern princes feel so bitter an aversion as
the residence of a European representative—a barbarian eye,
as they term it—at their courts.

Remarks on   This was the first occasion on which the British
the war, 1826. arms were carried beyond the confines of India,
and great fears were entertained lest the Company should
thus be drawn into collision with the various Indo-Chinese
nations; but the apprehension has proved groundless. The
Burmese war was also more expensive and less recuperative
than any which had preceded it. The great Mahratta and
Pindaree war cost the Government only a crore of rupees,
which was more than covered by a year's revenue of the
provinces acquired by it. The Burmese war cost thirteen
crores, and the return consisted in three impoverished and
thinly inhabited provinces. A fatality seemed, moreover, to
mark every arrangement in this war, and in the presence of a
contemptible enemy, it was remarkable only for want of
judgment and perpetual delay. Its character was not redeemed by a single stroke of generalship. A great outcry
was consequently raised against Lord Amherst in England;
he was denounced in the Court of Proprietors as in every way
unfit, by education, habits, and character, for the Government

of India, and repeated attempts were made to procure his recall. But Sir Thomas Munro, whose opinion was entitled to more confidence than that of any other statesman of the day, considered that there was great injustice in the idle clamour raised against the Governor-General. The Court of Directors, he said, were unreasonable in expecting to find every day for the Supreme Government such men as Cornwallis, and Wellesley, and Hastings, who appeared only once or twice in an age. Lord Amherst was as good a Governor-General as they were likely to send out. His situation was an arduous one; he was necessarily influenced by Captain Canning and the military authorities around him; he was new to India, and the Burmese were entirely unknown to us. But we lose sight of the mismanagement of the war when we view the prosperous condition which the provinces it gave us presents after the lapse of forty years. The energy and enterprize of the interlopers whom the Court of Directors endeavoured to exclude from India in 1813, have contributed in no small degree to augment the resources and the strength of the empire. They have covered Assam with tea gardens. The desolate and pestilental swamp of Aracan has become the granary of the Bay of Bengal, and hundreds of vessels are annually employed in conveying its produce from the port of Akyab to India, China, and Europe. Moulmein, the capital of the Tenasserim provinces, which contained only half a dozen fishermen's huts when it was first occupied, has become a flourishing port, with a population of fifty thousand, and a trade of half a million a-year.

Mutiny at Barrackpore, 1824.   The progress of the Burmese war gave rise to another sepoy mutiny. The Aracan expedition was composed of two regiments of Europeans and of several native corps from Madras and Bengal. The Madras troops embarked with extraordinary alacrity; these from Bengal, owing to their religious aversion to the sea, were directed to march down the coast. The disaster at Ramoo had diffused throughout the army a great dread of the Burmese soldiers who were represented as magicians, and

created a passionate repugnance to the service. The Bengal
sepoys had been accustomed to provide for the transport of
their own baggage out of their pay, but the public demand
for cattle had not only doubled the price, but exhausted the
local supplies. Towards the end of October, the 47th Native
Infantry at Barrackpore, one of the regiments warned for
service, · presented a respectful memorial setting forth the
extreme difficulty of procuring the means of conveyance.
The representation was just and reasonable, and might have
been investigated without any peril, but the military chiefs,
accustomed to the stringent discipline and implicit obedience of
European regiments, resented the slightest appearance of back-
wardness in the native army, and the sepoys were informed
that they would receive no assistance from Government, and
must procure their own cattle at their own expense, without
delay. Discontent was thus ripened into insubordination;
excited meetings were held in the cantonments; the sepoys
rose in their demands, and solemnly pledged themselves not
to march without a supply of cattle, and also an increase of
pay. To augment the embarrassment of the crisis, the whole
army had been recently remodelled, and officers transferred
from one regiment to another. Those of the 47th had been
only three months with the corps, and had not acquired any
influence over the men. On the 1st November, the 47th was
paraded in marching order, but scarcely a third of the regiment fell in; the rest assembled tumultuously in the adjacent
lines. The commandant of the station and other officers of
rank attempted to reason with them, but were repulsed with
vehement gestures and vociferations. The Commander-in-
chief then resolved to crush the mutiny by force of arms.
Two regiments of Europeans, a detachment of horse artillery,
and the Governor-General's body-guard, were marched over
night to Barrackpore and drawn up, unperceived, in the vicinity
of the parade ground. In the morning, the Commander-in-
chief came on the ground with his staff. The regiment was
paraded, and officers, whom the men were accustomed to

respect, were sent to remonstrate with them, but without success. The sepoys were ordered to march forthwith, or to ground arms. They stood still in a state of stupid desperation, resolved not to yield, but making no effort at resistance. A volley was discharged by the artillery, when they cast away their arms with a loud shriek, and fled in dismay. The European troops then fired on them, and the body-guard sabred the fugitives. The slaughter on the ground and on the line of pursuit was very severe, and some were drowned in attempting to swim across the river. The ringleaders were subsequently tried by court-martial, and executed; and others were sentenced to hard labour in irons. A Court of Inquiry was held, which came to the decision that the "mutiny was an ebullition of despair at being compelled to march without the means of doing so." There was no intention of resistance on the part of the sepoys, as scarcely one of the muskets left on the ground was found to be loaded, though each man had forty rounds of ammunition. When the corps had reached a state of actual mutiny, armed coercion was the only course which could be adopted, but the military authorities incurred a heavy responsibility by treating their legitimate representations with scorn. The Bengal sepoys are, after all, but a mercenary militia, bound to serve their foreign rulers within the limits of their own country. A little consideration for men required to march into an unknown region, peopled by the terrors of their imagination with goblins who had destroyed their fellow-soldiers, would have averted the catastrophe; but the sharpness of the remedy served to secure the subordination of the native army for sixteen years. In the following year Lord Amherst availed himself of the conquest of Aracan, to grant a free pardon to all the prisoners, but so little did they appreciate this act of kindness, that they asked, as they left the jail, what compensation they were to receive for the brass *lotas*, or water-pots, they had lost on the morning of the mutiny.

General spirit of   The condition of India at the beginning of the

disaffection,   Burmese war was such as to create much dis-
1824.
quietude, though no alarm. Nothing is so soon
forgotten in India as our successes, and nothing so long and
so heartily remembered as our reverses. The recollection of
the splendid triumphs of the Mahratta and Pindaree war had
begun to fade, and some of the princes whom we had rescued
from oppression were impatient under the restraints imposed
on them, and the punctual demand of the tributes they had
agreed to pay. There were few districts in Hindostan in
which disaffection was not, more or less, manifested; the
Mahratta states were not free from disorders, and one of the
old Pindaree chiefs emerged from obscurity and collected a
small band of followers. This fermentation in various and
widely separated provinces was important chiefly from its
common origin in the contempt which was growing up for
British power. The withdrawal of troops for the Burmese war,
and the reports which were diligently circulated of our non-
success, as well as of the talismanic prowess of the Burmese,
produced no small agitation among the natives. They had
been accustomed to see a campaign begun and ended in a few
months; but in the second year of the Burmese war, the
army had scarcely advanced a third of the way to the capital.
The hopes of our downfall, always fondly cherished by the
princes of India, were again revived. But in no instance was
Bhurtpore, 1825.   the defiance of our power so bold and significant
as at Bhurtpore. Runjeet Sing, the Jaut chief,
who had baffled Lord Lake in 1805, bequeathed the kingdom
to his son in 1823, on whose death, without issue, it devolved
on his brother. He was infirm in health, and applied to Sir
David Ochterlony, the British representative in Malwa and
Rajpootana, to recognize his son, a child of six years, as his
successor. The question was referred to Calcutta, and, in
obedience to the express orders of the Governor-General in
Council, the investiture was performed by one of the political
officers of the Residency. A twelvemonth after he ascended
the throne, on the death of his father, under the guardianship

of his maternal uncle. But before a month had elapsed, Doorjun Saul, the nephew of the deceased raja, an ambitious and impetuous youth, having succeeded in corrupting the troops, put the guardian to death, and placed his cousin in confinement. Sir David, acting on his own responsibility, and with his usual energy, zeal, and promptitude, lost no time in issuing a proclamation to the Jauts to rally round their lawful sovereign, and in ordering a force of 16,000 men with a hundred guns into the field to support his rights, and vindicate the authority of the British Government. But the Governor-General disapproved of this proceeding. He denied that we were bound to uphold the young raja by force of arms. He considered it imprudent to embark the small disposable force in the north-west in a new war during the hot weather, while we were engaged in a conflict in Burmah, the extent, or duration, or demands of which could not be foreseen. Considering all the circumstances of the time, the Government was prudent in hesitating to incur the risk of a second siege of Bhurtpore. "A failure there," wrote Sir Charles Metcalfe, " would have given a shock to our power in every part of India, shaken the confidence of our army, and confirmed the fatal belief that we could be successfully resisted."

Communication to and from Sir David Ochterlony, 1825.

The opinion of Government might, however, have been communicated to Sir David Ochterlony in a manner worthy of his long and eminent services, but for some time past there had been a strong desire in Calcutta to remove him from his post, and he had been repeatedly thwarted in his proceedings. He had latterly exhibited some of the infirmities of age, though it could not be denied that in the present instance he had manifested all the vigour of youth. Accustomed, moreover, as he had long been, to the exercise of great authority, and feeling a just confidence in his own experience, he was, perhaps disposed to stretch the exercise of his power beyond the limits of his subordinate position. The unauthorized assemblage of a field force presented the occasion which had long been desired, of getting rid of him. He was informed that he had acted on imperfect and unsatisfactory information, and that his measures were precipitate' and unjustifiable; he was ordered to countermand the march of the troops and to recall his proclamation. The letter was intended to provoke him to a resignation, and Sir Charles Metcalfe was summoned from Hyderabad to supersede him before he could receive it. He replied to this communication with much, and perhaps with undue, warmth. He said the usurpation would never have been attempted but under the strong impression then prevalent that the Government was no longer in a' position to punish insolence and to support right, and he affirmed that his military preparations fully justified the expectation that the fort would fall in a fortnight. As to the hot winds which had been adduced as an argument against the expedition, the old soldier remarked that the hour of necessity and the call of honour fixed the time for military operations. It was on this principle that, in his youth, the army had kept the field three years against Hyder, knowing no repose but during the rains, when the country was equally impassable for both parties. On this principle also, Lord Lake began the campaign of 1803, in the height of the rains, and remained under canvas during the hot winds of 1804, in the hottest province in Hindostan. He considered every moment of delay a submission to disgrace. But, in obedience to the orders he had received, he suspended the progress of the army, and issued another proclamation to the effect that the Government proposed, in the first instance, to investigate the merits of the question of the succession. He then tendered his resignation, stating that " as he had erred so egregiously in what he considered the proper and dignified course to pursue, he could no longer conceal from himself his unfitness for the situation he held." The ungenerous treatment to which he had been subjected, broke his heart, and he retired to Meerut, where he died within two months, as he said, with a bitter feeling, " disgraced," after an illustrious career of half a century, during

which there were few military operations in which he had
not taken an active part. In the camp which he formed for
the reduction of Bhurtpore in 1826, he discoursed with great
zest of his early campaigns in the Carnatic in the days of
Hastings and Coote. He was one of the brightest ornaments
of the Company's service, equally eminent in the cabinet and
in the field, a man born for high command and fitted to
strengthen the power and to sustain the dignity of Great
Britain in India. As the British representative in Malwa and
Rajpootana, he commanded universal deference, as well by
the equity of his decisions as by the magnificence of his
rétinue, which from time immemorial has always been an
element of power in eastern countries. He was not, however, without his weak side. The blind confidence which he
reposed in the natives around him was employed, as usual,
for the purpose of extortion, the odium of which fell on his
reputation. His moonshee had the presumption to place his
name on the pension list of the King of Delhi for a thousand
rupees a-month, where it remained till it was accidentally
discovered by his master; but he was happily the last of the
moonshees of European officers who created a princely fortune out of his position. Sir David's memory was more
especially cherished by the Indian army from the fact that he
was the first Company's officer who received the highest
honours of the Bath, which, down to the period of the Nepal
war, had been invidiously confined to the officers of the
Crown.

Proceedings of
Doorjun Saul
and the
Council, 1825. While Sir David was assembling the army,
Doorjun Saul manifested a spirit of entire sub-
mission to the British Government, and professed
to be satisfied with the regency, but when he found that the
troops were remanded, he assumed a higher tone, claimed
the throne itself, and prevailed on the chiefs of his tribe to
rally round him. His cause became popular, as soon as it
was understood that he intended to hold Bhurtpore against
the will of the Governor-General. Rajpoots, Jauts, Mahrat-

tas, Afghans, and not a few of the Company's own subjects, flocked to his standard, and a body of 25,000 men was speedily collected for the defence of the place. From the neighbouring Mahratta and Rajpoot chiefs he received every token of encouragement, and it was firmly believed that they were fully prepared to take part in the quarrel. The Supreme Council met to deliberate on this perilous state of affairs soon after the death of Sir David. The two civilian members of Council, and the Commander-in-chief maintained, that as the young raja had been invested with the insignia of royalty under the authority of the Governor-General, they were bound to support him against a usurper, at any hazard, more especially as the increasing disorders in the north-west threatened a general convulsion. Lord Amherst alone strenuously resisted all active measures from an overwhelming dread of a second failure at Bhurtpore. Happily Sir Charles Metcalfe arrived in Calcutta in August on his way to Delhi, and, after a careful examination of all the documents on the question, drew up a clear, bold, and masterly minute, which at once decided the policy of the Government. " We have, by degrees," he said, " become the paramount state in India. In 1817, it became the established principle of our policy to maintain tranquillity among the states of India. . . . . and we cannot be indifferent spectators of anarchy therein without ultimately giving up India again to the pillage and confusion from which we then rescued her. . . . . We are bound, not by any positive engagement to the Bhurtpore state, nor by any claim on her part, but by our duty as supreme guardians of general tranquillity, law, and right, to maintain the legal succession of Bulwunt Sing. . . Our supremacy has been violated, or slighted, under the impression that we were prevented by entanglements elsewhere from sufficiently resenting the indignity. . . . A display and vigorous exercise of our power, if rendered necessary, would be likely to bring back men's minds in that quarter to a proper tone, and the capture of Bhurtpore, if effected in a glorious manner, would do us more honour throughout India, by the removal of the hitherto unfaded impressions caused by our former failure, than any other event that can be conceived." Lord Amherst surrendered his opinion to Sir Charles Metcalfe, and had the candour and grace to place the fact on record. The Council was now unanimous, and on the 18th September, at a time when the Court of Directors maintained that " the settlement of ˙1818 had in no degree extended our right of interference in the internal concerns of other states, except as it had been provided by treaty," passed the following manly resolution : " Impressed with a full conviction that the existing disturbances at Bhurtpore, if not speedily quieted, will produce general commotion and interruption of the public tranquillity in Upper India, and feeling convinced that it is our solemn duty, no less than our right, as the paramount power and conservators of the general peace, to interfere for the prevention of these evils, the Governor-General in Council resolves that authority be conveyed to Sir Charles Metcalfe to accomplish the above object, and to maintain the succession of the rightful heir to the raj of Bhurtpore, if practicable, by expostulation and remonstrance ; and should these fail, by a resort to measures of force."

Capture of
Bhurtpore,
1826.

Sir Charles's expostulations and remonstrances, as might have been expected, were lost upon Doorjun Saul, who determined to hold the fortress to the last extremity, and it became necessary to resort to arms. To the astonishment of the princes of Upper India, who believed that the war in which the Company were engaged in Burmah had absorbed all their military resources, a British army of 20,000 men, together with a hundred mortars and heavy ordnance, suddenly sprung up in the midst of them. Bhurtpore was considered an insuperable check to British power, and the last bulwark of national independence, and the eyes of all India were fixed upon the siege, not without a general wish for its failure. The head-quarters of the Commander-in-chief, now Lord Combermere, were estab-

lished before it on the 10th December, and Sir Charles Metcalfe soon after joined the camp.   At a short distance from
the town there was a lake, separated from it by an embank-
ment, which the defenders had cut in the former siege, and
thus filled the ditch with water.   On the present occasion
they had commenced the same operation, but by the timely
arrival of a British detachment, and the energetic exertions of
Captain Irvine, the flow of water was checked, and the breach
repaired.   A delay of a few moments would have altered the
result of the siege.   The defences of this celebrated fort consisted of lofty and thick walls of clay, five miles in circumference, hardened in the sun, supported and bound by beams
and logs, rising from the edge of a ditch, fifty-five feet in
depth, and a hundred and fifty feet broad.   It was strengthened
by the outworks of nine gateways, and flanked by thirty-five
lofty mud bastions, one of which, called the "bastion of victory," was built to commemorate the defeat of Lord Lake, and,
as they vauntingly said, with the skulls and bones of those who
had fallen in the first siege.   For the level country in which it
was situated, the fortification was the strongest, and, so to
speak, the most impregnable which could be devised.   Thirty-
six mortars and forty-eight pieces of heavy ordnance played on
the ramparts for many days without making any impression on
the walls, or creating a practicable breach.   The heaviest shot
only caused the defences to crumble into rugged masses
falling down on each side of the conical wall, but leaving the
ascent scarcely less steep and inaccessible than before.   At
the commencement of operations Colonel Galloway, who had
been present at the former siege, and had written a valuable
treatise on Indian fortifications, and Lieutenant—afterwards
General—Forbes, had, unknown to each other, urged on Lord
Combermere the necessity of endeavouring to create a breach
by mining, but the proposal was treated with contempt.   It
was only when every effort to breach the wall by batteries
had hopelessly failed, that the chief engineer consented to
adopt this advice and to have recourse to mines, several of

which were completed and fired, but without any adequate
result. A great mine was at length completed, and charged
with ten thousand pounds of powder. The explosion, which
took place on the 18th January, seemed to shake the foundations of the earth; enormous masses of hardened earth, and
blocks of timber, mingled with heads, legs, and arms, were
sent flying into the air, and the sky was darkened with
volumes of smoke and dust. The column destined for the
assault, under General Reynell, rushed up the breach and
bayonetted the defenders, who fought to the last with the
greatest resolution. Six thousand—according to other
accounts double that number—were said to have fallen in the
siege, while the loss in the Company's army did not exceed a
thousand. Doorjun Saul was captured as he endeavoured
to make his escape, and sent first to Allahabad and then to
Benares, where he passed twenty-five years of his life, in
that asylum of disinherited princes, upon a pittance of five
hundred rupees a-month. The boy raja was conducted to
the throne by Sir Charles Metcalfe and Lord Combermere,
but the laurels of Bhurtpore were dishonoured by rapacity.
The siege was undertaken to expel a usurper and to restore
the throne to the rightful prince, yet all the state treasures
and jewels found in the citadel, to the extent of forty-eight
lacs of rupees, were unscrupulously pronounced by the military
authorities to be lawful prize, and at once distributed among
the officers and men. Six lacs fell to the share of the
Commander-in-chief. This procedure was defended by the
sophism that "as Doorjun Saul had been in quiet possession of
the throne, and acknowledged by all parties as the Maharaja,
no individual either openly or secretly supporting the claims
of Bulwunt Sing, naturally gave the former the full right to
all the property in the fort, and deprived the latter of any
claim which he might be supposed to have to it." This
spoliation was denounced by Sir Charles Metcalfe, in terms
of indignation : " Our plundering here," he wrote, " has been
very disgraceful, and has tarnished our well-earned honours.

Until I can get rid of the prize agents, I cannot establish
the sovereignty of the young raja, whom we came professedly
to protect, but have been plundering to the last *lotah*—water-
pot—since he fell into our hands."

Effect of the
capture, 1826.
The capture of Bhurtpore is a salient point in
the history of British progress in India. Though
absolute masters of the whole continent, our prestige still
seemed to be suspended upon the issue of the siege, which
was watched with extraordinary interest throughout the
country, and more particularly in the metropolis. Government
had been constrained to open a loan in the month of August,
but the moneyed classes hung back from it till the result of the
siege was known. The privilege of private posts had not
then been abolished, and the Calcutta bankers received daily
intelligence of the progress of operations before Bhurtpore
more speedily than the Governor-General obtained it through
the public mail, and the first intimation which the Government received of the capture of the town was from the sudden
influx of subscriptions to the loan, to the extent of thirty
lacs of rupees, as soon as the treasury opened for the
day. Bhurtpore was dismantled, 'and the proud walls which
had baffled the hero of Laswaree and Delhi were levelled with
the ground. The capture of the town and fort by the skill
of British engineers diffused a salutary feeling of awe
throughout India, and, combined with the simultaneous submission of the Burmese, dissolved the hopes of the disaffected, and strengthened the power of Government.

Honours con-
ferred on Lord
Amherst, 1826.
The gross mismanagement of the Burmese war
had created great discontent in England, but the
successful termination of it brought the Governor-
General a step in the peerage as Earl Amherst of Aracan—
though the most disastrous of his expeditions—and a vote of
thanks from the Court of Directors for " his active, strenuous,
and persevering efforts in conducting to a successful issue
the late war with the King of Ava." On the return of peace
he made a progress through the north-west, and held stately

durbars, and the native princes who had recently been medi-
tating the downfall of British power, hastened to offer their
homage to it.   In the summer of 1827 he proceeded to Simlah,
the delightful climate and majestic scenery of which was then
for the first time selected as a summer retreat by the head of
the Government.   His example has been followed by his successors, and this sanatarium has now become the annual resort
of European officers and residents in the north-west from the
heat of the plains to such an extent as to support a banking
establishment.   The financial result of Lord
Amherst's administration was calamitous.   The
wealth left in the treasury by Lord Hastings was dissipated ;
the surplus of revenue was converted into a deficit, and an
addition of ten crores was made to the public debt.   Of this
sum about one-fourth was obtained from the hoards of the
King of Oude, the perennial reservoir of the Calcutta treasury.
Large sums were likewise subscribed by native chiefs and
bankers after   and Bajee Rao himself was induced to invest in "Company's paper" some portion
of the accumulations of his annuity.   Lord Amherst, immediately after his arrival, and while new to the
country and to the community, was led by the
Tory members of the Government to continue
those truculent proceedings against the press which they
had originated.   But it was not long before he adopted a more
generous policy, and on his departure was complimented by
the journals in Calcutta "on the liberality and even magnanimity with which he had tolerated the free expression of
public opinion on his own individual measures, when he had
the power to silence them with a stroke of his pen."   It was
during his absence at Simlah, and without his concurrence,
that the Vice-President in Council revoked the licence of one
of the Calcutta papers, and ruined the proprietor for a racy
but innocent squib on the higher members of the service,
similar to those which form the weekly attraction of the
London "Punch."   This was happily the last interference on

Financial results, 1828.

Lord Amherst and the Press, 1824-28.

the part of the public authorities with the local press. Within ......act Lord William Bentinck ......and on his departure, Sir ......on a legal basis.

......Munro, the Governor of Madras, ...1824, but was ......expedition, and ......and the state ......to obey the call of ......draw from Lord ......acknowledgment, that ......sible to undertake

......to return to his ......attack of ......and united a ......with broad views of policy ......him for ......ment, that ......shed statesman, nor ......soldier." He ......to his ......shington, who ......to himself for the ......vernment of ....who have ......cessful and illus...... ......institutions of ....nlarged to its present ......the Peshwa, and one ....the Bombay code, which ......degree to enhance ......charged with ....after the deposit......

Appa Sahib, during the minority of his successor, and resigned it into his hands in 1826, when he came of age.   His administration was the most honest and beneficial the Bhoonslay kingdom had ever been blessed with, and was rendered the more memorable by the condition to which it relapsed when again subjected to native rule.   The same lamentable result followed the removal of Sir Charles Metcalfe to Delhi, and the consequent abandonment of the administrative system he had introduced into the domains of the Nizam.   By a singular coincidence, each of these statesmen, though civilians, had enjoyed an opportunity of acquiring laurels in the field, Sir Charles Metcalfe at Deeg, Mr. Elphinstone at Kirkee, and Mr. Jenkins at Seetabuldee; but it was the revenue settlement and civil administration of the large kingdoms confided to them at Hyderabad, Bombay, and Nagpore, which formed the chief distinction of their career.   They may be considered, in conjunction with Sir John Malcolm, Sir Thomas Munro, and Sir David Ochterlony, as forming that galaxy of talent which gave solidity and splendour to the Company's government during the first quarter of the present century.

Lord Amherst's departure, 1828.   Lord Amherst was constrained to leave Calcutta earlier than he had expected through the illness of his son, and embarked for England in February, 1828.   Mr. Bayley, the senior member of Council, a disciple of Lord Wellesley's school, succeeded temporarily to the office of Governor-General, and was for four months employed in discussing and maturing some of those great measures of reform which rendered the next administration memorable in the history of British India.

GLOSSARY.

Banian.—A Hindoo merchant; manager of a European's concerns

Balla.—A ... to troops in the field.

B....—The body of a noble or prince.

D.....—Hereditary and professional carriers of India.

C....—A Mahomedan judge and notary.

Chout.—The fourth of revenues exacted by the Mahrattas.

Cowrie.—The lowest coin in India; a shell.

C.....—... millions of rupees; one million sterling.

Darogha.—Superintendent of Police.

D....—The chief minister of finances; a head manager

D.....—... of the revenue ...

D.....—... court of justice.

D....—A country lying between any two rivers.

Darbar.—A levee; a public council.

F.....—... charter ...

...

Lac.—One hundred thousand ...

Maun.—... about 82 lbs.

...

O....—A noble.

...

P....

Peshcut....

P....

R....

Ryot.—... peasant.

...

S....—... soldier.

...

... governor of a Soobah.

... of the fourth or lowest caste.

S..... Adawluty.—The supreme civil court.

... office.

... representative;—an attorney.

Vizier.—... minister.

...

Z....

Ingram Content Group UK Ltd.
Milton Keynes UK
UKHW011826170323
418736UK00004B/333